Programming with Higher-Order Logic

Formal systems that describe computations over syntactic structures occur frequently in computer science. Logic programming provides a natural framework for encoding and animating such systems. However, these systems often embody variable binding, a notion that must be treated carefully at a computational level. This book aims to show that a programming language based on a simply typed version of higher-order logic provides an elegant and declarative means for realizing such a treatment. Three broad topics are covered in pursuit of this goal. First, a proof-theoretic framework that supports a general view of logic programming is identified. Second, an actual language called λProlog is developed by applying this view to a higher-order logic. Finally, a methodology for computing with specifications is exposed by showing how several computations over formal objects such as logical formulas, functional programs, λ-terms, and π-calculus expressions can be encoded in λProlog.

DALE MILLER is Director of Research at INRIA-Saclay and LIX, École Polytechnique where he is the Scientific Leader of the Parsifal team. He has been a professor at the University of Pennsylvania, the Pennsylvania State University, and the École Polytechnique, France. Miller is the Editor-in-Chief of the *ACM Transactions on Computational Logic* and has editorial duties on several other journals. He was awarded an ERC Advanced Grant in 2011 and is the recipient of the 2011 Test-of-Time award of the IEEE Symposium on Logic in Computer Science. He works on many topics in the general area of computational logic, including automated reasoning, logic programming, proof theory, unification theory, operational semantics, and, most recently, proof certificates.

GOPALAN NADATHUR is a Professor of Computer Science at the University of Minnesota. He has previously held faculty appointments at Duke University, University of Chicago, and Loyola University of Chicago. Nadathur's research interests span the areas of computational logic, programming languages, and logic programming. His work has been regularly funded by the National Science Foundation and has appeared in the *Journal of the Association of Computing Machinery*, *Information and Computation*, the *Journal of Automated Reasoning*, *Theoretical Computer Science*, and *Theory and Practice of Logic Programming* among other places.

PROGRAMMING WITH HIGHER-ORDER LOGIC

DALE MILLER
INRIA-Saclay, Île de France &
LIX, École Polytechnique

GOPALAN NADATHUR
University of Minnesota

CAMBRIDGE
UNIVERSITY PRESS

CAMBRIDGE
UNIVERSITY PRESS

University Printing House, Cambridge CB2 8BS, United Kingdom

One Liberty Plaza, 20th Floor, New York, NY 10006, USA

477 Williamstown Road, Port Melbourne, VIC 3207, Australia

314-321, 3rd Floor, Plot 3, Splendor Forum, Jasola District Centre, New Delhi - 110025, India

79 Anson Road, #06-04/06, Singapore 079906

Cambridge University Press is part of the University of Cambridge.

It furthers the University's mission by disseminating knowledge in the pursuit of education, learning and research at the highest international levels of excellence.

www.cambridge.org
Information on this title: www.cambridge.org/9780521879408

© Dale Miller and Gopalan Nadathur 2012

First published 2012

A catalogue record for this publication is available from the British Library

ISBN 978-0-521-87940-8 Hardback

To Catuscia, Nadia, and Alexis
— Dale

To the memory of my parents
— Gopalan

Contents

Preface

Formal systems in computer science frequently involve specifications of computations over syntactic structures such as λ-terms, π-calculus expressions, first-order formulas, types, and proofs. This book is concerned, in part, with using higher-order logic to express such specifications. Properties are often associated with expressions by formal systems via syntax-based inference rules. Examples of such descriptions include presentations of typing and operational semantics. Logic programming, with its orientation around rule-based specifications, provides a natural framework for encoding and animating these kinds of descriptions. Variable binding is integral to most syntactic expressions, and its presence typically translates into side conditions accompanying inference rules. While many of the concepts related to binding, such as variable renaming, substitution, and scoping, are logically well understood, their treatment at a programming level is surprisingly difficult. We show here that a programming language based on a simply typed version of higher-order logic provides an elegant approach to performing computations over structures embodying binding.

The agenda just described has a prerequisite: We must be able to make sense of a higher-order logic as a programming language. This is a nontrivial task that defines a second theme that permeates this book. Usual developments of logic programming are oriented around formulas in clausal form with resolution as the sole inference rule. Sometimes a semantics-based presentation is also used, expanding typically into the idea of minimal (Herbrand) models. Neither of these approaches is suitable in a higher-order setting: Model theory is not a well-developed tool here, and substitutions for predicate variables that can appear in a higher-order logic can take formulas in a restricted form, such as the conjunctive-normal clausal form, into new formulas that no longer adhere to this form. Faced with this situation, we have turned in our work to the sequent calculus of Gentzen. We have found this to be a versatile and flexible tool for understanding and analyzing the metatheory and computational properties of logics. Using it, we have been able to identify logic programming languages as ones that support a particular goal-directed approach to proof search. This viewpoint allows us to extend naturally the Horn clause logic that underlies languages such as Prolog to richer first-order logics that offer support at the programming level to scoping mechanisms. The same approach generalizes to higher-order logic and also to contexts that we do not explicitly treat here, such as linear logic and the dependently typed λ-calculus. Indeed, understanding proof search through the perspective of the sequent calculus seems to be an essential part of grasping the significance of logic as a tool for computing. We accordingly expose this line of thinking as we develop a higher-order logic for programming.

Gaining facility with new ideas in programming usually requires concrete experimentation with them. Many of the ideas that we expose here have an actual realization in the language λProlog. Programs written in λProlog often will be used to illuminate discussions of logic and theoretical principles. These programs can be run using the Teyjus implementation of λProlog that we provide an introduction to in the Appendix. The Teyjus system can be freely downloaded, and the distribution material accompanying it contains many programs, including the ones discussed in this book, that illustrate the special capabilities of λProlog. We anticipate that a reader of this book eventually will have enough expertise to develop his or her own programs in a number of application areas where binding is an important part of syntactic structure.

This book, then, covers three broad topics: a proof search–based view of computation, a higher-order logic–based approach to programming, and a particular language that realizes these ideas. We hope to leave the reader in the end with an appreciation of how higher-order logic may be used to specify computations and with the ability to use a logic programming language based on such a logic to build actual systems. We believe that this kind of background is becoming increasingly useful as demands of the programming process get more sophisticated. One pertinent application area is that where logic and deduction function as "gatekeepers" that ensure the security and integrity of lower-level processes; a specific example of this kind appears within the proof-carrying-code framework that has been proposed as a vehicle for ensuring, for instance, the safety of mobile code. Another application area is the mechanization of the metatheory of logics and languages that is the focus, for example, of the recently posed POPLmark challenge. This book develops a fruitful approach to specifying computations over logical expressions and program phrases, all of which are central to such metatheoretic manipulations. The λProlog language also provides a means for prototyping and implementing such specifications. While we do not discuss this issue significantly in this book, these λProlog specifications should further facilitate rich and interesting new approaches to reasoning about metatheoretic properties of the logics and languages encoded in them.

The material we present here owes a lot to collaborations with colleagues. The foundational ideas relating to logic programming were developed in the late 1980s in interactions with Frank Pfenning and Andre Scedrov. We also received valuable input from Natarajan Shankar during this phase. A Prolog-based implementation of λProlog followed soon after. The understanding we now have of the capabilities of this language derives significantly from the experiments conducted with this system by Amy Felty, Elsa Gunter, John Hannan, Fernando Pereira, Remo Pereschi, and Frank Pfenning, among many other researchers who we surely err in not mentioning explicitly. The language subsequently has received implementations in Common Lisp by Conal Elliott and Frank Pfenning; in C by Pascal Brisset and Olivier Ridoux; and in Standard ML by Conal Elliott, Amy Felty, Dale Miller, Frank Pfenning, and Philip Wickline. Gopalan Nadathur has led a long-term project focused on compiling this language in which Andrew Gacek, Steven Holte, Bharat Jayaraman, Keehang Kwon, Dustin Mitchell, Xiaochu Qi, and Zachary Snow have participated. This work has resulted in two different versions of the Teyjus system. We have received comments and helpful suggestions on this book from Jim Blandy, Iliano Cervesato, Giorgio Delzanno, Joern Dinkla, Zhiping Duan, Daniel Friedman, Andrew Gacek, Clément Houtmann, H. Krishnapriyan, Gary Leavens, Chuck Liang, Jim Lipton, Tong Mei, Catuscia Palamidessi, Olivier Ridoux, Jenny Simon, and Yuting Wang. INRIA has provided support during the writing of this book by facilitating a sabbatical visit by Gopalan Nadathur and through its "Equipes Associées" Slimmer. The National Science Foundation has funded the development of the ideas we present through grants at various points, most recently through the Grants CCF-0429572 and NSF/CCF-0917140. Any opinions, findings, and conclusions or recommendations expressed in this book are those of the authors and do not necessarily reflect the views of the National Science Foundation.

Palaiseau, France   *Dale Miller*
Minneapolis, MN, USA   *Gopalan Nadathur*
October 2011

Introduction

This book is about the nature and benefits of logic programming in the setting of a higher-order logic. We provide in this Introduction a perspective on the different issues that are relevant to a discussion of these topics. Logic programming is but one way in which logic has been used in recent decades to understand, specify, and effect computations. In Section I.1, we categorize the different approaches that have been employed in connecting logic with computation, and we use this context to explain the particular focus we will adopt. The emphasis in this book will be on interpreting logic programming in an expressive way. A key to doing so is to allow for the use of an enriched set of logical primitives while preserving the essential characteristics of this style of specification and programming. In Section I.2, we discuss a notion of expressivity that supports our later claims that some of the logic programming languages that we present are more expressive than others. The adjective "higher order" has been applied to logic in the past in a few different ways, one of which might even raise concern about our plan to use such a logic to perform computations. In Section I.3, we sort these uses out and make clear the kind of higher-order logic that will interest us in subsequent chapters. Section I.4 explains the style of presentation that we follow in this book: Broadly, our goal is to show how higher-order logic can influence programming without letting the discussion devolve into a formal presentation of logic or a description of a particular programming language. The last two sections discuss the prerequisites expected of the reader and the organization of the book.

I.1 Connections between logic and computation

The various roles that logic has played in analyzing and performing computations can be understood as falling under two broad categories that we call the *computation-as-model* and the *computation-as-deduction* approaches. We describe these below.

In the computation-as-model approach, computations are understood abstractly via mathematical structures that are based on notions such as nodes, transitions, and states. Logic is employed in an external sense in this context to make statements *about* such structures. That is, computations are treated as *models* for logical expressions. Intensional operators, such as the triples of Hoare logic or the modals of temporal and dynamic logics, are often employed to express propositions about change in state. This use of logic to describe and reason about computations probably represents the oldest and most broadly successful interactions between the two areas.

In contrast, the computation-as-deduction approach uses logical expressions such as formulas, terms, types, and proofs directly as elements of the specified computation. In this more rarefied setting, two rather different methods have been employed in describing computations. The *proof normalization* approach views the state of a computation as a proof term and the process of computing as reducing such a term to normal form via, say, β-reduction. This view of computation provides a theoretical basis for the *functional programming paradigm*. In the proof normalization approach, one uses the fact that a given program (proof) has at most one normalized value, and one focuses on producing this value. If types are used, they generally denote "abstract domains" of values, such as the integers and function spaces. In the alternative *proof search* approach, the state of a computation is viewed as a *sequent* that comprises a formula that is to be proved and a collection of assumptions from which the formula is to be established. The process of computing is identified with the search for a derivation of a sequent: The changes that take place in sequents during proof search capture the dynamics of computation. This view of computation can be used to provide a proof-theoretic basis for the *logic programming paradigm*.

Of course, proof search is a rather general activity. For example, mathematicians can be said to be searching for proofs when they try to determine the validity of a proposition. However, it is not sensible to identify the steps that mathematicians take in building proofs with the low-level steps that are used to propel computations associated with a logic program. A particularly important difference between proofs used to realize computations and unrestricted proofs is the fact that in general reasoning, lemmas are discovered and used routinely. In the general setting, the attempt to prove one proposition, say, B, often results in the enunciation of a lemma, say, C, and subsequent attempts to find proofs of C and $C \supset B$. This process may be repeated—another lemma D may be helpful in proving C, and so on—and the result could be a large number of lemmas whose proofs are all used to support the proof of B. In the *sequent calculi*, i.e., the calculi that have been proposed for proving sequents, the *cut rule* provides the mechanism for introducing lemmas in the course of proof search. As such, this rule is a frequent and critical component in any attempt to model genuine mathematical reasoning using such calculi.

Since choosing lemmas involves creativity, the cut rule poses a problem for the mechanization of reasoning. A result that has obvious connotations in this context is Gentzen's famous *cut-elimination* theorem (for classical and intuitionistic logic) that says that if a formula can be proved using the cut rule, then it also can be proved without the cut rule. The proof of this theorem is based intuitively on the observation that lemmas always can be *in-lined* or *re-proved* each time they are needed. The derivations that result from the elimination of uses of the cut rule are often huge and of little value to a mathematician. The fact that they can be constructed, however, is quite interesting from the perspective of computation. The in-lining of proofs, via cut elimination or the closely related operation of β-reduction, is the process that underlies computation in the functional programming paradigm. In the logic programming paradigm as we describe it here, the cut rule is excluded from the execution of logic programs, and computation is based on the search for *cut-free* proofs. The cut rule and the cut-elimination theorem, however, can be used to reason *about* logic programs; i.e., they are part of the metatheory of the paradigm.

I.2 Logical primitives and programming expressivity

In the logic programming setting, one generally partitions formulas into two classes. A formula can be a member of a *logic program*, and as such, it provides part of the computational meaning of the nonlogical constants that appear in it. A formula also can be a *goal* or *query*, and in this role, it represents something to be derived from a given logic program. We shall often idealize the state of the search for a proof by a collection of sequents. A *sequent* in this context will be an expression written as $\Sigma; \mathcal{P} \longrightarrow G$, comprising three parts: a *signature* Σ that is a set of typed, nonlogical constants; a logic program $\mathcal{P}$; and a goal G that is to be proved. The signature Σ denotes the set of constants and predicates that are available for building the terms and formulas in G and $\mathcal{P}$.

An important aspect of logic programming is that a complete proof strategy, in principle, can be structured in the following goal-directed fashion. If the goal formula is not an atom, that is, if its top-level symbol is a logical constant or quantifier, then the search for a proof is completely committed to dealing with that top-level logical constant. Thus the "search semantics" of the logical connectives is fixed and independent of the logic program. On the other hand, if the goal formula is atomic, then the logic program $\mathcal{P}$ is consulted to discover how that atom might be proved. Typically, this involves using *backchaining*, which is the process of finding in the logic program an implicational formula whose consequent matches the atom and then trying to prove its antecedent. Logic programming can be seen abstractly as a logical framework in which a strategy that alternates between goal reduction and backchaining is *complete*, i.e., is capable of finding a proof whenever one exists. This viewpoint is developed in more detail in Section 2.2.

The computational dynamics in logic programming arises from the way the signature, the program, and the query change during the search for a proof. We therefore can understand this dynamics qualitatively by considering the following question.

> Assume that during an attempt to prove the sequent $\Sigma; \mathcal{P} \longrightarrow A$, the search yields the attempt to prove the sequent $\Sigma'; \mathcal{P}' \longrightarrow A'$. What differences can occur when moving from the first to the second sequent?

In this book, we shall consider logic programs based on *Horn clauses* and on a more general class of formulas called *hereditary Harrop formulas*. If $\mathcal{P}$ is a Horn clause program (either first order or higher order), then Σ' and $\mathcal{P}'$ must be identical to Σ and $\mathcal{P}$, respectively. Thus the signature and logic program are global and immutable and have a flat structure during computation; in particular, Horn clauses do not support the capability of using some data structures and some clauses locally and only for auxiliary calculations. The differences between the atoms A and A' are determined, on the other hand, by the logic program $\mathcal{P}$, and these can be rich enough to capture arbitrary computations. Notice, however, that the dynamics of such computations has a largely *nonlogical* character; that is, it is dependent on the meaning associated with predicate symbols through the assumptions in the logic program. If programs are allowed to involve more logical primitives, more of the character of the dynamics of computation may depend on the *logical* structure, and as a result, the metatheory of the logic can be of more value in proving properties of those programs.

Using hereditary Harrop formulas improves the dynamics of proof search: In particular, both the signature Σ' and the program $\mathcal{P}'$ can be larger than Σ and $\mathcal{P}$, respectively. As a particular consequence, it is possible for a program to grow by the addition of clauses that can be used only in a local proof search attempt. Similarly, it is possible to introduce data constructors that are available only for part of the computation. In this way, the logical framework is capable of supporting the use of modular programming and data abstraction techniques.

We shall limit our attention to classical and intuitionistic logic as they are applied to Horn clauses and to hereditary Harrop formulas. If one were to consider proof search in the more general setting of linear logic, the alternation between goal reduction and backchaining still would yield a complete proof procedure (for a suitable presentation of linear logic), and the dynamics of proof search would improve beyond what we have observed for the two fragments of logic just discussed. Although this is an interesting direction to pursue, logic programming based on linear logic is beyond the scope of the topics we consider here.

I.3 The meaning of *higher-order logic*

The term *higher-order logic* has been used ambiguously in the literature. We identify three common interpretations below and then explain the sense in which we will be using the form in this book.

Philosophers of mathematics often distinguish between first-order logic and second-order logic. The latter logic, which is used as a formal basis for all of mathematics, involves quantification over the domain of all possible functions. A consequence of Kurt Gödel's celebrated first incompleteness theorem is that truth in this logic cannot be recursively axiomatized. Thus higher-order logic interpreted in this sense consists largely of a model-theoretic study, typically of the *standard model of arithmetic*.

Proof-theoreticians take logic to be synonymous with a formal system that provides a recursive enumeration of the notion of theoremhood. A higher-order logic is understood no differently. The distinctive characteristic of such a logic, instead, is the presence of predicate quantification and of comprehension, i.e., the ability to form abstractions over formula expressions. These features, especially the ability to quantify over predicates, profoundly influence the proof-theoretic structure of the logic. One important consequence is that the simpler induction arguments of cut elimination that are used for first-order logic do not carry over to the higher-order setting, and more sophisticated techniques, such as the "*candidats de réductibilité*" due to Jean-Yves Girard, must be used. Semantical methods also can be employed, but the collection of models now must include *nonstandard models* that use restricted function spaces in addition to the standard models used for second-order logic.

Implementers of deduction usually interpret higher-order logic as any computational logic that employ λ-terms and quantification at higher-order types, although not necessarily at predicate types. Notice that if quantification is extended only to non–predicate function variables, then the logic is similar to a first-order one in that the cut-elimination process can be defined using an induction involving the sizes of (cut) formulas. However, such a logic may incorporate a notion of equality based on the rules of λ-conversion, and the implementation of theorem proving in it must use (some form of) higher-order unification.

Clearly, it is not sensible to base a programming language on a higher-order logic in the first sense. Our use of this term therefore is restricted to the second and third senses. Notice that these two views are distinct. As we have already commented, a logic that is higher order in the third sense may well not permit quantification over predicates and thus may not be higher order in the second sense. Conversely, a logic can be higher order in the second sense but not in the third: There have been proposals for adding forms of predicate quantification to computational logics that do not use λ-terms and in which the equality of expressions continues to be based on the identity relation.

The actual higher-order logic that we shall use in this book is a simplified form of an intuitionistic version of the *Simple Theory of Types* that was developed by Alonzo Church. Our simplification leaves out axioms concerning extensionality, infinity, and choice that are needed for formalizing mathematics but that do not play a role in and indeed interfere with use of the logic in describing computations. The resulting logic extends first-order logic by permitting quantification at all types and replaces both first-order terms and first-order formulas by simply typed λ-terms complemented by a notion of equality based on β- and η-conversion. This logic does permit predicate quantification, which makes theorem proving in it particularly challenging. In first-order logic, substitution into an expression does not change its logical structure, and all the needed instantiations in a proof can be produced simply through the unification of atomic formulas. With the inclusion of predicate quantification, instantiations can introduce new occurrences of logical connectives and quantifiers in formulas, and as a result, unification is not rich enough to find all substitutions needed for proofs. However, we shall, restrict the uses of predicate variables in the logic programming languages we consider in such a way that unification becomes sufficient once again for finding all the necessary instantiations.

I.4 Presentation style

This book is intended to be an exposition of programming techniques based on the use of a higher-order logic. In order to discuss these techniques in detail, we need to be able to present actual logic programs. More specifically, a concrete syntax must be picked for programs and goals, language principles such as modularity and typing must be established, and strategies for dealing effectively with nondeterministic proof search must be chosen. Toward meeting these requirements, we introduce the programming language λProlog, which represents one way of addressing these pragmatic aspects. This language also gives us a setting in which to discuss relevant issues concerning the computational use of higher order logic. Thus goal-directed search for higher-order hereditary Harrop formulas must be translated into an operational semantics and, subsequently, an implementation of λProlog. Similarly, higher-order logic and a rich use of logical primitives raises the issue of solving equations between λ-terms modulo β- and η-conversion rules and in the presence of mixed quantifier prefixes. The λProlog language gives us a concrete setting in which to understand the structure of such issues as well as to appreciate practical approaches to solving them.

Although we discuss λProlog explicitly, this is not intended to be a book *about* λProlog. We introduce the syntax of this language and we display several λProlog programs, but we do not provide enough information about the language for this book to serve as a programming manual. Rather, the focus is on painting a broad picture of the interplay between proof search in higher-order logic and computational principles: This focus underlies the discussion of language structure initially and the presentation later of several applications where higher-order logic programming techniques lead to appealing and natural solutions. A reader who is not satisfied with this kind of exposure to the language and wants a more detailed, manual-like presentation should consult the documentation accompanying one of its implementations, such as the Teyjus system that is briefly described in the Appendix.

While our emphasis is on understanding high-level, logic-related aspects of programming, we emphasize that this book is not a formal development of logic in any sense. In particular, we try to build a good intuitive understanding of higher-order logic characteristics, but we do this without providing many formal definitions and theorems. Instead, most formal aspects of this logic are exposed through examples and probed by tracing computational behavior. However, detailed bibliographic references to literature containing such formal presentations are included at the end of many chapters for the interested reader.

I.5 Prerequisites

The ideal reader of this book would have had prior exposure to high-level programming and to the rudiments of logic and logic programming. We specifically assume that the reader knows how to write and execute simple programs in some dialect of Prolog. We use small programming examples in λProlog to bring out the different ideas we present. A reader who has a programming feel for Prolog will find these examples easy to understand because λProlog inherits many features and conventions from Prolog. Conversely, someone not familiar with how computations are organized in logic programming languages may have difficulty in understanding the λProlog examples in detail. Knowledge of "advanced" aspects of Prolog, however, is not necessary. In fact, such knowledge could be confusing: Advanced Prolog features often derive from nonlogical aspects of the language, whereas our focus here will be on finding logical solutions to the problems that have led to the proliferation of nonlogical solutions that are familiar to Prolog programmers.

I.6 Organization of the book

This book has four conceptual parts that are identified in Figure I.1 together with their dependencies.

The first part introduces a proof-theoretic foundation for logic programming in the setting of first-order logic. Chapter 1 describes how symbolic objects might be represented using simply typed first-order terms that are manipulated using first-order unification. Chapter 2 presents an abstract framework for logic programming and elaborates this framework using first-order Horn clauses. The resulting language then is extended in Chapter 3 by using a richer class of formulas known as first-order hereditary Harrop formulas.

The second part of this book generalizes the structure of logic programming languages discussed in the first part to the higher-order setting. Chapter 4 introduces simply typed λ-terms and exposes some of the properties of the reduction computation and the process of solving equations relative to these terms. Formulas are identified as the specific collection of simply typed λ-terms that have a certain type, and Church's Simple Theory of Types defines a logic over these formulas. Chapter 5 identifies higher-order versions of Horn clauses and hereditary Harrop formulas within this logic. These classes of formulas provide the basis for *higher-order logic programming*, some characteristics of which we also expose in this chapter.

The third part of this book deals with pragmatic issues related to programming. Chapter 6 shows how code-structuring possibilities can be realized by exploiting features of higher-order hereditary Harrop formulas. The Appendix

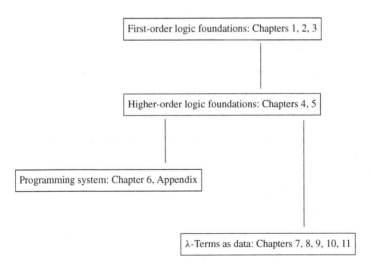

Figure I.1 Dependency and grouping of chapters.

describes how the logic specifications presented in this book can be written as λProlog programs and executed using the Teyjus implementation of λProlog.

The fourth part of this book is devoted to showing the benefits of the ability to compute directly on λ-terms. One part of this discussion consists of explaining the general structure that supports this approach. Chapter 7 illustrates how computations on λ-terms can be used to encode and manipulate syntactic objects that contain binding operators. Proof search in higher-order logic requires solving variously quantified equalities between λ-terms, and as a result, higher-order unification plays an important role in the implementation of such logic programming languages. Chapter 8 discusses the structure of procedures for higher-order unification and the more limited higher-order pattern unification that underlies computation in an important subset of higher-order hereditary Harrop formulas that is known as L_λ. The remaining chapters in this fourth part, which can be read independently of each other, present different applications that involve computing on symbolic structures encoded using λ-terms. In particular, Chapter 9 considers the problem of implementing natural deduction and sequent calculus proof systems as well as tactic-based provers, Chapter 10 considers several computations in the context of the untyped λ-calculus and a simple functional programming language built on it, and Chapter 11 considers specifications and computations related to the π-calculus.

1

First-Order Terms and Representations of Data

Our initial discussion of logic programming focuses on first-order languages. In this chapter, we limit our attention to the capabilities for representing data that are present in such languages. These capabilities are provided for by first-order terms. The terms that we use in our exposition of data representation here are similar to those in a conventional logic programming language such as Prolog with one difference: We shall be interested in a *typed* version of these terms. In the first two sections that follow, we describe the structure of the types that are employed to classify terms. Section 1.3 then introduces typed first-order terms, and the following section discusses the pragmatics of using such terms to represent structured and recursively constructed data. The last section in this chapter considers the operation of first-order unification, the primary mechanism for analyzing data that are encoded using first-order terms. To ground this discussion—in particular, to show how the type and term languages may be identified in a programming setting—we use the actual syntax of λProlog in our presentation.

1.1 Sorts and type constructors

The starting point for a type system is a set of atomic or unanalyzable types. We shall refer to such types as *sorts*. Most typed programming languages have a set of built-in sorts associated with them. In the case of λProlog, any implementation of the language is expected to support at least the following collection of sorts with the corresponding denotations:

int	an implementation dependent range of integers
real	an implementation dependent set of real numbers
string	sequences of characters
in_stream	character streams that can be read from

10

out_stream   character streams that can be written to and
o   formulas,

The last of these sorts has a special status in a logic programming language that we will discuss in later chapters. The first three sorts have a built-in collection of constants associated with them, as we explain in Section 1.3. To use the sorts in_stream and out_stream in a meaningful way in programming, we will need some means to associate them with specific files that reside within an encompassing file system. We will consider this issue in due course. For the moment, we focus simply on the *names* of these types and how they may be used in constructing larger type expressions.

The λProlog language also possesses built-in *type constructors* that are mechanisms for constructing new types from other types. An example of such a type constructor is list, which takes a type as argument and produces a new type that represents lists of objects that have the argument type. For example, the expression (list int) denotes the type of lists of integers. Once again, we delay a discussion of how objects of such a type may be constructed till Section 1.3.

Sorts and type constructors themselves can be thought of as typed objects in a language for constructing types. To elaborate on this idea, let us use the symbol type to denote the collection of type expressions. Then the sort int can be viewed as an object of the category type. Similarly, the constructor list can be conceived of as an object of the category type -> type; that is to say, list needs to be supplied an object of the category type to produce another object of this category. It is sensible, of course, to consider type constructors of arity greater than 1. For example, we can think of a constructor pair that takes two types and returns a new type corresponding to pairs of objects of the given types. This constructor, then, would be an object of the category type -> type -> type; we assume that -> associates to the right in this expression. Notice also that a sort can be seen as a special case of a type constructor, in particular, one that has the arity 0.

We refer to the "types" that we have just used to categorize sorts and type constructors as *kinds*, to be distinguished from the types that we will soon use to categorize terms. The language of kinds that is used in λProlog is simple and given by the following grammar:

$$\langle \text{kind exp} \rangle ::= \text{type} \mid \text{type} \; \text{->} \; \langle \text{kind exp} \rangle.$$

In principle, we can permit a richer collection of kind expressions. An interesting possibility is that of giving up on a strict hierarchy among kind, type, and term expressions, thus allowing the types of some data to be parameterized by other data. However, we do not explore such a direction in this book.

The λProlog language permits the user to extend the collection of built-in sorts and type constructors. In particular, new sorts and type constructors can be introduced using *kind* declarations, which have the structure

$$\texttt{kind} \quad \texttt{c1, ..., cn} \quad \langle\text{kind exp}\rangle.$$

Such a declaration identifies the symbols c1,..., cn as new type constructors that have ⟨kind exp⟩ as their kind. Thus we might write the declaration

```
kind   pair   type -> type -> type.
```

after which we will be free to use the newly declared constructor to form type expressions such as (pair string int). Application of type constructors associates to the left, a convention that matches the right associative reading of -> in kind expressions.

1.2 Type expressions

The λProlog language incorporates polymorphic typing in a manner that has similarities to that followed in modern functional programming languages. This polymorphism arises initially from including variables in type expressions. The full collection of types, in fact, is obtained by closing sorts and type variables under the operations of forming *constructed types* and *function types*. More specifically, this set is given by the following syntax rule

$$\langle\text{type exp}\rangle ::= \langle\text{type variable}\rangle \mid$$

$$(\langle\text{type exp}\rangle \text{ -> } \langle\text{type exp}\rangle) \mid$$

$$(\langle\text{tyc}\rangle \langle\text{type exp}\rangle \text{ ... } \langle\text{type exp}\rangle)$$

where ⟨tyc⟩ represents a type constructor. We assume here that each such type constructor is provided with as many arguments as it needs to produce an expression of kind type. Implicit also in this rule is the fact that we consider each (well-formed) type expression to have the kind type. The function type constructor is represented in concrete syntax by the symbol ->, written in infix form. We shall depict this symbol by → in mathematical notation. Notice that -> is also used for a similar purpose in kind expressions. However, the overloading that is present here is harmless because kind and type expressions will be used in distinct contexts. We also observe that unlike in the kinds language, there is no restriction on the use of the constructor -> in type expressions. In particular, this symbol may be nested within the type expression that appears to the left of a ->, and it also may appear in the argument provided to a type constructor.

The concrete syntax we use adopts the convention that tokens that begin with uppercase letters represent type variables and those that begin with lowercase letters represent type constructors. Notice that type variables are expressions of kind type, i.e., they cannot take types as arguments. We permit the omission of parentheses in writing type expressions by assuming that -> is right associative. Thus the type expression a -> b -> c is to be interpreted as a -> (b -> c). To further reduce the number of necessary parentheses, we use the convention that the application of a type constructor binds more tightly than the function type construction operation; e.g., the expression list A -> B corresponds to ((list A) -> B) in a fully parenthetized form. The expressions in the following list use the type constructors presented in the preceding section to illustrate the syntax of type expressions and the conventions for writing them that we have just described.

```
int -> int -> o
o -> int -> o
int -> real -> string
(int -> real) -> string
int -> real -> pair int real
list A -> (A -> B) -> list B -> o
list (list A) -> list A -> o
(A -> B) -> list (A -> B)
((A -> B) -> A) -> A
```

The right-associative reading of the function type constructor can be exploited to depict any type τ in the form

$$\tau_1 \to \cdots \to \tau_n \to \tau_0 \qquad (n \geq 0)$$

where τ_0 is a type expression that does not have a function type constructor at its top level. When written in this form, we say that τ_0 is the *target type* of ι and the types $\tau_1, \ldots, \tau_n$ are the *argument types* of τ. A type expression is a *functional type* if it has at least one argument type; otherwise, it is a *nonfunctional type*. A nonfunctional type that is not a variable is called a *primitive type*.

The *order of a type expression* τ, denoted by ord(τ), is defined by recursion on the structure of the expression:

$$\text{ord}(\tau) = 0 \quad \text{provided } \tau \text{ is non-functional}$$

$$\text{ord}(\tau_1 \to \tau_2) = \max(\text{ord}(\tau_1) + 1, \text{ord}(\tau_2))$$

Figure 1.1 shows examples of type expressions of different orders. Intuitively, the order of a type counts the number of times the function type constructor is nested to the left. A somewhat peculiar property is that the order of a type expression that contains variables can increase under the substitutions for those

Order	Examples of Types
0	`int, A, list (int -> int), pair int A`
1	`int -> int, string -> list (pair string int) -> o`
	`int -> string -> o, int -> string -> A`
2	`(string -> string) -> string, int -> (int -> o) -> o`
	`(int -> int) -> (int -> o) -> int`

Figure 1.1. Some example type expressions and their orders.

variables. For example, while the order of (`A -> list A -> o`) is 1, substituting a type expression of order 1 for `A` transforms it into a type expression of order 2. This kind of behavior will be absent in a first-order language, where we restrict types to be of order at most 1 and where we require that type variables be substituted for only with expressions of order 0. This peculiarity also will be harmless when we discuss higher-order languages later because the restrictions we place on syntax there will not be based on the orders of types.

1.3 Typed first-order terms

A term language is determined in significant part by its constant and function symbols. In a typed setting, each of these symbols has an associated type. It is customary not to distinguish between constants that have functional and nonfunctional types in a higher-order language such as λProlog, i.e., we refer in their context to what traditionally are known as function symbols in Prolog or first-order logic also as constants. However, we sometimes will use the term *value constructor* for a constant of functional type to emphasize its role in representing structured data.

The λProlog language provides a basic set of constants corresponding to the built-in sorts. We refer to these *built-in* constants also as *pervasive constants* because they are present in every setting.[1] We delay a presentation of the pervasive constants of type o until Chapter 2. Nonnegative integers, written as a sequence of digits, constitute built-in constants of the type `int`. There are, in addition, several constants of functional type that have `int` as their target type. These constants represent the usual arithmetic operators. One example of such a constant is ˜ of type `int -> int`, which represents the unary minus on integers. The term formation rules that we present more formally shortly allow ˜ to be applied to integer constants to construct expressions such as (˜ 1) that represent negative numbers. Constants such as + and ∗ that denote binary arithmetic operators have special conventions associated with them that permit them to be written as infix and left associative operators in terms. The pervasive constants

---

[1] The built-in sorts and type constructors similarly are called *pervasive type symbols*.

of type `real` correspond to the nonnegative real numbers and are written as two sequences of digits with an intervening period and such that at least one of the two sequences is nonempty. As is the case for integers, there are several additional constants of functional type that have `real` as their target type, serving to represent the arithmetic operators on reals. Pervasive constants of type `string` that denote strings are written as sequences of characters enclosed within double quotes; unprintable control characters are rendered into suitably chosen letters preceded by a backslash (i.e., the character \) in this sequence. Finally, we assume that the constant `std_in` of type `in_stream` represents the standard input stream and that the constants `std_out` and `std_err` of type `out_stream` represent the standard output and standard error streams.

The built-in type for lists illustrates the features of polymorphism and recursion in the data structures that are provided by λProlog. List objects are constructed using the constants `nil`, representing the empty list, and the value constructor `::`, pronounced "cons," that creates a new list by placing an element in front of an already existing list. The constants `nil` and `::` have the types (`list A`) and (`A -> list A -> list A`), respectively. Constants that have variables in their types are polymorphic: Such constants have all the types that can be obtained by possibly instantiating the type variables. Thus `nil` has simultaneously the types (`list int`), (`list (list int)`), and (`list A`), among other possibilities. The type of `::` is such that one of its argument types is identical to its target type. This property allows it to be used to construct a new data object by applying it to an object that is perhaps constructed in a similar fashion. For example, starting from `nil`, we can use `::` repeatedly to obtain the terms ((`:: 1) nil`), ((`:: 2) ((:: 1) nil)`), and so on of type (`list int`); we have assumed here a syntax and typing rules for forming terms using application that we will describe precisely later in this section. The constant `::` is defined to be an infix and right associative operator in λProlog so that the last two terms actually would be written thus:

```
1 :: nil
2 :: 1 :: nil
```

Another example of a list term that brings out the polymorphic nature of the constants for constructing lists is the following:

```
(2 :: 1 :: nil) :: (1 :: nil) :: nil
```

This term has the type (`list (list int)`). Notice especially that the first two occurrences of `nil` in this term have type (`list int`), whereas the last occurrence has the type (`list (list int)`).

We obviously have not presented a complete catalog of the built-in constants of λProlog here. For such a description, we refer the reader to the documentation for particular implementations of the language, such as the Teyjus system described in the Appendix. The λProlog language also allows the user to extend existing collections of constants. New constants are identified using *type declarations* that have the following structure:

    type   c1, ..., cn   ⟨type exp⟩.

A declaration of this kind defines the symbols c1, ..., cn to be constants that have the type ⟨type exp⟩. For example, the declaration

    type   pr   A -> B -> pair A B.

identifies pr as a constant for constructing representations of objects of the pair type that we considered earlier in this chapter. Using this constant, we can construct, for instance, the expression ((pr "three") 3) to denote a term of type (pair string int). The full language allows arbitrary type expressions to be used in type declarations. However, the first-order fragment that we are considering currently requires two conditions to be satisfied: The type expressions must be of order at most 1, and the sort o must not be used in them. Notice that these restrictions are satisfied by all the built-in constants we have considered up to this point.

The λProlog language allows the user to identify newly declared constants as operators of particular fixity and precedence. This is done via *operator declarations* that have the form

    ⟨fixity⟩   c1,..., cn   ⟨precedence⟩.

Here, ⟨fixity⟩ may be one of the keywords

    prefix, prefixr, postfix, postfixl, infix, infixl, and infixr

denoting operators that are prefix, postfix, or infix and possibly left- or right-associative as relevant. Further, ⟨precedence⟩ ranges over positive integers (in some implementation-dependent range) and indicates the precedence level of the defined operator. As an example, the declaration

    infixl   pr   5.

identifies pr as a left-associative infix operator with precedence level 5. After such a declaration, we may write (3 pr 4 pr "three") for the term ((pr ((pr 3) 4)) "three"). Operator and type declarations, of course, must be consistent with each other. For example, a constant that is defined to be an infix operator must have a functional type with at least two argument types, and its first argument type must have common instances with its target type if the constant, in addition, is identified as being left-associative. Violations of such conditions will show up at least in the ill-formedness of particular term expressions. A compiler for the language also may check type and operator declarations directly for this kind of compatability.

The other constituents of terms besides constants are *variables*; we will refer to these as *term variables* when it is necessary to distinguish them from the variables appearing in types. Variable occurrences can be explicitly bound in terms, as we shall see later. However, many occurrences of variables are also implicitly bound, and some convention then is necessary to distinguish them syntactically from constants. We will assume here that (unbound) tokens that begin with uppercase letters denote (implicitly bound) variables. Each variable must have a type associated with it. Such a type can be inferred by a process that we will presently describe. The type of a variable also may be indicated together with an operator that binds it, as we discuss in later chapters. In the first-order setting, the types of variables are limited to being of order 0, and they also must be distinct from o.

In the preceding discussions, we have assumed informally the ability to construct terms using application. Formally, given two terms t_1 and t_2, *application of t_1 to t_2* is represented by the expression $(t_1\ t_2)$. Not all such applications are well formed. To be well formed, t_1 must have the functional type $\alpha \to \beta$, where t_2 has the type α. The type of the overall term in this case is β. Typed first-order terms are all the expressions of nonfunctional type different from o that can be generated using well-formed application, starting from variables and constants that satisfy the first-order typing conditions we have described for them. There is a subtlety to how we may determine the types of *occurrences* of constants and variables related to the fact that the declared types of these symbols may have type variables in them. An occurrence of a constant can have any type that is obtained by instantiating these type variables. We note especially that different occurrences of the same constant in a given term may have different, even incompatible types. It is, in fact, only when types are picked in this way for the different occurrences of nil and :: that the term ((1 :: nil) :: nil) is determined to be well formed. The requirement is much more restrictive for a variable: No instantiation of type variables is permitted at any of its occurrences. Thus the term (X pr X) is well formed only if the type of pr that appears in it is an instance of (A -> A -> (pair A A)) and there is no possible assignment of types that would make the term ((X :: nil) :: X :: nil) well formed.

We make the preceding description of the structure of typed first-order terms precise by presenting in Figure 1.2 the inference rules for a type assignment calculus for these terms. These rules allows us to derive judgments of the form $\Sigma; \Gamma \Vdash_f t : \tau$ that assert that t is a term of type τ with respect to a *signature* Σ that assigns types to constants and a *context* Γ that assigns types to variables. In

$$\frac{c : \sigma \in \Sigma \quad \tau \vartriangleleft_f \sigma}{\Sigma; \Gamma \Vdash_f c : \tau} \qquad \frac{x : \tau \in \Gamma}{\Sigma; \Gamma \Vdash_f x : \tau}$$

$$\frac{\Sigma; \Gamma \Vdash_f g : \tau_1 \rightarrow \tau_2 \quad \Sigma; \Gamma \Vdash_f t : \tau_1}{\Sigma; \Gamma \Vdash_f (g\ t) : \tau_2}$$

Figure 1.2. Rules for defining typed first-order terms

the present setting, we assume that the types in Σ are of order at most 1, those in Γ are of order 0, and none of the types in these two sets contains occurrences of the sort o. We also assume that no symbol is given a declaration in both Σ and Γ. The typing rule for constants makes use of the relation $\tau \vartriangleleft_f \sigma$ between two first-order types τ and σ. This relation holds if τ and σ are such that the former results from the latter through the substitution of type expressions of order 0 that are distinct from o for type variables. Notice that $\vartriangleleft_f$ is an ordering relation on types: It is reflexive, transitive, and antisymmetric in the sense that if both $\tau \vartriangleleft_f \sigma$ and $\sigma \vartriangleleft_f \tau$ hold, then σ and τ are equal up to changes in the names of type variables.[2]

The type assignment rules are used by letting Σ be the assignment of types to the built-in and user-defined constants that are prevalent in a particular programming context. We also assume that terms have been preprocessed so as to transform operator occurrences into a standard applicative form. We then say that t is a *typed first-order Σ-term* if the judgment $\Sigma; \Gamma \Vdash_f t : \tau$ is derivable for some type τ that is of order 0 and distinct from o; noting that typing is intrinsic to our setting and that the knowledge of the specific signature may be irrelevant to the discussion at hand, we also may refer to t simply as a first-order term under these circumstances. In general, t may contain (unbound) variables, and Γ then must contain assignments of types to these variables. However, rather than requiring Γ to be determined beforehand, we can use the constraints imposed by the occurrences of variables and the typing rules to *infer* types for variables. In general, a *family* of typings can be inferred in this way for the variables and, correspondingly, for the overall term. For example, the term (X :: nil) :: nil is a well-formed first-order term if X has either the type int or the type (list int), yielding the types (list (list int)) or (list (list (list int))) for the overall term. An important fact about the terms that we are considering is that if there is a satisfactory assignment of types to a term and to the free variables appearing in it, then there is an assignment that is (pointwise) most general, up to the renaming of type variables, under the ordering relation

---

[2] Subscripts are used in $\vdash_f$ and $\vartriangleleft_f$ to signal a restriction to the first-order setting of the more general versions of these relations that will be described in Chapter 4.

$\triangleleft_f$. For example, in the case of the term (X :: nil) :: nil, a type assignment with this property is the one that associates the type A with X and the type (list A) with the full term. We discuss a procedure for inferring such types in more detail in Section 2.1. In the meantime, we use the existence of such a procedure to sometimes omit mention of types for variables in the first-order terms we consider.

Application is taken to be a left associative operator. This convention, which accords well with the right-associative reading of the function type constructor, allows us to reduce the number of parentheses in displaying terms; for example, we can write $(t_1\ t_2\ t_3)$ instead of $((t_1\ t_2)\ t_3)$. Based on this convention, we can describe a "canonical form" for typed first-order terms: Such a term is a variable, a constant, or an application of nonfunctional type that has the form $(f\ t_1\ \dots\ t_n)$, where f is a constant and $t_1, \dots, t_n$ are themselves typed first-order terms. In the last case, the term is said to have f as its *head* and the list of terms $t_1, \dots, t_n$ as its arguments. By an abuse of notation, we will allow n, the number of arguments, to be 0 in this form, thereby extending the terminology for applications to also cover constants.

1.4 Representing symbolic objects

In this section we consider the use of first-order terms in representing collections of structured data. Lists provide an example of such a collection. The first step in describing a suitable encoding consists usually of identifying a type, through the choice of a sort or a type constructor, to represent the data class as a whole. The data objects belonging to the class in many cases can be constituted in one of a few different ways. For instance, lists can be either empty or of a form that has a head element and a tail list. This kind of subdivision can be captured in a representation based on first order terms by using distinct value constructors that have a common target type and whose argument types are the types of the relevant subcomponents. Such a structure, in fact, is exhibited in the built-in representation of lists that uses two different constructors, nil and ::, to encode empty and nonempty lists. Structured data also can be recursive in nature. In this case, some of the argument types of the constructors that are used would be identical with their target type; the :: constructor whose second argument is also of list type exemplifies this aspect in the context of lists.

The ideas that we have just outlined have several uses, especially in encoding the abstract syntax of languages that we might wish to manipulate in a computational setting. We use examples from such contexts to provide detailed illustrations of the style of representation that we have described.

1.4.1 Representing binary trees

Like lists, binary trees are an example of a structured and recursively defined collection of data that is used frequently in computing. We will first describe a representation for such trees that is polymorphic in a way that is parameterized by the type of the elements in the tree. Toward this end, we identify a type constructor for this type as follows:

```
kind   btree   type -> type.
```

Using this constructor, the type of a binary tree whose elements are integers can be identified as (btree int), and the type of a binary tree of string elements would be written as (btree string).

As an object, a binary tree is either empty or a structure that consists of a data item and two subtrees. To encode these different possibilities, we introduce two value constructors through the following declarations:

```
type   empty   btree A.
type   node    A -> btree A -> btree A -> btree A.
```

Using the newly declared constants, we can represent specific binary trees through first-order terms such as

```
(node 3 (node 1 empty empty) (node 4 empty empty))
```

and

```
(node "dog" (node "cat" empty empty) (node "mouse" empty empty))
```

Notice that these two terms are of type (btree int) and (btree string), respectively.

The type and value constructors we have chosen here do not allow us to represent trees that contain data of a "mixed" variety. For example, the putative term

```
(node 3 (node "cat" empty empty) (node 4 empty empty))
```

that we might want to use to represent a tree that has both integer and string elements is ill formed for typing reasons. A characteristic of the representation that we have described is that while it can be used to encode binary trees whose elements are of arbitrary type, it must be the case that the types of all the elements in any given tree are identical. This type-based regularity results from two properties of our declarations: The type of a binary tree contains in it the type of the elements in the tree, and the variables in the argument types of each value constructor also appear in its target type. The "parametric polymorphism" that results from these restrictions has practical benefits: It allows more properties of data to be encoded in their types and to be checked in a compilation phase.

We will discuss this issue in more detail in Section 2.7, after we have presented a notion of computation to go along with data representation.

The type system of λProlog does not actually force adherence to parametric polymorphism. It is, for example, possible to describe a representation for binary trees that contain elements of mixed type. In fact, changing the declarations of the type and value constructors for binary trees to the ones shown below results in such a representation:

```
kind    btree    type.
type    empty    btree.
type    node     A -> btree -> btree -> btree.
```

Notice that under this representation, the type btree for binary trees no longer contains any information about the data elements that appear in the tree.

It is interesting to compare the encoding that we have described for trees using first-order terms with ones that might be provided for them in other programming languages. The most common approach in a C-like procedural language uses a structure to represent a node and a pointer to such structures to represent trees; the empty tree is represented by a null pointer. There is clearly a correspondence between constructed terms in our setting and the structures used in the described representation in procedural languages. Another common approach in a (procedural) object-oriented language such as Java is to use two distinct derived classes of an abstract binary tree class to represent empty and nonempty trees. This encoding resembles the one based on first-order terms that we have described here much more closely: Different value constructors for a particular type in λProlog are similar to different derived classes whose disjoint union makes up an abstract class in the object-oriented setting.

Procedural languages provide a view of data that exposes their machine representation. Thus, in both Java and C, it is necessary for the programmer to explicitly create objects corresponding to tree nodes rather than treating trees directly as values. These languages also do not allow for polymorphism in the controlled way that we have described here. Our encoding is, in this sense, much more like the one that typically is used in a typed functional programming language such as ML or Haskell. For example, a datatype declaration would be used in ML to identify a type constructor for binary trees together with value constructors that can be used to produce objects of this type. Such a declaration combines the separate kind and type declarations that we have shown for defining a data representation in λProlog. One difference that now becomes apparent is that the set of constructors for data objects can be extended in λProlog, whereas they are completely determined by a single declaration in ML. Another difference, illustrated by the second encoding for binary trees considered earlier, is that unlike in ML, type variables appearing in the argument types of a value constructor are not forced also to appear in the target type in λProlog; i.e., polymorphism can be nonparametric in λProlog. At the level of data objects, an important difference is that terms in a logic programming language can contain variables. This feature allows a term to describe a *class* of data objects that satisfy certain structural constraints.

1.4.2 Representing logical formulas

We now consider the use of first-order terms in encoding linguistic entities. The first example we consider is that of representing the formulas in an (untyped) first-order logic. There are two categories of expressions that are of interest in such a logic: terms and formulas. We accordingly introduce two sorts for representing these classes:

```
kind   term, form   type.
```

To represent the terms of the logic, we will need encodings of its constants and function symbols. Let us suppose that the logic has the two constant symbols a and b and a binary function symbol f. Encodings for these symbols are provided by the following declarations:

```
type   a, b   term.
type   f      term -> term -> term.
```

Terms in the logic also can contain variables. We could represent these by using variables from the metalanguage, i.e., variables from λProlog. However, such an encoding is not flexible. In particular, the scopes of variables in the object language will be governed entirely by the scoping rules of the metalanguage and cannot be controlled explicitly. An alternative is to use chosen constants to denote variables. A variant of this idea is to represent a variable such as x in the logic by the λProlog term (var "x"), where var is a constructor given by the declaration

```
type   var   string -> term.
```

We will adopt this second approach here. Using it, the term $f(a,f(x,b))$ in the object language will be represented by the expression (f a (f (var "x") b)) of type term in λProlog.

To represent formulas, we will first need to encode the vocabulary of predicate symbols of the logic. If this vocabulary consists of the unary predicate symbol q and the binary predicate symbol p, then it can be encoded by means of the following declarations:

```
type   p   term -> term -> form.
type   q   term -> form.
```

A similar set of declarations can be used to describe a representation for propositional connectives; in this case, we also may want to identify some of the constants as operators so as to be able to use syntax that has a more familiar structure. For concreteness, let us suppose that the logic that we want to encode includes the symbols ⊥ and ⊤ denoting the false and true propositions and the binary infix connectives ∧, ∨ and ⊃ denoting conjunction, disjunction, and implication. We might encode these through the following declarations:

```
type    ff,                     % encoding the false proposition
        tt    form.             % encoding the true proposition
type    &&,                     % encoding conjunction
        !!,                     % encoding disjunction
        ==>  form -> form -> form. % encoding implication
infixl  &&   5.
infixl  !!   4.
infixr  ==>  3.
```

These declarations also illustrate the use of *comments* in λProlog that begin with the occurrence of a % symbol and extend to the end of the line and that are meant to help the reader understand the declarations but are otherwise to be ignored. Subsequent to these declarations, we can write the term

```
(p a b) && (q a) !! (q (f a b)) ==> (p b (f b a))
```

to represent the formula $((p(a,b) \wedge q(a)) \vee q(f(a,b))) \supset p(b, f(b,a))$.

Extending the representation of quantifier-free formulas to formulas that include quantifiers is somewhat complicated. Suppose, for example, that we want to encode the formula $\forall x(p(a,x) \wedge q(x))$. One possible approach to doing this is to introduce a new constant all through the declaration

```
type    all   term -> form -> form.
```

and then to use the term

```
(all (var "x") ((p a (var "x")) && (q (var "x"))))
```

This expression reflects the recursive structure of the formula it is meant to represent, but it does not adequately capture the binding force of the quantifier. In particular, the connection between the binding and bound occurrences of the variable x in the formula is not governed by any principles underlying the first-order term language that we have used to represent it. Binding properties therefore will need to be accounted for explicitly in any user-defined computations over a term that contains the constructor all. This is a fundamental limitation of first-order approaches to the treatment of syntax. Chapter 7 presents ways to overcome this deficiency through the use of features found within higher-order logic.

It is sometimes necessary to encode classes of logics that possess a common set of connectives and quantifiers (such as the ones considered in this section) but that then extend this base in different ways. We will describe a modular approach to realizing a collection of such encodings in Chapter 6. The ability to declare value constructors in an incremental fashion, rather than being required to present them all in one datatype declaration, as in ML, plays an important role in making such an approach possible.

1.4.3 Representing imperative programs

The second kind of linguistic objects whose representation we consider are programs in a typed imperative language. For simplicity, we assume that the language of interest has only two types of values: integers and booleans.

In devising a representation for programs, a question to be addressed is how object language types should be treated. One possibility is to build these types into the metalanguage encoding, i.e., to use terms of different types in λProlog to represent integer- and boolean-valued program expressions. However, it is usually not a good idea to do this. To understand why, let us consider the encoding of object language identifiers. These identifiers share a collection of properties, such as the ability to appear on the left-hand side of an assignment expression, that are independent of the type of values they can hold. A uniform treatment of such properties is convenient for syntactic processing, but this requires representations of identifiers not to be distinguished based on their object language types. For reasons such as this, the preferred representation for programming language expressions is often type neutral; type distinctions that are necessary in particular analyses such as type checking are made explicit in later "semantics processing" phases.

Based on the preceding considerations, our representation of programs will use only two sorts: `expr` for expressions and `stmt` for statements. We encode identifiers by using a constructor `id` that converts their name, given by a string, into objects of type `expr`. We designate a constructor `c` for similarly coercing integers into expressions. Our encoding of the atomic boolean values is simpler: Since there are only two such values, we designate `t` and `f` as constants that represent them. Let us assume that the only operations available on program expressions of boolean type are conjunction and disjunction. We will represent these using the infix operators `&&` and `!!`. Similarly, let the operations on integer program expressions be restricted to addition, subtraction, multiplication, and less than; observe that the last of these operations yields a boolean value. We will encode these using the constructors `plus`, `minus`, `mult`, and `<`. Finally, suppose that the only statement forms in the programming language are assignments, conditionals, while loops, and statement composition. The following declarations constitute a signature for representing such programs:

```
kind stmt, expr      type.
type id              string -> expr.
type c               int -> expr.
type t, f            expr.
type &&, !!,
     plus, minus,
     mult, <         expr -> expr -> expr.
type :=              expr -> expr -> stmt.      % for assignment
type cond            expr -> stmt -> stmt -> stmt.   % for conditionals
type while           expr -> stmt -> stmt.      % for while loops
type seq             stmt -> stmt -> stmt.      % for composition
infixl &&, mult      5.
infixl !!,
       plus, minus   4.
infix  <             3.
infix  :=            2.
```

To illustrate the representation we have described, let us consider the following program, written using a C-like syntax for the object language:

```
v = 1; i = n;
while (0 < i) {
  v = v * i; i = i - 1;
}
```

This program would be represented by the first-order term

```
(seq ((id "v") := (c 1))
     (seq ((id "i") := (id "n"))
          (while ((c 0) < (id "i"))
                 (seq ((id "v") := (id "v") mult (id "i"))
                      ((id "i") := (id "i") minus (c 1))))))
```

The reader might notice a similarity between this encoding and what is referred to as the *abstract syntax* of the program. This similarity is a natural consequence of the fact that first-order terms are a generalization of the labeled trees that are used in depicting abstract syntax. Another aspect to note is that representations of "good" programs must satisfy syntactic constraints beyond those arising from types in the object language that we discussed earlier. For example, the left-hand side of an assignment in such a representation must be the encoding of a variable. We will see in Chapter 2 that such properties can be checked through logic programs that compute over first-order term–based representations.

1.5 Unification of typed first-order terms

The ability to analyze complex data objects into their subparts and to use such analyses in constructing new data objects plays an important role in programming. The unification operation on terms provides the basis for such capabilities in logic programming languages. We restrict our attention here to a version of this operation that applies to typed first-order terms, i.e., to *typed first-order unification*. In this setting, a *unification problem* is a finite multiset[3] of equations between first-order terms such that the two terms in each equation are of the same type. Such a multiset asks whether there is a type-preserving substitution of terms for variables that, when applied to the terms in the multiset, would make the two terms in each equation identical. A substitution that has this characteristic is said to be a *unifier for* the unification problem. As an example, if X and L are variables of type int and (list int), respectively, then the multiset

$$\{(\texttt{X :: L}) = (\texttt{1 :: 2 :: nil})\}$$

is a unification problem; note that we use the same notation for multisets as for sets, allowing the context to determine which one is meant in any particular instance. Writing substitutions as a collection of variable-term pairs, a unifier for this problem is given by the set $\{\langle \texttt{X}, 1\rangle, \langle \texttt{L}, 2\texttt{::nil}\rangle\}$.

The example just considered shows that unification can be used to decompose data structures: The term on the left-hand side of the equation constituting the multiset serves as a "pattern" for extracting the head of a list into a binding for X and the tail into a binding for L. The same pattern also functions as a structure recognizer: It will successfully unify only with lists that have at least one element and thus characterizes nonempty lists. Interestingly, a variable may have more than one occurrence in the same term. This feature endows considerable strength to the structure recognition capability of such patterns. For example, consider the term (node El T T) in the context of the representation for binary trees discussed in the preceding section. This term constitutes a pattern for recognizing nonempty binary trees in which the left and right subtrees are identical. Thus the unification problem

$$\{(\texttt{node El T T}) = (\texttt{node 1 (node 2 empty empty) (node 2 empty empty)})\}$$

has a solution, whereas the problem

$$\{(\texttt{node El T T}) = (\texttt{node 1 (node 2 empty empty) (node 3 empty empty)})\}$$

---

[3] A *multiset* is similar to a set except that the same item may appear more than once in a multiset. Alternatively, a multiset is like a sequence, with the difference that the order of elements is to be ignored. We use multisets of equations here to avoid having to find and remove duplicate elements in carrying out computations and because multiplicity does not cause problems at a conceptual level.

does not. Clearly, unification problems that provide deeper structural information of this kind about data require nontrivial effort to solve. When we consider higher-order terms later in the book, we will see that unification can be used to extract even more information about data and that it, correspondingly, becomes computationally more complex.

In a programming context, we can view the left-hand side of an equation as something that comes from a statically provided program and the right-hand side as something that arises dynamically as a result of user interaction. Observing now that variables can occur in terms on either side of an equation, we see that unification is a mechanism not just for decomposing data but also for constructing new structures. As an illustration, consider the following multiset of equations:

$$\{(\texttt{X :: L1}) = (\texttt{1 :: nil}), \texttt{L2} = (\texttt{2 :: nil}), (\texttt{X :: L2}) = \texttt{L3}\}.$$

Solving the first of the equations listed leads, as before, to the decomposition of an input value. However, once this decomposition has been carried out, a component extracted through it is combined with a second input value by means of the pattern (X :: L2). This newly constructed value is returned eventually in a binding for the "output" variable L3.

A unification problem can have more than one unifier. For example, consider

$$\{(\texttt{X :: L}) = (\texttt{Y :: Z :: nil})\},$$

assuming that the two terms in the sole equation in this multiset are of type (list int). One unifier for this problem is given by the substitution of Y for X and (Z :: nil) for L. A different unifier consists of substituting X for Y instead, leaving the substitution for L unchanged. Other unifiers can be obtained by picking particular integer values to substitute for X and Y and possibly choosing such a value for Z as well; the collection of such unifiers is, in fact, infinite. This situation raises the following question: Is it necessary to consider the entire set of unifiers for a given unification problem, or can all these be circumscribed in a finite, possibly unitary way?

Substitutions in a computational setting serve as constraints on the values of variables. For example, the substitution $\{\langle \texttt{X}, \texttt{Y}\rangle\}$ constrains the values of X and Y to be the identical. The substitution $\{\langle \texttt{X}, 1\rangle, \langle \texttt{Y}, 1\rangle\}$ satisfies the earlier constraint but further refines it by requiring the value of these variables to be chosen to be 1. Viewing substitutions in this way, we say that one substitution is *more general than* than another if the latter is obtained from the former by making further substitutions for variables. A desirable property for a unifier is that it be as general as possible: Such a unifier may become a constraint on a further computation, such as finding a unifier for a subsequent unification problem, and making it too specific may prevent a successful completion of that computation.

An important characteristic of (typed) first-order unification problems is that they have most general unifiers whenever they have unifiers. Moreover, these most general unifiers are unique up to substitutions that "rename" variables. For example, the substitution $\{\langle X, Y \rangle, \langle L, Z :: nil \rangle\}$ is a most general unifier for the unification problem $\{(X :: L) = (Y :: Z :: nil)\}$ that we considered earlier. This problem has $\{\langle Y, X \rangle, \langle L, Z :: nil \rangle\}$ as another most general unifier. Finally, these two substitutions differ only by a substitution that renames X to Y or vice versa.

Of course, we are interested in a method for finding most general unifiers. In describing such a method, we initially assume that there are no type variables in the types of the variables and constants that appear in unification problems. A general approach to structuring the search for unifiers is to apply transformations to the equations constituting a unification problem in such a way that the collection of unifiers is preserved, but the problem itself is successively simplified to a point where it is easy to tell that it does not have a unifier or a most general unifier can be read off immediately from it. Let $\bot$ represent a unification problem that has no unifiers. Then, using the canonical form for first-order terms that was described at the end of Section 1.3, we present the following set of transformations for resolving a unification problem given as the multiset of equations $\mathcal{E}$:

> *Term reduction.* Let $(f \; t_1 \; \ldots \; t_n) = (g \; s_1 \; \ldots \; s_m)$ be an equation in $\mathcal{E}$ for some constant symbols f and g. If f and g are distinct constants, or if they are occurrences of the same symbol with two different types, replace $\mathcal{E}$ with $\bot$. Otherwise, transform $\mathcal{E}$ by replacing this equation with the ones in the sequence $t_1 = s_1, \ldots, t_n = s_n$; notice that m and n must be identical in this case.
>
> *Reorientation.* Let $t = x$ be an equation in $\mathcal{E}$ where x is a variable but t is not. Replace this equation by $x = t$.
>
> *Variable elimination.* Let $x = t$ be an equation in $\mathcal{E}$ for some variable x that also has an occurrence in t or some other equation in $\mathcal{E}$. Suppose first that x occurs in t. In this case, remove the equation from $\mathcal{E}$ if t is identical to x, and replace $\mathcal{E}$ by $\bot$ if t is different from x. On the other hand, if x does not appear in t, then transform $\mathcal{E}$ by substituting t for x in the terms of all the other equations in $\mathcal{E}$.

Let us say that a first-order term is *rigid* if it is not a variable, i.e., if it has the structure $(f \; t_1 \; \ldots \; t_n)$, where f is a constant symbol and $n \geq 0$. Applying a substitution to this term produces the term $(f \; t_1' \; \ldots \; t_n')$, where $t_1', \ldots, t_n'$ are terms that result from $t_1, \ldots, t_n$ via the same substitution. In other words, the head of a rigid term remains unchanged under a substitution, and the substitution simply passes through to its arguments. Thus, if an equation has two rigid terms that have different heads, either because they have different names or because they have the same names but with different types, then no substitution can make the two sides of the equation identical. On the other hand, if the heads of the two terms are the same, then the set of substitutions that make their arguments identical must be the same as the set of substitutions that make the terms themselves identical. These observations underlie the term reduction transformation.

The second transformation is essentially a bookkeeping one that may be needed to reorient equations so that the variable elimination transformation can be applied to them. Underlying the last transformation is the observation that terms must be of finite size; this follows from the fact that the well-formedness rules discussed in Section 1.3 require them to be constructed in a finite number of steps starting from constants and variables. If terms have this property, then it is easy to see that an equation of the form $x = t$ cannot have a solution if x is a variable that has an occurrence in the first-order term t but is not t itself. If x does not appear in t, on the other hand, then this equation is solvable, but x must have the structure of t in any of its solutions. This "most general" constraint can be propagated to the other places where x appears to refine the search for unifiers, as the variable-elimination transformation does.

A multiset $\mathcal{E}$ of first-order term equations is in *solved form* if the left-hand side of each equation in it is a variable, and in addition, a variable occurring on the left of any equation does not occur elsewhere in $\mathcal{E}$. Such a multiset cannot have more than one equation with the same variable on the left. We therefore can read it as a substitution, with the term on the right of each equation being the mapping for the variable on the left. Confusing a solved multiset with a substitution in this way, it is easy to see that it must be its own most general unifier. Moreover, it can be shown that if we are careful not to use the variable-elimination transformation on the same (unchanged) equation more than once, then any sequence of applications of the transformations must terminate, reducing a given unification problem either to $\bot$ or to a solved form. Combining these two observations, it follows that the transformations we have presented define a nondeterministic algorithm for finding most general unifiers.

To illustrate the unification algorithm, let us consider the problem

```
{(node E1 T T) = (node 1 (node 2 empty empty) (node 2 empty empty))}
```

By applying term reduction to the only equation in this problem, we can transform it into

```
{E1 = 1, T = (node 2 empty empty), T = (node 2 empty empty)}
```

Using variable elimination with respect to the second equation now produces

```
{El = 1, T = (node 2 empty empty),
         (node 2 empty empty) = (node 2 empty empty)}
```

Applying term reduction based on the last equation further transforms the problem into

```
{El = 1, T = (node 2 empty empty), 2 = 2, empty = empty, empty = empty}
```

The last three equations can be removed using term reduction to produce the multiset {El = 1, T = (node 2 empty empty)} that represents a most general unifier for the original problem.

The algorithm we have described, of course, also will discover nonunifiability. One example of a unification problem that leads to such a conclusion is the following:

```
{(node El T T) = (node 1 (node 2 empty empty) (node 3 empty empty))}
```

Proceeding as in the earlier example, this multiset can be transformed into

```
{El = 1, T = (node 2 empty empty), 2 = 3, empty = empty, empty = empty}
```

Applying term reduction to the third equation in this multiset reduces the unification problem to $\perp$. The cause of the failure in this case is commonly referred to as a *constant clash*. Another problem that has no unifiers is {T = (bt 1 T T)}. In this case, failure is caused by the occurrence of T embedded inside the term on the right-hand side of the equation, a fact that would be discovered when trying to use variable elimination. The test that leads to failure in this case is often called an *occurs-check*.

We have simplified presentation of the unification algorithm by assuming that no type variables appear in the types of terms. We now consider how to proceed in the presence of such variables. Types enter into the calculation only in the term-reduction transformation, and moreover, this happens only when the heads of the two rigid terms have the same name. In this case, we have to match up the types of the two occurrences of this name. When there are no type variables in the types, this "matching up" is straightforward: The two types must be identical. When type variables are present, we also consider substitutions for these variables that could make the types of the two head symbols identical; unification in this sense, is considering refinements not only to term variables but also to (term) constants toward making the terms on the two sides of the equations in a unification problem identical. Of course, such substitutions should be as little constraining as possible. Now the language of types is seen easily to be a special instance of that of typed first-order terms, one, in fact, in which every well-formed expression has a (variable free) type constructed using only the sort type. Thus the algorithm that we have just described can be used to match up the types of head symbols encountered in term reduction in a most general way. Notice that including such a computation could result in the instantiation of type variables in the course of solving (term) unification problems.

We have assumed that the two terms in each equation in a unification problem have identical types. An interesting question is whether the satisfaction of this condition at the beginning eliminates the need to consider types any further in unification. The answer to this question is negative in the general case. More specifically, the need to consider types dynamically in unification arises from two aspects of our language. First, polymorphic constants can be used in terms at instances of their defined types, and looking at just their names therefore does not convey complete information about the types of their occurrences. Second, when such a constant is applied to other terms, the types of its arguments get "erased" from the type of the resulting term, making it necessary to look at these argument types explicitly in order to determine the identity of the constant. To illustrate these points, let us consider the multiset $\{(c\ 1\ Y) = (c\ X\ a)\}$, assuming that c and a are constants whose declared types are A -> A -> i and i, respectively, where i is a user-defined sort. The two terms in the equation have identical types, making this a bona-fide typed unification problem. However, if we do not consider types during unification for this reason, then we will generate the ill-typed unification problem $\{1 = X, Y = a\}$ and, consequently, also the ill-typed unifier $\{\langle X, 1\rangle, \langle Y, a\rangle\}$.

An observation about types in the first-order setting is that while they determine the well formedness of unification problems and hence the existence of solutions, they do not affect the shapes of the unifiers that exist if typing constraints are respected. Thus, if the well typedness of the intermediate multisets produced by versions of our transformations that do not look at types is guaranteed by the type correctness of the original multiset of equations, then types can be eliminated safely from the unification computation. A particular case of practical interest in which this happens is when term constructors are defined so that all the type variables in their argument types also appear in their target type.

We have imposed no limitations on the appearance of constants in the instantiations for variables in the discussions in this section. In a logical setting, and especially when we consider higher-order terms later in the book, constants usually correspond to universally quantified variables, and instantiatable variables similarly correspond to existentially quantified ones. Based on this identification, the unification problems that we have considered in this section can be represented by logical formulas of the form

$$\forall x_1 \ldots \forall x_n \exists y_1 \ldots \exists y_m [t_1 = s_1 \wedge \ldots \wedge t_p = s_p]$$

We will examine the relationship between finding unifiers for unification problems and proving such formulas in more detail in Section 4.4. Notice that the formulas corresponding to the unification problems considered here have a ∀∃ quantifier prefix; i.e., they have a prefix consisting of a sequence of universal quantifiers followed by a sequence of existential quantifiers. We will encounter situations later that have more complex alternations of quantifiers.

The occurs-check test is an important part of the variable elimination transformation as we have described it here: Success in this test must result in a failure to unify. Our rationale for failure in this case is that there can be no finite structure that constitutes a solution to the equation $x = t$ when x occurs in t but is distinct from it. This test is actually omitted in many implementations of unification with the justification that there is a structure with a finite circular description that can be substituted for x to yield a solution to the equation. However, we will require failure in any case where the occurs-check test is satisfied. Finiteness of terms, enforced through this test, will be important to encoding quantifier dependencies in the representations of logics and to capturing similar properties in many other applications that we will consider for our languages.

1.6 Bibliographic notes

Our discussion of the use of first-order terms to represent symbolic and recursive objects draws on standard techniques from logic programming. The reader who is not already familiar with such techniques and who is in search of a larger collection of examples can find them in a number of texts (Clocksin and Mellish 1984; Maier and Warren 1988; O'Keefe 1990; Sterling and Shapiro 1986).

A major difference between the usual treatment of first-order terms and the one we have adopted here is that we take types to be fundamental to their structure. λProlog (Nadathur and Miller 1988) appears to be the first logic programming language to have used a polymorphic typing discipline; however, see Mycroft and O'Keefe (1984) for an early proposal for adding polymorphic types to Prolog. The type system of λProlog was inspired by the one used in ML (Gordon et al. 1979; Damas and Milner 1982; Milner et al. 1990). However, as indicated in Section 1.4, there are differences in the precise form in which types are used in these languages. These differences, as well as the broader differences between functional and logic programming languages, have an impact on the way types affect the computational process. This matter is discussed in detail in Nadathur and Pfenning (1992); a brief discussion also appears in this book in Section 2.7. Type systems for logic programming languages are far from canonical, and many designs and uses of types are possible. For example, the Prolog/Mali (Brisset and Ridoux 1992) and the Gödel (Hill and Lloyd 1994) systems implement variations on the typing described here, whereas other versions based on interpreting types as sets of values were considered by Lakshman and Reddy (1991).

We have distinguished between three categories of expressions in our description of the syntax of terms: the kind expressions, the type expressions, and terms. We have maintained a separation between expressions in these categories, thinking of them in a strictly hierarchical fashion. Such a separation is not essential, and dependently typed λ-calculi such as the Edinburgh Logical Framework or LF (Harper et al. 1993) represent an alternative treatment. These dependently typed λ-calculi can be used as the basis for logic programming, as has been done in Twelf (Pfenning 1989; Pfenning and Schürmann 1999). Such languages permit rich constraints on the structures of objects to be presented through types. These constraints also can be captured in λProlog but require encoding dependent types in predicate definitions using the methods we discuss in Chapter 2 (Felty and Miller 1990; Snow et al. 2010).

First-order unification has a long history. Herbrand's thesis (Herbrand 1930) contains a description of how to solve such problems. Robinson (1965) introduced the idea of most general unifiers and then presented an algorithm similar to that of Herbrand that he proved correctly computed such unifiers. The worst-case complexity of Robinson's algorithm is exponential. Martelli and Montanari (1982) improved the algorithm to one that has almost linear worst-case complexity. Their algorithm begins with the idea of transforming multisets of equations, which is described in this chapter, but then imposes a particular order on the selection of equations and transformations to achieve its efficiency. Paterson and Wegman (1978) presented a different algorithm that is actually of linear worst-case complexity. Most Prolog implementations use Robinson's exponential algorithm because this requires fewer bookkeeping steps and has good behavior in most problems that occur in practice. Another practical matter is whether or not to implement the occurs-check. If this check is implemented naively, it can result in basic programming operations taking unacceptable amounts of time: Setting a variable to a term is often considered to be a constant-time operation, but performing an occurs-check makes it an operation that is linear in the size of the term. Leaving the occurs-check out can lead to unsound deduction. There are situations, however, in which this check can be omitted safely, and there are known implementation and compilation techniques for determining several of these cases. If infinite terms are permitted, it is possible to view unification without the occurs-check as a sound operation that also has programming applications (Colmerauer 1982).

2

First-Order Horn Clauses

Chapter 1 discussed the use of first-order terms to represent data. This chapter describes logic programming over such representations using a typed variant of *first-order Horn clauses*. We begin this presentation by developing a view of logic programming that will allow us to introduce extensions smoothly in later chapters, leading eventually to the full set of logical features that underlie the λProlog language. From this perspective, we will take this paradigm of programming to have two defining characteristics. First, languages within the paradigm provide a *relational approach* to programming. In particular, relations over data descriptions are defined or axiomatized through formulas that use logical connectives and quantifiers. Second, the paradigm views computation as a *search* process. In the approach underlying λProlog, this view is realized by according to each logical symbol a fixed search-related interpretation. These interpretations lead, in turn, to specific programming capabilities.

The first two sections that follow provide a more detailed exposition of a general framework for logic programming along the lines just sketched. The rest of the chapter is devoted to presenting first-order Horn clauses as a specific elaboration of this framework.

2.1 First-order formulas

The first step toward allowing for the description of relations over objects represented by first-order terms is to ease a restriction on signatures: We permit the target types of constants to be o. Constants that have this type are called *relation* or *predicate* symbols. Well-formed first-order expressions are otherwise constructed in the same fashion as that described in Section 1.3. Expressions that have the type o in this setting are referred to as *first-order atomic formulas*. When displayed in canonical form, such an expression must have a predicate symbol as its head and first-order terms as its arguments. As particular examples, the constants memb and append introduced through the declarations

```
type  memb      A -> list A -> o.
type  append    list A -> list A -> list A -> o.
```

are (first-order) predicate symbols. Atomic formulas are formed by applying such predicate symbols to as many terms as required to produce a term of type o. For example, the following are two such formulas.

```
memb 1 (1 :: 2 :: nil)
append (1 :: nil) (2 :: nil) (1 :: 2 :: nil)
```

Each of these formulas can be understood to represent the proposition that the objects denoted by their argument terms stand in the relationships named by their heads.

To permit the construction of complex formulas, we add to signatures a special, pre-defined set of *logical constants* or *propositional symbols*. Written in mathematical notation, the particular such constants that we include are $\top$ standing for the always true proposition, $\wedge$ standing for conjunction, $\vee$ standing for disjunction, and $\supset$ standing for implication. The concrete syntax used in λProlog for these constants is the following:

true	of type o representing $\top$
=>	of type o -> o -> o representing $\supset$
&	of type o -> o -> o representing $\wedge$
,	of type o -> o -> o representing $\wedge$
;	of type o -> o -> o representing $\vee$ and
:-	of type o -> o -> o representing implication written in reverse

Notice that many of these constants have the sort o as an argument type, a violation of a restriction placed earlier on the types of constants contained in signatures. We permit this violation in the first-order setting only with respect to the types of these logical constants. All but the first of the λProlog constants shown are defined to be infix operators. Further, the first two of these operators are taken to be right associative, the next two are considered to be left-associative, and the last is nonassociative. Finally, the precedences of these operators follow the order in which they are listed, and they all bind less tightly than application.

Well-formed expressions of type o that can be constructed with the enhancements up to this point constitute *quantifier-free first-order formulas*. Examples of such formulas that use the predicate symbols declared earlier are the following:

```
(memb 1 (2 :: 1 :: nil) :- memb 1 (1 :: nil)), memb 1 (1 :: nil)
memb 1 (1 :: nil) => memb 1 (2 :: 1 :: nil) & memb 1 (1 :: nil)
(memb 1 (1 :: nil) => memb 1 (2 :: 1 :: nil)) & memb 1 (1 :: nil)
(append nil nil nil ; memb 1 (2 :: nil)), append (1 :: nil) nil (1 :: nil)
```

The parentheses around the implication expression in the third formula are redundant by virtue of the assumed operator precedences; this formula is, in fact, structurally equivalent to the second one that omits the parentheses. The parentheses surrounding the implication in the first formula and the disjunction in the last formula are, however, essential for the readings intended in these cases. The first two formulas, which have an identical logical structure, illustrate a redundancy in the concrete syntax in that two different symbols are provided for representing conjunction and implication. In each of these cases, the different symbols are intended to be used in λProlog in distinct, mutually exclusive situations; we describe the convention governing their use later in this chapter.

The final addition that leads to the full set of first-order formulas is that of universal and existential quantification. Both forms of quantification range over explicit domains specified by types. In mathematical notation, the universal and existential quantification of x over the formula F at the type τ are written as $\forall_\tau x\, F$ and $\exists_\tau x\, F$, respectively. Both quantifiers bind a variable and establish a scope for its binding. In concrete syntax, the depicted expressions are written as (pi (x:T)\ F) and (sigma (x:T)\ F), respectively, where F, T, and x are themselves the concrete syntax renditions of the formula F, the type τ, and the variable x. While quantification must take place at a specified type, this type often can be left implicit, to be filled in in a most general way that we describe shortly. Thus we may depict quantified formulas simply as $\forall x\, F$ and $\exists x\, F$ in mathematical notation or as (pi x\ F) and (sigma x\ F) in concrete syntax. It is apparent from the representation of quantification that the backslash token plays the role of a binding operator. This role will become precise in Chapter 4 when it will be identified officially as an infix operator representing λ-abstraction. In that context, pi and sigma will be recognized to be polymorphic constants of the type (A -> o) -> o. For the moment, however, we treat pi x\ and sigma x\ simply as unanalyzed, concrete syntax forms for the quantifiers depicted by $\forall x$ and $\exists x$ in our metalinguistic discourse.

The following expression illustrates the concrete syntax for quantified formulas:

```
(pi x\ (pi z\ (append x z x =>
            (sigma y\ (append x y z, pi x\ (append y z x))))))).
```

By convention, the scope of a bound variable introduced by a backslash extends as far to the right as possible, limited only by parentheses and the end of the expression. Using this convention, the expression shown above can be written simply as

```
pi x\ pi z\ append x z x => sigma y\ append x y z, pi x\ append y z x.
```

The scope convention is especially useful in reducing parentheses when a series of quantifiers appears at the beginning of the formula. For example, the expression

```
pi x\ pi y\ pi z\ append x y z
```

that represents the closure of the atomic formula append x y z under universal quantification avoids the use of parentheses altogether. Further examples of quantified formulas are the following:

```
pi x\ pi k\ memb x (x :: k)
pi X\ pi L\ pi K\ pi M\ append (X::L) K (X::M) :- append L K M
sigma X\ pi y\ sigma h\ append X y h
```

The various examples also illustrate a rule that governs the syntax of bound variable names: These can be any contiguous sequence of characters beginning with an upper- or lowercase letter.

An important principle concerning quantification is that the pattern of binding is key and the names chosen for variables to indicate this structure are unimportant. A consequence of this principle is that the names of bound variables can be changed systematically without affecting the meaning of a quantified formula. For example, the following four formulas are all logically equivalent to each other.

```
pi x\ (p x) => sigma y\ (q x y, pi x\ (q y x))
pi x\ (p x) => sigma U\ (q x U, pi x\ (q U x))
pi z\ (p z) => sigma y\ (q z y, pi x\ (q y x))
pi z\ (p z) => sigma y\ (q z y, pi v\ (q y v))
```

In Chapter 4 we shall see that these equivalences are actually a consequence of the notion of α-convertibility for λ-terms.

The syntax that we have described for (typed) first-order formulas can be formalized through an extension of the type assignment calculus presented in Section 1.3. In the extended setting, we assume that signatures contain the necessary association of types with logical constants and that the types they associate with other (nonlogical) constants may have o as their target type. We then augment the typing rules presented in Figure 1.2 with the rules in Figure 2.1, which treat expressions containing quantifiers; the third rule in this figure, which is justified by the principle of bound variable renaming, may need to be used in type assignment derivations in order to satisfy the proviso associated

$$\frac{\Sigma; \Gamma, x : \tau \Vdash_f B : o}{\Sigma; \Gamma \Vdash_f \forall_\tau x\, B : o} \qquad \frac{\Sigma; \Gamma, x : \tau \Vdash_f B : o}{\Sigma; \Gamma \Vdash_f \exists_\tau x\, B : o}$$

provided x is not assigned a type by either Σ or Γ.

$$\frac{\Sigma; \Gamma \Vdash_f B : \tau}{\Sigma; \Gamma \Vdash_f C : \tau}$$

provided B and C differ only in the names of bound variables.

Figure 2.1. Rules added to those in Figure 1.2 for typing expressions with quantifiers.

with the first two rules. Finally, we say that an expression F is a *typed first-order Σ-formula* if the judgment $\Sigma; \emptyset \Vdash_f F : o$ is derivable in the resulting calculus; noting that typing is intrinsic to our setting, we may in such a case also refer to F as a first-order Σ-formula or, simply, as a first-order formula when the identity of the signature is not important to the discussion at hand.

The preceding characterization of first-order formulas assumes that each occurrence of a variable in such a formula is within the scope of a quantifier that binds the variable, i.e., that the formula is *closed*. Each such quantifier is also assumed to indicate explicitly the type of the domain of quantification. In reality, the concrete λProlog syntax allows this type to be left implicit, and indeed, this is the preferred way of writing quantified expressions. This style can be accommodated because the missing types can be filled in by a type inference process. Formally, this process tentatively associates a new type variable with the variable of quantification in the augmented contexts shown in the premises of the first two rules in Figure 2.1. This type variable then is refined incrementally in as minimal a way as possible so as to ensure a continued adherence to the typing rules in the course of type assignment. The unification computation described in Section 1.5 can be applied to type expressions to realize such refinements and thereby to infer an association of types with quantified variables that is most general with respect to the $\lhd_f$ relation. We assume such a type inference process to be operative in all future discussions.

2.2 Logic programming and search semantics

Four ingredients are essential to our abstract presentation of logic programming: (1) signatures, (2) program clauses, (3) goals or goal formulas, and (4) a calculus for constructing proofs. Signatures identify the nonlogical constants that can be used to build data objects and to state the relationships that hold between these objects. Once the signature Σ has been fixed, we assume that the logical context makes precise the collection of well-formed terms and formulas that we will refer to as Σ-*terms* and Σ-*formulas*; we have seen how these notions are formalized in the first-order setting. Some of the Σ-formulas are now identified as program clauses. These formulas are the ones that might be used as assertions or axioms to partially define the relations denoted by the predicate symbols in Σ. A collection of such formulas constitutes a logic program. Another, possibly different class of Σ-formulas is admitted as the collection of goal formulas, also called *queries*. These formulas are the ones whose derivations may be attempted from a given logic program.

We make use of sequent calculi to describe the structures of proofs. For our purposes here, a sequent is a triple consisting of a signature Σ, a set $\mathcal{P}$ of Σ-formulas (the logic program), and a Σ-formula G (the goal). Such a sequent will be written as $\Sigma; \mathcal{P} \longrightarrow G$. We also sometimes shall talk of a signature-program pair $\langle \Sigma, \mathcal{P} \rangle$ that defines a context in which varied queries can be posed. The sequent $\Sigma; \mathcal{P} \longrightarrow G$ denotes the judgment, which may or may not hold, that the formula G can be proved from the assumptions $\mathcal{P}$ and the signature Σ. Sequent calculi are characterized by particular collections of inference rules that permit a sequent judgment to be derived from a possibly empty collection of premises that are themselves sequent judgments. Such calculi have been described for classical, intuitionistic and linear logic as well as many other logics.

Goal-directed proof search can be presented through a collection of transition or reduction rules that transform the task of solving a given sequent into the task of solving other related sequents. We use the following rules to associate a search behavior with each of the logical constants and quantifiers:

AND   Reduce $\Sigma; \mathcal{P} \longrightarrow B_1 \wedge B_2$ to the two sequents $\Sigma; \mathcal{P} \longrightarrow B_1$ and $\Sigma; \mathcal{P} \longrightarrow B_2$.

OR   Reduce $\Sigma; \mathcal{P} \longrightarrow B_1 \vee B_2$ to either $\Sigma; \mathcal{P} \longrightarrow B_1$ or $\Sigma; \mathcal{P} \longrightarrow B_2$; the sequent that is selected must be solved to yield a solution to the original sequent.

INSTAN   Reduce $\Sigma; \mathcal{P} \longrightarrow \exists_\tau x\, B$ to $\Sigma; \mathcal{P} \longrightarrow B[t/x]$, for some term Σ-term t of type τ; the resulting sequent thus is parameterized by the chosen Σ-term t.

AUGMENT   Reduce $\Sigma; \mathcal{P} \longrightarrow B_1 \supset B_2$ to $\Sigma; \mathcal{P}, B_1 \longrightarrow B_2$.

GENERIC   Reduce $\Sigma; \mathcal{P} \longrightarrow \forall_\tau x\, B$ to $c : \tau, \Sigma; \mathcal{P} \longrightarrow B[c/x]$, where c is a token that is not in the current signature Σ. We shall refer to c as a *new constant*.

TRUE   The sequent $\Sigma; \mathcal{P} \longrightarrow \top$ is provable immediately and does not need to be reduced further.

These rules assign a *fixed* search semantics that is independent of the signature and the program to each of the logical symbols. For example, the connectives

$$\frac{}{\Sigma; \mathcal{P} \longrightarrow \top} \top R \qquad \frac{\Sigma; \mathcal{P} \longrightarrow B_1 \qquad \Sigma; \mathcal{P} \longrightarrow B_2}{\Sigma; \mathcal{P} \longrightarrow B_1 \wedge B_2} \wedge R$$

$$\frac{\Sigma; \mathcal{P} \longrightarrow B_1}{\Sigma; \mathcal{P} \longrightarrow B_1 \vee B_2} \vee R \qquad \frac{\Sigma; \mathcal{P} \longrightarrow B_2}{\Sigma; \mathcal{P} \longrightarrow B_1 \vee B_2} \vee R$$

$$\frac{\Sigma; \mathcal{P}, B_1 \longrightarrow B_2}{\Sigma; \mathcal{P} \longrightarrow B_1 \supset B_2} \supset R$$

$$\frac{\Sigma; \mathcal{P} \longrightarrow B[t/x] \qquad \Sigma; \emptyset \Vdash_f t : \tau}{\Sigma; \mathcal{P} \longrightarrow \exists_\tau x \, B} \exists R \qquad \frac{c : \tau, \Sigma; \mathcal{P} \longrightarrow B[c/x]}{\Sigma; \mathcal{P} \longrightarrow \forall_\tau x \, B} \forall R$$

The $\forall R$ rule has the proviso that c is not declared in Σ.

Figure 2.2. Right-introduction rules.

$\wedge$ and $\vee$ in goals are always mapped into AND and OR search steps regardless of the signature-program context in which they are encountered.

The reduction rules just listed treat sequents as if they are characterizations of the state of an interpreter. Specifically, $\Sigma; \mathcal{P} \longrightarrow G$ might be read in the context of these rules as an attempt to solve G given the signature-program pair $\langle \Sigma, \mathcal{P} \rangle$. However, we also have noted a logical interpretation for such a sequent: It represents the judgment that the Σ-formula G is true whenever the Σ-formulas in $\mathcal{P}$ are true for a suitable notion of truth. Under this second viewpoint, it makes sense also to reverse the reduction rules, reading them as inference rules of logic instead. Interpreted this way, the INSTAN rule, for example, translates into the following: If the sequent $\Sigma; \mathcal{P} \longrightarrow B[t/x]$ can be proved for some Σ-term t of type τ, then we have a justification for the sequent $\Sigma; \mathcal{P} \longrightarrow \exists_\tau x \, B$. Figure 2.2 displays the inference rules corresponding in this manner to each of the reduction rules. These inference rules are called *right-introduction rules* because they justify the introduction of a logical symbol to the right of the arrow in the sequent constituting the conclusion of the rule, i.e., in the sequent that appears below the horizontal line in the presentation of the rule. We have adopted some conventions commonly used with sequent calculi in displaying the inference rules in Figure 2.2: In the $\supset R$ rule, the expression $\mathcal{P}, B_1$ denotes the set $\mathcal{P} \cup \{B_1\}$ of formulas, and in the $\forall R$ rule, the expression $c : \tau, \Sigma$ denotes the set $\{c : \tau\} \cup \Sigma$ of type declarations. Notice also that we have used the judgment $\Sigma; \emptyset \Vdash_f t : \tau$ in the $\exists R$ rule to formalize the requirement that t must be a Σ-term of type τ. This is somewhat limiting in that it assumes a restriction to the first-order setting. A more general form of this rule will be presented in Section 5.2 after higher-order terms have been introduced.

We have, at this point, two views of sequents and, thereby, of logic programming: an abstract, declarative interpretation based on logic and an operational interpretation based on understanding logical symbols as specific search instructions. The desire is, of course, that these two interpretations coexist. This naturally raises the question of the extent to which the inference rules in Figure 2.2 correspond to logic. It is easy to see that each of these inference rules is sound in any interesting logic; i.e., if the premise sequents—the sequents above the horizontal line in each rule—are provable, then the conclusion sequent also must be provable. The converse property, that of logical completeness, can be phrased as follows: If a sequent with a nonatomic goal is provable, then must the premise sequent(s) of the rule corresponding to such a goal also be provable? Completeness is a more intricate question and depends both on the formulas we permit in programs and queries and on the logic that we use to provide the declarative semantics. To illustrate some of the issues involved, let us take the signature Σ to be $\{p : o,\ q : o,\ r : i \to o,\ a : i,\ b : i\}$, where i is some fixed sort. Then we observe the following:

1. The OR rule reduces the sequent $\Sigma;\ p \vee q \longrightarrow q \vee p$ to either $\Sigma;\ p \vee q \longrightarrow q$ or $\Sigma;\ p \vee q \longrightarrow p$. Neither of these sequents is provable, although the original sequent is provable in classical and intuitionistic logics.
2. The OR rule reduces $\Sigma;\ \longrightarrow p \vee (p \supset q)$ to either $\Sigma;\ \longrightarrow p$ or $\Sigma;\ \longrightarrow p \supset q$. The first sequent cannot be proved. The second sequent reduces by virtue of the AUGMENT rule to $\Sigma;\ p \longrightarrow q$, which also cannot be proved. However, in classical logic—a logic that is often used to formalize mathematical arguments—$p \vee (p \supset q)$ is a tautology. Within this logic, it is assumed that any given proposition is either true or false. Using this assumption in the situation at hand, if p is true, then the disjunction $p \vee (p \supset q)$ is true, and if p is false, then $p \supset q$ is true, and again, the disjunction is true.
3. The INSTAN rule reduces the sequent

$$\Sigma;\ (r\,a \wedge r\,b) \supset q \longrightarrow \exists_i x\,(r\,x \supset q)$$

to the sequent $\Sigma;\ (r\,a \wedge r\,b) \supset q \longrightarrow r\,t \supset q$, where t is some Σ-term of type i. However, there is no possible choice for t that makes this sequent provable: If we pick t to be a, then the AUGMENT rule reduces this sequent to the unprovable sequent

$$\Sigma;\ (r\,a \wedge r\,b) \supset q,\ r\,a \longrightarrow q.$$

Similar observations apply if we pick t to be b or something different from a and b. While no sequent it reduces to can be proved, the original sequent itself is true (and, hence, provable) in classical logic according to the following reasoning: We know that $r\,a$ is either true or false. If it is false, then $\exists_i x\,(r\,x \supset q)$ is true (by picking a for x). If $r\,a$ is true, then $(r\,a \wedge r\,b) \supset q$

is equivalent to $r\ b \supset q$, from which it follows easily that $\exists_i x\ (r\ x \supset q)$ again must be true.

Completeness is important to the integrity of the framework we have described. A central question concerning the design of logic programming languages therefore becomes the following: Is it possible to restrict the program and goal formulas and to choose the underlying logic in such a way that interesting and useful programming behavior is supported on the one hand and completeness is assured on the other? We shall need to think of both kinds of refinements in developing the logical basis of λProlog. As the first example illustrates, it seems likely that we will have to prohibit disjunctions from appearing in our programs. In fact, the formulas we eventually allow in programs are also called *definite formulas* because they do not contain indefinite information of the kind let in by disjunctions. The last two examples illustrate that this step by itself may not be enough because classical logic, as we have seen, has a kind of indefinite assumption built into it: It assumes that $B \vee \neg B$ is true for any formula B. This assumption is known as the *principle of the excluded middle*. To overcome the problem raised by it, we shall move to intuitionistic logic, a weaker logic than classical logic in which the principle does not hold.

The focus on search semantics has led to our describing reductions only for nonatomic goals. We must, of course, also consider how to reduce atomic goals. Clearly, progress when these are encountered should depend on the program. At a logical level, inference rules that introduce logical symbols in the program that appears to the left of the sequent arrow, i.e., *left-introduction rules*, should govern what happens at this point. From a pragmatic perspective, features of the atomic goal, such as the predicate symbol at its head, should influence the particular choice of rules. We will see these intuitions being substantiated in the particular logics that we propose for programming. However, we do not build them into the framework for two reasons. First, we are presently interested only in an abstract characterization of search behavior in which the logical symbols in goals are the primary players. Second, greater specificity in the treatment of atomic goals requires detailed assumptions about the structure of the formulas permitted in programs, something that is to be avoided in describing a general framework.

We have presented computation as the process of solving a query or, equivalently, searching for a proof. There is, of course, also interest in what the eventual result of such a computation should be. If the attempt to solve the goal is unsuccessful, the answer is easy: The result should be an indication of the failure. If the attempt is successful, the result could be the proof that has been found. However, proofs are complete traces of computations, and in programming situations, it is often useful to provide back only a summary of a computation. The INSTAN rule indicates a possible way to satisfy this requirement. By virtue of this rule, an existential goal is solved by finding a particular instance of it that is solvable. The term that yields this instance then can be considered to be the result of the computation. Extending the idea a bit further, we may allow a goal to contain free variables with the interpretation that these variables are existentially bound at the head. The result of solving such a goal—which we refer to as an *answer substitution*—is then the mapping from these variables to terms that leads to the successful computation.

In the rest of this chapter we consider a particular example of the framework for logic programming that we have just described. This example, called the logic of *first-order Horn clauses*, or `fohc`, provides the logical foundations for the programming language Prolog. The syntax of goals in the Horn clause setting is restricted in such a way that the AUGMENT and GENERIC reduction rules become redundant. We shall remove these restrictions in Chapter 3 to obtain a more expressive language. Later we will extend the language further to incorporate a richer term structure and quantification over predicate and function symbols while preserving the principle of goal-directed proof search discussed here.

2.3 Horn clauses and their computational interpretation

Let A be a syntactic variable denoting first-order atomic formulas. Goals and program clauses in the setting of `fohc` are then the first-order formulas corresponding to the syntactic variables G and D that are given, respectively, by the following rules:

$$G ::= \top \mid A \mid G \wedge G \mid G \vee G \mid \exists_\tau x\, G$$

$$D ::= A \mid G \supset D \mid D \wedge D \mid \forall_\tau x\, D$$

We have used here the richest of different but logically equivalent ways to describe these classes of formulas. In this formulation, only $\supset$ and $\forall$ are disallowed at the top level in G-formulas, and only $\vee$ and $\exists$ are disallowed at the top level in D-formulas.

The program clauses that we have described include formulas of the form

$$\forall_{\tau_1} x_1 \ldots \forall_{\tau_m} x_m\, (A_1 \wedge \ldots \wedge A_n \supset A_0)$$

for $m, n \geq 0$; we let $m = 0$ denote the situation where there are no universal quantifiers at the front of the formula and $n = 0$ denote the situation where there is no implication. A formula that has this structure should be familiar from Prolog, where it serves as a partial definition of the predicate symbol that appears as the head of A_0. Notice, however, that such formulas are only special cases of our program clauses. In particular, in our setting, the right-hand side of an implication need not be an atomic formula: What we might think of as the eventual "head" of an implication may be to the right of further implications and buried under conjunctions and universal quantifiers.

Given a set of program clauses $\mathcal{P}$ and a goal formula G defined over the signature Σ, computation in the model we described in the preceding section consists of attempting to construct a derivation for the sequent $\Sigma; \mathcal{P} \longrightarrow G$. The previously presented reduction rules determine the manner in which to proceed in the case where G has a complex structure. To complete this picture, it is necessary to explain what is to be done when G has been reduced to an atomic formula. Considering some simple cases leads us naturally to an answer to this question. If the goal G is the atomic formula A and the program $\mathcal{P}$ contains this formula, then clearly the computation should succeed immediately. Similarly, if $\mathcal{P}$ contains a clause of the form $G' \supset A$, then it should suffice to derive G' from $\mathcal{P}$: From a logical perspective, since $G' \supset A$ and G' follows from $\mathcal{P}$, so must A. Thus, in this case, one possibility would be to reduce the sequent $\Sigma; \mathcal{P} \longrightarrow A$ to $\Sigma; \mathcal{P} \longrightarrow G'$.

The process that we just described for advancing proof search when the goal is atomic is commonly known as *backchaining*. Since program clauses in our setting can be more than atomic formulas or implicational formulas with atomic consequents, we need to describe backchaining in a more general way for it to be adequate. The inference rules in Figure 2.3 provide such a description. The sequent $\Sigma; \mathcal{P} \xrightarrow{D} A$ in these rules is used to indicate that an attempt is being made to prove the atomic goal A by backchaining on the program clause D. The first rule in Figure 2.3 has the proviso that D appears in $\mathcal{P}$, and it encodes the selection of D as the clause on which to backchain. The second rule has an obvious connotation: If the atom that we are attempting to derive is identical to the one on which we are backchaining, then the computation along this branch ends. If, on the other hand, the formula chosen for backchaining is the implication $G \supset D$, then we must do two things: derive G from the same program and continue the backchaining process using D in place of $G \supset D$. This behavior is encoded in the third rule. The next two rules allow for reducing backchaining on a conjunction to backchaining on either conjunct. The last rule describes backchaining on universal formulas: The selected universally quantified formula is instantiated by a chosen Σ-term, and the resulting formula becomes the basis for backchaining.

The backchaining rules other than the first one in Figure 2.3 can be compiled into a simple and familiar form when the structure of program clauses is restricted to that in Prolog, i.e., when they are all of the form

$$\forall_{\tau_1} x_1 \ldots \forall_{\tau_m} x_m (A_1 \wedge \ldots \wedge A_n \supset A_0)$$

$$\frac{\Sigma;\mathcal{P} \xrightarrow{D} A}{\Sigma;\mathcal{P} \longrightarrow A} \text{ decide} \qquad \frac{}{\Sigma;\mathcal{P} \xrightarrow{A} A} \text{ initial} \qquad \frac{\Sigma;\mathcal{P} \xrightarrow{D} A \quad \Sigma;\mathcal{P} \longrightarrow G}{\Sigma;\mathcal{P} \xrightarrow{G \supset D} A} \supset L$$

In the decide rule, D is a formula that is selected from $\mathcal{P}$.

$$\frac{\Sigma;\mathcal{P} \xrightarrow{D_1} A}{\Sigma;\mathcal{P} \xrightarrow{D_1 \wedge D_2} A} \wedge L \qquad \frac{\Sigma;\mathcal{P} \xrightarrow{D_2} A}{\Sigma;\mathcal{P} \xrightarrow{D_1 \wedge D_2} A} \wedge L \qquad \frac{\Sigma;\mathcal{P} \xrightarrow{D[t/x]} A \quad \Sigma;\emptyset \vdash_f t : \tau}{\Sigma;\mathcal{P} \xrightarrow{\forall_\tau x \, D} A} \forall L$$

Figure 2.3. Rules for backchaining.

where $m, n \geq 0$. In particular, if D is such a formula, then the inference rule

$$\frac{\Sigma;\mathcal{P} \longrightarrow A_1\theta \qquad \cdots \qquad \Sigma;\mathcal{P} \longrightarrow A_n\theta}{\Sigma;\mathcal{P} \xrightarrow{D} A}$$

suffices to describe backchaining. This rule has an associated "side condition" that θ must be a substitution for the variables $x_1, \ldots, x_m$ that maps each x_i to a Σ-term t_i of type τ_i and that is such that A is equal to $A_0\theta$. The soundness of this rule in a logical sense can be seen as follows: Assume that $A_1\theta, \ldots, A_n\theta$ follow from $\mathcal{P}$ (i.e. that the premises of the inference rule are derivable). Since $\mathcal{P}$ contains the clause $\forall_{\tau_1} x_1 \ldots \forall_{\tau_m} x_m (A_1 \wedge \ldots \wedge A_n \supset A_0)$, the instance $(A_1\theta \wedge \ldots \wedge A_n\theta \supset A_0\theta)$ also must follow from $\mathcal{P}$. But then, using modus ponens, it must be the case that $A_0\theta$ follows from $\mathcal{P}$.

The formula that appears above the sequent arrow in the rules in Figure 2.3 can be thought of as being a part of the left side of the sequent; placing it above the arrow merely puts the focus on using it in the next step in the derivation. Interpreting this formula in this way makes these inference rules instances of *left-introduction rules*: They introduce a new occurrence of a logical connective in the formulas appearing on the left of the sequent arrow in the sequent that constitutes the conclusion of the rule. These rules thus complement the right-introduction rules in Figure 2.2, and when read bottom-up, these two sets together with the rules in Figure 1.2 for identifying first-order Σ-terms provide a collection of reductions that can be used in deriving a goal. These reductions actually yield a proof procedure for the logic of first-order Horn clauses that is complete with respect to both classical and intuitionistic logic. More specifically, let us call a proof that is constructed using the inference rules from Figures 1.2, 2.2, and 2.3 an *O-proof*. A known result, then, is that if $\mathcal{P}$ is a logic program and G is a goal in `fohc`, then $\Sigma;\mathcal{P} \longrightarrow G$ has an *O*-proof if and only if it has a proof in classical logic or, equivalently, a proof in intuitionistic logic.

As discussed in Section I.2, an important measure of the expressiveness of a logic programming language is the different ways in which sequents in that language can change during proof search. For `fohc`, we have the following property: Every sequent in an O-proof of the sequent $\Sigma; \mathcal{P} \longrightarrow G$ is of the form $\Sigma; \mathcal{P} \longrightarrow G'$ or $\Sigma; \mathcal{P} \xrightarrow{D} A$, for some A, G', and D. Thus every goal formula that is encountered during a computation ends up having to be proved with respect to the *same* signature-program pair. Another way to understand this is that signatures and programs are *flat* and *global* in fohc: Every clause and every constant that is needed during the construction of a proof must already be a member of the initial logic program and signature. In later chapters we will extend the syntax of formulas in fohc so that the AUGMENT and GENERIC rules become applicable to them. These rules support the capability of enlarging both the program and the signature during a computation.

2.4 Programming with first-order Horn clauses

The preceding two sections have provided an abstract view of computation based on a fragment of first-order logic. We now turn to understanding the use of this framework in actual programming tasks. We begin by taking a more concrete, system oriented view of fohc that is based on λProlog. In particular, we present a concrete syntax for program clauses and queries, and we describe a mode of interaction that corresponds to constructing derivations for sequents. We then explore the programming capabilities afforded by this setup by considering its use in encoding search related problems and in the specification of relations over recursively structured data.

2.4.1 Concrete syntax for program clauses

Programs are presented in λProlog as a sequence of clauses, each terminated with a period. The program clauses that we want to write often have several universal quantifiers at the outermost level. To make such clauses simpler to write and display, the following conventions are used:

- A token in a program clause that is not explicitly quantified or otherwise reserved is assumed to be a variable that is implicitly universally quantified over the entire clause if it begins with an uppercase letter and to be a constant otherwise. Type declarations must be included in the program that make explicit the types of nonpervasive constants that appear in any clause. The λProlog system attempts to infer types for implicitly quantified variables using the process discussed earlier.[1]
- The underscore symbol _ also may be used to denote a variable that is implicitly universally quantified over the entire clause. Each occurrence of

---

[1] The user also may indicate types for these variables, as we discuss in Section 2.7.3.

this symbol corresponds to a distinct variable. Such variables are said to be *anonymous*.

- Quantifiers also may be included explicitly in clauses. The names of the variables that such quantifiers bind may begin with either an uppercase or a lowercase letter. Types may be provided for these variables at the binding site. If they are not provided, the λProlog system will try to infer them.

Let append be a constant that is identified by the following type declaration:

```
type  append  list A -> list A -> list A -> o.
```

Then the following program fragment illustrates these conventions:

```
append nil L L.
append (X :: L1) L2 (X :: L3) :- append L1 L2 L3.
```

These clauses also may be written in more verbose form as

```
pi L\ append nil L L.
pi X\ pi L1\ pi L2\ pi L3\
            append (X :: L1) L2 (X :: L3) :- append L1 L2 L3.
```

Regardless of which syntax is used, λProlog will certify the clauses as being well typed, inferring the type (list A) for L in the first clause and the types A for X and (list A) for L1, L2, and L3 in the second clause. The second presentation also can be modified to

```
pi l\ append nil l l.
pi x\ pi l1\ pi l2\ pi l3\
            append (x :: l1) l2 (x :: l3) :- append l1 l2 l3.
```

Here, tokens beginning with lowercase letters have been used for variables that are explicitly quantified. As another example, consider the following type declaration and clause:

```
type sublist   list A -> list A -> o.
sublist L K :- append _ T K, append L _ T.
```

The clause here contains two occurrences of the anonymous variable and equivalently could have been written as

```
sublist L K :- append U T K, append L V T.
```

As noted in Section 2.1, there are two symbols in λProlog for conjunction, namely, & and the comma. There is also a redundancy in the representation of implication in that => is available for writing "implies" and :- can be used to write "is implied by." Stylistic conventions for using the different symbols motivate these redundancies. The symbol & is intended to be used when forming the conjunction of two program clauses, whereas the comma is to be used to construct a conjunction of two goal formulas. Similarly, the symbol :- is to be used to represent the implication that appears in the syntax rules for *D*-formulas, and => is to be used for implications that appear at the top level in queries. Since *fohc* does not permit implications in queries, the last convention makes the => symbol redundant in this setting and has a positive impact only in the richer logics we consider later. The conventions that we have described can be ignored without affecting the well-formedness of expressions, but following them can ease the reading of program clauses and queries.

It is possible to embed conjunctions and implications in program clauses, and this allows us to write the same programs in different ways. For example, suppose that we are given the kind and type declarations shown below:

```
kind   bool          type.
type   neg           bool -> bool.
type   and, or, imp   bool -> bool -> bool.
type   ident          bool -> bool -> o.
```

Consider then the following clauses:

```
ident (neg B)   (neg D)    :- ident B D.
ident (and B C) (and D E) :- ident B D, ident C E.
ident (or  B C) (or  D E) :- ident B D, ident C E.
ident (imp B C) (imp D E) :- ident B D, ident C E.
```

The "bodies" of the last three clauses are identical. Using the fact that the right-hand sides of implications in program clauses can contain conjunctions, this part can be factored out, as in the following set of clauses.

```
ident (neg B)   (neg D)    :- ident B D.
ident (and B C) (and D E) &
ident (or  B C) (or  D E) &
ident (imp B C) (imp D E) :- ident B D, ident C E.
```

Recall here that the precedence of & is higher than that of :-. It is possible to compress this presentation of clauses even further into the following single clause:

```
ident (neg B)    (neg D)    &
(ident (and B C) (and D E) &
 ident (or  B C) (or  D E) &
 ident (imp B C) (imp D E) :- ident C E) :- ident B D.
```

Implicit in this discussion is the fact that all three forms presented here are equivalent in terms of the goals that can be derived from them as well as in terms of any observable operational behavior that results from them. This observation follows from examining the way the backchaining rules structure the use of the clauses in the different presentations.

Rather than aiding in readability, a compact representation sometimes may make programs more difficult to understand and so should be used with care. From an execution perspective, a naive application of the rules in Figure 2.3 when a program clause is in compressed form can be costly. A more sophisticated implementation therefore might use the structure of the backchaining rules to preprocess a program clause in the form presented last into the first set of program clauses.

2.4.2 Interacting with the λProlog system

The search for a derivation can begin only after a sequent $\Sigma; \mathcal{P} \longrightarrow G$ has been presented. In the typical programming scenario, the left-hand side of the sequent is specified first. There is a part of this signature-program pair that comes with the λProlog system and therefore is always available. The signature part of this *ambient* or *pervasive* signature-program pair includes all the type and value constructors for representing integers, strings, reals, and streams that were discussed in Chapter 1 and the logical constants described in Section 2.1 of this chapter. For the program part, we assume that it contains built-in definitions of certain predicates that are broadly useful or that are difficult to encode in a purely logical manner. For instance, included in this component are the following:

`<, >, =<, >=`	each of type `int -> int -> o`, representing the usual comparison operators on integers and correctly used only when both arguments are instantiated to numbers
`read`	of type `A -> o`, which reads a line from the standard input stream (`std_in`), parses the portion of it up to a period, and succeeds if this unifies with the argument and
`print`	of type `string -> o`, which prints the argument to the standard output stream (`std_out`); this predicate is meaningfully used only when its argument is instantiated to a string constant.

We introduce more pervasive predicates as we need them in various parts of this book.

A programmer can add declarations and program clauses by using the module system of λProlog, which is discussed in detail in Chapter 6. For the moment, it suffices to view a module as a named collection of signature declarations and program clauses. The following code provides an example of a module called lists that declares the predicate constant append and provides program clauses defining it:

```
module lists.
type  append    list A -> list A -> list A -> o.
append nil L L.
append (X::L) K (X::M) :- append L K M.
end
```

When initiating an interaction session, the user of the system must provide the name of the module whose signature and clause declarations are to augment the ambient signature-program pair before parsing and solving queries. If the user indicates lists to be this module, then the system will build the relevant left-hand side of the sequent and present the user with the prompt

```
[lists] ?-
```

At this stage, the system enters a mode of interaction that is referred to as the *read-prove-print loop*. Although interactions take place relative to modules, we shall simplify the prompt to just ?- if the name of the module is not important for understanding the issues in a given context.

The read phase

At this stage, all that remains to initiate a computation is providing a query, which is done at the prompt. An example of this is the following:

```
[lists] ?- sigma X\ sigma Y\ append X Y (1 :: 2 :: nil).
```

Notice that queries are terminated by a period.

In Section 2.4.1 we noted a convention for omitting quantifiers at the head of a program clause. A dual convention applies to goals typed in at the prompt: Tokens that are not explicitly quantified and which start with an initial uppercase letter are assumed to be implicitly existentially quantified with outermost scope, and all other tokens that are not special symbols or explicitly bound are taken to be constants that must be declared in the signature. Using this convention, the following queries are equivalent to the one presented earlier, at least in terms of the search behavior to which they give rise:

```
[lists] ?- sigma Y\ append X Y (1::nil).
[lists] ?- append X Y (1::nil).
```

As with program clauses, the symbol _ can be used to represent an anonymous variable. Thus these queries also may be written as

```
[lists] ?- append _ _ (1::nil).
```

There is, however, a pragmatic difference between these varied forms that will be explained in the presentation of the print phase below.

The prove phase

The prove phase corresponds to trying to find an O-proof for a sequent.[2] It is in this phase that computation takes place in λProlog. Later in this chapter we consider in more detail the manner in which this computation might be structured. For the moment, we adopt a simplistic view of the search procedure that is oriented around the treatment of the goal under consideration. If the goal has a logical connective as its top-level symbol, the procedure tries a right rule from Figure 2.2; for example, if the goal is a conjunction, then an attempt is made to construct two separate proofs, one for each conjunct. If the goal is atomic, then backchaining is initiated by the decide rule from Figure 2.3 and is elaborated by the other rules in the same collection. Such a proof search can have three outcomes: A proof might be found, it may be determined that no proof exists because all possible paths to a proof have led to failure, or the search may never terminate. We note that the provability of a goal formula from a set of program clauses in *fohc* is an undecidable question in general. Thus the possibility of nontermination is one faced by any interpreter for this language and is not a facet merely of a simple-minded search engine.

The print phase

If a proof has been found, or if it has been determined that no proof exists, then this needs to be reported to the user. In the latter situation, i.e., when it is known that no proof exists, the system simply can respond with a no. For example, we may have the following interaction:

```
[lists] ?- append (1::nil) (2::nil) (3::nil).
no

[lists] ?-
```

On the other hand, if a proof is found, then the system might respond with an indication of success:

```
[lists] ?- append (1::nil) (2::nil) (1::2::nil).
```

---

[2] For brevity, we shall refer to an O-proof simply as a proof in what follows.

```
solved
```

```
[lists] ?-
```

The response also can be more informative in the case of a success. One
possibility is to show the successful proof. However, this is too verbose, as
we have noted previously. The common practice in logic programming languages is to present instead a trace of the proof in the form of instantiations
for the implicitly existentially quantified and named variables in the original
query that result in the success. Such instantiations are what we have previously referred to as an *answer substitution*. Viewing such a substitution as the
outcome of the computation does not change the response when success is
encountered in the earlier query because there are no variables to instantiate in
it. However, this idea underlies the result that λProlog shows in the following
interaction:

```
[lists] ?- append (1::nil) (2::nil) X.
X = (1::2::nil)
```

```
[lists] ?-
```

Under the convention described, instantiations for explicitly quantified variables and for anonymous variables are not presented. This is illustrated by the
following interactions:

```
[lists] ?- sigma X\ append (1::nil) (2::nil) X.
solved
```

```
[lists] ?- append (1::nil) (2::nil) _.
solved
```

```
[lists] ?-
```

It is also possible to mix the different kinds of variables, as illustrated in the
following queries:

```
[lists] ?- sigma Y\ append X Y (1::nil).
X = nil
```

```
[lists] ?- append X _ (1::nil).
X = nil
```

```
[lists] ?- append X Y (1::nil).
X = nil
```

```
Y = (1::nil)
```

```
[lists] ?-
```

These queries all result in an attempt to prove the same sequent, but there are differences in what is presented back to the user.

Multiple solutions

There might, of course, be more than one proof of a sequent, each with a different answer substitution. In light of this, when an answer substitution is presented, the system will pause for the user to provide input on what to do next. The user can signal that no additional proofs are needed by typing in a carriage return; this is what occurs in the last of the preceding queries. Alternatively, the user may request a search for another proof by typing in a semicolon. The following variation on the last preceding interaction illustrates this possibility:

```
[lists] ?- append X Y (1::nil).
X = nil
Y = 1::nil;

X = 1::nil
Y = nil;

no

[lists] ?-
```

Two proofs are found here, and the corresponding answer substitutions are displayed. The final no in response to the user's request for yet one more proof indicates that there are no others to be found.

2.4.3 Reachability in a finite-state machine

As our first illustration of the programming capabilities of *fohc*, we consider its use in encoding and solving search-related problems. The particular task we consider is that of determining whether or not a finite-state machine accepts a given word.[3] This task is an example of a *reachability* problem that has a rather natural encoding in a logic programming language: The existence of a path can be linked directly to the existence of a proof.

---

[3] We assume familiarity here with such machines and the notions related to them.

```
kind state, letter        type.
type q1, q2, q3, q4, q5   state.
type a, b                 letter.
type start, final         state -> o.
type path, trans          state -> list letter -> state -> o.
type accept               list letter -> o.


path S nil S.
path S Letters T :- trans S Arc M, append Arc Rest Letters,
                    path M Rest T.
accept W :- start S, path S W F, final F.
```

Figure 2.4. Declarations for encoding finite-state machines and tracing transitions in them.

```
start q1 & final q2 & final q3.
trans q1 (a::nil) q1    & trans q1 (b::nil) q1.
trans q1 (a::b::nil) q2 & trans q1 (b::a::nil) q3.
```

Figure 2.5. Predicate definitions for a three state nondeterministic machine.

```
start q1 & final q4 & final q5.
trans q1 (a::nil) q2   &   trans q1 (b::nil) q3.
trans q2 (a::nil) q1   &   trans q2 (b::nil) q4.
trans q3 (a::nil) q5   &   trans q3 (b::nil) q1.
trans q4 (a::nil) q5   &   trans q4 (b::nil) q3.
trans q5 (a::nil) q2   &   trans q5 (b::nil) q4.
```

Figure 2.6. Predicate definitions for a five-state deterministic machine.

A finite-state machine is determined by an alphabet, a set of states, an enumeration of the labeled transitions between states, and the designation of a start state and a set of final states. Figure 2.4 contains declarations that identify types and constants that can be used to encode finite-state machines. These declarations provide for an alphabet that has only the letters (labels) a and b and for machines that have at most five states. This can, of course, be changed by modifying the declarations that enumerate the letters and the states. Notice also that we can cater to a potentially unlimited number of states by using the built-in domain of integers to generate the set of states via a constructor of type int -> state. Figure 2.4 also contains a definition of the predicate path that explores transitions between states and the predicate accept that uses path to find accepting transitions and thereby to identify accepted words.

Figures 2.5 and 2.6 present two different finite state machines that both accept the same language, namely, the set of all words over the alphabet $\{a, b\}$ that end in either the string ab or ba; this language is denoted by the regular expression $(a + b)^*(ab + ba)$. The first machine is nondeterministic, whereas the second is deterministic. If we collect the definition of append and the code in Figures 2.4 and 2.5 into a module called fsm1, then the following interaction is possible:

```
[fsm1] ?- accept (b::b::a::b::nil).
solved

[fsm1] ?- accept (b::a::X::Y::nil).
X = a
Y = b ;

X = b
Y = a ;

no

[fsm1] ?-
```

The answer to the first query confirms that the string *bbab* is accepted by this machine, and the answer to the second query shows that there are only two four-letter words starting with *ba* that are accepted by this machine.

To explore a bit more the set of accepted words, one could systematically generate all lists of letters and then check them for acceptance. The polymorphic predicate lists defined by the code

```
type lists    list A -> o.
lists nil.
lists (_::L) :- lists L.
```

identifies all lists. This predicate also can be used to *generate* all lists: A depth-first search engine, such as that underlying λProlog, will systematically produce lists of increasing length. Thus, if we assume that this definition of lists is also part of the module fsm1, then the following interaction is possible:

```
[fsm1] ?- lists L.
L = nil ;

L = T1 :: nil ;

L = T1 :: T2 :: nil ;

L = T1 :: T2 :: T3 :: nil

[fsm1] ?- lists L, accept L.
```

```
L = a :: b :: nil ;
```

```
L = b :: a :: nil ;
```

```
L = a :: a :: b :: nil ;
```

```
L = a :: b :: a :: nil ;
```

```
L = b :: a :: b :: nil
```

```
[fsm1] ?-
```

Notice that both these queries have an unbounded number of successful proofs, each with a different answer substitution.

The reader should confirm that if the specification in Figure 2.6 were to replace the one in Figure 2.5 in the preceding interactions, then exactly the same behavior would be observed.

2.4.4 Defining relations over recursively structured data

Section 1.4.1 describes the encoding of data objects such as lists and trees using first-order terms: In such an encoding, one recognizes the recursive structure of the objects, and one chooses constructors to represent the base and recursive cases. Program clauses complement this style of representation by providing a natural way of defining relations over these encodings. Such relations can be described first for the objects constituting the base cases of the type through program clauses that are the (implicit) universal closures of atomic formulas. These definitions then can be extended to cover all objects of the type through program clauses whose bodies are "rules" of the form $G \supset A$; here, A corresponds to a description of the relation relative to a recursive case that may be conditioned, via G, on the relation holding for subcomponents of the same type.

This structure underlies the definition that we have already seen of the append predicate, which is a relation among three lists that is defined by recursion on the structure of the first list. When this list is nil, the second and third lists must be identical for the relation to hold. This fact is asserted by the clause

```
append nil L L.
```

When the first list has a head element, then the relation holds if that element is also the head of the third list and if the rest of the third list is in the append relation to the tail of the first list and the second lists. This is the intended reading of the second clause

```
append (X :: L1) L2 (X :: L3) :- append L1 L2 L3.
```

that completes the definition of `append`.

The same idea also may be applied to the definition of relations over binary trees whose representation is based on the following declarations:

```
kind  btree    type -> type.
type  empty    btree A.
type  node     A -> btree A -> btree A -> btree A.
```

For example, suppose that we wish to define an `insert` relation between an integer and two ordered, integer binary trees that holds just in the case that the second tree corresponds to the result of inserting the given integer in the first. This relation is given by the following clauses:

```
type    insert    int -> btree int -> btree int -> o.
insert X empty (node X empty empty).
insert X (node A L R) (node A NL R) :- X < A, insert X L NL.
insert X (node A L R) (node A L NR) :- X >= A, insert X R NR.
```

The recursion in this definition is on the structure of the "input" tree.

Let us suppose that the definitions pertaining to binary trees presented in this section are collected into a module called `btree`. The following interaction uses the `insert` relation:

```
[btree] ?- insert 4 (node 3 (node 2 empty empty) empty) T.
T = node 3 (node 2 empty empty) (node 4 empty empty)

[btree] ?-
```

An important observation about this specification is that since the arguments of the comparison operators must satisfy the constraints described for them in Section 2.4.2, `insert` is well defined only when its first and second arguments are restricted to closed terms.

2.4.5 Programming over abstract syntax representations

In Chapter 1 we discussed how first-order terms can be used to realize traditional abstract syntax representations. Given the recursive structure of these expressions, program clauses in *fohc* provide a natural means for describing relations over abstract syntax. We illustrate this idea through the encoding of a provability relation over logical formulas.

$$\overline{\Gamma, \bot \longrightarrow \Delta} \; \bot L \qquad \overline{\Gamma, A \longrightarrow \Delta, A} \; \text{initial}$$

$$\frac{\Gamma, A \longrightarrow \Delta \quad \Gamma, B \longrightarrow \Delta}{\Gamma, A \vee B \longrightarrow \Delta} \; \vee L \qquad \frac{\Gamma \longrightarrow \Delta, A, B}{\Gamma \longrightarrow \Delta, A \vee B} \; \vee R$$

$$\frac{\Gamma, A, B \longrightarrow \Delta}{\Gamma, A \wedge B \longrightarrow \Delta} \; \wedge L \qquad \frac{\Gamma \longrightarrow \Delta, A \quad \Gamma \longrightarrow \Delta, B}{\Gamma \longrightarrow \Delta, A \wedge B} \; \wedge R$$

$$\frac{\Gamma \longrightarrow \Delta, A \quad \Gamma, B \longrightarrow \Delta}{\Gamma, A \supset B \longrightarrow \Delta} \; \supset L \qquad \frac{\Gamma, A \longrightarrow \Delta, B}{\Gamma \longrightarrow \Delta, A \supset B} \; \supset R$$

Figure 2.7. Inference rules for a propositional fragment of logic.

Section 1.4.2 described an encoding of formulas constructed using the logical constant $\bot$ and the connectives $\wedge$, $\vee$, and $\supset$. That encoding was based on the following declarations:

```
kind   term, form    type.
type   ff, tt         form.
type   &&, !!, ==>    form -> form -> form.
infixl &&             5.
infixl !!             4.
infixr ==>            3.
type   a,b            term.
type   f              term -> term -> term.
type   p,q            term -> term -> form.
```

Let us now suppose that we wish to define provability for sequents of the form $\Gamma \longrightarrow \Delta$, where Γ and Δ are multisets of formulas. In a mathematical setting, this relation is given by the rules in Figure 2.7. In using these rules, we assume that a multiset matches with an expression of the form Γ, P just in the case that P is a formula in it, and the rest of the multiset corresponds to Γ. What we desire now is a translation of these inference rules into an *fohc* program.

In the encoding we describe, we use lists to represent multisets. In this context, the predicate memb_and_rest, defined by the following clauses, provides a means for selecting an item from a multiset:

```
type  memb_and_rest   A -> list A -> list A -> o.
memb_and_rest X (X :: L) L.
memb_and_rest X (Y :: L) (Y :: L1) :- memb_and_rest X L L1.
```

The inference rules in Figure 2.7 lead to provability judgments about sequents that can be encoded as a relation between the two lists of formulas constituting the left and right sides of sequents. The following type declaration introduces a binary predicate that provides the basis for such an encoding:

```
type  prv   list form -> list form -> o.
```

Inference rules can be translated into program clauses defining `prv` in the following way: The conclusion of the rule can be encoded by A and the premises of the rule by G in a clause of the form $G \supset A$. Specifically, the sequent rules in Figure 2.7 yield the following set of λProlog clauses:

```
prv Gamma Delta :- memb_and_rest ff Gamma _.
prv Gamma Delta :- memb_and_rest A Gamma _,
                   memb_and_rest A Delta _.
prv Gamma Delta :-
     memb_and_rest (A && B) Gamma Gamma',
     prv (A :: B :: Gamma') Delta.
 prv Gamma Delta :-
     memb_and_rest (A !! B) Gamma Gamma',
     prv (A :: Gamma') Delta, prv (B :: Gamma') Delta.
prv Gamma Delta :-
     memb_and_rest (A ==> B) Gamma Gamma',
     prv Gamma' (A :: Delta), prv (B :: Gamma') Delta.
prv Gamma Delta :-
     memb_and_rest (A && B) Delta Delta',
     prv Gamma (A :: Delta'), prv Gamma (B :: Delta').
prv Gamma Delta :-
     memb_and_rest (A !! B) Delta Delta',
     prv Gamma (A :: B :: Delta').
prv Gamma Delta :-
     memb_and_rest (A ==> B) Delta Delta',
     prv (A :: Delta) (B :: Gamma').
```

Notice that the schema variables Γ, Δ, A, and B that possibly appear in an inference rule translate into the variables `Gamma`, `Delta`, `A`, and `B` that are implicitly universally quantified over the program clause encoding the rule.

Let all the declarations in this subsection be collected into a module called `logic`. We then would pose the query `prv nil (F :: nil)` relative to this module in order to determine if a formula represented by `F` is provable. For instance, the interaction

```
[logic] ?- prv nil (((p a b) !! ((p a b) ==> (q a a))) :: nil).
solved

[logic] ?-
```

shows that the formula $(p\ a\ b) \lor ((p\ a\ b) \supset (q\ a\ a))$ is provable.

2.5 Pragmatic aspects of computing with Horn clauses

We consider briefly the practical issues associated with constructing a derivation for a goal formula from a program in the `fohc` setting. When read with an upward proof-search orientation, the right-introduction rules of Figure 2.2 and the backchaining rules of Figure 2.3 provide the structure for a procedure for finding such derivations. Since nondeterminism is involved in the application of some of these rules, we must specify how choices are to be resolved so that the behavior of an interpreter is more predictable; such predictability is essential for understanding the computations that actually result from a given logic program. For this reason, unlike automatic theorem provers, where rich and sophisticated methods are often used to search for proofs, the procedure for λProlog employs a simple and rigid search strategy. Using such a strategy has certain implications. First, the proof search that is conducted may be incomplete: There may be sequents that have derivations but for which no derivations will be found because of the strategy. In fact, the chosen strategy even can cause indefinite looping when a more flexible search strategy might be able to find a proof. However, since the search strategy is known beforehand, it usually will be possible to restructure programs so as to avoid incomplete behavior. Second, since a search strategy is the vehicle that carries a logic program into an actual series of computation steps, a simple strategy means that a programmer can predict to a large degree the computational resources such as time and space that the execution of a logical specification will consume. This kind of transparency is important for a programming paradigm.

Turning to the details, we see that there are two possible rules that can be used when the goal is a disjunction or the formula selected for backchaining is a conjunction. The convention in these situations is to always try the rule that involves the left subformula before the one involving the right subformula. Another choice that must be made in a sequential implementation concerns the subgoal to try first when a conjunctive goal is encountered. Here again, a left-to-right textual ordering guides the search; i.e., a derivation of the left premise of the ∧R rule is constructed first, before one for the right premise is attempted. Yet another place where a selection must be made pertains to the choice of the formula from $\mathcal{P}$ that is to be used in the decide rule of Figure 2.3. In making this choice, a program $\mathcal{P}$ is viewed as a list rather than as a set; i.e., the order and multiplicity of formulas in $\mathcal{P}$ affects the way proofs are attempted. More specifically, a program is presented as a module that occurs textually in a file, and such a presentation naturally imposes a listing order on the clauses that appear in it. The search strategy uses this order to determine the (next) formula to try in the decide rule.

The only remaining choices pertain to the term t that is to be used to instantiate the existential quantifier in the $\exists$R rule of Figure 2.2 and the universal quantifier in the $\forall$L rule of Figure 2.3. Both inference rules have $\Sigma; \emptyset \Vdash_f t : \tau$ as one of their premises. If there are a small number of terms of type τ, as is the case in the example in Section 2.4.3, where there are just two terms corresponding to the type letter, then using this typing judgment to step through all the terms of that type might be an effective approach to proof search. However, many types have an infinite number of terms corresponding to them. A more reasonable strategy, therefore, is to use the other premise in these rules to constrain the terms to be considered in the typing judgment. *Logic variables*, used in combination with *unification*, provide a means for doing this. A logic variable serves as a "placeholder" for a value for t in the $\exists$R and $\forall$L rules. Unlike the usual variables in a proof system but rather like the variables considered in Section 1.5, these variables can be instantiated during the course of proof search. Using these variables, the $\exists$R and $\forall$L rules take the form

$$\frac{\Sigma; \emptyset \Vdash_f X : \tau \quad \Sigma; \mathcal{P} \longrightarrow B[X/x]}{\Sigma; \mathcal{P} \longrightarrow \exists_\tau x \, B} \quad \text{and} \quad \frac{\Sigma; \mathcal{P} \xrightarrow{D[X/x]} A \quad \Sigma; \emptyset \Vdash_f X : \tau}{\Sigma; \mathcal{P} \xrightarrow{\forall_\tau x \, D} A}$$

respectively, where X is a logic variable that is new in the sense that it has not been used previously in this proof search computation. The place where the choice of instantiation for such variables becomes significant is in the application of the initial rule of Figure 2.3. In determining suitable instantiations in the fohc setting, the unification operation discussed in Chapter 1 can be used. In particular, the initial rule can be modified to

$$\frac{}{\Sigma; \mathcal{P} \xrightarrow{A'} A} \quad \text{initial}$$

with the proviso that A and A' are unifiable and the requirement that the substitutions for the logic variables that are chosen to unify them be percolated all over the derivation that has been constructed thus far. Of course, all the remaining, delayed typing judgments must be provable for instances of the logic variables, something that is guaranteed to be true if typed unification is used.

A naive scheme for implementing the decide rule will try every clause that is available in the program context. This approach can be improved on by precomputing the effects of applying the $\supset$L and $\land$L rules, thereby transforming the original program into a listing of clauses that have the form

$$\forall_{\tau_1} x_1 \ldots \forall_{\tau_m} x_m \, (G_1 \land \ldots \land G_n \supset A)$$

where A is an atomic formula and $G_1, \ldots, G_n$ are G-formulas.[4] Such a transformation preserves the operational interpretations of program clauses, as mentioned previously, and is also justified at a logical level by the discussions in the next section. Now, in trying to solve an atomic goal with a specific predicate as its head, only the clauses in this form in which the head of A_0 is identical to the predicate in question need be considered by the decide rule; in all other cases, unification will quickly lead to failure. Thus the clauses in a large program can be partitioned into separate subsequences indexed by predicate names. Further, in a model that supports compilation, each of these subsequences can be realized as code for the separate clauses surrounded by instructions that cause them to be tried one after another. The use of a particular clause eventually leads to an attempt to unify the head of the clause with the query to be solved. Since this head is known statically, several decisions that have to be made in unification are predetermined and hence also can be compiled. Finally, it is possible in some cases to make quick checks on the form of the arguments in an atomic query to rule out the use of specific clauses before a full-fledged, and potentially costly, unification computation is invoked. This idea can be realized through special code that allows for an indexed access to clauses even within those pertinent to a particular predicate name. These various ideas usually are deployed in practical, compiled implementations of logic programming based on *fohc*.

2.6 The relationship with logical notions

Our presentation of logic programming up to this point has been predominantly operational. In Section 2.2 we characterized logical connectives and quantifiers in goals as vehicles for specifying search. When we introduced *fohc*, we once again focused on the backchaining rules that have the flavor of being directed by the atomic goal that is to be solved. This operational notion of provability is, however, related to truth in well known and well understood logical systems. In fact, an underlying theme of logic programming is a duality between a declarative and an operational interpretation of formulas: We would like the solvability of a goal from a program to be an assertion of both the fact that it follows from the program in a relevant logical system and the fact that a certain kind of derivation can be constructed for it. As we pointed out in Section 2.3, this duality finds exact expression in the fact that the O-proofs using *fohc* are sound and complete for both intuitionistic and classical logic.

---

[4] As usual, we let $m = 0$ represent the case in which there are no universal quantifiers at the beginning of the clause and $n = 0$ denote the situation in which there is no implication.

2.6.1 The cut rule and cut-elimination

Finding proofs in a mathematical setting can demand cleverness and invention. A common technique in such a context is the invention of a sequence of lemmas that breaks a proof into small pieces. The justification for this approach is provided by the *cut rule* (which has no connection to Prolog's pruning operator !).

The cut rule has the following form:

$$\frac{\Sigma; \mathcal{P} \longrightarrow B \qquad \Sigma; \mathcal{P}, B \longrightarrow G}{\Sigma; \mathcal{P} \longrightarrow G}$$

In trying to prove G in the context $\langle \Sigma, \mathcal{P} \rangle$, this rule allows a formula B to be used in the proof after this formula has been shown to hold in the context. The intuition here is that a well-chosen B can shorten the proof for G considerably. While attempting to automate the selection of such lemmas is an interesting problem, the ingenuity involved makes it fall outside the domain of mechanisms that can be used in the execution of even a high-level programming language such as λProlog. Focusing on proofs that do not involve the use of lemmas means that we are not really thinking of automating provability in a rich mathematical setting: Proofs of nontrivial mathematical theorems are manageable only through the use of lemmas. Our goals are much more modest in that we are thinking of using logic in computations such as those involving sorting and merging of lists or the manipulation of abstract syntax.

While the cut rule is not used in effecting computation (i.e., in carrying out proof search), it has a role to play in reasoning about computation. A result known as the *cut-elimination theorem* tells us that this rule can be added to both classical and intuitionistic logic without changing the set of sequents that are derivable. The completeness of the limited derivation system for fohc implies that a suitably adapted form of the cut rule is also admissible in that system. One consequence of such a cut-elimination or cut-admissibility theorem, then, is that if we replace a subformula in a logic program with a logically equivalent subformula, the resulting logic program proves the same goals (in the sense of O-provability, although maybe not under a depth-first search strategy). We exploit this aspect of logical equivalence to provide alternative formats for Horn clauses.

2.6.2 Different presentations of fohc

The definition of fohc program clauses introduced in Section 2.3 is the most liberal of a few roughly equivalent alternatives. A different, and perhaps more common, definition for these clauses is given by the following grammar:

$$F \quad ::= A \mid F \wedge F$$
$$D \quad ::= A \mid F \supset A \mid \forall_\tau x \, D$$

In this version, program clauses have the form

$$\forall_{\tau_1} x_1 \ldots \forall_{\tau_m} x_m \, (A_1 \wedge \ldots \wedge A_n \supset A_0)$$

for $m, n \geq 0$. A compact presentation for `fohc` program clauses also can be given by identifying them simply as

$$D \quad ::= A \mid A \supset D \mid \forall_\tau x \, D$$

In this definition, program clauses are formulas that are formed using only implications and universal quantifiers with the additional proviso that the nesting of implications and universal quantifiers can occur only in the conclusion of an implication and not in its premise. Note that we change the syntax of only the program clauses in these alternative presentations; the original syntax for goal formulas is retained.

These three ways of defining program clauses give rise to logical languages of the same expressive power in the sense that a program clause in one definition is classically (and also intuitionistically) equivalent to a set of program clauses in any of the other definitions. This is easily shown through use of the following logical equivalences:

$$\forall x \, (B_1 \wedge B_2) \equiv (\forall x \, B_1) \wedge (\forall x \, B_2)$$
$$B_1 \supset (B_2 \supset B_3) \equiv (B_1 \wedge B_2) \supset B_3$$
$$B_1 \wedge (B_2 \vee B_3) \equiv (B_1 \wedge B_2) \vee (B_1 \wedge B_3)$$
$$B_1 \vee (B_2 \wedge B_3) \equiv (B_1 \vee B_2) \wedge (B_1 \vee B_3)$$
$$(B_1 \vee B_2) \supset B_3 \equiv (B_1 \supset B_3) \wedge (B_2 \supset B_3)$$
$$B_1 \supset (B_2 \wedge B_3) \equiv (B_1 \supset B_2) \wedge (B_1 \supset B_3)$$
$$B_1 \supset (\forall x \, B_2) \equiv \forall x \, (B_1 \supset B_2)$$
$$(\exists x \, B_2) \supset B_1 \equiv \forall x \, (B_2 \supset B_1)$$

In the last two equivalences, the assumption is that x is not free in B_1.

If we take the size of a program to be the number of occurrences of logical connectives it contains, programs that use the definition in Section 2.3 generally are smaller than ones equivalent to them that are based on syntax rules presented in this section. For example, a program clause of the form $G \supset (D_1 \wedge D_2)$ is logically equivalent to the formula $(G \supset D_1) \wedge (G \supset D_2)$, but the second formula, in which G is duplicated, could be much larger than the first. Thus, prohibiting conjunctions on the right side of implications can cause the size of the formula to grow, in the worst case exponentially. As another example, consider the following propositional program clause permitted by our original definition:

$$((p \vee r) \wedge (q \vee t)) \supset s$$

Using the preceding equivalences, most notably the distributivity of conjunction over disjunction, this formula can be transformed into the following set of clauses that is based on the first definition in this section:

$$(p \wedge q) \supset s \qquad (r \wedge q) \supset s \qquad (p \wedge t) \supset s \qquad (r \wedge t) \supset s$$

The cumulative size of the formulas in this collection can be much more than the original formula because it contains two occurrences each of p, r, q, and t, and each of these could themselves be large formulas. In general, this kind of conversion can lead to an exponential growth in the number of symbols in the set of formulas. Another important point to note is that the transformation used here is not guaranteed, in general, to preserve operational behavior. For example, if the original formula is selected by the decide rule in Figure 2.3, then there is at most one derivation that will be constructed for p. However, in the transformed version, there are two different clauses in which p occurs, and a separate derivation will have to be constructed for it when each of these formulas is selected by the decide rule.

The problems just described actually can be avoided if we are willing to introduce new predicate constants. For example, if the propositional constants pr and qt are introduced to denote the disjunctions $p \vee r$ and $q \vee t$, then the program clause

$$((p \vee r) \wedge (q \vee t)) \supset s$$

can be transformed instead into the collection containing the clauses

$$p \supset pr \qquad r \supset pr \qquad q \supset qt \qquad t \supset qt \qquad (pr \wedge qt) \supset s$$

Replacing disjunctions in this fashion can cause a growth in the sizes of formulas that is at most linear in the number of disjunctions they contain. Since we have introduced new constants, the original formula is not logically equivalent to the new set of formulas. The following statement about their relationship can, however, be made: Let D_1 denote the original program clause, and let Σ_1 be the signature $\{p : o, \ q : o, \ r : o, \ s : o, \ t : o\}$. Further, let Σ_2 be the union of $\{pr : o, \ qt : o\}$ and Σ_1, and let $\mathcal{D}_2$ denote the collection of program clauses shown earlier that are obtained by transforming D_1. Then, for any goal formula G that is also a Σ_1-formula, the sequent $\Sigma_1; \mathcal{P}, D_1 \longrightarrow G$ is provable if and only if $\Sigma_2; \mathcal{P}, \mathcal{D}_2 \longrightarrow G$ is provable. If we are concerned only with provability over the original signature, a transformation that satisfies such a property is acceptable. We shall return to this transformation again after we introduce higher-order Horn clauses in Chapter 5.

2.7 The meaning and use of types

Types are an integral part of the logic that we have presented in that they help to identify the expressions that are well formed. Types also have a conceptual role in the programming language, and they affect computations. We discuss these aspects in this section.

2.7.1 Types and the categorization of expressions

The typical interpretation of types is that they classify expressions. In the first-order setting, the main distinction that types force is that between propositions and other kinds of expressions. All other distinctions can be suppressed by restricting the language to having exactly one sort in addition to o. In the higher-order setting that we shall encounter later, a further distinction that realizes a functional hierarchy based on the order of types is forced. Of course, even in the first-order setting, we have chosen to build in more distinctions by including additional sorts for integers, strings, etc. and by including a constructor for list types. We also have provided the programmer with the ability to augment these collections further and hence to add to the distinctions that are possible.

It is important to understand the exact nature of the sets of expressions that types denote. An important notion in this context is that of equality between syntactic expressions. In λProlog, two closed expressions are equal only if they are exactly the same.[5] For example, the expressions 2 + 3, 3 + 2, and 5 all have the type int, but they are different elements of that type. This is in contrast to the viewpoint taken in the setting, say, of functional programming: In that context, the expressions 2 + 3, 3 + 2, and 5 all have type int and are also equal in that type because of an underlying meaning attached to the + operator. Thus, in λProlog, the goal formula (2 + 3 = 5) fails, whereas in functional programming, this expression evaluates to true. Similarly, the type o denotes a set of formulas in λProlog rather than a set of truth values. As we shall see later, understanding types as sets of *expressions* rather than as sets of more abstract *values* allows us to carry out interesting computations on expressions of functional type that are not possible in functional programming: Testing equality at a functional type in our context reduces to checking whether the "code" has the same shape and does not require determining equality of the

---

[5] When we introduce λ-terms, we will extend this notion to include λ-conversion.

(possibly infinite) graphs of functions that are their "values." Computation in functional programming corresponds to the rewriting of an expression until it has been converted into a normal form that may be thought of as a representation of its value. In λProlog, there is no rewriting phase: Expressions of a given type are themselves the intended members of that type. Computation in the logic programming setting is based not on rewriting but on the search for proofs.

It is, of course, useful even in the logic programming context to know that the expressions 2 + 3, 3 + 2, and 5 all denote the same mathematical value (the number 5). For this reason, λProlog is equipped with a simple evaluator that is invoked through a special nonlogical predicate called is (see Section A.4.1 of the Appendix). Although such evaluation and rewriting can be accommodated in logic programming, it is important to note that they are not part of the logical foundations.

2.7.2 Polymorphic typing

One way to understand a type declaration in λProlog is to think of the keyword type as a predicate relating a token and a type; we ignore here the problem of what type to associate with the predicate type itself. The type variables that appear in types would, in this rendition, translate into quantified term variables. A question that arises here is what the scope of the quantifier over the type variables should be in such an interpretation. Thus we could view the type association with nil as being given either by the clause

$$\forall A \ (\text{type nil (list A)})$$

or by the clause

$$\text{type nil} \ (\forall A \ (\text{list A}))$$

The first rendition is closest to the way we have been viewing variables in types: nil has many types associated with it, but all of these are substitution instances of a particular structure. Similarly, the type association with the append predicate can be given by the clause

$$\forall A \ (\text{type append (list A -> list A -> list A -> o)})$$

It is interesting to note the consequence of such a type association: append can be applied to three lists, all of which have to have the same type of elements, but the particular value of this type is not fixed.

Consider a type expression of order 1 written in the canonical form $\tau_1 \rightarrow \cdots \tau_n \rightarrow \tau_0$. A type variable that appears in τ_0 is called a *transparent type variable* for that expression. If all the type variables in a type are transparent, then that expression is said to be *determinate*. Knowing the target type of a determinate type allows the argument types to be determined uniquely, a fact that has an interesting consequence for recursively constructed terms. For example, the types we have chosen for `nil` and `::` ensure that the types of all the elements in any given list must be the same. However, if we had used the constructors `null` and `cons` identified by the following declarations

```
kind lst     type.
type null    lst.
type cons    A -> lst -> lst.
```

that do not have transparent types, then a term of type `lst` would represent sequences of elements of heterogeneous type. A similar observation was made in Section 1.4.1 relating to the representation of binary trees.

2.7.3 Type checking and type inference

Type checking is a process that determines whether a given term or formula is built correctly using the typed constants that have been declared. This process essentially uses the rules in Figures 1.2 and 2.1 to establish typing judgments. A characteristic of the type system of λProlog is that once the types of all the constants and variables occurring in an expression have been specified, type checking of the expression can be done statically. Languages that have this character are said to be *strongly typed*. Strong typing is useful for detecting statically many situations that otherwise would cause errors at run time. For example, a program that successfully passes the type checking phase is likely to have all the arguments to predicates present and in the right order and to have the names of all the constant symbols it uses spelled correctly.

In describing strong typing, we assumed that the types of all the variables appearing in an expression are known before the type-checking phase. As noted in Section 2.1, this is not necessarily true in λProlog: Types may be missing for variables, in which case these will need to be *inferred* in a most general form in the course of type checking. We recall, in this context, that every occurrence of a variable in an expression is expected to have the same type, although different occurrences of a constant can have different types. For example, the formula

```
append (1::nil) (2::nil) X, append ("abc"::nil) ("efg"::nil) Y.
```

is well typed and requires X and Y to have the types `list int` and `list string`, respectively. Notice also that the two occurrence of the constant `append`, whose declared type appeared earlier in this section, are given the following two types:

```
list int -> list int -> list int -> o.
list string -> list string -> list string -> o.
```

Finally, observe that if Y is replaced by X, then the formula will not pass type checking because there is no type that can be given to X that would be acceptable at both its occurrences.

Thus not only does λProlog check types, but it also infers types for variables. Not all types have to be inferred: Some also can be supplied by the user. One way to do this is by indicating it at the binding occurrence of a variable, as illustrated by the expression

```
pi (X:list int)\ append X X Y.
```

The type also may be presented at an (implicitly) bound occurrence of the variable, as shown in the expression

```
append (X:list int) X Y.
```

When a type is provided in one of these ways, the actual type attributed to the variable must be some instance of the one shown, and once again, an identical type must be used at all occurrences.

2.7.4 Types and run-time computations

Since λProlog makes use of *typed* unification, types play more than a static role: They also may be needed during execution. In the higher-order setting that we look at later, types can determine unifiability as well as affect the shape of unifiers. Relative to first-order terms, types have a more benign effect in that they influence only the existence of unifiers and do not have a bearing on their structure.

In a statically type checked language, one may imagine that all the type information relevant to a program is already available at compile time and therefore that types do not need to be computed at run time even if they are used in the course of unification. This image does not fit with the reality for two reasons. First, because of polymorphism, we may not know the precise run-time types of constants and variables prior to execution. Second, since types are not required to be determinate and specifically cannot be so for polymorphic predicates, it may be necessary to look dynamically at the type of an argument.

An illustration of the need for run-time computations on types is provided by the declarations and clauses in Figure 2.8. This code identifies constructors for building heterogeneous lists. The list constructor cons used here has a type that is not determinate. The predicate separate, whose definition also appears in this figure, can be used to separate a heterogeneous list containing only integers and reals into two homogeneous lists, one containing only integers and the other containing only reals. Computationally, the type that is shown for X in the first two clauses for separate must be matched with the type of the head element

```
kind lst          type.
type null         lst.
type cons         A -> lst -> lst.
type separate     lst -> list int -> list real -> o.

separate (cons (X:int) L) (X::K) M :- separate L K M.
separate (cons (X:real) L) K (X::M) :- separate L K M.
separate null nil nil.
```

Figure 2.8. Heterogeneous lists.

```
kind numb         type.
type inj_int      int  -> numb.
type inj_real     real -> numb.
type separate     list numb -> list int -> list real -> o.

separate ((inj_int  X)::L) (X::K) M :- separate L K M.
separate ((inj_real X)::L) K (X::M) :- separate L K M.
separate nil nil nil.
```

Figure 2.9. Lists contain only integers and reals.

of the incoming list argument to effect the desired separation; i.e., a dynamic processing of types is essential to realize the intent of this code.

Figure 2.9 contains another specification of the separate predicate with a related functionality. Here, the run-time determination of which clauses to select for processing the first element of the list that is the first argument of separate is provided by examining terms and not types: If the first item of the list in the first argument has the top-level function symbol inj_int (intended to be read as "inject an integer"), then the first clause is selected; otherwise, if it has the top-level function symbol inj_real, then the second clause is selected.

To contrast the two different implementations of separate, consider proving the goal

```
separate (cons 1.0 (cons 2 (cons 3.0 null))) L K
```

relative to the definition in Figure 2.8 and the goal

```
separate ((inj_real 1.0)::(inj_int 2)::(inj_real 3.0)::nil) L K
```

relative to the definition in Figure 2.9. In both cases, the query will be solved by binding K to (2 :: nil) and L to (1.0 :: 3.0 :: nil). A natural question at this point is which of these implementations is to be preferred. We discuss below some reasons for preferring programs in which constructors are defined to have determinate types. The conclusion from this is that the second implementation of separate should be favored.

Better static analysis is possible When data constructors have determinate types, the type of the composite expression places constraints on the type of its subexpressions. Conversely, knowledge about the type of a subexpression can be used to deduce information about other parts of the expression. For example, in the homogeneous list structure, if one element of the list is determined to be of a particular type, every other element of that list also must be of that type. As a result, the static process of type checking is likely to provide more useful information about a program. In the context of the two different definitions of the separate predicate, for example, we know from a static examination that the second definition is meaningful only when it is applied to a list of elements of type numb that, from other type declarations, is clearly meant to correspond to integers and reals. By contrast, the first specification will permit queries to be constructed that involve lists with elements that have a type different from int and real. An error of this kind will be observed only as a run-time failure of a goal that is actually expected to always succeed by separating a given list into its integer and real elements.

More type information can be omitted during proof search One way to understand the role of types in λProlog is to think of constants and variables as being given by their names as well as their types. Under this model, when checking the equality of two constants, not only will we have to determine whether their names are the same, but we also will have to check the unifiability of their types. The declarations occurring in a program already fix a considerable part of the type of a constant statically. This structure therefore can be assimilated into the name of the constant, making it necessary only to record the bindings of the variables that appear in this "type skeleton." In a setting where types affect only unifiability, we can even go a step further: We can dispense with types altogether if we can determine otherwise that unification over them is bound to succeed. A particular situation where this is possible occurs when the types of constants are determinate. In this case, noting that unification examines terms in an outside-in fashion, once we have checked that the type bindings of the top-level constructors are compatible, no further type checking need be done. In the concrete setting of the practical computational model we elaborated in Section 2.5, the use of determinate types for all but predicate constants ensures that all the type information that is needed can be supplied by a few extra arguments to predicates.

The type system of λProlog allows us to identify the type of a constant as just a variable, leading potentially to a trivialization of typing. For example, it is possible to give the constructors cons and null the type A, i.e., to define these constants as having every possible type. It then would be possible to build terms such as (null (cons cons) cons) using these constants, many of which have nothing to do with list structures. Of course, the use of these kinds of type declarations is not helpful either to a programmer or to program analysis and ought to be avoided.

2.8 Bibliographic notes

The metatheory of first-order Horn clauses has been considered in a number of papers (Apt and van Emden 1982; van Emden and Kowalski 1976). Most of these papers have based their analyses on resolution refutations. Resolution refutations, however, have a number of characteristics that make them undesirable for all but the most simple designs of logic programming languages. For example, resolution (Bachmair and Ganzinger 2001; Robinson 1965) generally is applicable only to formulas that are in the intersection of a variety of normal forms: conjunctive normal form, prenex normal form, Skolem normal form, etc. An arbitrary formula can be transformed into a satisfiability-equivalent one that adheres to all these normal forms in the setting of classical logic. However, such a transformation can cause the size of the formula to increase dramatically and also can force some information such as quantifier alternation to be encoded in different and not entirely equivalent ways [via, say, Skolemization (Miller 1992a)]. There is also something unsatisfactory about using *refutations* rather than *proofs*: As we have observed in this chapter, the activity of a logic programming interpreter profitably is seen as that of trying to find proofs, leading to a search behavior that alternates naturally between goal-directed reductions and backchaining. A more serious problem for resolution is that some of the normal forms are meaningful only for first-order classical logic. In the chapters that follow we wish to describe logic programming languages that are also based on intuitionistic logic and on higher-order quantification. Although variations of the resolution method have been described for higher-order logic (Andrews 1971; Huet 1973b) and for intuitionistic logic (Fitting 1987), there are other elegant and well understood proof formats, such as the sequent calculus, for these logical systems.

The sequent calculus was introduced as a vehicle for formulating and studying logical provability by Gentzen (1969). Gentzen's paper also introduced the cut rule and established the fundamental property of cut-elimination for first-order classical and intuitionistic logic. The sequent calculus is a convenient setting for describing the high-level structure of computation in logic programming: For example, normal forms for program clauses and goals are not required, and sequent calculi for both classical and intuitionistic logic are well known. Many textbook treatments of the sequent calculus are available (Gallier 1986; Girard et al. 1989; Troelstra and Schwichtenberg 1996). Miller

(2002, 2006) has considered uses of the cut rule and the cut-elimination theorem to reason about logic programs.

Early in our work on the foundations of logic programming, we used the sequent calculus to develop the metatheory of first-order and higher-order Horn clauses (Miller and Nadathur 1986; Nadathur 1987; Nadathur and Miller 1990). In collaboration with colleagues, we later went on to introduce the technical device of *uniform proofs* within the sequent calculus as a way to formalize the notion of goal-directed proof search (Miller et al. 1987, 1991). The term *abstract logic programming language* also was proposed by us as a name for a logical language in which a procedure that searches for uniform proofs constitutes a complete proof procedure. Both *fohc* and the logic of hereditary Harrop formulas that is presented in Chapter 3 are examples of abstract logic programming languages. The idea of uniform proofs has been used to demonstrate that other logics, such as those based on Girard's linear logic (Girard 1987), are abstract logic programming languages (Hodas and Miller 1994; Miller 1996).

Provability in the sequent calculus presented here is characterized using two phases: the goal-reduction phase (using right-introduction rules) and the backchaining phase (using left-introduction rules). An abstract logic programming language is one where this two phase proof structure is complete. Andreoli (1992) generalized this two-phase proof structure to what he called *focused proofs* and showed that these are complete for linear logic. Focusing conceptually groups several "small" inference rules (such as those in Figure 2.2) into "larger" inference rules (such as the backchaining in Figure 2.3). Liang and Miller (2009) described comprehensive focused-proof calculi for intuitionistic and classical logic. The completeness of the focused-proof system LJF of Liang and Miller (2009) provides an alternative proof of the completeness of O-provability.

A common application area of logic programming is the manipulation of the syntax of languages, both natural and artificial. A number of books cover approaches to performing computations on natural languages using Prolog (Covington 1994; Pereira and Shieber 1987). Prolog has been used often to manipulate Prolog programs: This kind of *meta-level programming* has included building interpreters, type checkers, static analyzers, declarative debuggers, and partial evaluators for Prolog and logic programming–related systems (Hill and Lloyd 1994; Shapiro 1983). A large number of the applications of λProlog involve using it to represent and reason about specification and programming languages, including first-order logic formulas, λ-terms, functional programs, and π-calculus expressions. A common feature of all these languages is the presence of bound variables in expressions. A declarative treatment of this aspect requires higher-order techniques that we present in Chapter 7. We therefore delay a discussion of these applications until that point.

The type system of λProlog is inspired by that for ML (Milner et al. 1990), and the type inference algorithm is similar to that used in ML and other polymorphic languages (Damas and Milner 1982). There are differences, however, in what types mean and how they affect computation in our setting. We have discussed some of these differences here. Nadathur and Pfenning (1992) have provided a more detailed analysis. Caires and Monteiro (1994) developed an approach to strengthening λProlog typing to allow for richer polymorphisms. We have taken a prescriptive view of types here, assuming that they are an integral part of the logical language. Other views are possible within the context of logic programming (Pfenning 1992). Many type systems are essentially "static" in that they treat typing as an issue to be considered and dispensed with prior to execution of a program. As we have seen, types in λProlog also can play a role during program execution. The run-time impact of typing has been analyzed in a number of papers (Kwon et al. 1994; Brisset and Ridoux 1992; Nadathur and Qi 2005).

We have used o to denote the type of propositions. This usage comes directly from Church's use of the Greek letter omicron as the type of formulas in his *Simple Theory of Types* (Church 1940). The choice of pi and sigma to denote universal and existential quantification also mimics Church's use of the Greek letters Π and Σ for the same purpose.

We have touched briefly on the implementation of a logic programming language based on *fohc*. Work on this topic by several researchers culminated eventually in a virtual machine structure known as the *Warren Abstract Machine* (Warren 1983). Aït-Kaci (1991) provides a tutorial exposition of this machine. While implementation techniques have evolved considerably since its description, the structure of this machine still underlies many current Prolog implementations.

3

First-Order Hereditary Harrop Formulas

A logic programming language that is based on the logic of first-order Horn clauses or $fohc$ does not make very strong use of the structure afforded by logic in general even while providing significant computational capabilities. Part of this weakness arises from the fact that goal formulas and the bodies of program clauses in the setting of $fohc$, are not permitted to contain implications and universal quantifiers. In the first section of this chapter, we introduce the logic of *first-order hereditary Harrop formulas*, or $fohh$, that eases this restriction. The computational interpretation of these additional logical symbols then leads to a logic programming language in which programs and signatures can grow dynamically in the course of searching for a proof. We consider some of the pragmatic benefits of these capabilities in the second and third sections of this chapter; a full realization of the richness arising especially from universal quantifiers must await the introduction of higher-order features later in this book. In the last section of this chapter, we discuss logical aspects of $fohh$, relating, for example, its operational semantics to provability in classical, intuitionistic, and minimal logic.

3.1 The syntax of goals and program clauses

Let A denote first-order atomic formulas. Goal formulas and program clauses in the setting of $fohh$ then are the first-order formulas corresponding to the syntactic variables G and D given by the following rules:

$$G ::= \top \mid A \mid G \wedge G \mid G \vee G \mid \exists_\tau x\, G \mid D \supset G \mid \forall_\tau x\, G$$

$$D ::= A \mid G \supset D \mid D \wedge D \mid \forall_\tau x\, D$$

In contrast to the situation in the context of $fohc$, goal formulas now are allowed to contain all four logical connectives ($\top$, $\wedge$, $\vee$, and $\supset$) and both quantifiers ($\forall$ and $\exists$). Goals are, however, still not freely generated from atomic formulas using

75

these logical symbols. In particular, the premise of an implication appearing at the top level in a goal formula is restricted to being a *D*-formula. The structure of a program clause also is restricted, in a sense more so than that of a goal formula: Program clauses cannot contain disjunctions and existential quantifications at the top level, and the premise of a top-level implication must be a *G*-formula. The limitations on program clauses are, in fact, identical to the ones present in the `fohc` setting, but the resulting formulas represent a larger class than before because the syntax of *G*-formulas is now more permissive. A *D*-formula that is given by the preceding syntax rules will be called a *first-order hereditary Harrop formula*. This terminology is somewhat ambiguous because we also refer to the framework for logic programming that results from the present choices for goal formulas and program clauses as the *logic* of first-order hereditary Harrop formulas, or `fohh`, but the context always will clarify the intended usage.

When implications are present in formulas, it becomes meaningful to talk about their *positive* and *negative* subformula occurrences. These notions are defined as follows:

- *B* is a positive subformula occurrence of *B*.
- If *C* is a positive subformula occurrence of *B*, then *C* is a positive subformula occurrence of $B \wedge B'$, $B' \wedge B$, $B \vee B'$, $B' \vee B$, $B' \supset B$, $\forall_\tau x\, B$, and $\exists_\tau x\, B$, and *C* is a negative subformula occurrence of $B \supset B'$.
- If *C* is a negative subformula occurrence of *B*, then *C* is a negative subformula occurrence of $B \wedge B'$, $B' \wedge B$, $B \vee B'$, $B' \vee B$, $B' \supset B$, $\forall_\tau x\, B$, and $\exists_\tau x\, B$, and *C* is a positive subformula occurrence of $B \supset B'$.

In other words, if *C* occurs to the left of an even number of occurrences of implications in *B*, then it is a *positive* subformula occurrence of *B*, and if *C* occurs to the left of an odd number of occurrences of implication in a formula *B*, then it is a *negative* subformula occurrence of *B*.

Given the recursive definition for `fohh`, it is clear that positive subformulas of *G*-formulas are *G*-formulas, and negative subformulas of *G*-formulas are *D*-formulas. Dually, positive subformulas of *D*-formulas are *D*-formulas, and negative subformulas of *D*-formulas are *G*-formulas. Also notice that if *G* is a goal formula in `fohc`, then *G* has no negative subformulas. We also can characterize a hereditary Harrop formula as a formula in which no positive subformula occurrence is either disjunctive or existentially quantified.

The *clausal order* of a first-order formula is defined by the following recursion on its structure:

$$\text{clausal}(A) = 0 \quad \text{if } A \text{ is atomic or } \top$$

$$\text{clausal}(B_1 \wedge B_2) = \max(\text{clausal}(B_1), \text{clausal}(B_2))$$

$$\text{clausal}(B_1 \vee B_2) = \max(\text{clausal}(B_1), \text{clausal}(B_2))$$

$$\text{clausal}(B_1 \supset B_2) = \max(\text{clausal}(B_1) + 1, \text{clausal}(B_2))$$

$$\text{clausal}(\forall x\ B) = \text{clausal}(B)$$

$$\text{clausal}(\exists x\ B) = \text{clausal}(B)$$

Notice that in fohc, goal formulas have clausal order 0, and clauses have clausal order of either 0 or 1. In fohh, both goals and clauses can have arbitrary clausal order. If we interpret the implication symbol as the function type constructor $\rightarrow$, then the clausal order of a formula has a definition that is similar to that given in Section 1.2 for the order of a type. The identification of $\supset$ with $\rightarrow$ and, consequently, the similarity in the definitions of order in the two cases are not accidental, and we will have opportunities to use this similarity in describing computations. For example, we will provide a description of equality and substitution for terms containing constants of higher-order types in Section 7.6 that will use a clause of clausal order n for a constant that has a type of order n.

The framework that we have described in Section 2.2 already provides the search semantics for implications and universal quantifiers that appear at the top level in goals: These are to be treated by the AUGMENT and GENERIC reduction rules. To complete the picture, we also have to decide how to proceed when the goal has been reduced to an atomic form. Here we use, once again, the backchaining rules in Figure 2.3. Notice that this is possible because D-formulas have exactly the same structure in fohh as in fohc, modulo the structure of G-formulas. As with fohc, we shall use the term O-proof for a derivation that is constructed in the fohh setting using the rules in Figure 1.2, 2.2, and 2.3.

3.2 Implicational goals

An attempt to prove the goal $D \supset G$ from the signature Σ and the program $\mathcal{P}$ results in an augmentation of the program: The AUGMENT rule transforms the objective into one of trying to prove the goal G from the same signature but the larger program $\{D\} \cup \mathcal{P}$. To take a more involved example, attempting to prove the goal

$$(D_0 \supset ((D_1 \supset G_1) \wedge (D_2 \supset G_2))) \wedge G_3$$

from the program $\mathcal{P}$ will result in attempts to prove G_1 from the program $\{D_1, D_0\} \cup \mathcal{P}$ and G_2 from $\{D_2, D_0\} \cup \mathcal{P}$ and, finally, G_3 from the program $\mathcal{P}$. In Section 2.3 we noted that during proof search in fohc, both programs and signatures remained fixed. As seen from this example, implicational goals allow logic programs to grow and shrink following a stack-based discipline during proof search. In Section 3.3, universal quantifiers in goals will be seen to allow signatures to change similarly in the course of computation.

In the depth-first search procedure that is used in implementations of logic programming languages such as λProlog, the order in which clauses are tried in the course of backchaining becomes important: Using different orders for the same clauses can have different outcomes. In this setting, programs are best thought of not as sets but rather as lists of clauses where the list ordering determines the order of use. When new clauses are added to the current context, it is important to know where these new clauses are placed in the list. λProlog uses the rule that when an implicational goal augments the current program, it does so by adding the new clauses at the front of the program: That is, the most recently added clauses are the first to be used in backchaining. To illustrate this convention, assume that the current context contains just the atomic formula (p 1) for some predicate p of type int -> o. Then the following queries should yield the corresponding answer substitutions in the order that they are shown:

```
?- p 2 => p 3 => p X.
X = 3;
X = 2;
X = 1

?- (p 2 & p 3) => p X.
X = 2;
X = 3;
X = 1

?-
```

3.2.1 Inferences among propositional clauses

As a simple example of using implications in goals, we consider proving entailments among propositional Horn clauses of the form $(A_1 \wedge \ldots \wedge A_n) \supset A_0$, where $n \geq 0$ and $A_0, \ldots, A_n$ are propositional constants. Let the symbols q, r, s, t, and u all denote propositional symbols; i.e., let them all have the type o, and consider the logic program composed of the following propositional Horn clauses:

```
s :- r, q.
t :- q, u.
q :- r.
```

Although these clauses do not have any atomic consequences, other clauses can be proved from them. For example, the Horn clauses

```
t :- r, u.
```

and

```
s :- r.
```

are both provable from the shown logic program. To work the second of these out in more detail, the query

```
?- s :- r.
```

which, following the conventions described in Chapter 2, is better written as

```
?- r => s.
```

would result in an attempt to prove the goal s from a program obtained by extending the current program with the clause r. At this point, traditional Horn clause reasoning would provide a proof of s, thereby leading to a successful conclusion to the original query from the starting program. In a similar fashion, the formula

```
(r => u) => (r => t)
```

can be seen to be provable. In this case, the conclusion will follow from attempting to prove the goal t after the the program has been extended with the two propositional Horn clauses r and r => u.

As a final example, consider the query

```
?- (q :- (q => q)) => (q :- (q => q)).
```

which is an formula of the form $B \supset B$. The reader should be able to show that there is an O-proof of this query from the empty program. Unfortunately, there are limitations to what can be done using a depth-first search procedure: It is not too difficult to conclude that such a procedure will not terminate on the given query.

3.2.2 Hypothetical reasoning

Implications in goals can be used to formulate hypothetical reasoning. Figure 3.1 contains an encoding of some simple database-like facts about courses completed by students, rules for inferring who is a computer science major and who graduates, and a constraint that says that it is inconsistent for someone to have completed the two courses numbered 210 and 250. Relative to these definitions, the following query can be interpreted as asking whether

```
kind entry                type.
type fact                 entry -> o.
type false                o.
kind person               type.
type kim, dana            person.
type finished             person -> int -> entry.
type cs_major, graduates  person -> entry.

fact (finished kim  102) & fact (finished dana 101).
fact (finished kim  210) & fact (finished dana 250).

fact (cs_major X)  :-
    (fact (finished X 101); fact (finished X 102)),
    fact (finished X 250), fact (finished X 301).
fact (graduates X) :-
    (fact (finished X 101); fact (finished X 102)),
    (fact (finished X 210); fact (finished X 250)),
    fact (finished X 301).

false :- fact (finished X 210), fact (finished X 250).
```

Figure 3.1. An encoding of a small course-related database.

there is a course such that if Dana completed it, then the database would become inconsistent:

```
?- fact (finished dana X) => false.
X = 210;
no

?-
```

The answer indicates that the course numbered 210 is such a course (and that it is the only course that leads to such an inconsistency). Similarly, one can ask the hypothetical question, "If person X took just one more course Y, will he or she graduate with a CS degree?" The following query provides the one answer:

```
?- fact (finished X Y) => (fact (graduates X), fact (cs_major X)).
X = dana
Y = 301;
no

?-
```

We can try to find out what courses Kim should take in order to graduate and be a computer science major. The response to the preceding query indirectly implies that there is no single course she can take to achieve that goal. The following query considers the same question but this time allowing Kim to take two courses:

```
type db                          o.
kind command                     type.
type do                          command -> o.
type enter, query, whatif, check entry -> command.
type quit, consis                command.


db :- print "Command?", read Command, do Command.


do quit.
do (enter Fact) :- fact Fact => db.
do (query Q) :- (fact Q, !, print "yes\n"; print "no\n"), db.
do (whatif Conjecture) :- (fact Conjecture => db),
                          print "Resuming\n", db.
do consis :- false, print "no\n", !; print "yes\n".
do (check Entry) :- (fact Entry, print "yes\n", !;
                     fact Entry => false, print "no\n", !;
                     print "no, but it could be true\n"),  db.
```

Figure 3.2. A program that allows hypothetical queries against an encoded database.

```
?- fact (finished kim X) => fact (finished kim Y) =>
                (fact (graduates kim), fact (cs_major kim)).
X = 250
Y = 301

?-
```

Thus Kim can graduate as a computer science major by taking courses 250 and 301. Unfortunately, taking these two courses leads to an inconsistency:

```
?- fact (finished kim 250) => fact (finished kim 301) => false.
solved

?-
```

A little reflection on the given database leads to the conclusion that there is no consistent way for Kim to graduate as a computer science major.

A simple interactive database program that is capable of considering hypothetical situations is presented in Figure 3.2. In this program, the predicate db implements a loop that repeatedly reads a command from the keyboard and carries out that command. As is common with interactive programs, this code uses several nonlogical predicates of λProlog. We have discussed all the predicates used in Chapter 2 except for the "cut" (!) predicate that we assume the reader to be familiar with from a previous exposure to Prolog. The following interaction sequence illustrates the use of this code:

```
?- db.
Command? query (graduates dana).
```

```
no
Command? whatif (finished dana 301).
Command? query (graduates dana).
yes
Command? query (cs_major dana).
yes
Command? quit.
Resuming.
Command? query (finished kim 101).
no
Command? query (graduates kim).
no
Command? whatif (finished kim 301).
Command? query (graduates kim).
yes
Command? query (cs_major kim).
no
Command? whatif (finished kim 250).
Command? query (cs_major kim).
yes
Command? consis.
no
Command?
```

3.3 Universally quantified goals

The GENERIC reduction rule transforms the attempt to prove the universal goal $\forall_\tau x\, G(x)$ from the signature-program pair $\langle \Sigma, \mathcal{P} \rangle$ into an attempt to prove $G[c/x]$ from the signature-program pair $\langle \Sigma \cup \{c : \tau\}, \mathcal{P} \rangle$ for some token c that does not occur in Σ. While there are several choices for the token c here, it is a property of O-proofs that the particular selection does not matter from the perspective of finding a derivation as long as c is picked so as to not be a member of Σ. In the proof-theoretic setting, a token that satisfies this kind of constraint is often called an *eigenvariable*. Since such eigenvariables do not get instantiated (i.e., they do not vary) during computation, we will also refer to them as *scoped constants*. The reader might notice a similarity in the interpretation of implicational goals and universal quantifiers: Implicational goals cause the existing program to be augmented for a part of the computation, and universal quantifiers cause a similar augmentation but to the existing signature.

For a simple illustration of the use of universal quantifiers in goals, consider the following problem. Assume that a jar is sterile if every bug (germ) in it is dead, that a bug in a heated jar is dead, and that a given jar has been heated. These assumptions about jars and bugs are encoded by the following λProlog program:

```
kind jar, bug          type.
type j                 jar.
type sterile, heated   jar -> o.
type dead, bug         bug -> o.
type in                bug -> jar -> o.

sterile J :- pi x\ bug x => in x J => dead x.
dead B    :- heated J, in B J, bug B.
heated j.
```

Notice that the signature corresponding to this program does not provide for any particular constants of type bug, and hence no assumption is being made in the program about the existence of any bugs. Now consider solving the goal sterile j from this logic program. Backchaining on the first clause yields the goal

```
pi x\ bug x => in x j => dead x.
```

To solve this universal goal, we proceed by selecting a constant, say, g, that does not occur in the current signature. Using this constant, the goal gets transformed into

```
bug g => in g j => dead g.
```

This goal would succeed if the goal dead g were to follow from the original program augmented with the program clauses bug g and in g j. A few straightforward backchaining steps suffice to convince us that this is indeed the case. After this goal succeeds, the constant g is removed from the signature, and the two clauses bug g and in g j are similarly removed from the program.

This example shows that the interpretation of universal quantifiers in *fohh* is *intensional* in nature: Proofs of universal goals do not make any assumptions about the structure of the domain of quantification, and in fact, the same *generic* proof must work for *every* element of the domain. Universal statements also can be treated *extensionally*, i.e., their proofs can be given by showing, possibly in different ways, that every one of their instances over the domain of quantification holds. In the case that τ represents an inductively given set, such as the set of natural numbers or lists, a common way to provide a proof of an extensionally interpreted goal of the form $\forall_\tau x \, G$ is to use induction. However, the *fohh* logic does not encompass rules for induction and therefore is

incapable of providing such proofs. To illustrate this fact, let us consider the
λProlog program given by the following declarations:

```
kind nat     type.
type zero    nat.
type succ    nat -> nat.
type plus    nat -> nat -> nat -> o.
```

```
plus zero L L.
plus (succ N) M (succ P) :- plus N M P.
```

First, notice that the generic treatment of the universal quantifier will not allow
the query

```
?- pi N\ plus N zero N.
```

to be proved from the program shown even though plus N zero N is true for
every instantiation of N with a closed term of type nat. To pursue the example
further, an inductive proof of the universal query would proceed by choosing
an invariant and then showing that it holds for the base and inductive cases
of closed terms of type nat. In the example being considered, the base and
inductive cases of the obvious invariant can, in fact, be proved in the setting of
fohh. More specifically, the following goal is provable:

```
?- plus zero zero zero,
   pi N\ plus N zero N => plus (succ N) zero (succ N).
```

However, there is no rule in the fohh setting that allows these facts to be used
to conclude that pi N\ plus N zero N is true, so this universal goal remains
unprovable in that logic.

3.3.1 Substitution and quantification

As we have seen in Section 2.6, Horn clauses can be presented as formulas
of the form $\forall_{\tau_1} x_1 \ldots \forall_{\tau_m} x_m (A_1 \wedge \ldots \wedge A_n \supset A_0)$, where $A_0, \ldots, A_n$ are
atomic formulas. When this format is used, only universal quantifiers appear
in these formulas, and they also appear only at the outermost level. Moreover,
backchaining over such a clause can be viewed as a process that simultaneously instantiates all these quantifiers. In this situation, substitution becomes
a particularly simple operation: Given a formula $\forall_{\tau_1} x_1 \ldots \forall_{\tau_m} x_m D$, where D
has no quantifiers in it, to instantiate its quantifiers with the terms $t_1, \ldots, t_n$, we
simply replace the occurrences of $x_1, \ldots, x_n$ in D with these terms.

The quantificational structure of program clauses in a language that is based
on fohh can be more complex. While we will describe restricted versions of

fohh in Section 3.4.3 that use program clauses of a simpler form than that presented in Section 3.1, these formulas still can have occurrences of quantifiers whose scopes are narrower than the entire formula. Thus, in the *fohh* setting, substitutions may have to be applied to formulas containing bound variables. The simple replacement operation just described may not be a logically correct realization of substitution in this situation. For example, consider substituting (f y) for X in the formula

```
p X :- pi y\ q X y.
```

Notice that the token y occurs as a constant in the substitution term and as a bound variable in the formula. If we implement substitution via a naive replacement, we will get

```
p (f y) :- pi y\ q (f y) y.
```

This formula is not a logical consequence of the one that was "instantiated": Where there was only one bound occurrence of y in the original formula, there are two such occurrences in the formula produced from it. The reason for this discrepancy is that an illegal *variable capture* has occurred in the process of blind replacement. Proper substitution must avoid such captures.

Let x be an occurrence of a free variable in a formula B, and let t be some term of the same type as x. We say that t *is free for x in B* if no free occurrence of x in B is in the scope of a quantifier that binds a variable free in t. The replacement of x with t in B, written as $B[t/x]$, is a sound substitution operation if t is free for x in B. Notice that if t is not free for x in B, it is always possible to change bound variables names in B to obtain an equivalent formula B' for which t is free for x in B'. Of course, there are many choices for such a B', but they differ only in the names used for bound variables and therefore are equivalent to each other as well as to B. If we pick any such B', we can carry out the substitution naively on it to realize a logically sound version of the desired operation. Thus, to continue the example considered earlier, the result of correctly substituting (f y) for X is a formula such as

```
p (f y) :- pi z\ q (f y) z.
```

where many other tokens could have been used instead of z. We shall assume that substitution is always performed in this logically sound fashion.

Possibly the simplest example illustrating the relevance of quantifier scopes in computation is the query

```
?- sigma x\ pi y\ x = y.
```

This query is not provable because (pi y\ t = y) is not provable for any term t in which y does not appear. While this expression is true in a model with exactly one object in the domain, which then also must be the denotation of t, not all models are required to have singleton domains. Thus this formula generally is not true. Proof search as we have presented it here correctly determines that this formula is not derivable. In particular, the GENERIC goal reduction step generates a new scoped constant, say c, and attempts to prove the equality c = t, which must fail. One could try to solve the goal (sigma x\ pi y\ x = y) by choosing the variable y to instantiate the existential quantifier. However, the capture avoiding aspect of substitution will end up producing an expression of the form (pi z\ y = z) as a result of this instantiation and the earlier discussion applies to this formula.

3.3.2 Quantification can link goals and clauses

As discussed in Section 2.5, implementation of the ∃R and ∀L quantifier rules often uses a combination of instantiatable or logic variables and unification to delay the determination of actual substitution terms. Thus, although the query and the program at the start of a computation do not contain such variables, intermediate values of both kinds of objects may end up containing them. In Prolog, where the program remains fixed throughout the computation, logic variables find their way only into goal formulas. However, such variables also may appear eventually in program clauses in λProlog.

The ability to have logic variables in program clauses can be useful in programming. To illustrate this, let us consider first the specification of the list-reversal predicate reverse that is shown in Figure 3.3. The definition of this predicate uses an auxiliary predicate rev whose definition has a tail-recursive structure. The clauses for rev are assumed only for the duration of addressing a query involving reverse. Notice that the universal quantification that is written explicitly in these clauses cannot be dropped: Doing so will change the scope of the quantification and hence also the meaning of the predicate the clauses define.

Let the code in Figure 3.3 determine the ambient setting. Then the query

```
?- reverse (1::2::nil) P.
```

effectively reduces to the query

```
?- rev (1::2::nil) P nil.
```

with the existing program being augmented with the clauses

```
rev nil L L.
rev (X::L) K M :- rev L K (X::M).
```

```
type reverse    list A -> list A -> o.
type rev        list A -> list A -> list A -> o.

reverse L K :-
   ((pi L\ rev nil L L) &
   (pi X\ pi L\ pi K\ pi M\ rev (X::L) K M :- rev L K (X::M)))
       => rev L K nil.
```

Figure 3.3. An implementation of the reverse using a three-place auxiliary predicate.

```
type reverse, rev    list A -> list A -> o.

reverse L K :-
   (rev nil K &
   (pi X\ pi L\ pi K\ rev (X::L) K :- rev L (X::K)))
       => rev L nil.
```

Figure 3.4. Another implementation of the reverse using a two-place auxiliary predicate.

The rest of the computation proceeds as expected, leading eventually to the instantiation of P with the term (2::1::nil).

There is another way to visualize the reversal computation. First, observe that if we start with the program

```
rv nil (c::b::a::nil).
rv (X::N) M :- rv N (X::M).
```

then we should be able to prove the goal (rv (a::b::c::nil) nil). Generalizing on this observation, we see that if (c::b::a::nil) in the first clause above is replaced with any list L, then we will be able to prove the atomic goal (rv K nil) if and only if L and K are reverses of each other. While this is a natural approach to specifying reverse, perhaps more natural than the first definition of reverse that we considered, it is not possible to code it directly in *fohc* because to do so we require the ability to "tie" the binding for a variable in the specification of the reverse predicate to one that appears in a goal at a particular point in the computation. It is easy, however, to write this relation in *fohh*: This is, in fact, what is done in Figure 3.4. With respect to that specification, the query

```
?- reverse (1::2::nil) P.
```

reduces to the query

```
?- rev (1::2::nil) nil.
```

with the program being augmented with the clauses

```
rev nil K.
rev (X::L) K :- rev L (X::K).
```

Notice, however, that the variable K in the first clause is not like the usual implicitly universally quantified variables that appear in clauses because its binding is tied to that of P in the original query; our convention for displaying clauses using implicit quantification actually becomes somewhat misleading when such variables can appear in clauses, but we will continue to use it with the appropriate qualifications. Proceeding further with the computation, the rev goal is reduced using the second rev clause to (rev (2::nil) (1::nil)) and then to (rev nil (2::1::nil)). This final goal now succeeds by binding the variable K and hence P to the list (2::1::nil). Since P is implicitly existentially quantified in the original query about the reverse of the list (1::2::nil), its binding is reported as the answer substitution for the overall computation.

3.4 The relationship with logical notions

One reason for using logic as the basis of programming is that useful metatheoretic principles then become available in analyzing programs. For example, if B and C are program clauses or queries that are logically equivalent when viewed as formulas, a fact that is denoted by writing $B \equiv C$, then we might expect that these can be used interchangeably in programming contexts. If the logic programming language allows for side effects or for incomplete proof search, such replacements actually may not preserve computational behavior. For example, in logic, conjunction is commutative, that is, $G_1 \wedge G_2 \equiv G_2 \wedge G_1$, but switching the order of goals does not always leave the computational significance unaltered. Thus, switching the order of the conjuncts in the goal print "yes", print "no" causes different side effects. Similarly, switching the order of the conjuncts in the goal loop, fail, where loop is defined by the sole clause

```
loop :- loop.
```

and fail is an atom with no defining clauses, yields different behaviors under a depth-first prover: One goal loops forever, whereas the other fails quickly.

Nevertheless, logic still might be useful in understanding idealized behavior. In particular, if we rule out programs with side effects and consider complete proof-search strategies, then logical equivalences can be used meaningfully in reasoning about logic programs. It is in this spirit that we make connections in this section between first-order hereditary Harrop formulas understood through the prism of O-proofs and their interpretation as formulas in classical, intuitionistic, and minimal logics.

3.4.1 Classical versus intuitionistic logic

It was observed in Section 2.3 that the rules of inference restricted to `fohc` were complete with respect to both classical and intuitionistic logics. The situation is different for `fohh`: The operational semantics for sequents in `fohh` is sound and complete for intuitionistic logic, but classical logic is not sound for this operational semantics. The latter fact can be demonstrated through varied examples.

As a first example, consider constructing an O-proof for the formula $p \vee (p \supset q)$ from the empty program. This formula (as a goal) is provable if and only if either p is provable from the empty program or q is provable from the program containing just the atomic propositional symbol p. Since neither of these cases holds, the goal is not provable. This conclusion about O-proofs also coincides with provability in intuitionistic logic. In classical logic, however, the following equivalences all hold:

$$B_1 \vee (B_2 \supset B_3) \equiv B_1 \vee \neg B_2 \vee B_3 \equiv (B_2 \supset B_1) \vee B_3 \equiv B_2 \supset (B_1 \vee B_3)$$

As a consequence, the interpretation we desire for implication as a scoping mechanism is not valid in classical logic. More precisely, classical logic allows scopes to be "extruded" over disjunctions: The formula $p \vee (p \supset q)$ is equivalent to $p \supset (p \vee q)$ in classical logic, and the latter formula is clearly provable.

As additional examples, the reader can check that none of the following goal formulas has an O-proof, although every one of them is provable in classical logic:

$$(r\,a \wedge r\,b \supset q) \supset \exists x\,(r\,x \supset q)$$

$$((p \supset q) \supset p) \supset p$$

$$\exists x\,\forall y\,(p\,x \supset p\,y)$$

The middle formula is also commonly known as *Pierce's formula*. It is clear from all these examples that classical logic cannot provide the declarative semantics of λProlog.

3.4.2 Intuitionistic versus minimal logic

Negation of the formula B, usually written as $\neg B$, can be defined in a logical setting as $B \supset \bot$, where $\bot$ is a logical constant denoting the false proposition. Of course, we must include inference rules for $\bot$ in order to make sense of this translation. There are two common ways to describe the meaning of $\bot$, and they lead to rather different interpretations of negation. The *minimal logic* approach treats $\bot$ as, essentially, a *nonlogical* constant. The intuitionistic logic approach provides an additional inference rule for ⊥, namely, that one can infer any formula from it; this logical principle is called *ex falso quodlibet*. In particular, intuitionistic logic contains the following inference rule:

$$\frac{\Sigma; \mathcal{P} \longrightarrow \bot}{\Sigma; \mathcal{P} \longrightarrow B}$$

We say that a logic program $\mathcal{P}$ is *inconsistent* if it entails ⊥. Thus the preceding rule says that if a logic program $\mathcal{P}$ is inconsistent, then it, in fact, entails any formula.

Within λProlog, the weaker form of falsity can be accommodated by picking a propositional constant, say, `false`, to denote ⊥. Since `false` is a nonlogical constant, the rule "from false, anything can be proved" is not available for this proxy of falsehood. The (weak) form of negation that results from translating $\neg B$ to $B \supset \bot$ and this interpretation of falsity is called *minimal logic negation*. There are programming uses for this notion, as we illustrated in Section 3.2.2.

Although the λProlog interpreter does not support intuitionistic negation directly, it can be extended to do so. Toward this end, before failing on a given query, the interpreter would try to determine if `false` is provable. If it is, then it would have to succeed on the query in question. Such a check for inconsistency would have to be coordinated with each (sub)query that leads to the program being augmented.

Minimal logic is weak but does satisfy some laws generally connected with negation. For example, the following implications in which p and q are constants of type o are provable queries in λProlog:

```
(p => q) => ((q => false) => (p => false)).
p => ((p => false) => false).
```

The converse of these implications are provable neither in minimal logic nor in intuitionistic logic but are provable in classical logic.

The query

```
?- p; (p => false).
```

which encodes a particular instance of the principle of the excluded middle, is not provable in the logic of *fohh*. The doubly negated version of this formula, written as the goal formula,

```
?- ((p; (p => false)) => false) => false.
```

is provable. A proof of this is interesting to see and is indicated through the display of a partial list of the queries that arise from attempting to solve this goal from an initially empty program. In this display we show the formulas that get added to the program prior to the invocation of a subgoal by writing them to the left of the symbol ?- used to indicate queries.

```
(p; (p => false)) => false ?- false.
(p; (p => false)) => false ?- p; (p => false).
(p; (p => false)) => false ?- p => false.
p, (p; (p => false)) => false ?- false.
p, (p; (p => false)) => false ?- p; (p => false).
p, (p; (p => false)) => false ?- p.
```

This last query succeeds immediately because the goal p is also in the program at that point.

It is a theorem that when $\mathcal{P}$ is a *fohh* logic program and G is a *fohh* goal formula (both over the signature Σ), then the sequent $\Sigma; \mathcal{P} \longrightarrow G$ has an O-proof if and only if it is provable in minimal logic. Now program clauses and goal formulas in *fohh* do not actually contain any occurrences of $\perp$ and negation—in the preceding discussions we have used only a *nonlogical constant* to simulate their presence. Minimal and intuitionistic provability therefore are indistinguishable with respect to sequents containing only these formulas. For this reason, we shall say that the declarative semantics of λProlog is also given by intuitionistic logic.

3.4.3 Notable subsets of fohh

Goal formulas and program clauses in *fohh* were defined through the following mutually recursive syntax rules in Section 3.1:

$$G ::= \top \mid A \mid G \wedge G \mid G \vee G \mid \exists x \, G \mid D \supset G \mid \forall x \, G$$
$$D ::= A \mid G \supset D \mid D \wedge D \mid \forall x \, D \tag{3.1}$$

It is interesting to consider whether this rich collection of formulas might be restricted without limiting the kind of specifications that could be written. In this section we present two restrictions that have this property.

It can be shown, in a manner analogous to that sketched in Section 2.6, that program clauses written using the preceding syntax can be preprocessed without changing their essential operational interpretation into a form where all the top-level implications in them have atomic conclusions. In other words, program clauses in *fohh* could be restricted to those adhering to the following syntax rule:

$$D ::= A \mid G \supset A \mid D \wedge D \mid \forall x \, D \tag{3.2}$$

The restriction in syntax also can be justified at a declarative level: Any *D*-formula satisfying the definition (3.1) is equivalent in intuitionistic (and minimal) logic to a set of *D*-formulas based on the definition in (3.2).

We also can consider a simplification that eliminates all occurrences of disjunctions and existential quantification in goals. In this case, the *G*- and *D*-formulas will be given by the rules

$$G ::= A \mid G \wedge G \mid D \supset G \mid \forall_\tau x\, G$$
$$D ::= A \mid G \supset A \mid D \wedge D \mid \forall x\, D$$

Notice that now the *G*- and *D*-formulas are identical. Thus another restriction of *fohh* results from letting both program clauses and goal formulas be given by the rule

$$D ::= A \mid D \supset D \mid D \wedge D \mid \forall x\, D \tag{3.3}$$

In this version, goal formulas and program clauses are constructed from atomic formulas via unrestricted use of implications, conjunctions, and universal quantifications.

The relationship between the versions of *fohh* given by the syntax rules (3.1) and (3.2) and the version in (3.3) that excludes disjunctions and existential quantifiers is not based on logical equivalences. To see this, observe that the formula

$$(p \supset (q \vee r)) \supset s$$

is a legal program clause using (3.2) but it is not equivalent in intuitionistic logic to any set of *D*-formulas using the syntax described by (3.3). This formula does imply

$$((p \supset q) \supset s) \wedge ((p \supset r) \supset s)$$

in intuitionistic logic, but the converse implication does not hold.[1] As program clauses, however, these two formulas prove exactly the same atomic formulas, so the former can be replaced by the latter in the limited context of *fohh*. Another way to remove disjunctions and existential quantifiers is to treat them as nonlogical predicates and to realize their proof-search impact via Horn clauses. This approach requires using *higher-order Horn clauses*, and we shall consider it in Section 5.6.

---

[1] The reader might notice that the two formulas in question *are* equivalent in classical logic.

3.5 Bibliographic notes

Extensions to Horn clauses that permit implications in goals have been considered by several researchers. Gabbay and Reyle (1984) described such an extension and used intuitionistic logic to provide the semantics of the resulting language. Their motivation for considering implicational goals was largely that this allowed the language to capture more of its own metatheory. For example, the demo predicate of Bowen and Kowalski (1982) can be encoded using implication: The goal demo(D,G), which should succeed if the goal G is provable from the program D, can be encoded as the goal D => G. Warren (1984) investigated a simpler version of the logic we have described here as the basis for a database updating program. His "modal" operator $assume(A)@G$ can be approximated by $A \supset G$. Warren also provided a possible worlds semantics for this modal operator. Miller (1986, 1989c) presented implicational goals as a means for supporting modular structuring of code. The proof theory of implications in goals also has been developed by Hallnäs and Schroeder-Heister (1990). A stronger logical language, which includes full intuitionistic negation and universally quantified goals, was investigated by McCarty (1988a,b) as the basis for knowledge representation and commonsense reasoning.

It is of interest to understand the circumstances under which the provability of the formula $F_1 \vee F_2$ in intuitionistic logic guarantees that either F_1 or F_2 is provable, and similarly, the provability of $\exists x\, F$ guarantees that there is a term t such that $F[t/x]$ is provable. Harrop (1960) showed that if all the assumption formulas, i.e., the formulas on the left-hand side of a sequent, are restricted to ones given by the syntax rules

$$H ::= \top \mid A \mid H \wedge H \mid B \supset H \mid \forall_\tau x\, H$$

in which A represents an atomic formula and B an arbitrary formula, then the so-called disjunctive and existential properties hold. These H-formulas, which are often called *Harrop formulas*, essentially disallow appearances of disjunctions and existential quantifiers in the top-level positive context of a formula. Notice that Harrop's restrictions guarantee that the disjunctive and existential properties hold only at the root of a proof, whereas we have wanted them to hold at *all* points in the proof. To get the latter effect, we prohibit disjunctions and existential quantifiers not just at the top level but *hereditarily* at *all* positive locations in the formula. The resulting formulas are what have been called *hereditary Harrop formulas* (Miller 1987a; Miller et al. 1987, 1991). The higher-order version of these formulas, presented formally in Section 5.2, can be used to provide a declarative basis for modularity and abstract datatypes in logic programming (Miller 1990).

Classical and intuitionistic logic are distinguished at a semantic level by providing different notions of models for them. Satisfiability for classical logic is defined relative to a world that fixes the interpretation of predicate, constant, and function symbols, whereas the more general notion of *Kripke models* that is used for intuitionistic logic allows these interpretations to vary based on a set of possible worlds (Doets 1996; Fitting 1969; Hodges 1997). Logic programming in *fohh* can be considered as satisfying the "open-world assumption": If we identify worlds as signature-program pairs, then computations can carry us from one world to another, larger world. It is possible to build a Kripke model for hereditary Harrop formulas based on this kind of interpretation of the open-world assumption (Miller 1992b). The open-world assumption does not allow for an interesting notion of negation: The formula $A \supset \bot$ for atomic A can never be true because there is always some future world in which A is true (simply add it to the program in the current world). To achieve an interesting notion of negation, one must move to a *closed-world* assumption and not allow signatures and programs to grow during proof construction.

In contrast to the situation for *fohc*, computations in *fohh* can give rise to goals in which there are alternations between essential existential and universal quantifiers. If logic variables are used to delay instantiations for existentially quantified variables in this setting, then unification must be modified from what was described in Section 1.5 so as to ensure that quantifier scopes are respected. Miller (1989b) and Nadathur (1993) have presented proof procedures for *fohh* that take this aspect into account. Unification problems can be generalized to include explicit quantifiers, as we shall see in Section 4.4. The issue of finding unifiers for problems in this form in a higher-order setting is discussed in Chapter 8.

The intensional and extensional readings of the universal quantifier touched on in Section 3.3 can be distinguished in the form of *generic* and *universal* judgments. A generic judgment is justified by an argument that is parametric in some new object (the eigenvariable or scoped constant). In contrast, a universal judgment is valid for every possible term in a domain. Clearly, a generic reading of the goal $\forall_\tau x \, G$ implies the universal reading: Just substitute the scoped constant with a term in the formula and the proof. On the other hand, under the "open-world assumption," where signatures and programs can grow during computation (as is the case with proof search in *fohh*), the universal reading of $\forall_\tau x \, G$ implies the generic reading: Just consider extending the type τ with a new constant c, and we know that $G[c/x]$ is provable. If one embraces the "closed-world assumption," then, of course, there are distinctions to be made between generic and universal judgments. Miller and Tiu (2005) have introduced the ∇-quantifier to capture generic quantification in that setting.

In Section 3.4.1 we used the term *scope extrusion*. This term is borrowed from the π-calculus (Milner et al. 1992a) where it also applies to an abstraction extending its scope over parallel composition. The π-calculus will be discussed in more detail in Chapter 11.

The problem of removing all occurrences of disjunctions from program clauses that was discussed in Section 3.4.3 has been addressed by Miller (1989c).

4

Typed λ-Terms and Formulas

The previous chapters have dealt with logic programming in the context of first-order logic. We are now interested in moving the discussion to the setting of a higher-order logic. The particular logic that we will use for this purpose is one based on the simply typed λ-calculus, generalized to allow for a form of polymorphic typing. This underlying calculus has several nontrivial computational characteristics that themselves merit discussion. We undertake this task in this chapter, delaying the presentation of the higher-order logic and the logic programming language based on it until Chapter 5.

The first two sections of this chapter describe the syntax of the simply typed *λ-calculus* and an equality relation called λ-conversion that endows the expressions of this calculus with a notion of functionality. The λ-conversion operation brings with it considerable computational power. We discuss this aspect in Section 4.3. In the logic programming setting, λ-conversion will not be deployed directly as a computational device but instead will be used indirectly in the course of solving unification problems between λ-terms. A discussion of this kind of unification, commonly called *higher-order unification*, is the focus of the second half of this chapter. Section 4.4 presents a general format for such problems, introduces terminology relating to them, and tries to develop intuitions about the solutions to these problems. Section 4.5 begins to develop the structure for a procedure that might be used to solve higher-order unification problems; this discussion is incomplete and meant only as a prelude to the more detailed treatment of higher-order unification that appears in Chapter 8. The last section of this chapter provides illustrations of the computational power that is contained in higher-order unification. In particular, it shows how two problems that are known to be undecidable—the Post correspondence problem and Hilbert's Tenth Problem—can be translated into higher-order unification problems.

4.1 Syntax for λ-terms and formulas

Typed λ-terms are built from typed collections of constants and variables using the syntactic operations of application and abstraction. Application, denoted by juxtaposition, has already been used in the construction of first-order terms. Abstraction, however, is a new operation that takes an expression in which a particular (typed) variable possibly appears free and creates from it a term denoting a function ranging over values for that variable. If t is the expression and x is the variable that has the type α, then the function expression, which is said to be *an abstraction that binds x and whose body is t*, is written in mathematical notation as $\lambda(x : \alpha)\, t$. In concrete syntax, abstraction is written in infix form, being denoted by a backslash placed between the bound variable and its type on the one hand and the abstraction body on the other. Thus, if T is the representation of the term t in which the token x is used to denote the variable x and A is the representation of the type α, the term $\lambda(x : \alpha)\, t$ is written as $(x:A)\backslash$ T. The type of the variable also can be omitted—i.e., this expression may be written simply as $\lambda x\, t$ in mathematical notation or as x \ T in concrete syntax—in which case the type will be filled in using an inference process that we explain later in this section.

When an abstraction is being read, its body is to be understood to go as far to the right as is possible, given the presence of delimiting parentheses and the end of the expression. This convention implies that application binds more tightly than does abstraction and that abstraction is right associative. As examples, the terms $\lambda f\, \lambda x\, (f\ (f\ (f\ x)))$, $\lambda x\, (f\ (g\ \lambda y\, (h\ x\ y))\ x)$, and $\lambda x\, \lambda y\, x$ in mathematical notation can be written in concrete syntax as f\x\ f (f (f x)), x\ f (g y\ h x y) x, and x\y\ x, respectively. We shall assume that the concrete syntax disallows a backslash in the name of a constant or variable. No space therefore is needed before or after this symbol in writing an abstraction term.

The syntax of typed λ-terms can be formalized through a type assignment calculus in a manner similar to that done for first-order terms and formulas. The judgments for this calculus have the form $\Sigma; \Gamma \Vdash t : \tau$. These judgments generalize the ones of the form $\Sigma; \Gamma \Vdash_f t : \tau$ that we described in Section 2.1. As before, we assume that Σ provides an assignment of types to constants that include the logical constants and that Γ is an assignment of types to variables. However, in contrast to the first-order setting, there are no longer any restrictions on the types that can be assigned by Σ and Γ. The rules defining the new judgment appear in Figure 4.1. There are several noteworthy differences between these rules and the first-order typing rules presented cumulatively in Figure 1.2 of Chapter 1 and Figure 2.1 of Chapter 2. First, the judgment $\tau \lhd_f \sigma$ is replaced by $\tau \lhd \sigma$, although this judgment continues to hold between any two types τ and σ if τ is a substitution instance of σ; as with the main typing judgment, the dropping of the subscript signals the shift away from the first-order

$$\frac{c:\sigma \in \Sigma \quad \tau \lhd \sigma}{\Sigma;\Gamma \Vdash c:\tau} \qquad \frac{x:\tau \in \Gamma}{\Sigma;\Gamma \Vdash x:\tau} \qquad \frac{\Sigma;\Gamma \Vdash g:\tau_1 \to \tau_2 \quad \Sigma;\Gamma \Vdash t:\tau_1}{\Sigma;\Gamma \Vdash (g\ t):\tau_2}$$

$$\frac{\Sigma;\Gamma,x:\tau \Vdash t:\sigma}{\Sigma;\Gamma \Vdash \lambda(x:\tau)\,t:\tau \to \sigma}\ (\dagger) \qquad \frac{\Sigma;\Gamma \Vdash B:\tau}{\Sigma;\Gamma \Vdash C:\tau}\ (\ddagger)$$

The proviso ($\dagger$) requires that x is not declared as a type or kind in Σ or Γ, and the proviso ($\ddagger$) requires that B and C differ only in the names of bound variables.

Figure 4.1. Rules for typing λ-terms.

restrictions. Second, we have a new rule for typing abstractions. Finally, we no longer have special rules for typing existential and universal quantifications. These quantifiers are captured using abstractions and two new logical constants, as we note below, and the rules for typing applications and abstractions then suffice also for typing judgments pertaining to them.

An expression t is said to be a *well-formed λ-term over the signature* Σ or, alternatively, a *well-formed (higher-order)* Σ-*term* exactly when there is a context Γ and a type τ such that the judgment $\Sigma;\Gamma \Vdash t:\tau$ is derivable. We are typically interested only in well-formed λ-terms, and the signature also may not be directly relevant to the discussion. We therefore will often refer to t as a λ-term or, more simply, as a term under these circumstances. A term is *closed* if there is a derivable judgment $\Sigma;\Gamma \Vdash t:\tau$ for which Γ is empty. Terms that are not closed are *open*.

In the general case, the type assigned to a term or to one of its subcomponents may contain variables in it. Terms that do not contain type variables in this way are called *simply typed λ-terms*. While we usually will treat all typed λ-terms, it will be necessary occasionally to restrict our attention to simply typed λ-terms. This happens especially when we discuss the details of a unification procedure for these terms.

Given the way we have presented λ-terms and the associated typing rules, the bound variable of each abstraction is expected to be annotated with a type. When this principle is followed, it can be shown that the type associated with each well-formed λ-term is unique up to the renaming of type variables. It is often convenient, however, to omit the types of bound variables. In this case, we can fill in the missing types through a type inference process that is similar to the one described for quantified variables in the first-order setting: A new type variable is assigned tentatively to the variable bound by the abstraction, and this assignment then is refined in as minimal a way as possible in the course of checking adherence to the typing rules. The type that is obtained for the λ-term in this way is, once again, guaranteed to be unique up to type variable renaming.

We will often write abstractions without type annotations and expect their types to be inferred in this way.

Well-formed λ-terms that have type o are also called formulas. This class already contains expressions that can be formed using propositional connectives such as those for conjunction, disjunction, and implication. In Section 2.1 we had introduced special notation for quantifiers. This notation can be given formal status in the present context as follows: First, we extend the global signature Σ to include the constants $\forall$ and $\exists$ that have the type $(A \rightarrow o) \rightarrow o$, where A is a type variable. These constants are represented in concrete syntax by the symbols `pi` and `sigma` that we have already presented. Now, using these constants, we write the universal and existential quantification of the variable x over the term F as $\forall (\lambda x \, F)$ and $\exists (\lambda x \, F)$, respectively. Finally, consistent with the syntax described in Chapter 2, we use here $\forall x \, B$ and $\exists x \, B$ as alternative notation for $\forall (\lambda x \, B)$ and $\exists (\lambda x \, B)$, respectively. Sometimes it may be important to depict the type of the bound variable, and we shall do this by adding a type subscript to the quantifier symbol in this notation. Thus the expressions $\forall (\lambda(x : \tau) \, B)$ and $\exists (\lambda(x : \tau) \, B)$ may be rendered as $\forall_\tau x \, B$ and $\exists_\tau x \, B$, respectively.

For an example of a quantified formula and the association of a type with it, assume that Σ is a signature such that the judgment $\Sigma; \Gamma, x : \sigma \Vdash B : o$ is provable, where σ is some type expression. Thus B is a formula that may contain the variable x free. Using the typing rule for λ-abstractions, we obtain a derivation for $\Sigma; \Gamma \Vdash \lambda x \, B : \sigma \rightarrow o$. Since Σ is assumed to contain $\forall : (\tau \rightarrow o) \rightarrow o$, we can derive the judgment $\Sigma; \Gamma \Vdash \forall : (\sigma \rightarrow o) \rightarrow o$. Combining this with the earlier derivation, we obtain a derivation for $\Sigma; \Gamma \Vdash \forall (\lambda x \, B) : o$, thereby showing that $\forall x \, B$ is a well-formed term. As another example, this time using λProlog syntax, we can apply an instance of the logical constant `pi` that has type `(list int -> o) -> o` to the abstraction term

```
y\ append (1::2::nil) y X.
```

which has type `list int -> o` to get the quantified formula

```
pi y\ append (1::2::nil) y X.
```

The removal of restrictions on the types that can be assigned by a signature makes it possible to construct terms in which logical connectives appear inside the arguments of nonlogical symbols. Higher-order programming, which we discuss in Chapter 5, is based substantially on this possibility. To understand the kinds of terms that can be constructed now, consider the following type declaration:

```
type foreach   (A -> o) -> list A -> o.
```

This declaration identifies a constant that yields an atomic formula when provided with two arguments. The first of these arguments must be a predicate over the type A, and the second argument must be a term denoting a list of items of type A. A concrete example of an atomic formula that can be formed using this constant is

```
foreach (x\ x > 5, x < 9) (3::10::6::8::nil).
```

Notice that in this atomic formula the subterm (x > 5, x < 9) appears within an argument of the nonlogical symbol foreach. This subterm has in it an occurrence of the logical constant corresponding to conjunction.

Our higher-order logic contains only one binding operation, namely, abstraction. As we have just seen, this binding operation can be used to form the ones associated with the universal and existential quantifiers. We shall see later that other binding operations in terms and formulas also can be encoded using abstraction in an analogous manner.

4.2 The rules of λ-conversion

The *rules of λ-conversion* partially formalize the intended interpretation of abstraction and application as the operations of function definition and function application in the context of λ-terms. To define these rules, we must generalize terminology governing the substitution of terms into quantified formulas that we presented in Section 3.3.1. We shall say that the λ-term t is *free for* a variable x *in* the λ-term s if the free occurrences of x in s are not in the scope of any abstractions that bind free variables of t. For example, the term $(f\ x)$ is free for u in $\lambda w\ (g\ u\ w)$, whereas the term $(f\ w)$ is not free for u in $\lambda w\ (g\ u\ w)$. If x and t are, respectively, a variable and a term that have the same type and t is free for x in s, then $s[t/x]$ denotes the result of replacing all free occurrences of x in the term s by t. The "free for" proviso is needed in this substitution operation for reasons similar to those encountered in the context of quantified formulas in Chapter 3: If it is not satisfied, free variables in t will get bound in a logically unsound way in the course of substitution.

The rules that are of interest now comprise the following operations on terms:

- Replacing a subterm $\lambda x\ s$ by $\lambda y\ s[y/x]$, provided that y is free for x in s and y is not free in s, is called an *α-rewriting*. The reflexive, symmetric, and transitive closure of α-rewriting is called *α-conversion*.
- Replacing a subterm $(\lambda x\ s)\ t$ by $s[t/x]$, provided that t is free for x in s, is called *β-contraction*. The converse operation is call *β-expansion*. The reflexive and transitive closure of the union of α-conversion and β-contraction is

called *β-reduction*, and the symmetric and transitive closure of *β*-reduction is called *β-conversion*.

- Replacing a subterm *λx* (*s x*) by *s*, provided that *x* is not free in *s*, is called *η-contraction*. The converse operation is call *η-expansion*. The reflexive and transitive closure of *η*-contraction is called *η-reduction*, and the symmetric and transitive closure of *η*-reduction is called *η*-conversion.

As an illustration of these relations, consider the following terms in concrete syntax:

```
x\y\ f (g x) y
X\Y\ f (g X) Y
x\ f (g x)
x\y\ f ((u\v\v) (2 + 3) (g x)) y
```

The first two terms are related by *α*-conversion. The third term results from the first through an *η*-contraction. Finally, a *β*-contraction on the fourth term yields

```
x\y\ f ((v\v) (g x)) y
```

and another *β*-contraction on this term yields the first term.

The transitive closure of *α*-, *β*-, and *η*-conversion is called *λ-conversion*. This relation is clearly an equivalence and congruence. It also will be taken as the notion of *equality* within higher-order logic. If we use this relation for equality, it will not be possible to distinguish among the four terms displayed above in the logic. It also will be impossible to write a specification in the logic that determines the name of the bound variable in an abstraction: This follows from the fact that the name of such a variable always can be changed using *α*-conversion while maintaining equality with the original term.

For convenience, we extend the notation $s[t/x]$ to the case where *t* is not necessarily free for *x* in *s*. We do this by first picking a term s' that is *α*-convertible to *s* and such that *t* is free for *x* in s' and then setting $s[t/x]$ to the result of substituting *t* for *x* in s'. Although the result depends on the actual term s' that is picked, all possible results themselves will be *α*-convertible and hence equal. In this sense, the extended operation $s[t/x]$ is well defined. Moreover, this extension allows us to modify *β*-contraction to cover the replacement of a subterm of the form (*λx s*) *t* by the term $s[t/x]$ with no restrictions on *t*. We assume this more liberal interpretation henceforth.

4.3 Some properties of λ-conversion

A term of the form (*λx s*) *t* that can be the target of a *β*-contraction is also called a *β*-redex. Similarly, a term of the form *λx* (*t x*) in which *x* does not occur free in t is referred to as an *η-redex*. A term t that contains no *β*-redexes is said to be a *β-normal form*, and it is said to be a *λ-normal form* if, in addition, it contains no *η*-redexes. Sometimes, a λ-normal form is also referred to as a *βη-normal* form.

If t is a λ-normal form and s is λ-convertible to t, then t is said to be a λ-normal form of s. It is well known that every λ-term in our typed language has a λ-normal form and that this normal form is unique up to *α*-conversion. We denote the λ-normal form of s by $\lambda norm(s)$. There is an easy algorithm for computing such a normal form for a term: We repeatedly replace subterms of the form $(\lambda x \, s) \, t$ by $s[t/x]$ to produce a *β*-normal form and then repeatedly replace subterms of the form $\lambda x \, (s \, x)$ with s provided that x is not free in s. From this, we also obtain an algorithm for determining if two λ-terms of the same type are equal (modulo λ-conversion): We first compute their respective λ-normal forms and then determine if these are equal up to *α*-conversion.

As we have already observed, λ-terms can contain logical constants. For example, let p and q be predicates of type $i \rightarrow o$. The expression $\lambda x \, (p \, x) \wedge (q \, x)$ (also of type $i \rightarrow o$) contains an occurrence of the conjunction symbol. While logical constants can appear in terms, the equality of expressions containing them is not affected by any logical equivalences pertaining to them. For example, the λ-term above is not equal (as a term) to the term $\lambda x \, (q \, x) \wedge (p \, x)$. This situation is consistent with the view presented in Section 2.7 that types (such as $i \rightarrow o$ that is relevant in this case) are inhabited by expressions and not more abstract values such as the set of objects that satisfy a particular property.

The computation of λ-normal forms is a rich operation largely because of the presence of *β*-reduction. When $(\lambda x \, s) \, t$ is replaced by $s[t/x]$, there may be many or no occurrences of x in s. If there are many, then $s[t/x]$ may contain many copies of the term t. Also, while both t and s may be in λ-normal form, the term $s[t/x]$ may not be in such a form. Given these complexities, it is not surprising that λ-normalization can be used as a device for computing.

To appreciate this possibility in more detail, let us see how λ-terms and *β*-reduction can be used to encode functions over natural numbers. To begin with, we need an encoding of the natural numbers themselves. Let i be a sort, and assume that there are no constants of type i. The only closed λ-normal forms of the (second-order) type $(i \rightarrow i) \rightarrow i \rightarrow i$ then are those which are *α*-convertible to one of the following:

$$\lambda f \, \lambda x \, x, \quad \lambda f \, \lambda x \, (f \, x), \quad \lambda f \, \lambda x \, (f \, (f \, x)), \quad \ldots, \quad \lambda f \, \lambda x \, (f^n \, x), \quad \ldots$$

We write $f^n \, x$ here to denote the n-fold application of f to x, i.e., the expression that written out in full form would be $f \, (f \, \cdots \, (f \, x) \cdots)$ with n occurrences of f. The terms displayed above are called the *Church numerals* and can be used to denote the nonnegative integers by encoding the number $n \geq 0$ as $\lambda f \, \lambda x \, (f^n \, x)$.

Once we have picked this representation for the nonnegative integers, it is an easy matter to write down λ-terms that encode functions such as those for producing the successor of such a number or for adding or multiplying two of these numbers. Thus consider the λ-term $\lambda n \, \lambda f \, \lambda x \, f \, (n \, f \, x)$. This term represents the successor function for the following reason: When it is applied to the encoding of a nonnegative integer, we get a new term that is equal modulo λ-conversion to the encoding of the successor or that integer. To take a concrete example, consider its application to the encoding of the number 3:

$$(\lambda n \, \lambda f \, \lambda x \, f \, (n \, f \, x)) \, (\lambda f \, \lambda x \, f \, (f \, (f \, x)))$$

This term has the normal form $\lambda f \, \lambda x \, f \, (f \, (f \, (f \, x)))$ that is the encoding of 4, the successor of 3. In a similar fashion, addition and multiplication on nonnegative integers can be encoded by the λ-terms

$$(\lambda n \, \lambda m \, \lambda f \, \lambda x \, n \, f \, (m \, f \, x)) \quad \text{and} \quad (\lambda n \, \lambda m \, \lambda f \, \lambda x \, n \, (m \, f) \, x)$$

respectively. Since a λProlog interpreter computes the λ-normal form of expressions prior to printing them out, we can use it to see these functions in action, so to speak. For example, to compute the multiplication of 2 with 2 using Church numeral encoding, one simply can pose the query[1]

```
?- N = ((n\m\f\x\ n (m f) x) ((f:i -> i)\x\ f (f x)) (f\x\ f (f x))).
N = f\x\ f (f (f (f x)))

?-
```

The result is, as expected, the Church numeral for 4.

While a large collection of functions over nonnegative integers can be encoded by our λ-terms using the preceding ideas, it turns out that the functions that can be so represented are limited to the polynomial ones. The presence of types and the fact that we have used closed terms of a particular type—the type $(i \to i) \to i \to i$—to represent the nonnegative integers greatly limits what can be expressed by these terms.

Define the *size of a λ-term* to be the number of occurrences of application within the term. The encoding examples discussed earlier can be used to show that the size of a λ-term can be made at least polynomially larger by passing to its λ-normal form. For a more dramatic example of the increase in size, consider

---

[1] We assume here and below that the ambient λProlog signature includes the sort i corresponding to the sort shown as *i* in mathematical notation.

the series of λ-terms of which the following are the first four (switching to the concrete syntax of λProlog):

```
(g\e\ e)           (e\f\ e (e f)) (f\x\ f (f x)).
(g\e\ g e)         (e\f\ e (e f)) (f\x\ f (f x)).
(g\e\ g (g e))     (e\f\ e (e f)) (f\x\ f (f x)).
(g\e\ g (g (g e))) (e\f\ e (e f)) (f\x\ f (f x)).
```

We assume here the following types for the bound variables:

```
x : i
f : i -> i
e : (i -> i) -> i -> i
g : ((i -> i) -> i -> i) -> (i -> i) -> i -> i.
```

The subterms that start with `g\e\` are a version of Church numeral but with the type `i` replaced with the type `(i -> i) -> i -> i`: For example, the term `g\e\ g (g e)` has the fourth-order type

```
(((i -> i) -> i -> i) -> (i -> i) -> i -> i) ->
 ((i -> i) -> i -> i) -> (i -> i) -> i -> i.
```

The $(n + 1)^{\text{th}}$ term of this series has the size $n + 6$. The normal form of the first term in this series is `f\x\ f (f x)`, encoding the numeral 2, whereas the normal form for the second term is the encoding of the numeral 4. The third λ-term normalizes to

```
f\x\ f (f (f (f (f (f (f (f (f (f (f (f
           (f (f (f (f x)))))))))))))))
```

which encodes the numeral 16. The fourth λ-term normalizes to the encoding of the numeral 256. It is easy to show that the $(n + 1)^{\text{th}}$ term of this series has a λ-normal form that is of size

$$
\left. 2^{2^{2^{\cdot^{\cdot^{2}}}}} \right\} n+1
$$

(i.e., there are $n + 1$ occurrences of 2). Even for small values of n, this increase in the size of terms is dramatic and is not the kind of value that one expects to be calculating within any practical computational setting.

When we consider logic programs that contain λ-terms, such blow-ups in the sizes of λ-normal terms generally do not occur during the search for proofs. There are at least three reasons for this.

- When computing with structures such as integers, we make use of built-in integers instead of those constructed from λ-terms, as above. Thus computations on integers are carried out in a familiar and efficient fashion. Similarly, while it is possible to encode other structures, such as binary trees, using closed typed λ-terms with no special constants, this is typically not the way it is done. The usual practice is instead to introduce new nonlogical constants that serve as constructors for such structures.

- When λ-abstraction within a term is needed, bound variables generally have types that are of order 0. If all the bound variables in a term T have primitive types, then the dynamics of β-reduction is simple. In particular, if in the β-redex $(\lambda x \, s) \, t$ both s and t are λ-normal, then the β-reduction $s[t/x]$ is in λ-normal form: While substituting t for x may yield many copies of t at several different positions, no new β-redexes are created.
- There is a subset of higher-order logic programs that belongs to a sublanguage, called L_λ (described in Section 7.8), in which β-contraction is restricted to β_0-contraction, which involves replacing a subterm of the form $(\lambda x \, s) \, x$ with s. Notice that with this restriction on β-contraction and, correspondingly, on β-reduction, passage to the λ-normal form produces smaller terms.

4.4 Unification problems as quantified equalities

In Section 1.5, a unification problem was defined to be a finite multiset of equations of the form $\{t_1 = s_1, \ldots, t_p = s_p\}$, where, for $1 \le i \le p$, t_i and s_i are first-order terms of the same type. We also observed there that such a problem is related to a logical formula of the form

$$\forall y_1 \ldots \forall y_m \exists x_1 \ldots \exists x_n \, [t_1 = s_1 \wedge \cdots \wedge t_p = s_p]$$

where the variables $y_1, \ldots, y_m$ correspond to the constants of the language, and $x_1, \ldots, x_n$ is a listing of the variables that are free in the terms in the multiset of equations. We now adopt such formulas as the preferred style of presentation for unification problems. Solutions to unification problems in the earlier style will correspond to proofs of the associated quantified formulas in a sense that we make precise later in this section.

We actually shall generalize the preceding kind of presentation in one important respect: We shall allow for *arbitrary* quantification in the prefix over the conjunction of equations between terms. More specifically, a *(generalized) unification problem* henceforth will be a formula of the form

$$Q_1 x_1 \ldots Q_n x_n \, [t_1 = s_1 \wedge \ldots \wedge t_m = s_m]$$

where $n, m \ge 0$, Q_i is either $\forall$ or $\exists$ for $1 \le i \le n$, and $t_1, s_1, \ldots, t_m, s_m$ are λ-terms such that, for $1 \le j \le m$, t_j and s_j are of the same type. Notice that in the present higher-order context, the bound variables $x_1, \ldots, x_n$ are allowed to have types of arbitrary order.

As a result of this generalization, a unification problem will have a *mixed prefix* of quantifiers. The reasons for wanting a more complicated prefix are twofold. First, while the earlier form was adequate from the perspective of implementing proof search in `fohc`, proof search in `fohh` naturally gives rise to unification problems where existential and universal quantifiers can appear in any order. For example, consider the query

```
?- pi y\ X = y.
no

?-
```

The associated unification problem, written in mathematical notation, is $\exists x \forall y \, [x = y]$. The order of the quantifiers *is* important: The query fails because instances of X cannot contain the eigenvariable used to instantiate y. Second, binders that may be present in λ-terms are closely related to universal quantifiers that appear *inside* the scope of existential quantifiers in unification problems. For example, consider the query

```
?-  (y\ X) = (y\ y).
no

?-
```

The unification problem associated with this query is $\exists x \, [(\lambda y \, x) = (\lambda y \, y)]$. Since the equation $(\lambda y \, t) = (\lambda y \, s)$ and the universally quantified equation $\forall y \, [t = s]$ are logically equivalent, one can argue that the unification problem being considered is logically the same as $\exists x \forall y \, [x = y]$. It follows then that the second query fails for essentially the same reason as the first: No instance of X can contain a variable that gets bound by the abstraction within whose body X occurs.

In the `fohc` setting, ∀∃-unification problems, i.e., problems in which the quantifier prefix consists of a sequence of universal quantifiers followed by a sequence of existential quantifiers, form a natural class. When we allow higher-order terms into this setting, these problems correspond more accurately to ∀∃∀-unification problems, i.e., ones that have prefixes in which a block of existential quantifiers can be preceded and followed by blocks of universal quantifiers. The outer ∀ quantifiers arise, as we have noted already, from constants. As for the inner universal quantifiers, we see that equations between λ-terms of type $\tau \to \sigma$ can be replaced by universally quantifying a variable of type τ around an equation between terms of type σ and that these quantifiers can be moved to scope over the entire conjunction of equations. To illustrate this sequence of transformations, let f and a be constants of type $i \to i$ and i, respectively, and consider the unification problem initially given by

$$\exists G\, \exists H\, [(\lambda w\; f\; a) = (\lambda w\; f\; (G\; w)) \wedge (\lambda w\; f\; w) = (\lambda w\; H\; (H\; w))]$$

It is easy to see that the types of H and G must be $i \to i$ here. Making the quantifiers over the constants explicit yields the (closed) unification problem

$$\forall f\, \forall a\, \exists G\, \exists H\, [(\lambda w\; f\; a) = (\lambda w\; f\; (G\; w)) \wedge (\lambda w\; f\; w) = (\lambda w\; H\; (H\; w))]$$

Next, using the equivalence mentioned earlier between the equation $(\lambda y\; t) = (\lambda y\; s)$ and the quantified equation $\forall y\, [t = s]$, we can transform the preceding unification problem into

$$\forall f\, \forall a\, \exists G\, \exists H\, [\forall w\, [(f\; a) = (f\; (G\; w))] \wedge \forall w\, [(f\; w) = (H\; (H\; w))]]$$

This is not a unification problem in the accepted form, but we can obtain from it one in such a form by moving the $\forall w$ quantifiers to the prefix, getting, for example,

$$\forall f\, \forall a\, \exists G\, \exists H\, \forall w\, \forall w'\, [(f\; a) = (f\; (G\; w)) \wedge (f\; w') = (H\; (H\; w'))]$$

It is possible to consider unification problems that are not in prefixed form. In particular, we may allow quantifiers to also appear internal to the conjuncts. Such a generalization might, in fact, be preferable because moving quantifiers out to the prefix can lead to the introduction of variable dependencies that are not genuine aspects of a given unification problem. However, such dependencies are logically harmless, and we find it more convenient here to assume that all quantification is contained entirely within the prefix.

4.4.1 Simplifying quantifier prefixes

Using higher-order variables, it is possible to transform a unification problem with an arbitrary prefix into one with only a $\forall\exists\forall$ prefix. To see how this can be done, consider the two formulas $\forall y\, \exists x\, G$ and $\exists h\, \forall y\, G[h\; y/x]$, where the bound variables x, y, and h have types τ, σ, and $\sigma \to \tau$, respectively. It is easy to show that one of these formulas can be proved if and only if the other formula can be proved. In one direction, assume that the first formula can be proved by substituting the new constant c for y and the term t, which possibly may contain c, for x. Then the second formula can be proved by substituting $\lambda c\; t$ for h and c for y; notice that c is not free in $\lambda c\; t$. For the converse, assume that the second formula is proved by substituting the term s for h and the new constant c for y. In this case, c cannot be free in s. The first formula then is proved by substituting c for y and substituting the term $(s\; c)$ for x. Using equivalences of this kind, we can move any existential quantifier that is to the right of an (explicit) universal quantifier to be on the left of that universal quantifier instead. The cost of this transformation, which is called *raising*, is that the type of the variable that is existentially quantified needs to be "raised" by the type of the universally quantified variable. By repeatedly applying this raising transformation, a unification problem with an arbitrary quantifier prefix can be changed into one in which there is only a ∀∃∀ (or even just an ∃∀) prefix.

Raising bears some resemblance to the technique of *Skolemization*, which is known from automated reasoning contexts. To understand the relationship between the two, let us first recall how Skolemization is used. Suppose that $\forall x \, \exists y \, D$ is an assumption. Let x and y have the types σ and τ here. Then Skolemization applied to this formula produces the formula $\forall x \, D[f \, x/y]$, where f is a new function constant of type $\sigma \to \tau$; this kind of constant is typically called a *Skolem constant*. Since goals are the duals of assumptions, the roles of the quantifiers gets switched in Skolemizing them. Thus the Skolemization of the goal $\exists x \, \forall y \, G$ yields $\exists x \, G[f \, x/y]$, where f is again a new function constant; we assume that the types of x, y, and f are as before. Given our earlier comments about constants, we see that this goal formula alternatively is written as $\forall f \, \exists x \, G[f \, x/y]$.

From the preceding discussion, we see that Skolemization is a dual to raising in two senses. First, Skolemization moves an existential quantifier to a smaller scope, whereas raising moves a universal quantifier to a smaller scope. Second, Skolemization causes the introduction of a new constant (eigenvariable) of a raised type, whereas raising causes the introduction of a new existentially quantified variable of a raised type. These observations notwithstanding, there are differences between Skolemization and raising at a logical level. In particular, relating unifiers for Skolemized unification problems to original, un-Skolemized unification problems is problematic, especially when unification involves variables of higher-order type.

4.4.2 Unifiers, solutions, and empty types

We wish to tie the existence of a solution to a unification problem as described in Section 1.5 to the provability of the quantified formula that we associate with the problem. The connection is a bit more complicated than might appear at first glance. Consider, for example, the set of equations $\{X = X\}$, which is a unification problem in the terminology of Chapter 1. We now wish to describe this problem by the formula $\exists x \, [x = x]$; we assume here that X and x are both variables of some primitive type i. The original unification problem has a trivial solution. To prove the quantified formula, on the other hand, we have to use the following rule

$$\frac{\Sigma; \mathcal{P} \longrightarrow B[t/x] \qquad \Sigma; \emptyset \Vdash t : \tau}{\Sigma; \mathcal{P} \longrightarrow \exists_\tau x \, B}$$

which is an adaptation of the $\exists$R rule in Figure 2.2 that appears in Chapter 2 to the higher-order context. This rule has *two* premises. Applied to the formula at hand, it requires us to construct a closed term t and to show that $t = t$. While the second task is trivial once we have a closed term of type i, showing that there is such a term is more involved and requires an examination of the available signature. As another example, consider the quantified formula $\exists x \, \exists y \, \exists z \, [x = (f \ y) \wedge y = (f \ z)]$, which corresponds to the unification problem

$$\{X = (f \ Y), Y = (f \ Z)\}$$

in the style of Chapter 1; we assume here that f is a constant of type $i \to i$ and that x, y, z, X, Y, and Z are all variables of type i. Following the earlier description, we can conclude that this unification problem has the most general unifier $\{\langle X, f \ (f \ Z)\rangle, \langle Y, (f \ Z)\rangle\}$. The existence of a proof of the associated quantified formula, on the other hand, depends on whether or not there are closed terms of type i.

Consider the unification problem given by the $\forall\exists\forall$-formula

$$\forall u_1 \ \ldots \ \forall u_p \, \exists x_1 \ \ldots \ \exists x_n \, \forall w_1 \ \ldots \ \forall w_q \, [t_1 = s_1 \wedge \cdots \wedge t_m = s_m]$$

where p, q, n, $m \geq 0$, the types of the variables $x_1, \ldots, x_n$ are $\tau_1, \ldots, \tau_n$, respectively, and the ambient signature is Σ. Let θ be a substitution for the existentially quantified variables in the prefix, i.e., for the variables $x_1, \ldots, x_n$. The *range* of θ is the set $\{\theta(x_1), \ldots, \theta(x_n)\}$. We shall consider legitimate only those substitutions in which the variables $w_1, \ldots, w_q$ do not appear free in any term in the *range* of θ. If θ is such a substitution, then it is said to be a *unifier* for the problem in question just in the case that the terms $\theta(t_j)$ and $\theta(s_j)$ are λ-convertible to each other for $j = 1, \ldots, m$. Furthermore, θ is said to be a *solution* to a unification problem if θ is a unifier and the only variables that appear free in the terms in the range of θ are those contained in the list $u_1, \ldots, u_p$. As the examples we have considered in this section illustrate, it is possible for a unification problem to have a unifier but not a solution. It is the solution to a unification problem that ensures the provability of the quantified problem that represents it.

Notice that in Section 1.5, the term solution was used as a synonym for the term unifier. There are certain technical reasons underlying our desire to now distinguish these terms. In most treatments of first-order classical logic, the domain of every type is assumed to be nonempty. In higher-order intuitionistic logics, however, such an assumption generally is not made. For example, in Section 4.3 we took each term of type $(i \to i) \to i \to i$ to be a Church numeral. This identification is possible only if there is no closed term t of type i; otherwise, the term $\lambda f \, \lambda x \, t$ would be a closed term of type $(i \to i) \to i \to i$, that is not a Church numeral. For reasons such as this, we shall not always assume that types are inhabited by closed terms.

4.4.3 Examples of unification problems and their solutions

Let i be a type and let $g : i \rightarrow i \rightarrow i$ be a constructor for this type. The unification problem $\forall a \, \exists F \, [(F \ a) = (g \ a \ a)]$ has four solutions corresponding to the instantiation of F by one of the terms $\lambda x \, g \, a \, a$, $\lambda x \, g \, x \, a$, $\lambda x \, g \, a \, x$, and $\lambda x \, g \, x \, x$. If we now switch the order of the quantifiers, we get the problem $\exists F \forall a \, [(F \ a) = (g \ a \ a)]$, which has the instantiation of F by $\lambda a \, g \, a \, a$ as its unique solution.

Suppose now that the only constructors that have i as a target type are u and v and that both these constructors have the type $i \rightarrow i$. In this case, there are no closed terms of type i. Further, all closed terms of type $i \rightarrow i$ can be viewed as words over a two letter alphabet with one letter being u and the other being v. Thus $\lambda w \, w$ corresponds to the empty string, $\lambda w \, u \, w$ to the string "u," and $\lambda w \, u \, (v \, (u \, w))$ to the string "uvu." In this context, the unification problem

$$\exists F \, \exists G \, [(\lambda w \, F \, (G \, w)) = (\lambda w \, u \, (v \, (u \, w)))]$$

in which F and G are variables of type $i \rightarrow i$, has four solutions: the substitutions that bind F and G, respectively, to $\lambda w \, u \, (v \, (u \, w))$ and $\lambda w \, w$, or $\lambda w \, u \, (v \, w)$ and $\lambda w \, u \, w$, or $\lambda w \, u \, w$ and $\lambda w \, v \, (u \, w)$, or $\lambda w \, w$ and $\lambda w \, u \, (v \, (u \, w))$. In general, any unification problem obtained from this one by preserving the term on the left of the equation while replacing the one on the right by some other closed term can be viewed as an attempt to find all pairs of words over the two-letter alphabet whose concatenations yield the word corresponding to the term on the right. The unification problem

$$\exists F \, [(\lambda w \, u \, (F \, (u \, w))) = (\lambda w \, u \, (v \, (v \, (u \, w))))]$$

has as its only solution the substitution that binds F to $\lambda w \, v \, (v \, w)$. The term on the left in this case can be thought of as a pattern for checking if the first and last letter of the word represented by a closed term of type $i \rightarrow i$ is the letter u. The unification problem

$$\exists F \, [(\lambda w \, u \, (F \, w)) = (\lambda w \, (F \, (u \, w)))]$$

has as a solution any substitution that binds F to one of the terms from the infinite sequence $\lambda w \, w$, $\lambda w \, u \, w$, $\lambda w \, u \, (u \, w)$, $\lambda w \, u \, (u \, (u \, w))$, etc.

Finally, suppose that the type i has as its constructors at least the constants a, b, c, and d, all of type i. In this setting, the unification problem

$$\exists F \, [(F \ a) = b \wedge (F \ c) = d]$$

has no solution. The first equation is solved uniquely by instantiating F with $\lambda x\, b$, but this instantiation does not solve the second equation. This example clearly illustrates that our typed λ-terms embody a relatively weak notion of functionality: While there clearly is a function that maps a to b and c to d, such a function is not expressible using these terms.

4.5 Solving unification problems

In Chapter 8 we shall consider in detail how the unification of simply typed λ-terms, often called *higher-order unification*, can be structured as a search procedure. Here, we develop vocabulary for that discussion and also provide high-level insights useful in predicting unifiers and solutions to unification problems.

A typed λ-term that is in β-normal form has the structure

$$\lambda x_1 \ldots \lambda x_n\, (h\, t_1\, \cdots\, t_p) \qquad (n, p \geq 0)$$

where h is either a constant or a variable, and the terms t_i (for $i = 1, \ldots, p$) are also in β-normal form. The list of variables $x_1, \ldots, x_n$ is the *binder* of this term, the symbol h is its *head*, the terms $t_1, \ldots, t_p$ are its *arguments*, and the application $(h\, t_1\, \cdots\, t_p)$ is its body.

A $\beta\eta$-*long normal form* is a variant of a β-normal form that also takes into account η-conversion. A typed λ-term is in this form if it has the structure

$$\lambda x_1 \ldots \lambda x_n\, (h\, t_1\, \cdots\, t_p) \qquad (n, p \geq 0)$$

where h is either a constant or a variable, the terms t_i (for $i = 1, \ldots, p$) are also in $\beta\eta$-long form, *and* the body $(h\, t_1 \ldots t_p)$ has nonfunctional type.[2] Any β-normal form can be converted into a $\beta\eta$-long normal form that is equal to it by using η-expansions. For example, if f is of type $((i \to i) \to i)$, where l is a sort, then the term f itself is in β-normal form. Using a η-expansion on it yields the term $\lambda w\, f\, w$, where the type of w is $(i \to i)$. This term is not yet in $\beta\eta$-long normal form: The subterm w has nonprimitive type. Using η-expansion again yields $\lambda w\, f\, (\lambda u\, w\, u)$, where the type of u is i. This term is in $\beta\eta$-long normal form.

Given a β-normal form $\lambda x_1 \ldots \lambda x_n\, (h\, t_1\, \cdots\, t_p)$, there are three possibilities for what its head h might be: It might be a variable that is bound by a universal quantifier, a member of the binder $x_1, \ldots, x_n$, or an existentially quantified variable. In the first two cases, this term is said to be *rigid*, and in the third case, it is said to be *flexible*. This terminology is meant to be suggestive:

---

[2] If we restrict our attention to only simply typed λ-terms, the body of a $\beta\eta$-long form must have a primitive type.

If a term is rigid, then the β-normal form of any substitution instance of it will have the same head, but if it is flexible, then a substitution can alter its head.

Suppose that we wish to unify two rigid terms of the same type that have the forms $\lambda x_1 \ldots \lambda x_n \ (h \ t_1 \ \cdots \ t_p)$ and $\lambda x_1 \ldots \lambda x_n \ (k \ s_1 \ \cdots \ s_q)$; notice that the presence of α- and η-conversion allows us to assume that the binders of these β-normal forms are identical. Since the heads of these forms cannot be modified by substitution, a necessary condition for the existence of a unifier for the original terms is that the heads h and k are the same symbols.

As concrete examples of the preceding observation, consider the following unification problems:

$$\{(\lambda x \ (d \ (c \ (F \ x)))) = (\lambda x \ (c \ (d \ (G \ x))))\}$$

$$\{(\lambda x \ (x \ (F \ x))) = (\lambda x \ (c \ (G \ x)))\}$$

$$\{(\lambda x \, \lambda y \ (x \ (F \ x \ y))) = (\lambda x \, \lambda y \ (y \ (G \ x \ y)))\}$$

Capital letters in these expressions denote instantiatable or logic variables, and the symbols c and d are constants. We have reverted here to showing unification problems as multisets of equations. Using more precise notation, the first problem might have been written instead as

$$\exists F \ \exists G \ [(\lambda x \ (d \ (c \ (F \ x)))) = (\lambda x \ (c \ (d \ (G \ x))))]$$

or, making the quantification over constants also explicit, as

$$\forall c \, \forall d \ \exists F \ \exists G \ [\lambda x \ (d \ (c \ (F \ x))) = \lambda x \ (c \ (d \ (G \ x)))]$$

Returning to the actual unification problems, we see that none of them have unifiers. The two terms in each of the equations are rigid, and they have different heads.

Another important structural property of substitution is that it cannot introduce new variables into a term that end up being captured by any of the existing abstractions in the term. Thus, if a variable in the binder of a β-normal form has no free occurrence in its body, then any substitution instance of this term also will not have any free occurrences of that variable in its body. For example, the unification problem

$$\{(\lambda x \, \lambda y \, x \ (F \ x \ y)) = (\lambda x \, \lambda y \, G \ y \ y)\}$$

cannot have a unifier because the body of any instance of the first (rigid) term always will contain an occurrence of the variable bound by the outermost abstraction, whereas the body of no substitution instance of the second term can contain such an occurrence. In a manner similar to what we saw in Section 3.3.1, it is possible to instantiate G with a term containing x free, but this will not result in the introduction of a new binding occurrence of x in the second term above.

Notice that a flexible term can be transformed by substitution into almost any term (of the appropriate type) except for the way this term uses the variables in the binder. Thus the term $\lambda x \, \lambda y \, F \, (f \, x \, (G \, x))$ can be transformed via substitution into *any* term of the form $\lambda x \, \lambda y \, t$, where t does not contain x and y free. A substitution instance of the given term also may have occurrences of x free in its body (e.g., $\lambda x \, \lambda y \, (f \, x \, x)$ is an instance of it), but none of its instances can have y free in the body.

As an extension of the preceding observations, consider unifying the pair of flexible terms $\lambda x \, \lambda y \, G \, x$ and $\lambda x \, \lambda y \, H \, y$. Instances of the first term leave the binding for y vacuous, and instances of the second term leave the binding for x vacuous. Thus any common instance of these two terms must be a term of the form $\lambda x \, \lambda y \, t$, where neither x nor y occurs free in t. As we shall see in Chapter 8, the "most general" unifier for the two given terms is the substitution of $\lambda w \, T$ for both G and H, where T is a new free variable of suitable type.

When a unification problem is presented as a formula involving quantifications over a conjunction of equations between β-normal terms, a term occurrence in the equations is classified as either rigid or flexible as follows: If its head is a variable that occurs in its binder or is bound by a universal quantifier in the prefix, then the term occurrence is rigid, and if the head variable is bound by an existential quantifier in the prefix, then the occurrence is flexible. An equation $t = s$ in such a presentation is classified as *rigid-rigid*, *rigid-flexible*, *flexible-rigid*, or *flexible-flexible* depending on the status of the terms t and s. Finally, a unification problem is called flexible-flexible if all the equations in it are flexible-flexible. This classification of equations and unification problems will be used in the presentation of higher-order unification in Chapter 8.

4.6 Some hard unification problems

Undecidable problems are encountered often in the course of trying to carry out deduction. For example, determining whether or not an atomic formula is derivable from a collection of `fohc` program clauses is, in general, undecidable. Similarly, it is not always possible to decide if two typed λ-terms are unifiable modulo the λ-conversion rules. In this section we present reductions from two different undecidable problems to unification problems that establish the latter fact. Although these examples show that unification problems can encode rich computations, the approach to constructing logical specifications using higher-order logic that we develop in later chapters will give rise to unification problems that have a much tamer computational behavior.

4.6.1 Solving Post correspondence problems

Consider the two letter alphabet $\{u, v\}$, a number $n \geq 1$, and two lists of strings $s_1, \ldots, s_n$ and $t_1, \ldots, t_n$ over the alphabet $\{u, v\}$. The *Post correspondence problem* given these inputs is the problem of determining whether or not there is a nonempty sequence $i_1, \ldots, i_k$ such that $1 \leq i_j \leq n$ for $1 \leq j \leq k$ and $s_{i_1} \cdots s_{i_k} = t_{i_1} \cdots t_{i_k}$. This problem is known to be undecidable in the general case. We establish the undecidability of higher-order unification by showing how to transform an arbitrary instance of the Post correspondence problem into an equivalent unification problem.

First, we need an encoding of strings over u and v. We have seen how to do this in Section 4.4.3 if we have a sort i and two constants u and v of type $i \to i$: The string $r = r_1 \cdots r_m$, where $r_1, \ldots, r_m$ are letters, can be represented by the term $\hat{r} = \lambda w \, (r_1 \, (\cdots \, (r_m \, w) \, \cdots))$. Using this encoding, the concatenation of the strings r and q is given by the term $\lambda w \, (\hat{r} \, (\hat{q} \, w))$.

In what follows, we assume the existence of a sort i that has *no* constructors at the outset; the needed constructors will be introduced by universal quantifiers. In this context, the Post correspondence problem given by the two lists of strings $s_1, \ldots, s_n$ and $t_1, \ldots, t_n$ is encoded by the unification problem

$$\exists F \, \exists G \, \forall u \, \forall v \, [(F \, \hat{s}_1 \, \cdots \, \hat{s}_n) = (F \, \hat{t}_1 \, \cdots \, \hat{t}_n) \wedge (F \, u \, \cdots \, u) = \lambda w \, (u \, (G \, u \, w))]$$

where u and v are both of type $i \to i$, $(F \, \hat{s}_1 \, \cdots \, \hat{s}_n)$ has type $i \to i$, G has type $(i \to i) \to i \to i$, and the representations $\hat{s}_1, \hat{t}_1, \ldots, \hat{s}_n, \hat{t}_n$ of the given strings are built using the universally quantified variables u and v as the needed constants. As an example, the Post correspondence problem given by the two lists of words uv, u and u, vu is encoded as the unification problem

$$\exists F \, \exists G \, \forall u \, \forall v \, [(F \, (\lambda w \, u \, (v \, w)) \, u) = (F \, u \, (\lambda w \, v \, (u \, w))) \wedge (F \, u \, u)$$
$$= \lambda w \, (u \, (G \, u \, w))]$$

In this particular case, F and G have the (second-order) types $(i \to i) \to (i \to i) \to i \to i$ and $(i \to i) \to i \to i$, respectively.

To prove that this encoding is correct, notice that the only closed instantiations for F are terms of the form $\lambda x_1 \ldots \lambda x_n \lambda w \, d$, where d is a term of type i that is built from the variables $x_1, \ldots, x_n$ and w. Moreover, since there are no constructors for i in the ambient signature, the only possibility for the shape of d is $x_{i_1} (\cdots (x_{i_k} w) \cdots)$, where $k \geq 0$ and $\{i_1, \ldots, i_k\} \subseteq \{1, \ldots, n\}$. If this unification problem has a solution, the structure of d describes a solution to the Post correspondence problem except in the case that $k = 0$. The second equation is used to rule out this degenerative case: If the substitution for F is (part of) a solution for this second equation as well, then k cannot be 0.

The opposite direction, that of constructing a solution to the unification problem from a solution to the given Post correspondence problem, is easy.

The preceding argument showed that there is a *solution* to a particular unification problem just in the case that there is a solution to the associated Post correspondence problem. It is straightforward to strengthen this argument to show that a *unifier* to the unification problem also yields a solution to the Post correspondence problem. It is similarly possible to remove the restriction that the type i has no constructors.

4.6.2 Solving Diophantine equations

Let **N** denote the set of natural numbers. Diophantine equations (over **N**) are equations constructed from variables and natural numbers using only the operations of addition and multiplication. A solution to a set of such equations is an assignment of natural numbers to the variables that satisfy the equations. Hilbert's Tenth Problem then is the following question: Does there exist a universal algorithm for solving Diophantine equations? A seminal result in computability theory is that no such algorithm can exist and that the existence of solutions to such equations is in general undecidable.

We outline here a reduction of the question of solvability of a set of Diophantine equations into the question of existence of a solution to a unification problem. We initially limit the equations to be encoded to one of the following forms: $x = 1$, $x + y = z$, or $x \times y = z$, where x, y, and z are (**N**-valued) variables. We also assume a sort i with no constructors for this type. Thus the only closed terms of the type $(i \to i) \to i \to i$ are the Church numerals that we saw in Section 4.3. We shall write $\lceil n \rceil$ to denote the encoding of $n \in \mathbf{N}$ as a Church numeral.

We now observe the following facts, assuming that all the existentially quantified variables in the formulas below have the type $(i \to i) \to i \to i$: (1) The (flexible-flexible) unification problem

$$\exists N \left[(\lambda f\, \lambda x\, N\, f\, (N\, f\, x)) = (\lambda f\, \lambda x\, (N\, f\, (f\, x))) \right]$$

has the unique solution $\{(N, \lceil 1 \rceil)\}$, (2) the flexible-flexible unification problem

$$\exists M\, \exists N\, \exists P\, \left[(\lambda f\, \lambda x\, (N\, f)\, (M\, f)\, x) = (\lambda f\, \lambda x\, P\, f\, x) \right]$$

has the solution $\{(N, r), (M, s), (P, t)\}$ if and only if for some $n, m \geq 0$, r is $\lceil n \rceil$, s is $\lceil m \rceil$, and t is $\lceil n + m \rceil$, and (3) the flexible-flexible unification problem

$$\exists M\, \exists N\, \exists P\, \left[(\lambda f\, \lambda x\, N\, (M\, f)\, x) = (\lambda f\, \lambda x\, P\, f\, x) \right]$$

has the solution $\{(N, r), (M, s), (P, t)\}$ if and only if for some $n, m \geq 0$, r is $\lceil n \rceil$, s is $\lceil m \rceil$, and t is $\lceil n \times m \rceil$. Using these observations, it is easy to see that any finite set of equations in the limited forms above can be transformed into a flexible-flexible unification problem that has a solution if and only if there is an assignment of natural numbers to the variables appearing in the equations that make each of them true. In this encoding, each variable that appears in the equation gives rise to an existentially quantified variable and each equation translates into a flexible-flexible equation. Further, as already noted, the existentially quantified variables in this encoding have types of order at most 2; the unification problem in this case is said to be of third order.

The reduction just described can be extended in an obvious way to treat sets of *arbitrary* Diophantine equations. Since the problem of determining if there is an **N**-valued solution to such a set of equations is known to be undecidable, the problem of determining whether a (third-order) flexible-flexible unification problem has a solution also must be undecidable.

The reduction of Diophantine equations that we have described is based on *solutions* to unification problems rather than on the less restrictive notion of *unifiers*. In fact, our encoding gives rise to a unification problem that always has a unifier. Such a unifier can be obtained by first picking a (new) variable U of type i and then instantiating every variable that is existentially quantified in the prefix with the term $\lambda f\, \lambda x\, U$. Of course, such a term is not closed, and hence this unifier is not also a solution.

4.7 Bibliographic notes

Church (1936, 1941) invented the λ-calculus and subsequently used a simply typed version of it to formulate a higher-order logic (Church 1940). There are a number of good references that cover the details, background, and history of the λ-calculus; e.g., see (Barendregt 1984, 1992) and Hindley and Seldin (1986). Statman (1979b) has analyzed various aspects of the computational complexity of λ-conversion in the simply typed λ-calculus.

The unification of simply typed λ-terms was first given a full and systematic presentation by Huet (1975). Snyder and Gallier (1989) provided an alternative presentation of Huet's search procedure using transformations on sets of term equations. Miller (1991b, 1992a) developed the presentation of unification problems as quantified conjunctions and described the use of raising and Skolemization to simplify quantifier alternations in the prefixes of unification problems.

Huet (1973a) originally developed the reduction of Post correspondence problems (Post 1946) to third-order unification. The presentation in Section 4.6.1 is modeled closely on his ideas. Goldfarb (1981) showed how to reduce the task of solving Diophantine equations to that of finding unifiers to second-order unification problems. The reduction outlined in Section 4.6.2 is due to Miller (1992a). This reduction uses ideas from Goldfarb's development but differs from it in two important respects: The transformation here is to a third-order unification problem, and it shows that the question of existence of *solutions*—as opposed to *unifiers*—to such problems is undecidable.

All the formal results about the λ-calculus that we have described here concern the simply typed λ-terms in which types do not contain variables. In this setting, Church (1940) encoded "polymorphic" constants by using a distinct constant at each of the instance types; thus the universal quantifier was represented by an infinite number of constants Π_τ, one for each type τ. We have allowed type variables into the type system because these provide significant convenience at a programming level. For example, in λProlog, a single type declaration that uses a type variable suffices for identifying the constant pi. In our description of unification, however, we have not permitted substituting for type variables. In this situation, these variables behave like sorts, and all the results for the simply typed λ-calculus continue to hold even when such variables are allowed into type expressions. Another, possibly more useful approach is to let these type variables be instantiated in the course of unification. Caires and Monteiro (1994) describe a treatment of unification under such an interpretation of type variables and approximations to this approach also have been used in implementations of λProlog such as the first version of the Teyjus system. Nadathur and Qi (2005) describe a comprehensive treatment of this kind of polymorphism in the context of a restricted form of higher-order unification known as L_λ unification.

5

Using Quantification at Higher-Order Types

First-order logic programming uses first-order terms to represent objects and predicate constants to represent relations between such objects. In Chapter 4 we presented an enrichment to formulas that replaces first-order terms with λ-terms and that permits quantification over predicate names. These additions can have significant practical benefits: For example, since predicates correspond to procedures, the ability to treat predicates as variables can be used as the basis for higher-order programming. Before we can harness this potential, however, it is necessary to explain how the enhanced logic can be used to define a logic programming language. We do this in the first two sections of this chapter. The rest of the discussion concerns the practical utility of the resulting language. Specifically, we explore in detail the use of predicate variables in realizing conventional forms of higher-order programming. We also show that function variables, when combined with λ-terms and higher-order unification, can lead to a new kind of programming capabilities. Several subsequent chapters explore varied applications that exist for these capabilities.

5.1 Atomic formulas in higher-order logic programs

In Chapter 3 we defined the logic programming language of first-order hereditary Harrop formulas, or (`fohh`), which is based on goal formulas and program clauses given, respectively, by the following syntax rules:

$$G ::= \top \mid A \mid G \wedge G \mid G \vee G \mid \forall x\, G \mid \exists x\, G \mid D \supset G$$
$$D ::= A \mid G \supset D \mid \forall x\, D \mid D \wedge D$$

The language of first-order Horn clauses, or `fohc`, corresponds to the subset of `fohh` that is obtained by disallowing universal quantifiers and implication in goal formulas. In these definitions, all the quantification is limited to being first order. Now that we have permitted quantification at higher-order types in the logic, it is possible to consider extensions to `fohh` and `fohc` that exploit this flexibility. In these extensions, we would like to preserve the top-level logical structure permitted in program clauses and goal formulas in the corresponding first-order versions. Apart from higher-order quantification, the main change, then, is in what is allowed for the atomic formulas A in the preceding syntax rules. In the higher-order setting, these formulas may contain arbitrary occurrences of function and predicate variables as well as of logical symbols. It turns out that we will need to restrict the latter two possibilities to obtain languages that are suitable for logic programming. We motivate these restrictions below in preparation for a formal definition of the higher-order versions of `fohc` and `fohh`.

5.1.1 Flexible atoms as heads of clauses

The λ-normal form of a higher-order atomic formulas has the shape $(h\ t_1\ \cdots\ t_n)$, where h is either a variable or a nonlogical constant, and $t_1, \ldots, t_n$ are terms. If h is a (nonlogical) constant, this formula is a *rigid atom*. If h is a variable, it is a *flexible atom*. Allowing flexible atoms to appear in goal formulas is essential for a natural treatment of higher-order programming, as we see, for example, in Section 5.3. Allowing the formula A in the definition of program clauses to be a flexible atom, on the other hand, is problematic for at least two reasons.

We say that a theory (or logic program) is *inconsistent* if any arbitrary formula is provable from it and that the theory is *consistent* if it is not inconsistent. It is easy to show that any logic program based on `fohc` or `fohh` is consistent. In fact, consistency of a logic program seems to be a desirable property for programming. Otherwise, if an interpreter is to be complete, it must establish that the program is consistent before it can decide that a given goal is not provable from it. Such a check might be sensible in the context of databases with "integrity constraints," but it seems to be unacceptable in a programming-language setting. More specifically, the syntax of the programming language should be structured in such a way that it prevents inconsistent programs from being constructed.

Allowing flexible atoms in the syntax rule for program clauses leads to a language in which it is possible to construct inconsistent programs. For example, consider the two clauses

```
P 5 :- q.
q.
```

Let B be any formula over the ambient signature of the (full) logic program. To prove B, we simply backchain over the first clause above, instantiating P with

$\lambda x \, B$. This leads to the goal q, which is provable. Thus any formula is provable from this "program." An even simpler example of an inconsistent program is that consisting of the single clause $\forall p \, p$.

The second reason for wanting to disallow flexible atoms as program clauses arises from the way we want to think of such clauses in a programming situation. Consider a clause of the form

$$\forall x_1 \, \ldots \, \forall x_m \, (A_1 \wedge \ldots \wedge A_n \supset A_0)$$

where $A_0, \ldots, A_n$ are atomic formulas. We typically interpret this clause as part of the specification of a relation named by the head of A_0. If that head is a variable, then such a clause has to be considered as adding meaning to *every* predicate, a possibility that seems to be counter to modularity and effective implementation.

For the two reasons just described, the definition of higher-order hereditary Harrop (*hohh*) formulas that we will adopt will require atomic formulas to be rigid to qualify as program clauses. Despite the rationale we have provided, this restriction appears to be draconian in some respects: There are situations in which it may be useful to allow flexible atoms to be program clauses. We present two examples of this kind below. However, we argue that even in these cases, the restriction may be justifiable.

Leibniz's definition of equality states that two terms are equal if and only if they satisfy the same properties. Thus the equation $x + 0 = x$ could be specified using the two clauses

```
P (X + 0) :- P X.
P X :- P (X + 0).
```

Given these clauses, any attempt to prove a goal containing an occurrence of a subterm of the form X + 0 can be replaced by the attempt to prove the same goal but with that subterm replaced with X (and vice versa). While this style of reasoning is meaningful logically, it is operationally problematic because it introduces into proof search too many choices and looping computations. For example, if a goal has $n \geq 0$ occurrences of the term, say, 5 + 0, then there are 2^n different ways to abstract those occurrences to form an instance for P. Even if the goal has no occurrences of such a subexpression, there still remains one way to use the first clause in backchaining.

Disallowing flexible atoms as the head of clauses also means that it is not possible to construct a formula by means of a computation and then to use that formula as a program clause. For example, suppose that we are given a program that contains clauses that define the binary predicate convert that relates descriptions of programs given as terms to the actual syntactic structure of program clauses. In this context, consider the "query"

```
?- convert d P, P => g.
```

where g is some formula, P is a variable of type o, and d is closed term describing a particular program. Intuitively, this query embodies a computation that constructs a logic program from d and then invokes the goal g relative to this program. Such a computation is related to the eval function in Lisp that allows a term to be evaluated. Notice that the second occurrence of P in the purported query shown above is in a position where a program clause is expected. Thus, ruling out flexible atoms as program clauses disallows it as a query and hence also disallows the evaluation-like computations that such queries embody. However, a little thought reveals that supporting such computations can be complicated. In particular, there seems to be no simple yet general way to statically guarantee that the value bound to P by the convert predicate in any particular instance actually will have the structure expected of a legal program clause.

5.1.2 Logical symbols within atomic formulas

The higher-order language we have described allows logical symbols to appear within atomic formulas. We show later in this chapter that arguments of atomic formulas that contain such symbols provide the basis for many natural higher-order programming capabilities. Allowing implications to occur within such arguments, however, is problematic: The language that results from permitting such occurrences does not constitute a logic programming language in the sense that formulas then can be constructed that should be provable in any reasonable logic but that do not have goal-directed proofs. For example, consider the formula

$$\exists Q \, [\forall p \, \forall q \, [r \, (p \supset q) \supset r \, (Q \, p \, q)] \wedge Q \, (t \vee s)(s \vee t)]$$

where r is a constant of type $o \rightarrow o$, s and t are constants of type o, Q is a variable of type $o \rightarrow o \rightarrow o$, and p and q are constants of type o. In order to prove the first formula in the conjunction, the existentially quantified variable Q must be instantiated with the term $\lambda x \, \lambda y \, (x \supset y)$, which makes the second formula in the conjunction equal to $(t \vee s) \supset (s \vee t)$. This formula should be provable, but it cannot be derived using only the rules for goal-directed proof construction presented in Chapter 2.

When implications are not allowed in terms, there is a natural and useful way to define the *polarity* of all logical symbols. For example, in the language of higher-order hereditary Harrop formulas that we present in the next section, an occurrence of a logical symbol is considered to be positive if and only if it is either within an atomic formula or is in the scope of only logical constants and to the left of an even number of implications. All other occurrences of logical symbols are taken to be negative. As the search for (cut-free) proofs proceeds and formulas within sequents are rearranged, positive occurrences remain positive occurrences, and negative occurrences remain negative. As the preceding example shows, if implications are allowed within atomic formulas, this invariant fails. In particular, both occurrences of the disjunction are positive in the original query, but after instantiation of the quantifier for Q, one of these occurrences becomes negative.

5.2 Higher-order logic programming languages

We present in this section a higher-order version of the Horn clause language that we call $hohc$ and two higher-order versions of the hereditary Harrop formulas language that we call $hohh$ and $hohh^+$, respectively. Two special classes of λ-terms, each parameterized by a signature that is assumed to contain at least all the logical constants, will be useful in describing these languages. The *Herbrand universe for* $hohc$ based on the signature Σ is denoted by $\mathcal{H}_1^\Sigma$ and is defined to be the set of all (possibly open) λ-normal terms over Σ that do not contain the logical constants $\forall$ and $\supset$. Note that terms in $\mathcal{H}_1^\Sigma$ may contain the constants $\top, \wedge, \vee$, and $\exists$ and that there is also no restriction on the types of these terms. The *Herbrand universe for* $hohh$ based on the signature Σ is denoted by $\mathcal{H}_2^\Sigma$ and is defined to be the set of all (possibly open) λ-normal terms over Σ that do not contain the logical constant $\supset$; thus the constants $\top, \wedge, \vee, \forall$, and $\exists$ may appear in the terms of $\mathcal{H}_2^\Sigma$. The difference between $\mathcal{H}_1^\Sigma$ and $\mathcal{H}_2^\Sigma$ is that terms in the latter can have occurrences of $\forall$.

5.2.1 Higher-order Horn clauses

We assume an ambient signature Σ that, of course, contains all the logical constants. In this context, let A be a syntactic variable ranging over atomic formulas in $\mathcal{H}_1^\Sigma$, and let A_r be a syntactic variable ranging over rigid atoms in $\mathcal{H}_1^\Sigma$. Then the goals formulas and program clauses of the *higher-order Horn clause* or $hohc$ language are defined to be the collections of formulas whose λ-normal forms are given by the following syntax rules:

$$G ::= \top \mid A \mid G \wedge G \mid G \vee G \mid \exists_\tau x\, G$$

$$D ::= A_r \mid G \supset D \mid D \wedge D \mid \forall_\tau x\, D$$

There are no restrictions here on what τ, the type of the quantified variable, might be. Notice that G-formulas are exactly the formulas in $\mathcal{H}_1^\Sigma$. The D formulas just defined are also called *higher-order Horn clauses*.

Computation in the hohc language involves constructing a derivation for a sequent of the form $\Sigma; \mathcal{P} \longrightarrow G$, where $\mathcal{P}$ is a set of closed program clauses and G is a closed goal formula. Goal-directed proof search for higher-order Horn clauses is given, as in the first-order case, by the inference rules in Figures 2.2 and 2.3. There are, however, some differences in how these rules are interpreted.

One difference is the use of λ-conversion for equality. Concretely, this means that we assume that the formulas in a sequent are in λ-normal form when we try to match this sequent with the lower sequent of any of the inference rules in question. A related observation is that we must take into account α-convertibility in applying the initial rule. Thus this rule is modified to be

$$\frac{}{\Sigma; \mathcal{P} \xrightarrow{A'} A} \text{ initial}$$

with the proviso that A' and A are α-convertible formulas.

Another important difference is in the kind of terms that might be picked for instantiating the quantifiers in the $\forall L$ and $\exists R$ rules. These terms must, of course, now be λ-terms. Thus the two rules in question must be replaced by the following:

$$\frac{\Sigma; \mathcal{P} \longrightarrow B[t/x] \qquad \Sigma; \emptyset \Vdash t : \tau}{\Sigma; \mathcal{P} \longrightarrow \exists_\tau x\, B} \exists R \qquad \frac{\Sigma; \mathcal{P} \xrightarrow{D[t/x]} A \qquad \Sigma; \emptyset \Vdash t : \tau}{\Sigma; \mathcal{P} \xrightarrow{\forall_\tau x\, D} A} \forall L$$

However, this change alone is not enough. The coherence of the operational semantics defined by the collection of inference rules depends on the formulas to the left and above the sequent arrow being program clauses and the formula to the right of the sequent arrow being a goal formula. If we allow t to be an arbitrary λ-term in the quantifier rules just shown, this "normal form" for sequents may be lost. For example, instantiating the goal formula $\exists p\; p$ with the term $\forall x\; q\; x$ (for some suitable predicate constant $q \in \Sigma$) produces the formula $\forall x\; q\; x$, which is not itself a goal formula.

To overcome the difficulty just described, we limit t in the two quantifier rules to being terms from $\mathcal{H}_1^\Sigma$. This requirement suffices at a technical level because substituting a term from $\mathcal{H}_1^\Sigma$ into a goal formula or a program clause preserves its categorization. The restriction also has considerable intuitive appeal: It is, in a sense, merely stating that we should not substitute into a program clause or goal formula something that cannot appear as the argument of an atomic formula or in the structure of a goal formula. A set of terms that functions in logical contexts in the way $\mathcal{H}_1^\Sigma$ does in our inference rules is called a *Herbrand universe*, thereby justifying our terminology for this set. Another interesting observation, which we do not explore here in any detail, is that derivability for goal formulas from program clauses in a calculus with these restrictions coincides exactly with provability in classical higher-order logic.

5.2.2 Higher-order hereditary Harrop formulas

Let Σ once again be a signature that contains all the logical constants, let A be a syntactic variable ranging over atomic formulas in $\mathcal{H}_2^\Sigma$, and let A_r be a syntactic variable ranging over rigid atoms in $\mathcal{H}_2^\Sigma$. The goals formulas and program clauses of the *higher-order hereditary Harrop* or hohh language then are defined by the following syntax rules:

$$G ::= \top \mid A \mid G \wedge G \mid G \vee G \mid \exists_\tau x\, G \mid D \supset G \mid \forall_\tau x\, G$$

$$D ::= A_r \mid G \supset D \mid D \wedge D \mid \forall_\tau x\, D$$

Notice that goal formulas for hohh are richer than the set of formulas in $\mathcal{H}_2^\Sigma$: In particular, goal formulas are allowed to contain implications, whereas no formula or term in $\mathcal{H}_2^\Sigma$ contains an implication. The D-formulas given by this definition are also called *higher-order hereditary Harrop* formulas.

As before, computation in the hohh language involves constructing a derivation for a sequent of the form $\Sigma; \mathcal{P} \longrightarrow G$, where $\mathcal{P}$ is a set of closed program clauses and G is a closed goal formula. Once again, the rules in Figures 2.2 and 2.3 are modified to treat λ-convertibility and to take into account the fact that we are now dealing with λ-terms. The only additional issue to consider is the collection of terms to use in the $\exists R$ and $\forall L$ rules. These must be restricted for reasons similar to those in the hohc context. However, we can be more liberal about the terms we use in this case: Any term drawn from $\mathcal{H}_2^\Sigma$ is acceptable, where Σ here is the signature in existence at the point in the derivation where the rule is used. The terms that are used in quantifier instantiations thus are limited to those which can appear in the arguments of atomic predicates. The logical constants that can appear in such terms are more restrictive than what is permitted at the top level in goal formulas for the reason discussed in Section 5.1.2: Substituting a term that includes an implication into a goal formula can produce a formula that is not itself a goal. An interesting observation from a logical perspective is that derivability for goal formulas from programs defined in this way coincides with provability in higher-order intuitionistic logic for the same sequents.

The higher-order Horn clause language shares with its first-order counterpart the property that the signature and the program remains fixed throughout a computation. In particular, the $\forall R$ and $\supset R$ rules play no role in its semantics. This aspect changes with the hohh language in a manner similar to the one we have observed at the first-order level.

5.2.3 Extended higher-order hereditary Harrop formulas

It is possible to further extend the collections of goal formulas and program clauses in the *hohh* language without changing its essential computational behavior. In particular, we can allow the head of an atomic program clause to be a variable, but only if this variable is bound by an essentially universal quantifier that contains this clause in its scope. The rationale for relaxing the constraint on atomic program clauses in this way is the following. When the enclosing goal formula is encountered in the course of computation, the universal quantifier will be instantiated with a constant that is added to the signature at that point. Thus, by the time the clause containing this atomic formula becomes a part of the program, it satisfies the requirements of program clauses in the *hohh* language.

The language that results from liberalizing program clauses in this manner is what we call the $hohh^+$ language. To understand the practical interest in this extension, note first that universal quantifiers in goals limit the visibility of the names they bind in the program. Thus, when this kind of quantification is applied at predicate type and combined with the enrichment to program clauses just described, it becomes possible to introduce definitions for predicates that are "closed"; i.e., they are completely independent of the environment to which they are added.

To concretely illustrate the benefits of the extended syntax allowed by $hohh^+$, we show how it helps in improving the definition of the `reverse` relation presented in Figures 3.3 and 3.4. In the earlier specifications, the scope of two clauses for the auxiliary predicate `rev` was limited to a goal appearing in the body of the `reverse` program clause. However, the visibility of the name `rev` was not limited. In particular, those definitions cannot guarantee that the context in which the `reverse` program is invoked does not already have program clauses that provide part of the meaning of `rev`; if there are such clauses, the reverse relation may not be defined as intended. By using a universal quantifier, however, it is possible to limit the visibility of the name `rev` and hence to circumscribe its definition. The specifications in Figure 5.1 and 5.2 modify the earlier specifications by adding such a universal quantifier. In attempting to prove the goal `(reverse (1::2::3::nil) K)` from the clause in, say, Figure 5.1, an interpreter would first generate a new predicate symbol, say, c, then add the Horn clauses

```
pi L\ c nil L L.
pi X\ pi L\ pi K\ pi M\ c (X::L) K M :- c L K (X::M).
```

to the current program, and then try to prove `(c (1::2::3::nil) K nil)`. After the answer substitution `K = (3::2::1::nil)` is discovered, both c and the new clauses pertaining to c would be removed from the program context.

```
type reverse    list A -> list A -> o.

reverse L K :-  pi rev\
  (pi L\ rev nil L L) &
  (pi X\ pi L\ pi K\ pi M\ rev (X::L) K M :- rev L K (X::M))
  => rev L K nil.
```

Figure 5.1. Definition of reverse in Figure 3.3 modified to hide the name of the auxiliary predicate.

```
type reverse    list A -> list A -> o.

reverse L K :- pi rv\
  (                rv nil K &
  (pi X\ pi N\ pi M\ rv (X::N) M :- rv N (X::M)))
  => rv L nil.
```

Figure 5.2. Definition of reverse in Figure 3.4 modified to hide the name of the auxiliary predicate.

5.3 Examples of higher-order programming

Figure 5.3 presents examples of program clauses in λProlog syntax that use predicate quantification. These clauses define relations that can be understood as follows. If the goal (mappred P L K) is provable, then L and K are lists of equal length, and corresponding members of these lists are related through the predicate P. If the goal (forsome P L) is provable, then L is a list in which some member satisfies the predicate P. If the goal (foreach P L) is provable, then L is a list all of whose members satisfy the predicate P. Finally, if the goal (sublist P L K) is provable, then K is a list of some of the elements of L that preserves the original order and is such that all its elements satisfy P. The order of the clauses in the specification of sublist is such that maximal solutions are found first if the usual sequencing of search options is used.

The following sequence of queries uses the specifications in both Figures 5.3 and 5.4.

```
?- mappred age (ned::bob::sue::nil) L.
L = (23::23::24::nil)


?- mappred age L (23::24::nil).
L = (bob::sue::nil);


L = (ned::sue::nil)


?- sublist male (ned::bob::sue::nil) L.
L = ned::bob::nil;
```

```
type foreach, forsome   (A -> o) -> list A -> o.
type mappred            (A -> B -> o) -> list A -> list B -> o.
type sublist            (A -> o) -> list A -> list A -> o.


foreach P nil.
foreach P (X::L) :- P X, foreach P L.


forsome P (X::L) :- P X; forsome P L.


mappred P nil nil.
mappred P (X::L) (Y::K) :- P X Y, mappred P L K.


sublist P (X::L) (X::K) :- P X, sublist P L K.
sublist P (X::L) K :- sublist P L K.
sublist P nil nil.
```

Figure 5.3. Examples of higher-order relational programs.

```
kind name          type.
type bob, sue, ned  name.
type age            name -> int -> o.
type male, female   name -> o.

age  bob 23 & age sue 24 & age  ned 23.
male bob    & female sue & male ned.
```

Figure 5.4. A simple collection of facts.


```
L = ned::nil;


L = bob::nil;


L = nil;
no


?- forsome female (ned::bob::sue::nil).
solved


?- foreach female (ned::bob::sue::nil).
no


?-
```

The following declarations specify the reflexive, symmetric, and transitive closures of a binary relation:

```
type ref, sym, trans  (A -> A -> o) -> A -> A -> o.
```

```
ref    R X Y :- X = Y; R X Y.
sym    R X Y :- R X Y; R Y X.
trans R X Y :- R X Y.
trans R X Z :- R X Y, trans R Y Z.
```

To illustrate the content of the predicate definitions provided here, assume that we are additionally given the following specification of a graph:

```
kind node    type.
type a, b, c, d, e    node.
type adj              node -> node -> o.

adj a b & adj b c & adj b d & adj d c & adj c e.
```

These clauses then will support the following interaction

```
?- trans adj a d.
solved

?- sym adj b a.
solved

?-
```

which shows that a and d are related by the transitive closure of adj and that b and a are related by the symmetric closure of adj. The equivalence closure of adj can be written simply as (trans (sym (ref adj))). Since the reflexive closure of a relation is not defined recursively, it is easy to write a λ-term that captures such a closure applied to adj. In particular, the λ-term (x\y\ x = y ; adj x y) will do. Similarly, the symmetric closure of adj also can be expressed through the λ-term (x\y\ adj x y ; adj y x). Describing transitive closure in a similar way is more challenging. From a declarative point of view, the expression

```
x\y\ pi p\
  (pi U\ pi V\ adj U V => p U V) =>
  (pi U\ pi V\ pi W\ adj U V => p V W => p U W) =>  p x y
```

captures the transitive closure of adj. However, this term is not a legal $\mathcal{H}_2^\Sigma$ term (for any relevant Σ) because it contains occurrences of the implication symbol. As a result, such a characterization of transitivity cannot be used as an argument of a λProlog goal.

We exploit the specifications in Figures 5.3 and 5.4 to provide further illustrations of using predicate variables and λ-terms of predicate type. The two λ-terms

```
x\ age jane x        and       n\ age n 24
```

are of types `int -> o` and `name -> o`, respectively. Notice that the first term is η-convertible to just `(age jane)`. The query

```
?- (n\ age n 24) W.
```

is equal modulo β-conversion to

```
?- age W 24.
```

and this goal has one answer substitution, the one that binds `W` to `sue`. The following interactions further illustrate the possible uses of λ-terms in atomic goal formulas.

```
?- mappred (x\y\ age x y) (ned::bob::sue::nil) L.
L = (23::23::24::nil)

?- mappred (x\y\ age y x) (23::24::nil) K.
K = (bob::sue::nil);

K = (ned::sue::nil)

?- foreach (x\ sigma y\ age x y) (ned::bob::sue::nil).
solved

?- foreach (x\ age x A) (ned::bob::sue::nil).
no

?-
```

The penultimate query succeeds because every person in the list has an age. The last query fails because not everyone in the list has the same age `A`. By contrast, the query

```
?- foreach (x\ age x A) (ned::bob::nil).
A = 23

?-
```

succeeds and returns the age that is common to both `ned` and `bob`.

The higher-order predicate definitions in Figure 5.5 support further familiar computations on relations. For example, if `R` and `S` are two binary relations, then `(union R S)` is the union of their extensions, and `(compose R S)` is their

```
type union          (A -> B -> o) -> (A -> B -> o) -> A -> B -> o.
type compose        (A -> B -> o) -> (B -> C -> o) -> A -> C -> o.
type foldl          (A -> B -> B -> o) -> list A -> B -> B -> o.

union   R S X Y :- R X Y; S X Y.
compose R S X Y :- R X Z, S Z Y.

foldl P nil     X X.
foldl P (Z::L) X Y :- P Z X W, foldl P L W Y.
```

Figure 5.5. More examples of higher-order relational programs.

relational composition (natural join). Notice that since union and compose are not defined recursively, they can be expressed using λ-terms: The predicate denoted by (union R S) can be written instead as the expression

```
x\y\ R x y; S x y.
```

and the predicate denoted by (compose R S) can be written instead as the expression

```
x\z\ sigma Y\ R x Y, S Y z.
```

If P is an A-indexed set of binary relations over B, that is, if it has type

```
A -> B -> B -> o
```

then (foldl P) iteratively composes P to get a predicate of type

```
list A -> B -> B -> o.
```

Part of the code in Figure 5.6 provides a specification of a stack. The two constructors emp and stk are used to represent stacks: For example, the stack that has 1 as its top element, 2 below it, and 3 as its bottom-most element is built as (stk 1 (stk 2 (stk 3 emp))). The predicate empty serves to initialize stacks, and the predicates enter and remove are logic programming versions of pushing and popping functions on stacks. Figure 5.6 also contains another definition of the predicate reverse that relates a list to its reverse. This definition uses a stack in conjunction with the earlier described higher-order predicates on relations. Intuitively, a list can be reversed by pushing its elements one by one onto a stack and then unloading the stack into another list. The predicate foldl is used twice in this process, once to put items from a list into a stack and once to move items from the stack to a list. These two phases are combined using the compose predicate.

Using higher-order quantification, it is possible to convert any purely Horn clause program into one that contains only *binary clauses*, i.e., clauses whose

```
kind stack            type -> type.
type emp              stack A.
type stk              A -> stack A -> stack A.
type empty            stack A -> o.
type enter, remove    A -> stack A -> stack A -> o.
type reverse          list A -> list A -> o.

empty  emp.
enter  X S (stk X S).
remove X (stk X S) S.

reverse L K :- compose (foldl enter L) (foldl remove K) emp emp.
```

Figure 5.6. An implementation of list reverse.

bodies consist of at most one, possibly complex atomic formula. This transformation illustrates what can be called the *continuation passing style* (CPS) approach to programming within logic programming. Specifically, for each predicate p of type $\tau_1 \to \cdots \to \tau_j \to o$, let us introduce a new predicate p' of type $\tau_1 \to \cdots \to \tau_j \to o \to o$. Further for every atomic formula A of the form $(p_i \; t_1 \cdots t_j)$, let us write A' to denote the term $(p'_i \; t_1 \cdots t_j)$ of type $o \to o$. Then the binary form of the Horn clause

$$\forall \bar{x} \, [A_1 \wedge \ldots \wedge A_n \supset A_0] \qquad (n > 0)$$

is the clause

$$\forall \bar{x} \, \forall K \, [(A'_1 \, (\ldots \, (A'_n \; K) \ldots)) \supset (A'_0 \; K)]$$

and the binary clause form of the atomic clause $\forall \bar{x} \, A_0$ is the clause $\forall \bar{x} \, \forall K \, [K \supset (A'_0 \; K)]$. Of course, K is a variable of type o. In the translation that is produced, top-level conjunctions will have been replaced by explicit sequencing of goals. To take a concrete example, if this transformation is applied to the collection of Horn clauses

```
adj a b.
adj b c.
path X Y :- adj X Y.
path X Y :- adj X Z, path Z Y.
```

it would produce the following set of higher-order Horn clauses

```
adj' a b K :- K.
adj' b c K :- K.
path' X Y K :- adj' X Y K.
path' X Y K :- adj' X Z (path' Z Y K).
```

It is easy to see that query

```
type fib_memo   int -> ((int -> int -> o) -> o) -> o.

fib_memo N G :-
  pi memo\ pi loop\
     memo 0 0 => memo 1 1 =>
     (pi F1\ pi F2\ pi F3\ pi C\ pi C'\
        (loop C F1 F2 :- (C >  N, (G memo)) ;
                         (C =< N, C' is C + 1, F3 is F1 + F2,
                          memo C F3 => loop C' F2 F3))) =>
     loop 2 0 1.
```

Figure 5.7. A "memo-ized" version of the Fibonacci predicate.

```
?- path X Y.
```

is provable if and only if the query

```
?- path' X Y true.
```

is provable.

All the examples that we have presented so far use the higher-order version of Horn clauses; i.e., they are all contained within the *hohc* language. Figure 5.7 contains a logic program from the *hohh*[+] fragment of logic that mixes higher-order programming and the dynamic addition of clauses during computation. Goals of the form V is M + N bind to the variable V the sum of the integer expressions M and N. The predicate fib_memo computes and stores an initial part of the Fibonacci relation in the context: It then calls a goal in that extended context. That goal is parameterized by the name of the binary predicate that is used to store the Fibonacci relation. For example, using this code, the following query could be used to search for all numbers $0 \le n \le 20$ such that the nth Fibonacci number is n^2.

```
?- fib_memo 20 (fib\ sigma M\ fib N M, M is N * N).
```

There are exactly three values for N that make this atom provable.

5.4 Flexible atoms as goals

We have already seen examples of flexible goals in the higher-order programs considered in the preceding section. Such a goal appears, for example, in the definition of the mappred predicate in Figure 5.3. In all the cases considered there, however, the predicate head of the flexible goal is instantiated by the time invocation of the goal is considered. We could, of course, consider dynamically invoking a predicate goal that is flexible. An example of such a goal is the flexible atom (P bob 23). Suppose that we try to prove this goal from the clauses in Figure 5.4. One possible answer substitution for this query is the substitution

```
kind i                                type.
type jane, mary, john                 i.
type mother, father, wife, husband    i -> i -> o.
type primrel, rel                     (i -> i -> o) -> o.

primrel father & primrel mother & primrel wife & primrel husband.

rel R :- primrel R.
rel (x\y\ sigma z\ R x z, S z y) :- primrel R, primrel S.

mother jane mary & wife john jane.
```

Figure 5.8. An example of computing relations from other relations.

$(x\y\ $ age x y$)$ (or simply age) for P. However, many other substitutions also lead to a provable goal. For example, substituting

```
x\y\ age x 23, age ned y
```

for P also works in this sense. In fact, the substitution $x\y\g$ for P for any closed goal g that is provable will lead to the goal (P bob 23) being provable. Thus $(x\y\$ age sue 24$)$ and $(x\y\$ memb 4 (3::4::5::nil)$)$ (if the clauses defining the basic list operations are included in the current context) both can be considered to be answer substitutions for P. Clearly, there are a large number of answer substitutions for this goal, many of which seem to have little to do with the actual query that was posed. It seems undesirable for an interpreter to search for all of these systematically. A flexible goal seems, in this sense, to be *underconstrained*.

Of course, not all flexible goals that are written in a program have this character. Whether a flexible goal is constrained or underconstrained depends on when the goal is invoked. For example, a computation may restrict the range of substitutions for a predicate variable through suitably defined clauses before it attempts to search through these possibilities for one that satisfies a given goal. Thus, consider the program in Figure 5.8. Simply asking for a predicate *R* that is satisfied by john and mary is not meaningful in its context. The programmer can, however, specify some collection of predicates that are considered relevant or interesting and then restrict the choice of substitutions for the predicate variable to that collection. For example, the query

```
?- rel R, R john mary.
```

is one that *is* meaningful. This query is solvable only if R is substituted for by the term

```
x\y\ sigma Z\ wife x Z, mother Z y.
```

The predicate rel, also defined in Figure 5.8, provides structure to the kinds of answer substitutions that we want to consider as being meaningful for the query R john mary.

In light of the preceding discussion, three different approaches seem possible in treating a flexible goal that is encountered during computation in a higher-order language:

1. Such a goal may be suspended in the hope that processing other goals will further instantiate the predicate variable at its head. If some later substitution changes this goal from flexible to rigid, then the search for a proof for it may be resumed. In the event that all rigid goals have been solved and only flexible ones are left, all the remaining goals may be solved immediately by instantiating the predicate variable at the head of each of them with a term of the form $\lambda x_1 \ldots \lambda x_n \top$, where $n \geq 0$ is the number of argument types in the type of that variable. The instantiation proposed here represents the universally true relation of the correct type; this substitution is the (extensionally) largest one that works.
2. Instead of suspending a flexible goal, we may solve it eagerly by using the universally true relation described earlier as a substitution for the predicate variable at its head.
3. A run-time error message may be issued when such a goal is encountered.

The first option has been shown to be complete with respect to provability in intuitionistic higher-order logic. The latter two are incomplete. Experience with implementations of λProlog suggests that the third choice is most useful for developing code. In practice, the flexibility of an atomic goal at the time this goal is encountered using the usual depth-first search strategy usually has been traceable to a mistake—such as the mistyping of a predicate constant with a capital letter—made by the programmer. Thus it seems best to generate an error message in these cases rather than rearranging goals in unexpected ways.

5.5 Reasoning about higher-order programs

One of the virtues of the logic programming view that we have developed here is that computation is clearly specified through a high-level operational semantics description. Moreover, there is a connection with logics for which several deep properties have been established previously. These properties give us a means for reasoning about the programs we write in this framework. In the higher-order context, this reasoning capability can be enhanced when we use the ability provided by the $hohh^+$ language to hide predicate names and thereby to tightly circumscribe the definitions of such predicates.

We use the definition of the `reverse` predicate presented in Figure 5.2 to illustrate the reasoning possibility just described. Let us suppose that we wish to show that the relation corresponding to this predicate is symmetric. To develop an intuition about how to prove this, consider the attempt to show that `reverse` holds of the two lists `[a,b,c]` and `[c,b,a]`. This goal causes the "hidden" predicate `rv` to be invoked successively with the following pairs of arguments:

```
(a :: b :: c :: nil)   nil
(b :: c :: nil)  (a :: nil)
(c :: nil)  (b :: a :: nil)
   nil   (c :: b :: a :: nil)
```

The fact that reverse is a symmetric relation now can be seen by noticing that if we flip the columns and flip the rows in the preceding "table," we get a valid computation trace to demonstrate that the reverse of `[c,b,a]` is `[a,b,c]`.

We shall use this observation to develop an actual proof of the symmetry property of `reverse`. Specifically, we shall assume that `(reverse L K)` is provable from the definition in Figure 5.2, and we shall then show that `(reverse K L)` is also provable. Now, there is only one way to prove the atom `(reverse L K)`, and that is by backchaining on the definition of `reverse`. Thus the formula

```
pi rv\ ( rv nil K &
        (pi X\ pi N\ pi M\ rv (X::N) M :- rv N (X::M)))
        => rv L nil
```

must be provable. Since this universally quantified expression is provable, by logical principles, any instance of it also must be provable. Let us then instantiate it with the λ-term `x\y\ (not (rv y x))`, where we are using `not` to denote logical negation (instead of negation-as-failure). Intuitively, the swapping of the order of the arguments in this term gives us one of the flips in the informal proof, and the negation gives us the other flip. The formula resulting from the instantiation is

```
not(rv K nil) &
        (pi X\ pi N\ pi M\ not(rv M (X::N)) :- not(rv (X::M) N))
        => not(rv nil L).
```

This formula can be simplified by using the contrapositive rule from logic for negation and implication ($p \supset q$ is equivalent to $\neg q \supset \neg p$), yielding

```
rv nil L & (pi X\ pi N\ pi M\ rv (X::M) N :- rv M (X::N))
    => rv K nil.
```

Since the contrapositive equivalence is classically valid, the resulting provability is classically valid. Since this is a deduction involving only (first-order) Horn clauses, and since classical logic and intuitionistic logics coincide on Horn clauses (see Section 2.3), we also can conclude that this is an intuitionistic entailment. If we now universally generalize on rv, we again have proved the body of the reverse clause, but this time with L and K switched. Thus we have proved that (reverse K L) also holds.

This proof exploits the explicit hiding of the auxiliary predicate rv, which provides a site into which a "reimplementation" of the predicate can be placed. Notice that the description of goal-directed search alone does not suffice for constructing this proof of symmetry of the reverse predicate. Knowledge of the metatheoretic properties of the specification logic is also needed; in particular, the proof uses the correspondence between goal solvability in that logic and provability in classical and intuitionistic logic.

5.6 Defining some of the logical constants

The *hohc* program clauses in Figure 5.9 provide a definition of the logical constants $\bot$, $\top$, $\vee$, and $\exists$. This definition is a partial one because the clauses describe only how to prove goals in which these symbols are the top-level ones and not how to use such formulas as an assumption or program clause. For example, the rule of cases, which describes how a disjunctive assumption can be used in a proof, is not specified by these clauses. In the language of the sequent calculus (Section 2.6), the clauses in Figure 5.9 specify the right-introduction rules but not the left-introduction rules for the connectives under consideration. Notice that there are no clauses defining ff: The behavior of this constant as a goal is encapsulated in the fact that trying to prove it results in failure.

If one uses *hohh*[+] formulas, then goal formulas with these four logical connectives can be rewritten in terms of universal quantification and implication as follows: The *hohh* goal $\forall p\, p$ can be used for $\bot$ and the *hohh*[+] goals

$$\forall p\,(p \supset p) \quad \forall p\,((B \supset p) \supset (C \supset p) \supset p) \quad \text{and} \quad \forall p\,((\forall x\,(G\,x \supset p)) \supset p)$$

can be used for $\top$, $B \vee C$, and $\exists x\,(G\,x)$, respectively.

```
type tt, ff   o.
type or        o -> o -> o.
type exists   (A -> o) -> o.

tt.                    % true
or P Q :- P.           % disjunction
or P Q :- Q.
exists B :- B T.       % existential quantifier
```

Figure 5.9. The "definition" of some logical constants.

Of course, an encoding of these logical symbols is not needed in λProlog: An implementation can treat them as primitive and build in their proof search behavior directly.

5.7 The conditional and negation-as-failure

The built-in vocabulary of Prolog includes several predicates whose operational behavior includes aspects of the "cut" operator that prunes search. The relationship between cut and some of these predicates can be made explicit in an λProlog setting.

One such operator is the "conditional" if. This operator is used to construct a goal from three other goal formulas. This conditional can be defined in λProlog as follows

```
type if    o -> o -> o -> o.
if P Q R :- P, !, Q.
if P Q R :- R.
```

Proving a goal of the form (if P Q R) involves first attempting to prove P and, if that succeeds, then attempting to prove Q. If the proof attempt for P fails, only then is an attempt made to prove R.

The negation-as-failure predicate can be defined similarly using the code

```
type not   o -> o.
not P :- P, !, fail.
not P.
```

Instead of the two preceding clauses, we also could use the following:

```
not P :- if P fail true.
```

The use of predicates such as these that rely on the pruning operator ! can lead logic programming rather far from its roots in logic. For example, the query

```
?- X = 2, not (1 = X).
```

succeeds, whereas switching the order of these two goals, namely,

```
?- not (1 = X), X = 2.
```

fails. Thus even a basic property such as commutativity of conjunctions becomes invalid in this setting. For this reason, we will use these predicates extremely sparingly. In the cases where we use them, we will discuss explicitly our reasons for doing so.

5.8 Using λ-terms as functions

The programming examples considered up to this point in this chapter have focused on the use of predicate variables that are instantiated by λ-terms and that then go on to form expressions that are invoked as goals. The logic we have described also allows for higher-order variables that are not of predicate type. When these variables are instantiated, they can give rise to expressions that need to be evaluated using the rules of λ-conversion. We provide illustrations of this possibility in this section. As we have seen Chapter 4, the class of functions that can be expressed and computed in this way using our typed λ-terms is quite weak. They are much weaker, in fact, than ones that can be encoded through predicate definitions and goal invocation. This weakness, however can be an asset for a different kind of computation: Rather than instantiating function variables with λ-terms, we can think of finding values for them by solving unification problems. The ability to express such computations is perhaps the single most novel aspect of higher-order logic programming and one that has a large number of interesting applications. We present only simple examples here to illuminate this possibility, leaving a detailed discussion to later chapters.

5.8.1 Some basic computations with functional expressions

Figure 5.10 contains the definition of the mapfun predicate that is a natural "functional" counterpart to the mappred predicate seen earlier. This predicate relates a term of functional type to two lists of equal length if the elements of the second list are the result of applying that functional term to corresponding elements of the first list. Of course, function computation here is simply $\beta\eta$-conversion for typed λ-terms. For example, suppose that the ambient signature defines a type i, four constants a, b, c, and d of this type, and a constant g of type i -> i -> i, and then consider the query

```
?- mapfun (x\ g a x) (a::b::nil) L.
```

There is exactly one answer substitution to this query:

```
L = ((g a a)::(g a b)::nil).
```

```
type mapfun    (A -> B) -> list A -> list B -> o.
type reducefun (A -> B -> B) -> list A -> B -> B -> o.

mapfun F nil nil.
mapfun F (X::L) ((F X)::K) :- mapfun F L K.

reducefun F nil Z Z.
reducefun F (H::T) Z (F H R) :- reducefun F T Z R.
```

Figure 5.10. Program clauses that use higher-order function variables.

To produce this substitution, an interpreter would form the terms ((x\ g a x) a) and ((x\ g a x) b) and λ-normalize them.

The example just considered shows that the (function) evaluation that is embodied in uses of mapfun is mainly *β*-reduction. By contrast, calls to mappred produce expressions that constitute goals of arbitrary complexity and that are invoked as such to produce the elements of the "output" list. It is of little surprise, therefore, that mappred can encode much stronger computations than mapfun can. A vivid demonstration of this difference is the fact that we could have defined mapfun alternatively as follows:

```
mapfun F L K :- mappred (x\y\ y = F x) L K.
```

The weakness of the functional computation carried out by mapfun actually allows us to think of running this computation in reverse; i.e., given a list of arguments and a list of results, ask for the function that may relate the two. An example of such a query is the following:

```
?- mapfun F (a::b::nil) ((g a a)::(g a b)::nil).
```

This goal is solvable and has exactly one answer substitution: The one that binds F to the term (x\ g a x). In producing this result, an interpreter for the higher-order language would need to consider unifying the pair of terms (F a) and (g a a) and also the pair of terms (F b) and (g a b). The first of these unification problems has four unifiers that correspond to substituting the following terms for F:

(x\ g x x)   (x\ g a x)   (x\ g x a)   (x\ g a a)

Only the second of these substitutions will work as a unifier for (F b) and (g a b). Thus, if the interpreter picks any substitution other than this one first, it will have to backtrack in its computation to eventually select the right answer.

The kinds of function terms that can be synthesized in this way are quite weak. To understand this, consider the following goal:

```
?- mapfun F (a::b::nil) (c::d::nil).
```

This goal actually will fail because there is no typed λ-term that maps a to c
and b to d—this despite the fact that we can conceive of an infinite number of
functions that map a and b in this way. (Recall a related discussion at the end
of Section 4.4.3.)

Figure 5.10 contains the definition of another predicate called reducefun.
The following interaction illustrates some possible uses of this predicate:

```
?- reducefun (x\y\ x + y) (3::4::8::nil) 6 R.
R = 3 + (4 + (8 + 6));

?- reducefun F (4::8::nil) 6 (1 + (4 + (1 + (8 + 6)))).
F = x\y\ 1 + (4 + (1 + (8 + 6)));

F = x\y\ 1 + (x + (1 + (8 + 6)));

F = x\y\ 1 + (x + y);
no

?-
```

The second query has three answer substitutions. If the query is modified by
replacing the occurrences of 6 in it by a variable that is quantified universally inside the scope of the (implicit) quantifier binding F, then only the last
substitution works as an answer:

```
?- pi z\ reducefun F (4::8::nil) z (1 + (4 + (1 + (8 + z)))).
F = x\y\ 1 + (x + y);
no

?-
```

The reason why substitutions such as the first two for the previous query do not
work in this case is that instantiations of F cannot contain occurrences of the
new constant introduced for z in proving the universal goal.

5.8.2 Functional difference lists

From a programming point of view, logic variables provide a means for marking
locations in data structures into which additional information can be inserted.
An interesting exploitation of this perspective appears in a data structure called
the *difference list*. This data structure describes a list by providing two lists, the
second of which is intended to be a suffix of the first: The list that is actually

represented is the prefix of the first component that is obtained by removing the elements of the second component from it.

Part of the declarations in Figure 5.11 implement the traditional first-order version of this data structure in λProlog. The type constructor dlist allows the type of any given difference list to be parameterized by the type of its elements. Using the constant dl, we represent a difference list of type (dlist A) as (dl L K), where L and K are both of type (list A). For example, (dl (1::2::3::4::5::nil) (4::5::nil)) and (dl (1::2::3::L) L) are both difference lists. Moreover, both of them denote the same "regular" list, namely, (1:2::3::nil). If a representation such as the second one is used for lists, it becomes possible to implement the concatenation of lists without an explicit recursion over either of the input lists. The definition of the predicate concat in Figure 5.11 shows how this can be done. As another illustration, difference lists are used in the definition in Figure 5.11 of the predicate collect that forms a list of the elements in a binary tree by carrying out an in-order traversal over it.

A higher-order language allows for another approach to realizing difference lists: A λ-term in which the abstracted variable is used to isolate the suffix of

```
kind dlist        type -> type.
type dl           list A -> list A -> dlist A.

type concat       dlist A -> dlist A -> dlist A -> o.
concat (dl L1 L2) (dl L2 L3) (dl L1 L3).

kind btree        type -> type.
type empty        btree A.
type bt           A -> btree A -> btree A -> btree A.

type collect      btree A -> list A -> o.
type aux          btree A -> dlist A -> o.
collect Bt L :- aux Bt (dl L nil).
aux empty         (dl A A).
aux (bt N L R) (dl A B) :- aux L (dl A (N::C)), aux R (dl C B).

kind fdlist       type -> type.
type fdl          (list A -> list A) -> fdlist A.

type collect'     btree A -> list A -> o.
type aux'         btree A -> fdlist A -> o.
collect' Bt (A nil) :- aux' Bt (fdl A).
aux' empty        (fdl x\ x).
aux' (bt N L R) (fdl x\ A (N::(B x))) :- aux' L (fdl A),
                                         aux' R (fdl B).
```

Figure 5.11. Difference lists and functional difference lists and examples of their use.

the list may be used. Figure 5.11 contains further declarations illustrating this approach. Specifically, consider the type (fdlist A)—fdlist here is the type constructor for *functional difference lists*—and its one constructor fdl, which takes an argument of type list A -> list A. Using these, we can construct the term (fdl x\ (1::2::3::x)) of type (fdlist int) that denotes the usual list (1::2::3::nil) while also maintaining a "pointer" to the tail of this list. The head and tail of a list represented in this way can be extracted by unifying it with x\(H::(T x)): The head is directly the binding found for H, whereas the tail is given as a functional difference list by (fdl T). Similarly, the last element and the list of all but the last element of the list can be obtained by unifying its representation with the term x\ F (Y::x): Here, Y will be bound to the last element, and (fdl F) will be a functional difference list representation of the front of the list. The concatenation of two functional difference lists (fdl A) and (fdl B) is given by (fdl x\ A (B x)); conceptually, the concatenation is formed by composing the two function terms A and B. Figure 5.11 contains the definition of the predicate collect', which uses functional difference lists to collect the elements in a binary tree into a list based on an in-order traversal of the tree.

For another example of the use of functional difference lists, suppose that we want to define a predicate that determines whether or not a given list is a *palindrome*, i.e., a list that reads the same both forward and backward. Since it is possible to access the first and last elements of a functional difference list in one unification step, this predicate has a particularly simple specification if such a representation is used for a list:

```
type palindrome    fdlist A -> o.
palindrome (fdl x\x).
palindrome (fdl x\ Y::x).
palindrome (fdl x\ Y::(F (Y::x))) :- palindrome (fdl F).
```

The following interaction illustrates the use of this definition:

```
?- palindrome (fdl x\ a::b::c::b::a::x).
solved

?- palindrome (fdl x\ a::b::a::(F x)).
F = x\ x;

F = x\ b::a::x;

F = x\ a::b::a::x;
```

```
F = x\ Y::a::b::a::x;

F = x\ Z::Z::a::b::a::x;

F = x\ Y::Z::Y::a::b::a::x;

F = x\ Y::Z::Z::Y::a::b::a::x;

F = x\ Y::Z::U::Z::Y::a::b::a::x;

F = x\ Y::Z::U::U::Z::Y::a::b::a::x
```

?-

The second query asks for a "functional difference list" F such that concatenating this with the "difference list" (x\ a::b::a::x) yields a palindrome. There are an infinite number of answers to this query, some of which are displayed above.

An important point to note about objects of the types (dlist A) and (fdlist A) is that they must satisfy certain structural properties for it to be possible to interpret them as lists, but these properties are not enforced by the type. Thus neither of the terms

(dl (1::2::3::nil) (4::5::nil))   and   (fdl x\ (1::2::3))

represents a list in the sense intended for difference lists, but these terms are, nevertheless, well formed and have the right types.

5.9 Higher-order unification is not a panacea

Learning to use a programming paradigm well involves learning also how *not* to write programs within it. Since combining unification with λ-terms is a rather novel programming idiom, one needs to learn to avoid pitfalls in its use. We discuss a couple of these in this section.

Consider the problem of abstracting over all occurrences of a constant in a given structure. For example, given the signature

```
kind i      type.
type a,b    i.
type f      i -> i -> i.
```

we may be interested in abstracting over the occurrences of a in the term (f a (f a b)) to produce the term (x\ f x (f x b)). Now, one may imagine

that this problem can be solved by higher-order unification as in the definition
of the predicate `extract_a` presented below:

```
type extract_a   i -> (i -> i) -> o.
extract_a (F a) F.
```

Unfortunately, this specification turns out to be a poor solution. Consider the
following:

```
?- extract_a (f a (f a b)) F.
F = x\ f x (f x b);

F = x\ f x (f a b);

F = x\ f a (f x b);

F = x\ f a (f a b);
no

?-
```

There are several solutions to this query, only one of which is the desired
expression. In general, if there are n occurrences of a in a term, there are 2^n
possible ways to "extract" a from that term using this predicate.

If unifiers are produced in the order just shown, it is possible to use a Prolog-
like cut predicate to eliminate all but the first answer substitution above by
defining `extract_a` as follows:

```
extract_a (F a) F :- !.
```

However, this is a rather nondeclarative solution and also relies on an inti-
mate knowledge of how unification is implemented. A more satisfying solution
involves changing the scopes of the quantifiers in the query. For example, while
the query

```
pi a\ sigma F\ (F a) = (f a (f a b)).
```

has four different proofs involving four different instantiations for F, the query

```
sigma F\ pi a\ (F a) = (f a (f a b)).
```

has exactly one proof, and in that proof, F is instantiated with the term
`x\ (f x (f x b))`.

The recourse to reordering the quantifiers in the query may, however, not
always be available. In this case, the `extract_a` predicate could be written as
a recursion over the syntax of terms instead of using higher-order unification

directly. The following definition of extract_a, for example, implements this idea:

```
extract_a a x\x.
extract_a b x\b.
extract_a (f T S) (x\ f (U x) (V x)) :- extract_a T U, extract_a S V.
```

Of course, unlike a unification-based approach, this encoding uses information about the signature of the type i in organizing the recursion. The payback is that there is more control over the steps in the computation and over the set of valid solutions.

A second task in which we might think of using higher-order unification is that of term rewriting. We could, for instance, define the predicate rewrite to encode (parallel) one-step rewriting based on some simple arithmetic identities:

```
type rewrite    int -> int -> o.

rewrite (0 + X) X.
rewrite (1 * X) X.
rewrite (X - X) 0.
rewrite (C X) (C Y) :- rewrite X Y.
```

The first three clauses specify the identities that are to be used. The last clause is a naive specification of the fact that two terms are equal if a subexpression is replaced by an equal subexpression.

Given the definition just shown, the goals

```
 rewrite ((5 - 5) + 6) (0 + 6)  and  rewrite ((1 * 5)   5) (5 - 5)
```

have derivations. Thus the definition captures the intended meaning in several cases. Unfortunately, there are far too many derivations for such goals for this definition to be computationally effective. For example, the goal rewrite ((1 * 5) - 5) (5 - 5) has an infinite number of derivations, each obtained by using the last clause a (chosen) finite number of times with C instantiated to x\x until eventually it is picked to be x\ x - 5.

A better, more controlled approach to rewriting can again be obtained by using an explicit recursion over the structure of terms. This solution, must of course, integrate the signature used in constructing terms into the program. Examples of this style of rewriting are provided at three other places in this book: Section 7.4.1, Section 9.4.1, and Section 10.3.2.

5.10 Comparison with functional programming

At this point it is worth contrasting the form of higher-order programming that we have considered in this chapter with the higher-order programming capabilities available within functional programming languages such as Scheme and ML. On the one hand, as the examples using mappred and sublist show, most of the higher-order programming capabilities in the functional framework can be transferred easily to the logic programming setting. On the other hand, there are at least two ways in which the notion of higher-order programming that we have described here is stronger than the notion found in functional programming. We discuss these differences below.

First, predicate variables, which allow capturing the idea of functions-as-data in functional programming, are only one kind of variable of functional type in logic programming. Since the proof theory of the general form of quantification at higher types is well understood, it is natural to design a logic programming language that exploits this more inclusive capability. The examples in Section 5.8 have illustrated new kinds of computations that become possible when the language includes nonpredicate function variables. We develop this idea further in Chapter 7, where we show that such variables can be used in manipulating the syntax of λ-terms and thereby to provide logic programming with an expressiveness not found directly in functional programming languages.

Even if we restrict our attention to predicate quantification, there is already a difference between higher-order notions in functional and logic programming. In languages such as Scheme and ML, it is not possible to compare functional expressions. By contrast, two predicate expressions are compared easily in the logic programming setting. For example, the following set of declarations is legal:

```
type eq_pred (A -> o) -> (A -> o) -> o.
```

```
eq_pred R R.
```

A goal with eq_pred as its head would succeed if its two arguments are equal (or, more precisely, unifiable) predicate expressions. Note, however, that such a check on equality is based on the *intension* and not the *extension* of the two expressions. For example, the query

```
?- eq_pred (x\ p x, q x) (x\ q x, p x).
```

will fail no matter what clauses provide the meaning for p and q. Equality is decided based only on the structure of λ-terms, and the fact that these terms denote sets that are equal is not considered. Functional programming does not allow for such checks between functions chiefly because the intended semantics of functional programming languages is an extensional one, and determining extensional equality is, in general, undecidable.

If our aim had been to generalize logic programming to capture only the higher-order capabilities of functional programming, then this could have been achieved by using a syntax that is more restricted than the one we have considered here. For example, quantification over higher-order nonpredicate types could have been disallowed. While a limited goal of this kind has its merits, adopting it would provide us with features that are already well appreciated at a programming level. The benefit of considering quantification at general higher-order types is that hitherto unknown and unexplored programming features begin to emerge. These new features—the use of λ-terms to represent syntactic objects encompassing binding notions and functional quantification to manipulate such objects—have provided much of the impetus for the development of λProlog.

5.11 Bibliographic notes

The Simple Theory of Types that provides the moorings for our treatment of higher-order notions in logic programming was first presented by Church (1940). The textbook of Andrews (1986) and the handbook article of Leivant (1994) are good starting points for learning about this logic. As a formal system, this logic is not complete with respect to the standard semantics for second order logic (Gödel 1965). Henkin (1950) developed a more liberal notion of models known as *general models* that provide an accurate semantical counterpart.[1] Many standard proof-theoretic results—such as cut-elimination (Girard 1986; Girard et al. 1989; Takahashi 1967), unification (Huet 1975), resolution (Andrews 1971), and Skolemization and Herbrand's theorem (Miller, 1987b)—have been established for the classical logic version of the Simple Theory of Types without the axioms of extensionality, infinity, and choice. Our use of the type o for formulas and of pi and sigma for the universal and existential quantification follows directly from Church's use of o as a type and Π and Σ as quantifiers (Church 1940).

The relevance of the model-theoretic view of second order logic for mathematical practice is discussed, for example, by Shapiro (1985). Variants of higher-order logic that do not contain, for example, λ-abstraction have been considered as the basis of adding higher-order programming features to logic programming (Chen et al. 1993; Wadge 1991).

---

[1] Henkin's original description of such models had a subtle error that was noticed and corrected by Andrews (1972).

The fact that goal-directed search in the context of *hohc* is complete with respect to both the classical and the intuitionistic versions of the Simple Theory of Types without the axioms of extensionality, infinity, and choice was established by Nadathur (1987) in his doctoral dissertation (see also (Nadathur and Miller 1990)). The critical part of this argument was noticing that predicate substitutions could be limited without loss of completeness to $\mathcal{H}_1^\Sigma$, the Herbrand universe for *hohc* described in Section 5.2; the cut-elimination result for the logic provided the rest of the machinery for the proof. These techniques were extended subsequently to show that goal-directed search in the context of *hohh* is complete with respect to an intuitionistic version of the same higher-order logic (Miller et al. 1991). These results provide the foundations for a unification-based interpreter for the respective languages that explicitly delays the consideration of flexible-flexible unification problems as well as flexible goals. Nadathur and Miller (1990) provided an interpreter for *hohc* that incorporates such delays.

The proceedings of the 1987 Symposium on Logic in Computer Science contain two closely related proposals for specification logics: the *hohh* logic first advanced by Miller, Nadathur, and Scedrov (1987) and the Logical Framework (LF) proposed by Harper, Honsell, and Plotkin (1987). These logics became the bases for the computer languages λProlog and Twelf (Pfenning and Schürmann 1999), respectively. An encoding of the dependently typed λ-calculus of LF into *hohh* that preserved provability was presented by Felty and Miller (1990) and Felty (1991). A less redundant and hence more efficient encoding that can be used as the basis for implementing Twelf through a translation into λProlog has been developed by Snow, Baelde, and Nadathur (2010). Another type system that is closely related to higher-order logic is the Calculus of Constructions (Coquand and Huet 1988). Felty (1993b) showed how to encode the Calculus of Constructions into higher-order logic. She also showed that if disjunctions and existentials are not allowed within formulas and terms, then it is possible to allow implications within terms and still maintain the completeness of goal-directed provability; this restriction should be contrasted with the one described in Section 5.2 that leads to *hohh*.

Combining functional and logic programming capabilities into one language has been an active topic for research. The logic programming language that we have described is sometimes thought to be such a combination, but this is a mistaken view: As we discussed in Chapter 4, the typed λ-terms are expressively rather weak and hence do not encompass a significant functional programming capability. For more on mixing functional and logic programming, we refer the reader to Hanus (1994).

Binary forms of Horn clauses have been used in the compilation of Prolog (Tarau 1992) and in the transformation of the operational semantics of simple function programming languages into abstract machines (Hannan and Miller 1992).

In Section 5.6 we illustrated how *hohc* clauses could be used to implement right-introduction rules for some logical connectives. Hallnäs and Schroeder-Heister (1991) describe a scheme for deriving the left-introduction rules from such *hohc* clauses.

As we shall show in Section 6.5.4, higher-order programming features can be mixed with modularity constructs in an unproblematic and natural way when *hohh* is used as the foundation of a logic programming language. In contrast, most other approaches to adding higher-order and modular programming features to Prolog are based on nonlogical mechanisms. As a result, the mixing of these two styles of programming can lead to ambiguities and may sometimes be beset with serious semantical problems (Haemmerlé and Fages 2006).

Some aspects of higher-order relational programming can be obtained in a first-order setting by using an encoding process, some of which are presented by D.H.D. Warren (1982) and Reddy (1994). The HiLog system of Chen, Kifer, and D.S. Warren (1993) provides a more systematic and declarative way of obtaining higher-order programming features while remaining within a first-order setting.

The functional version of difference lists presented in Section 5.8.2 has been explored in some detail by Brisset and Ridoux (1991).

There are only a few examples of using higher-order substitution to reason directly about logic programs. The proof in Section 5.5 that `reverse` is symmetric is due to Miller (2002). Miller (2006, 2008) also has presented a scheme for static analysis of Horn clauses using higher-order substitutions.

6

Mechanisms for Structuring Large Programs

In the early stages of developing a programming language or paradigm, the focus is on programming-in-the-small. As the language matures, programming-in-the-large becomes important and a second *modules* language is often imposed on the previously existing *core* language. This second language must support the partitioning of code and name spaces into manageable chunks, the enforcement of encapsulation and information hiding, and the interactions between separately defined blocks of code. The addition of such modularity features typically is manifest syntactically in the form of new constructs and directives, such as `local`, `use`, `import`, and `include`, that affect parsing and compilation. Since the second language is born out of the necessity to build large programs, there may be little or no connection between the semantics of the added modular constructs and the semantics of the core language. The resulting hybrid language consequently may become complex and also may lack declarativeness, even when the core language is based on, say, logic.

In the logic programming setting, it is possible to support some of the abstractions needed for modular programming directly through logical mechanisms. For example, the composition of code can be realized naturally via the conjunction of program clauses, and suitably scoped existential quantifiers can be used to control the visibility of names across program regions. This chapter develops this observation into the design of a specific module language.

6.1 Desiderata for modular programming

When designing a module system for logic programming, we should ask more than that it separate code elements and that it can be implemented efficiently. In particular, adhering to the following principles is also desirable:

• The additional syntax for programming-in-the-large should be natural and readable and should support

150

- Rich forms of abstraction, information hiding, and parametrization
- A high-level view of code interactions via the notion of interfaces
- Separate compilation and reusability of individual code components
- Constructs for modularization and encapsulation should not complicate the meaning of the underlying declarative core language. A particular challenge here is to ensure that higher-order programming works smoothly with modularity constructs; in the usual Prolog setting, this translates to getting the call/1 predicate to interact correctly with modules.
- Modules should support transitioning from high-level program specifications to lower-level program implementations. This entails that
  - There should be a nontrivial notion of module equivalence that guarantees that such replacements will not alter the semantics of a larger program; this property is sometimes called *representation independence*.
  - The notion of equivalence should facilitate a rich calculus of transformations pertaining to modules based on ideas such as partial evaluation, folding, and unfolding clauses and perhaps even encompassing compilation.

One approach to developing a principled modular programming language is to reduce programming-in-the-large to programming-in-the-small. In the logic programming setting, this can be done by explaining the constructs for modular programming completely in terms of the logical connectives of the underlying logical language. We develop this approach in the following sections. In particular, we describe a modules language that is designed initially to satisfy the first of the principles just described. We then show how a collection of modules would be mapped to a (possibly large) collection of (possibly large) formulas by exposing a correspondence between the combinators for module interaction and logical connectives. The second principle is naturally supported under this viewpoint, and the idea of logical equivalence becomes the basis for the third.

6.2 A modules language

Programming-in-the-small, as we have described it so far, consists of identifying sorts and type constructors through kind declarations, using these to declare constants through type and operator declarations, and finally, writing down clauses to describe relations that then may be queried. In a simplistic approach, we could view all these declarations as contributing incrementally to one monolithic collection. We introduce modules as a means for structuring this space.

The module construct actually serves not just to limit the scope of a set of declarations and program clauses but also to name such collections. In the proposed syntax—already briefly encountered in Chapter 2—the first line of the text for a module has the form

```
module <name>.
```

The argument of the keyword module is any token that satisfies the syntactic requirements of being an identifier. This line names the module that is composed of the sequence of kind, type, and clause declarations that follows this line. We use the keyword end to denote the end of the module. If modules are associated with disk files, the end point of a module declaration alternatively can be determined by the end of the file.

Figure 6.1 illustrates the use of the syntax just described in identifying a module called smlists. This module brings together a small collection of list-oriented predicate definitions. This code assumes the availability of the list type constructor and the associated data constructors nil and ::. As

```
module smlists.

type id              list A -> list A -> o.
type memb, member    A -> list A -> o.
type revapp          list A -> list A -> list A -> o.
type reverse         list A -> list A -> o.
type append          list A -> list A -> list A -> o.
type memb_and_rest   A -> list A -> list A -> o.

id nil nil.
id (X::L) (X::K) :- id L K.

memb X (X::L).
memb X (Y::L) :- memb X L.

member X (X::L) :- !.
member X (Y::L) :- member X L.

revapp nil L L.
revapp (X::L1) L2 L3 :- revapp L1 (X::L2) L3.

reverse L1 L2 :- revapp L1 nil L2.

append nil K K.
append (X::L) K (X::M) :- append L K M.

memb_and_rest X (X::L) L.
memb_and_rest X (Y::K) (Y::L) :- memb_and_rest X K L.

end
```

Figure 6.1. A module defining list operations.

explained in Chapter 1, certain sorts, type constructors, and constants—a collection that includes `list`, `int`, `real`, `string`, and the constants associated with these types—are assumed to be *pervasive* and can be used freely in any module or query.

It is often useful to be able to abstract away from the actual contents of a module, providing only an "interface" to it. A *signature* provides such an abstraction. Signature declarations begin with a line of the form

```
sig <name>.
```

This line is used to name the immediately following kind, type, and operator declarations. As with modules, the extent of a signature may be specified by the keyword `end` or, in a file-oriented view, by the end of file.

In the model we propose, each module must be mediated by a signature, and a common name links these two entities. Thus the signature shown in Figure 6.2 is associated with the module `smlists`. Such an association gives rise to certain consistency requirements. For example, the declarations in the signature must be matched exactly by any declarations of the same constants and type constructors that appear in the module. The signature also restricts the external visibility of the names defined in a module to exactly those which are mentioned in it. This restriction has an impact on the availability of predicate definitions: The definition of the predicate `revapp` is, for example, hidden within the module `smlists`. It is also possible to hide constants and data constructors within a module: Such hidden symbols remain hidden even through the results of computations. Later in this chapter we formalize the relationship between a module and its signature using the notion of *signature matching* and the translation of modules into logical formulas.

The simplest use of modules occurs at the query level. As we observed in Chapter 2, queries typically are posed relative to the definitions provided by a given module. The module that is in use in a particular interactive session is shown to the left of the ?- symbol in a prompt. For example, the prompt for

```
sig smlists.

type id              list A -> list A -> o.
type memb, member    A -> list A -> o.
type reverse         list A -> list A -> o.
type append          list A -> list A -> list A -> o.
type memb_and_rest   A -> list A -> list A -> o.

end
```

Figure 6.2. An interface specification for list operations.

queries that are to be evaluated against the definitions in the module smlists
has the form

```
[smlists] ?-
```

The exact way that a module is associated with a top-level query depends on
the implementation, and we do not discuss it any further here; the Appendix
provides an example of how this might be done by describing the manner in
which the Teyjus implementation of λProlog realizes this association. Assuming
that a module is associated with the top level, a query can use only pervasive
constants and types or those which appear in the signature corresponding to the
module determining the query context. Relative to the prompt just shown, this
means that a query about the append predicate is allowed, but one that involves
the revapp predicate is ill formed because that predicate constant is unknown
(out-of-scope) at that point.

When the contents exported by one module are needed to define predicates
in another module, we use the *accumulation* declaration that takes the form

```
accumulate <name1>, ..., <namen>.
```

and can be placed amid other declarations and definitions in a module. Conceptually, the effect of this declaration is to insert into the module in which it appears
all the code appearing in the modules in the list following the accumulate keyword. However, before such a textual insertion is carried out, the constants
and type constructors private to the module being inserted are renamed so as
to distinguish them from those appearing in the other accumulated modules
as well as the ones appearing in the accumulating module. This requirement
is formalized later via the logic-based interpretation of accumulation and the
associated definition of module elaboration.

Figure 6.3 contains an illustration of module accumulation. The module
smpairs that is defined here implements an association list data structure. In
doing so, it uses the predicates memb and member defined in the module smlists.
The code for these predicates is made available within the module smpairs
by using an accumulate declaration. Notice that the semantics of the modules
language ensures that the accumulated copy of smlists is entirely local to
smpairs: None of the predicates defined in smlists are exposed through the
signature of smpairs, and hence these are not directly available for use in a
context that accumulates smpairs or in queries posed against this module.

When it is pertinent to pass on definitions from accumulated modules,
one can include the declarations of relevant accumulated constants and type

```
sig smpairs.

kind pair     type -> type -> type.
type pr       A -> B -> pair A B.

type assoc, assod   A -> B -> list (pair A B) -> o.
type domain         list (pair A B) -> list A -> o.
type range          list (pair A B) -> list B -> o.

end

module smpairs.
accumulate smlists.

kind pair     type -> type -> type.
type pr       A -> B -> pair A B.

type assoc, assod   A -> B -> list (pair A B) -> o.

assoc X Y L :- memb (pr X Y) L.
assod X Y L :- member (pr X Y) L.

type domain         list (pair A B) -> list A -> o.

domain nil nil.
domain ((pr X Y)::Alist) (X::L) :- domain Alist L.

type range          list (pair A B) -> list B -> o.

range nil nil.
range ((pr X Y)::Alist) (Y::L)  :- range Alist L.
end
```

Figure 6.3. An illustration of module accumulation.

constructors in the signature of the accumulating module. Thus, by placing the declaration

```
type  append  list A -> list A -> list A -> o.
```

in the signature for smpairs, we make it possible to use the append predicate in any context where smpairs is accumulated or available. We sometimes even may want to export from an accumulating module *all* the definitions that emanate from an accumulated module. This, of course, can be done by including each declaration in the signature of the accumulated module again in the signature of the accumulating module. However, this is cumbersome. A simpler way to realize the same effect is to use *signature accumulation*, a declaration that takes the form

```
accum_sig  <name1>, ..., <namen>.
```

Conceptually, this declaration, which is analogous to module accumulation, results in the insertion in the place where it occurs of the signatures whose names follow the `accum_sig` keyword. As an example, we may add the line

```
accum_sig smlists.
```

to the signature `smpairs` to produce a module that implements both list operations and association list operations.

The accumulation of signatures was introduced as a means for composing signatures. Signatures also can be accumulated meaningfully into modules with a similar semantics.

6.3 Matching signatures and modules

A key part of the formalization of the modules language is making precise the intended relationship between signatures and modules. We deal with the syntactic aspects of this correspondence here by discussing the matching of a signature with a module, leaving the treatment of the logical and search related aspects to the next section.

Before we can discuss signature matching, it is necessary to understand how the full content of a given signature is to be extracted. This is done by a process that we call *signature elaboration* that also simultaneously determines if a signature is well formed. The process is easily defined in the case that the signature contains no accumulation directives: It simply collects all the kind and type declarations appearing in the signature. As for the well-formedness conditions, one set of these is obvious: All the type constructors used in the signature either should be defined in it or should be drawn from the globally available set, and each of these symbols should be used with its specified arity. The second set of conditions stems from the fact that kind, type, and operator associations must be functional in nature. For kind and operator declarations, this amounts to requiring that all such associations with any given token in the signature be identical. For type declarations, the requirement takes into account the presence of type variables: All the types associated with a token must be identical up to (type) variable renaming. If this requirement is fulfilled, any one of the alphabetic variants is treated as *the* type associated with the token by the extracted signature.

Signature elaboration for a signature that contains accumulation directives requires the notion of *signature merging*. A collection of elaborated signatures is mergeable if the following properties hold:

- If a token has a kind declaration in more than one signature in the collection, then all the declarations pertaining to it are identical.

- If a token has a type declaration in more than one signature in the collection, then all the types associated with it through such declarations are identical up to a renaming of type variables.
- If a token has an operator declaration in any one signature, then it has an identical operator declaration in any other signature that identifies it as a constant.

Now suppose that Σ is a signature that accumulates the signatures $\Sigma_1, \ldots, \Sigma_n$. A prerequisite for the well-formedness of Σ is that there be no accumulation cycles going through it; i.e., no sequence of accumulations starting at any one of $\Sigma_1, \ldots, \Sigma_n$ should include Σ. If this is the case, then the next requirement is that each of $\Sigma_1, \ldots, \Sigma_n$ should be well formed. Let this property also hold, and let $\Sigma'_1, \ldots, \Sigma'_n$ be the elaborations of these signatures. Then the third requirement for Σ to be well formed is that $\Sigma'_1, \ldots, \Sigma'_n$ be mergeable. Suppose this also to be true, and let Σ' be the signature obtained by replacing the accumulation directives in Σ by the elaborations $\Sigma'_1, \ldots, \Sigma'_n$. Then Σ' is the elaboration of Σ, and the latter signature is well formed only if the former (accumulation-free) one is.

Another important step in the syntactic checking of a module consists of verifying that it is well formed and simultaneously identifying an implicit signature for it. This step, once again, has an easy explanation in the case of a module that does not accumulate any other modules. The implicit signature here is determined by signature elaboration applied to the result of dropping all the clauses from the module. The module then is well formed if this signature is well formed, if every constant used in the clauses is defined in the signature or is drawn from the list of pervasive constants, if each such constant is used at an instance of its defined type and in a manner consistent with any operator declaration pertaining to it, and finally, if each clause is well typed.

To treat the general case, suppose that a module M accumulates, in this order, the modules $M_1, \ldots, M_n$ that have specified signatures $\Sigma_1, \ldots, \Sigma_n$. There are then three requirements for M to be well formed:

- M must not be part of a module accumulation cycle; i.e., no sequence of module accumulations starting at one of $M_1, \ldots, M_n$ should include M.
- Each of the modules $M_1, \ldots, M_n$ must be well formed and must match its specified signature.
- The module M' that is obtained from M by replacing the accumulation of modules $M_1, \ldots, M_n$ with an accumulation instead of the signatures $\Sigma_1, \ldots, \Sigma_n$ must be well formed by virtue of the criteria already described for modules that do not accumulate other modules.

```
module m1.                      sig m1.
kind   item   type.             kind   item   type.
type   p,q   item -> o.         type   p,q   item -> o.
type   a   item.                type   a   item.
type   r   list item -> o.      end
p X :- q X.
r (a :: nil).
end


module m2.                      sig m2.
kind   item   type.             kind   item   type.
type   q, r   item -> o.        type   q, r   item -> o.
type   a   item.                type   a   item.
q X :- r X.                     end
r a.
end


module m3.                      sig m3.
accumulate m1, m2.              kind   item   type.
type   s, t   item -> o.        type   s, t   item -> o.
type   b   item.                type   a   item.
s X :- p X.                     end
t b.
end
```

Figure 6.4. A set of modules for illustrating signature matching.

Suppose that all these conditions are met. The implicit signature for M then is identical to that associated with the module M' that we have just described.

Let M be a well-formed module with the implicit signature Σ. Then we say that M matches a signature Σ' just in the case that Σ and the (signature) elaboration of Σ' are mergeable.

We illustrate the ideas described in this section by considering the declarations shown in Figure 6.4. These declarations first present the modules m1 and m2 together with their associated signatures and then use these via module accumulation to define the module m3. It is easily seen that the modules and signatures m1 and m2 are well formed and that the modules match their respective signatures. For example, consider the module m1. The implicit signature corresponding to it is characterized by the following declarations:

```
kind   item   type.
type   p,q   item -> o.
type   a   item.
type   r   list item -> o.
```

We use concrete syntax here and below to show the (conceptual) associations of kinds and types with tokens. Now this signature contains (the elaboration of) the signature m1 and therefore must be mergeable with it.

Turning now to the module m3, we see that this also must be well formed: There are no module accumulation cycles beginning with m3, the accumulated modules m1 and m2 each are well formed and match with their defined signatures, and the module

```
module m3'.
accum_sig m1, m2.
type    s,t   item -> o.
type    b     item.
s X :- p X.
t b.
end
```

which is the result of replacing the accumulation of modules in m3 with an accumulation instead of their signatures, also can be shown to be well formed. We can observe further that module m3 matches its specified signature. The implicit signature for this module is identical to that for the module m3', which is

```
kind item type.
type p,q,r,s,t  item -> o.
type b           item.
```

This signature is clearly mergeable with (the elaboration of) the signature m3.

Suppose that the signature m1 has the following definition instead of the one shown in Figure 6.4:

```
sig m1.
kind    item    type.
type    p,q     item -> o.
type    a       item.
type    r       list item -> o.
end.
```

Then the signatures m1 and m2 will not be mergeable because they associate types with the common constant r that cannot be made identical simply by the renaming of type variables. The module m3' defined earlier therefore will not be well formed, and hence neither will m3.

6.4 The logical interpretation of modules

The modules language gives expression to two notions of scope: It allows queries to be relativized to predicate definitions emanating from a module, and it provides a means for controlling the visibility of names of predicates and data constructors used in different blocks of code. Implications and universal quantifiers that are permitted in goals in $hohh^+$ already lead to a treatment of both these aspects. Thus it appears possible to use a translation into the core language constituted by $hohh^+$ to formalize the meaning of the modularity constructs. There is, however, one issue that requires further consideration before a satisfactory translation can be provided: A logic-based mechanism must be described that allows names of constants to be localized to (sets of) program clauses. We show below how such a device may be obtained through a benign extension of $hohh^+$ syntax and then use this extended language to present a translation-based semantics.

6.4.1 Existential quantification in program clauses

Explicit universal quantifiers in goals provide a mechanism for designating the scope of constants. Thus consider a goal formula of the form $\exists y \forall x (D(x) \supset G(y))$. The universal quantification over x will lead to x being treated as a constant in the process of solving this goal, but this constant cannot be used in a term instantiating the existentially quantified variable y. Now suppose that x does not appear in the subformula $G(y)$. In addition to the restriction on instantiations just described, it is legitimate to think of x as a constant that is known only within $D(x)$, i.e., as one that is *local* to this program clause.

We would, of course, prefer a syntactic device that allows us to identify local constants directly with program clauses. A look at logical equivalences suggests a natural way for realizing this. In most logical systems, a formula of the form $\exists y \forall x (D(x) \supset G(y))$ is equivalent to one of the form $\exists y ((\exists x D(x)) \supset G(y))$ in the case that x is not free in $G(y)$. Thus, if our syntax is extended to permit existential quantifiers over program clauses at appropriate places, we would obtain a mechanism for signaling the locality of names directly with such clauses. A further useful equivalence is that between $\exists x (D_1(x) \land D_2)$ and $(\exists x D_1(x)) \land D_2$. This property justifies an extension of syntax that allows the scopes of existential quantifiers to be narrowed to subparts of a large program clause, thereby enabling a finer-grained control over the visibility of names.

We modify the syntax of $hohh^+$ in keeping with the preceding observations. In particular, we let program clauses and goal formulas to be given now by the

D- and G-formulas defined by the following syntax rules:

$$G ::= \top \mid A \mid G \wedge G \mid G \vee G \mid \exists x\ G \mid E \supset G \mid \forall x\ G$$

$$D ::= A_r \mid G \supset D \mid D \wedge D \mid \forall x\ D$$

$$E ::= D \mid E \wedge E \mid \exists x\ E.$$

The heads of atoms designated by A_r in the definition of hohh had to be constants (from a relevant signature Σ) or variables captured by a universal quantifier in a goal that embeds that atom. In hohh$^+$, this constraint is now expanded to allow such heads also to be variables that are bound by the existential quantifier in an E-formula inside which such atoms might appear.

The main change in the new version of hohh$^+$ is that the left contexts of implicational goals are now permitted to contain existential quantifiers that have program clauses in their scope. Some care is needed in the treatment of such formulas in the operational semantics associated with the language. If we naively use the $\supset R$ rule from Figure 2.2 in Chapter 2, namely,

$$\frac{\Sigma; \mathcal{P}, B_1 \longrightarrow B_2}{\Sigma; \mathcal{P} \longrightarrow B_1 \supset B_2}$$

then E-formulas would be added to programs, and this is problematic because programs are restricted to contain only D-formulas.

To resolve this problem, we reflect the logical equivalences that justified the introduction of existential quantifiers over program clauses into the treatment of implicational goals. Specifically, we replace the $\supset R$ rule with the set of rules shown in Figure 6.5 and introduce a new kind of sequent $\Sigma; \mathcal{P} - \langle \Delta \rangle \rightarrow G$, where Δ is a multiset of E-formulas. When reading proof rules bottom up, the $\supset R$ rule is replaced by a sequence of derivations that starts with $\supset R'$, ends with finish, and contains some number of occurrences of $\wedge L'$, $\exists L'$, and reclassify rules. This new phase designed to process E-formulas is essentially an extension to the goal-directed reduction phase, at least in the sense that all the inference rules in this new phase are invertible (i.e., no backtracking is needed). During this new phase, the local constants are introduced dynamically

$$\frac{\Sigma; \mathcal{P} - \langle E \rangle \rightarrow G}{\Sigma; \mathcal{P} \longrightarrow E \supset G}\ \supset R' \qquad \frac{\Sigma; \mathcal{P} \longrightarrow G}{\Sigma; \mathcal{P} - \langle\ \rangle \rightarrow G}\ \text{finish} \qquad \frac{\Sigma; \mathcal{P}, D - \langle \Delta \rangle \rightarrow G}{\Sigma; \mathcal{P} - \langle D, \Delta \rangle \rightarrow G}\ \text{reclassify}$$

$$\frac{\Sigma; \mathcal{P} - \langle E_1, E_2, \Delta \rangle \rightarrow G}{\Sigma; \mathcal{P} - \langle E_1 \wedge E_2, \Delta \rangle \rightarrow G}\ \wedge L' \qquad \frac{\Sigma, y; \mathcal{P} - \langle E[y/x], \Delta \rangle \rightarrow G}{\Sigma; \mathcal{P} - \langle \exists x E, \Delta \rangle \rightarrow G}\ \exists L'$$

The $\exists L'$ rule has the proviso that y is not present in Σ and hence is not free in the concluding sequent.

Figure 6.5. Modified proof rules for processing E-formulas.

into computation, and the clauses using these new constants are integrated with the ambient logic program.

The extended $hohh^+$ syntax allows (the more liberal) E-formulas to be used instead of D-formulas arbitrarily as the antecedents of implicational goals. We refine this syntax by restricting the expressions that a programmer might write within a module or in a query to those permitted by the original definition of the $hohh^+$ language, allowing the richer syntax to be used only in the translation of modularity constructs. Thus existential quantifiers over program clauses are used only to explain the localization of the scopes of constants to modules in the manner we discuss below.

6.4.2 A module as a logical formula

The logical semantics of a well-formed module and a well-formed matching signature are formalized by identifying an E-formula corresponding to the combination. The translation to such a formula is easy to describe in the case that the module in question does not accumulate any other modules. First, we collect the constants contained in the implicit signature for the module that do not also appear in the explicitly provided signature; these constitute the hidden or local constants of the module. We then construct a D-formula by conjoining all the program clauses contained in the module. Finally, we obtain the desired E-formula by inserting existential quantifiers over the hidden constants at the head of the D-formula.

The translation in the situation where the module accumulates other modules is only slightly more complicated. We proceed as before to identify the hidden constants for the module; notice that constructing the implicit signature will require us also to look at the (explicit) signatures of the accumulated modules in this case. We then extract an E-formula corresponding to each of the accumulated modules. This step involves a recursion that is well defined because of the absence of accumulation cycles. Next, we construct an E-formula by conjoining the E-formulas corresponding to the accumulated modules with the program clauses contained in the module. The formula to be associated with the given module now is obtained by existentially quantifying the hidden constants over this E-formula.

We illustrate the semantics that we have just described by considering the modules and signatures shown in Figure 6.4. As we have seen already, each of these is well formed, and each of the modules matches its respective signature. Examining the module m1, we observe that it has r as its sole local constant. Thus the E-formula corresponding to it is

$$\exists r((\forall x(q\ x \supset p\ x)) \land (r\ (a::nil)))$$

The module m2 has no local constants, and it therefore translates simply to the *D*-formula

$$\forall x (r\ x \supset q\ x) \land (r\ a)$$

Turning now to the module m3, we see that it hides the constants p, q, r, and b. Using the translation of module accumulation, we obtain the following *E*-formula for this module:

$$\exists p \exists q \exists r \exists b (\exists r ((\forall x (q\ x \supset p\ x)) \land (r\ (a::nil))) \land$$
$$(\forall x (r\ x \supset q\ x) \land (r\ a)) \land$$
$$(\forall x (p\ x \supset s\ x) \land (t\ b)))$$

6.4.3 Interpreting queries against modules

The informal description of posing a query against modules given in Section 6.2 now can be made more formal. As noted already, one role that modules play is a syntactic one: They provide a signature for interpreting terms and types used in the query. Formally, this signature is what we have called the explicit signature of the module. At a logical level, the query is treated as a request to solve an implicational goal in which the antecedent of the implication is the *E*-formula associated with the module and whose consequent is the query presented by the user. A point to emphasize concerning this translation is that the implicitly existentially quantified variables in the user presented query are treated as being quantified over the entire implicational goal. Thus consider an interaction depicted schematically as

```
[m] ?- g X.
```

Assuming that the formula associated with the module m is *E*, this query is logically equivalent to the request to solve the goal $\exists x (E \supset g\ x)$.

The explicit signature that mediates the external view of a module already leads to a static notion of scoping. Consider, for example, the modules shown in Figure 6.4. The predicate r that is defined in module m1 but is not exposed by its signature is unknown in an external context and hence cannot be confused with the predicate of the same name that appears in the module m2. As another example, the query

```
[m3] ?- p a.
```

is ill formed. Notice that this is the case even though the predicate p is known within the module m3; in fact, the query

```
[m3] ?- s a.
```

leads to an attempt to solve the same goal (p a) in the richer context internal to m3, and this results eventually in a success.

The E-formula-based interpretation of modules fits in well with this framework for giving names a scope while adding an interesting dynamic dimension to it. To see this, consider the query

```
[m3] ?- sigma x\ t x.
```

This query has a successful solution that is based on instantiating the existential quantifier with the constant b. By contrast, the seemingly identical query

```
[m3] ?- t X.
```

fails. Logically, the difference arises from the scope of the existential quantifier in the two cases. Pragmatically, we can understand this phenomenon as the difference between using a constant in the course of searching for a solution, as happens in the first query, and attempting to expose the identity of this constant externally, as happens in the second query.

6.4.4 Module accumulation as scoped inlining of code

The translation semantics for modules constructs a possibly large conjunction in which existential quantifiers have scopes over component formulas. The proof rules in Figure 6.5 break up such formulas into new scoped constants and new program clauses. Rather than executing these proof rules each time a module is queried, it is possible to preprocess a module so that it is devoid of accumulation directives and still maintains an equivalent behavior with respect to queries. We refer to this process as *module elaboration*: Its essential content is that of inlining accumulated signatures and modules while renaming local variables in a way that ensures that their relative scopes are preserved.

At a formal level, module elaboration associates a pair consisting of a signature and a list of clauses with each well-formed module; the composite module simply combines these two items together. The elaboration process has a straightforward definition if the module does not accumulate any other modules: The signature component is determined by signature elaboration applied to the result of dropping all the clauses from the module, and the list of clauses is obtained by dropping all directives to accumulate signatures and all the kind, type, and operator declarations. For the general case, suppose that a (well-formed) module M accumulates, in this order, the modules $M_1, \ldots, M_n$ for which module elaboration yields the signatures $\Sigma_1, \ldots, \Sigma_n$ and the clause lists $\mathcal{P}_1, \ldots, \mathcal{P}_n$, respectively. Further suppose that the implicit signature of M is Σ_0 and that the clauses contained in M form the list $\mathcal{P}_0$. Now, for $1 \leq i \leq n$, let

Σ_i' be obtained from Σ_i by possibly renaming sorts, type constructors, and constants that appear in it but not in the explicit signature of module M_i to ensure that these names do not appear in the implicit or explicit signature of M and are also distinct from the names used in Σ_j' for $1 \le j \le n$ and $i \ne j$. Moreover, for $1 \le i \le n$, let $\mathcal{P}_i'$ be obtained from $\mathcal{P}_i$ via the same renaming that produced Σ_i' from Σ_i. Then the signature and list of clauses associated with M by module elaboration are, respectively, the combination of the signatures $\Sigma_1', \ldots, \Sigma_n', \Sigma_0$, and the result of appending, in this order, the lists $\mathcal{P}_1', \ldots, \mathcal{P}_n', \mathcal{P}_0$.

To illustrate the process just described, consider, once again, the modules shown in Figure 6.4. The signature extracted by module elaboration for module m3 is

```
kind item type.
type p,q,r,r',s,t item -> o.
type a,b item.
```

and the list of clauses is

```
p X :- q X.
r' (a :: nil).
q X :- r X.
r a.
s X :- p X.
t b.
```

Here, r' is a new name for the constant r local to the module m1; this name is selected so as to avoid confusion with the constant of the same name that is exported from module m2. By combining these two components, we obtain a module that, when mediated by the signature m3, behaves the same with posed queries as does module m3.

6.5 Some programming aspects of the modules language

Notwithstanding its syntactic and semantic simplicity, the modules language that we have described is capable of supporting important aspects of programming-in-the-large. We illustrate a few of these aspects now.

6.5.1 Hiding and abstract datatypes

The signature associated with a module controls the visibility of the constants and types defined within it. By hiding the data constructors corresponding to a given type while exposing the type itself along with predicates using that type, one can build an *abstract datatype*. When designed in this way, objects

```
sig stack.
kind  store          type -> type.
type  init           store A -> o.
type  add, remove    A -> store A -> store A -> o.
end

module stack.
kind  store          type -> type.
type  emp            store A.
type  stk            A -> store A -> store A.
type  init           store A -> o.
type  add, remove    A -> store A -> store A -> o.
init emp.
add    X S (stk X S).
remove X (stk X S) S.
end
```

Figure 6.6. Implementing a stack abstract datatype.

of the abstract type can be used and manipulated by the exposed predicates wherever the module is available: At the same time, the details of the actual data representation can remain hidden.

The signature and the module defined in Figure 6.6 illustrate how to implement an abstract datatype. The code contained in the module defines a type constructor for a store, data constructors for stores, and the predicates for initializing a store and for adding and removing objects from it using a stack-based discipline. The signature associated with this module exposes the store type constructor and the predicates but not the data constructors. Thus the query

```
[stack] ?- init A.
```

that attempts to exhibit the representation of the empty stack to the user will fail. However, stack objects can be used "anonymously" even at the top level. For example, the query

```
[stack] ?- sigma A\ sigma B\ sigma C\ init A, add 1 A B, remove X B C.
```

that uses the stack representation to store and then retrieve the integer 1 will succeed by binding X to 1.

We illustrate the high level of functionality and abstraction afforded by both abstract datatypes and module accumulation by developing an implementation of a heuristic-based graph search procedure. Such a procedure would initialize a collection of states and then expand this set based on the rules for generating new states and an underlying strategy for selecting the next state for expansion. This procedure will need a mechanism for recording the set of states that are candidates for expansion. If the desire is to perform a (heuristics-driven) depth-first search, a natural choice for the store regimen would be a stack. The

```
sig graph_search.
kind  action  type.
type  graph_search  list action -> o.
end

module graph_search.
accumulate stack.
kind state, action type.
type graph_search list action -> o.
type init_open store state -> o.
type expand_graph store state -> list state -> list action -> o.
...
graph_search Soln :- init_open Open, expand_graph Open nil Soln.
init_open Open :- start_state State, init Op, add State Op Open.
expand_graph Open Closed Soln :-
    remove State Open Rest, final_state State, soln State Soln.
expand_graph Open Closed Soln :-
    remove State Open ROpen,
    expand_node State NStates,
    add_states NStates ROpen (State::Closed) NOpen,
    expand_graph NOpen (State::Closed) Soln.
...
end
```

Figure 6.7. The skeleton of a graph search module.

implementation of such a store can be obtained by accumulating the module
stack. Figure 6.7 displays part of the definition of a graph search module based
on this idea. The main predicate defined by this module is graph_search, which
ultimately produces a list of actions to achieve a desired goal. The definition of
this predicate depends on the predicates init_open, which initializes a list of
"open" nodes in the graph, and expand_graph, which expands a given graph by
selecting an open node and generating its successors based on the actions that
apply to it. These predicates must know of a type for stores, and their implementation will need operations for initializing stores and for adding to and removing
from them. These components are naturally provided by the accumulated module stack. Note that while the (universally quantified) variables in the program
clauses in the graph_search module can be instantiated with store representations, these representations are completely opaque; they can be examined and
manipulated only by means of the operations provided by the stack module.

6.5.2 Code extensibility and modular composition

In logic programming, it is possible for the definition of a predicate or procedure to be distributed across a set of clauses. Thus, in contrast to other
programming styles, an existing procedure definition always can be extended.
In the framework we have described, this kind of extensibility also applies to

data representations: New type declarations can be added to extend the constructors corresponding to an existing type, and these additions can occur in different modules.

The modules and signatures shown in Figure 6.8 illustrate the use of this capability. The purpose of this code is to build a theorem prover for a fragment of intuitionistic first-order logic. While the theorem prover itself is simple, the interesting part of this example is the manner in which it is built. First, the part of this prover that works on the propositional fragment of this logic is presented in the module `proplogic`. This code can be used in a stand-alone fashion or can be used to deal with the propositional fragment of different quantificational logics. In this particular example, it is accumulated into the module `quantlogic`, where it is extended to a first-order logic. (The treatment of encoded first-order quantifiers within the `quantlogic` module is fully explained in Chapter 7.) Notice that both the collection of constructors for objects of type `form` and the definition of the provability predicate are extended after the accumulation.

6.5.3 Signature accumulation and parametrization of modules

Module accumulation can be used to get a private copy of an existing functionality for new code that is being developed. In many cases, this is the right kind of interaction; this is especially true when the smaller components that are being used are the result of a stepwise refinement process and do not have significance in their own right. In other situations, however, the functionality that is needed in the code being developed is not intended to be of a restricted use, privately developed variety. Rather, it is expected to be something that is provided by an external "library" module. In this case, it is better to think of the module that is being built as one that is expecting to be given this library module before it can fulfill the functionality it promises. Thus the expected external module plays the role of a parameter. Of course, the parameter must satisfy certain requirements. These requirements can be specified by a signature.

Explicitly defined signatures and signature accumulation provide a natural way to capture such module parametrization. The essential idea is to accumulate a signature prescribing the needed capability into the module being defined and into its signature rather than accumulating the library capability directly. Of course, the module is complete only when it is combined with the expected functionality: This combination can be done at a subsequent level in the hierarchy by bringing the two modules together through a simultaneous accumulation. To illustrate this idea, consider the theorem prover in Figure 6.8. Both the `proplogic` and the `quantlogic` modules use list functions. In the code shown, this functionality is obtained by accumulating `smlists` immediately into

```
sig proplogic.
kind  form          type.
type  ff, tt         form.
type  and, or ==>  form -> form -> form.
type  prove list  form -> form -> o.
end

module proplogic.
accumulate smlists.
kind  form          type.
type  ff, tt         form.
type  and, or ==> form -> form -> form.
type  prove          list form -> form -> o.
prove L F :- member ff L.
prove L F :-
    memb_and_rest (and A B) L L', prove (A::B::L') F.
prove L (and F1 F2) :- prove L F1, prove L F2.
prove L (==> F1 F2) :- prove (F1::L) F2.
prove L F :- memb_and_rest (or A B) L L',
             prove (A::L') F, prove (B::L') F.
prove L (or F1 F2) :- prove L F1; prove L F2.
prove L F :- member F L.
prove L F :- memb_and_rest (==> F1 F2) L L',
             prove L F1, prove (F2::L') F.
end

sig quantlogic.
accum_sig proplogic.
kind term          type.
type all, some    (term -> form) -> form.
end

module quantlogic.
accumulate proplogic, smlists.
kind term          type.
type all, some    (term -> form) -> form.

prove L F :- memb_and_rest (some P) L L',
             pi c \ prove ((P c)::L) F.
prove L (all P) :- pi c\ prove L (P c).
prove L (some P) :- prove L (P T).
prove L F :- memb_and_rest (all P) L L',
             append L' [all P] L'', prove ((P T)::L'') F.
end
```

Figure 6.8. A first-order theorem prover in two modules.

the modules. Such an accumulation is at least wasteful: Two "private" copies of the smlists module are used where one library version would have sufficed. Moreover, the signatures of the two new modules do not clearly indicate the dependency on an implementation of lists.

```
sig mylogic.
accum_sig quantlogic.
type  a, b  term.
type  q  form.
type  p  term -> form.
end


module mylogic.
accumulate  quantlogic, smlists.
type  a, b  term.
type  q  form.
type  p  term -> form.
end
```

Figure 6.9. Combining functionalities to obtain an actual theorem prover.

An alternative development that overcomes these problems eliminates the accumulation of the `smlists` module from both the `proplogic` and the `quantlogic` modules and instead accumulates the *signature* of `smlists` into these modules and their signatures. Then, when we actually want to use the theorem prover (when the nonlogical vocabulary has been fixed), we simply accumulate all modules into the relevant context. Such accumulation is illustrated in Figure 6.9.

Another interesting observation is that the relationship between the modules `smlists` and `quantlogic` is different from that between `proplogic` and `quantlogic`. In the former case, the functionality that is provided by `smlists` is intended to be used *without modification*, whereas in the latter case, the meanings of the types and predicates are expected to change. Attaching annotations to predicates to indicate their fixed usage at module interfaces is useful as documentation for human readers and for compilers. The *Teyjus* implementation of λProlog includes mechanisms for providing such annotations.

6.5.4 *Higher-order programming and predicate visibility*

A higher-order logic programming language allows defining predicates that are parameterized by other predicates. For example, a collection of such higher-order predicates related to lists is shown in Figure 5.3. Such predicate definitions have general applicability and therefore may be usefully collected into a library module. The invocation of such predicates, of course, will supply them with specific predicate names as arguments. Prolog dialects that provide notions of both modules and higher-order predicates (e.g., the `call/1` predicate) need to determine how names of predicates that are provided as arguments to other predicates are interpreted. To see that such interpretations

```
sig comblibrary.                    module comblibrary.
type  call  o -> o.                 type  call  o -> o.
end                                 type  p  list int -> o.
                                    p (1 :: nil).
                                    call Q :- Q.
                                    end


sig test.                           module test.
type  test  list int -> o.          accumulate comblibrary.
end                                 type  test  list int -> o.
                                    type  p  list int -> o.
                                    p (2 :: nil).
                                    test X :- call (p X).
                                    end
```

Figure 6.10. Interpreting predicate names in higher-order programs.

can be problematic, consider the following query posed against the module in Figure 6.10.

```
[test] ?- test X.
```

The attempt to solve this query will lead to invocation of the goal `call (p X)`, which, in turn, will cause the goal `p X` to be called. What should be the definition of the name `p` when it is called? Two competing possibilities have been suggested: Its denotation may be determined by whatever is visible in the context where the predicate `call` is defined or by the environment in which the name is explicitly used. In this instance, the top-level query will succeed either way, but with different results depending on which answer one takes: X will be bound to `1 :: nil` in the first case and to `2 :: nil` in the second.

The second interpretation is the commonly used resolution. This interpretation has the advantage that the denotations of names are determined statically, an important requirement for any good notion of modularity. Notice that this interpretation is a natural consequence of the semantics that we have presented for our modules language. The possibility of two different interpretations arises from a separation between the calling and the called context. This separation plays no role in our semantics. The module `test` is, in fact, treated as *one* collection of declarations in which existential quantifiers with limited scope control the visibility and hence the identity of names. Using module elaboration, we see that the module `test` is equivalent to the following collection of declarations:

```
type  test  list int -> o.
type  call  o -> o.
type  p, p'  list int -> o.
```

```
p' (1:: nil).
p (2 :: nil).
call P :- P.
test X :- call (p X).
```

The name p has an unambiguous interpretation in this context, and the only answer substitution to the query shown earlier is the binding 2 :: nil for X.

6.6 Implementation considerations

In order for a module language to be effective, it should have an efficient implementation and support separate compilation. While a detailed discussion of these issues is beyond the scope of this book, we sketch possible ways to implement modules effectively.

Module elaboration can play an important role in the efficient realization of our module language. In the first instance, we can think of a preprocessor that carries out the inlining of various accumulated modules and signatures while carefully renaming constants to avoid clashes and inadvertent capture. Once a complete list of declarations without accumulations has been produced, standard compilation techniques can be used to generate code for the (elaborated) module. Some care is needed in the runtime treatment of the constants local to this module. However, the mechanisms that are already present in the language for treating alternating sequences of existential and universal quantifiers in goals suffice also for handling this aspect. The only additional requirement, then, is to make sure that local constants are annotated properly at the time the module is used to prove queries.

The main problem with the scheme that we have just described is that it depends on an explicit compile-time inlining of the code of accumulated modules. Rather than assimilating the code of an accumulated module and recompiling it each time the accumulating module is compiled, we might like to be able to compile this once and then somehow use the code that is produced anyplace where it is needed. Such a separate compilation strategy can be realized by moving the inlining of code to a linking phase and carrying it out over compiled code instead of source code. Of course, the compiler will have to produce additional information for use in the linking phase. For this scheme to be practically acceptable, the linking process must be designed so that it combines the separately generated code for blocks of clauses for a given predicate in such a way that the runtime performance of the resulting code is not significantly different from that of the code obtained via a compile-time inlining.

6.7 Bibliographic notes

As with all major programming paradigms, techniques for the modular construction of code have been of considerable interest within logic programming. Mechanisms for supporting modularity are, in fact, part of most advanced implementations of Prolog and also have been the topic of Prolog standardization (ISO/IEC, 2000). Much of this focus on modularity has been pragmatic and has dealt with questions such as the interpretation of metalogical predicates like call/1, the treatment of declarations that affect the interpretation of syntax, or the problem of language extensibility (Cabeza and Hermenegildo, 2000).

There have been number of papers dealing with more theoretical approaches to modularity in logic programming. Bugliesi et al. (1994) have surveyed this landscape. Their survey classifies the various approaches to modularity into two groups: those which treat modularity features as manifestations of an algebra for program composition built on top of a fixed core language and those which attempt to extend the underlying logical language to derive support for notions of scoping pertaining to names and predicate definitions. The first of these two approaches was initiated by O'Keefe (1985) and followed up in a more complete fashion by Sannella and Wallen (1992) and by Hill and Lloyd (1994) within the Gödel programming language.

The second approach, pioneered by Miller (1989c), extended Horn clauses with implications and universal goals in order to allow for varying and controlling the programs and signatures during the course of computation. A related idea for controlling predicate definitions was studied by Monteiro and Porto (1989) within their framework of contextual logic programming. The dynamic addition of program clauses means that previously existing predicates can change meanings, and hence the meaning of a module becomes dependent on the context in which it is used rather than being self-contained. Giordano and Martelli (1991) have described a way to ensure the fixity of predicate definitions by using modal interpretation of formulas. A later proposal by Miller (1994) includes the idea of module accumulation. As we have seen here, when combined with the use of existential quantifiers to narrow the visibility of names, this simple static device provides control over the availability of predicate definitions as well. Holte and Nadathur (2006) describe the particular modules language discussed in this chapter that realizes this combination.

The modularity constructs that we have described resemble the signatures and structures used in the language Standard ML (Milner et al. 1990). Moreover, our use of existential quantification in programs looks enticingly similar to existential types that underlie hiding in functional programming (Mitchell and Plotkin 1988). There are differences, however: Logic programming is based on proof search rather than on proof normalization, and much of our effort here has centered on explaining how well our modularity ideas fit with proof search. In contrast, Sannella and Wallen (1992) employ the constructs from Standard ML mainly as external mechanisms for organizing logic programs. Harper and Pfenning (1998) have adapted an ML-like approach to modularity to a logic programming language based on dependent types and consider the ramifications of using such an approach to modularity in the proof search paradigm.

The modules language described in this chapter is available in the *Teyjus* implementation of λProlog. The first implementation of *Teyjus* used the inlining approach in its realization (Nadathur and Tong 1999). A more recent implementation has refined this approach to incorporate separate compilation (Holte and Nadathur 2006).

7

Computations over λ-Terms

In Chapter 1 we observed that first-order terms can be used as data structures to represent a variety of symbolic objects. The higher-order language developed in Chapter 5 allows λ-abstraction to be used to build terms of higher-order type. We discussed briefly in that chapter how such terms can be used to encode data structures containing bindings, such as functional difference lists. We now explore in greater detail the uses of λ-terms in encoding data objects that contain bindings and show that the *hohh* language provides elegant and declarative means for describing a range of computations over such representations.

7.1 Representing objects with binding structure

There are many commonly used mathematical expressions that involve bindings. For example, the expressions

$$\int f(x)\, dx \qquad \frac{d(x^3 + 1)}{dx} \qquad \sum_{x=1}^{100} x^2$$

which represent integration, differentiation, and summation, all contain x as a bound variable. Similarly, in the programming language context, declarations of local variables and formal parameters usually constitute binders. Thus, in the Java code below, the tokens n, g, and i are all bound within the body of the function.

```
static List[] empty (int n) {
  List[] g;
  int i;
  g = new List [n];
  for (i=0; i <= n-1; i = i+1) {g[i] = null;}
  return(g); }
```

Likewise, in the following function definition in Standard ML, the variables n, this, prev, count, and iter are bound over relevant parts of the code.

```
fun fib 0 = 0 |
    fib n =
    let fun iter(this,prev,count) =
      if count = n then this
      else iter(this+prev,this,count+1)
    in iter(1,0,1)
    end;
```

Many other examples of this kind can be given. Quantifiers in logical formulas obviously involve binding variables. Expressions encountered in certain type systems, such as those based on polymorphic typing, often contain quantified type variables. Certain treatments of proofs introduce objects that contain abstractions over proofs and formulas. Expressions in the π-calculus, a framework for modeling concurrent processes, have binding operators that provide scope to communication channel names.

We are often interested in writing programs that compute over the kinds of objects just described: This happens, for instance, when we think of constructing symbolic differentiators for mathematical expressions or analyzers, compilers, interpreters, or transformers for programs written in Java or Standard ML. In such cases, it is useful to have a representation of the objects that explicitly recognizes the properties of the binding operators they contain. Many of these properties have a common structure. For example, in all these situations, there are closely related notions of *free* and *bound occurrences* of variables. Similarly, while the actual name used for a bound variable might be helpful for certain purposes, such as printing the object—in much the same way that good line breaks and indentations are helpful—this name is not semantically relevant, just as indentation generally has no bearing on meaning; in particular, the names used for these variables can be systematically changed to other ones without changing the intended semantics of the expression. Also, in all these contexts, there is a need for a notion of substitution associated with the binding operator. Thus quantifier instantiation in logical formulas involves substitution, and the evaluation semantics of some functional programming languages can be described by means of the substitution of actual parameters for the formal ones. A computational treatment of such binding-related notions is complicated, and programming language support for realizing them can be valuable.

There is actually a similarity between abstraction in the λ-terms that constitute the data structures of λProlog (Chapter 4) and the binding operator in the symbolic objects that we are presently considering. We show in this section how this similarity can be exploited to develop representations of such objects using λ-terms. There are a number of advantages to this kind of encoding. For example, if an implementation of λProlog already has grappled with the complexities of α- and β-conversion, then these representations considerably simplify the programmer's task in supporting substitution and variable renaming. Also, since the treatment of the conversion rules is internal to the logic rather than being provided by auxiliary library functions, our approach has a *declarative* nature, and reasoning about the programs that we write can benefit from foundational observations about the logic. We illustrate this perspective briefly in this section and use it later in this chapter to develop programs that carry out computations that are of broad interest.

7.1.1 Encoding logical formulas with quantifiers

Section 1.4.2 presented an encoding of first-order formulas. In particular, the sorts term and form were used to encode the syntactic categories of *object-level terms* and *object-level formulas*. Constants then were introduced through the following declarations:

```
type    ff,                         % encoding the false proposition
        tt    form.                 % encoding the true proposition
type    &&,                         % encoding conjunction
        !!,                         % encoding disjunction
        ==>   form -> form -> form. % encoding implication
type    neg   form -> form.         % encoding negation
infixl  &&    5.
infixl  !!    4.
infixr  ==>   3.
```

to represent *object-level logical connectives*; these constants could be used to construct terms of type form. We also described an encoding for quantifiers using only first-order terms, but that representation did not capture the binding aspect of quantifiers.

This situation can be rectified by using the abstraction present in λ-terms. For concreteness of discussion, suppose that we have the following additional declarations that introduce some of the nonlogical constants of the object logic:

```
type    p    term -> form.
type    q    term -> term -> form.
type    f    term -> term.
type    a    term.
```

By virtue of these declarations, p and q denote predicates of one and two arguments, respectively, f denotes a function symbol of one argument, and a denotes a constant. The following expressions denote terms of type `term -> form` that can be thought of as a new *syntactic type* for an abstraction of a term over a formula:

```
x\ (p x) ==> (p (f x))     Z\ (p Z) ==> (p (f Z))     Z\ (p Z) && (p (f Z))
```

Notice that the first two expressions here are equal as λ-terms because they differ only in the name of bound variables. Now the abstraction that is used in these terms captures the scoping effect of a quantifier over the body of the corresponding term. However, none of these terms are themselves representations of formulas because their type is `term -> form` rather than `form`. To obtain the representation of quantified formulas from them, we introduce two constants through the following declaration:

```
type  all, some     (term -> form) -> form.
```

These constants, whose types are of order 2, can be applied to the preceding abstractions to yield expressions of type `form`. For example, consider the λ-terms

```
all x\ (p x) ==> (p (f x))     some Z\ (p Z) && (p (f Z))
```

These terms are both of type `form` and can be viewed as the representations of the formulas

$$\forall x \, (p(x) \supset p(f(x))) \quad \text{and} \quad \exists Z \, (p(Z) \wedge p(f(Z))),$$

respectively. Notice that the mechanism that we have described divides the encoding of the object logic quantifiers into two parts: a second order constant that identifies the quantifier and an abstraction that captures its binding effect.

This style of encoding extends smoothly to formulas with multiple occurrences of quantifiers that do not necessarily scope over the entire expression. For example, the formula $\forall x \, \forall y \, (q(x, y) \supset \exists z \, (p(z) \wedge q(z, y)))$ is encoded by

```
all x\ all y\ (q x y) ==> some z\ p z && q z y.
```

7.1.2 Encoding untyped λ-terms

For another example, consider encoding *untyped* λ-terms. If the object language terms are pure, i.e., no special object-level constants occur in them, then we need only two meta-level constants, one denoting application and the other denoting abstraction, for the encoding. These can be given by the following declarations:

```
kind   tm      type.
type   app     tm -> tm -> tm.
type   abs     (tm -> tm) -> tm.
```

We list below several examples of untyped λ-terms and their representation using the preceding constants:

$\lambda x\, x$	`(abs x\x)`
$\lambda x\, (x\; x)$	`(abs x\ (app x x))`
$\lambda x\, \lambda y\, x$	`(abs x\ abs y\ x)`
$\lambda x\, \lambda y\, y$	`(abs x\ abs y\ y)`
$\lambda x\, \lambda y\, (y\; x)$	`(abs x\ abs y\ app y x)`
$\lambda x\, \lambda y\, \lambda z\, ((x\; z)\, (y\; z))$	`(abs x\abs y\abs z\ (app (app x z) (app y z)))`
$(\lambda x\, (x\; x))\, (\lambda x\, (x\; x))$	`(app (abs x\ app x x) (abs x\ app x x))`

Notice that for every implicit application in an untyped term, there is an occurrence of the constant app in its encoding, and for every occurrence of a λ-abstraction in the untyped term, there is an occurrence of abs followed by an occurrence of a meta-level λ-abstraction in its encoding. The latter aspect reflects, once again, the idea of dividing the representation of a binding operator into a constant that identifies the operator and an abstraction that captures its scoping effect. For readability, we have given corresponding bound variables in the untyped terms and in their encodings the same name. This is, of course, not necessary.

It is useful to introspect briefly on how terms of type tm are built. Notice first that the constant app needs to be given two expressions of type tm in order to yield a new expression of the same type. From this, it follows easily that no closed terms of type tm can be built by using just app. The constant abs will yield a term of type tm if it is given a term of type tm -> tm. This (meta-level) type *does* contain terms: For example, both x\x and x\ app x x are of this type. The meta-level abstraction serves also to introduce new objects of the type tm that can be used in the body of the abstraction. For example, if a term starts with the two abstractions abs x\ abs y\, then what follows can be built from app and abs as well as from the two "constructors" x and y, each of type tm. In this sense, the type tm can be seen as admitting new constructors as one descends under binders.

7.1.3 Properties of the encoding of binding

In the preceding two examples, the syntactic categories that are needed for encoding first-order formulas (term and form) and untyped λ-terms (tm) make use of additional syntactic categories (respectively, term -> form and tm -> tm) for encoding abstractions over syntax. The equality notion that applies to these categories has α-conversion built into it. This is a useful property from the perspective of the object language because equality typically is invariant under the renaming of bound variables.

Since α-conversion is included within the logical notion of equality, it is impossible to access the names of bound variables. While this fact may appear initially to be a deficiency, a little reflection shows that it is, in fact, a strength. Since no importance is given to the names of bound variables that are also a semantically meaningless part of the objects being encoded, programmers using the *hohh* language can give more attention to the conceptually significant aspects of the computation. Furthermore, an implementer of the language has the freedom to use names for bindings or to abandon them altogether. Of course, since syntax is treated in a more abstract fashion, print and parsing of such syntactic objects can be a bit more complex: For example, human-readable names of bindings may need to be generated in order to conveniently print such syntactic expressions.

Beside α-conversion, meta-level equality also includes β- and η-conversion. Much of the rest of this chapter explores the usefulness of β-conversion in computation. The impact of η-conversion is rather mild: It allows us to identify expressions that, in the simply typed λ-calculus setting, seem rather natural to identify. For example, if f is a constant of type, say, $i \rightarrow i$, then η-conversion identifies f with $\lambda x (f\ x)$. This conversion rule also implies that the object-level formula $\forall x (p\ x)$ can be encoded as either (all x\ p x) or (all p). Thus not only does the *hohh* language abstract away from names of bindings, but it also sometimes allows one to abstract away from the presence of actual binders.

7.2 Realizing object-level substitution

Substitution for bound variables is germane to many computations involving syntax with bindings. Since equality in our logic includes β-conversion, we have an immediate and elegant approach to performing substitutions into such syntactic expressions. We provide examples to illustrate this observation in this section.

A common operation on quantified formulas is that of instantiation. Thus, given the formula $\forall x (p\ x \supset \exists y (q\ x\ y))$ and a term t, we might want to construct the formula that results from instantiating the top-level quantifier with t; this formula is what we often write as $(p\ x \supset \exists y (q\ x\ y))[t/x]$. Given our representation of formulas, such a substitution can be effected simply by constructing a suitable application. To see this, observe first that the formula being considered is represented by the term

```
all x\ p x ==> some y\ q x y
```

of type *form*. The application of the argument of *all* to the term (f a) of type *term* is given by the expression

```
(x\ p x ==> some y\ q x y) (f a)
```

of type form. By virtue of β-conversion, this term is equal to

```
p (h a) ==> some y\ q (f a) y.
```

This is what we expect to have as a result of carrying out the desired substitution.

This technique for instantiating bound variables can be used within logic programs: The following clauses specify the predicate `list_instan` that relates a list of $n \geq 0$ terms and an object-level formula with at least n outer most universal quantifiers with the result of instantiating the first n of the quantifiers with the corresponding terms in the list.

```
type list_instan      list term -> form -> form -> o.
list_instan nil B B.
list_instan (T::Ts) (all B) C :- list_instan Ts (B T) C.
```

The head of the second clause for `list_instan` has the expression (all B), which, using η-conversion, is equal to (all x\ B x). The body of this clause contains the expression (B T), which, as we have just seen, is equal to the result of substituting T for x in the expression B x. Thus the substitution for a bound variable is realized simply by writing down (B T).

As another example, consider the interpreter for object-level Horn clauses shown in Figure 7.1. The predicate `interp` defined here relates the encoding of a program to that of a goal just in the case that the latter is derivable from the former. The declarations in Figure 7.2 that define a predicate `prog` show how programs are encoded in this context; here, Horn clauses describe a small graph via its adjacency relation and also define the path relation over graphs. One case to focus on in the definition of `interp` is the treatment of existentially

```
type interp      form -> form -> o.
type backchain   form -> form -> form -> o.
type atom        form -> o.

interp D tt.
interp D (G1 && G2)  :- interp D G1, interp D G2.
interp D (G1 !! G2)  :- interp D G1; interp D G2.
interp D (some   G)  :- interp D (G X).
interp D A           :- atom A, backchain D D A.
backchain D A A.
backchain D (D1 && D2) A   :- backchain D D1 A; backchain D D2 A.
backchain D (all D1) A     :- backchain D (D1 X) A.
backchain D (G ==> D1) A   :- backchain D D1 A, interp D G.
```

Figure 7.1. An interpreter for *fohc* written in *hohc*.

```
type a, b, c      term.
type adj, path    term -> term -> form.
type prog         form -> o.

atom (adj _ _) & atom (path _ _).
prog ((adj a b) && (adj b c) &&
      (all x\ all y\ (adj x y) ==> (path x y)) &&
      (all x\ all y\ all z\ (adj x y) && (path y z) ==>
                                          (path x z))).
```

Figure 7.2. Encoding of a sample object-level *fohc* program.

```
type cbn, cbv     tm -> tm -> o.

cbn (abs R) (abs R).
cbn (app M N) V :- cbn M (abs R), cbn (R N) V.

cbv (abs R) (abs R).
cbv (app M N) V :- cbv M (abs R), cbv N U, cbv (R U) V.
```

Figure 7.3. Encodings of call-by-name and call-by-value evaluation for the untyped λ-calculus.

quantified goals represented by expressions of the form (some G). Such quanti-fiers are instantiated by forming the expression (G X). A similar computation is generated by the definition of backchain for instantiating universal quantifiers in program clauses that are given by expressions of the form (all D1). The def-inition of interp also makes use of the atom predicate to recognize encodings of atomic formulas. This predicate is defined by identifying all the predicate constants in the object logic. The query

```
?- prog P, interp P (path a X).
```

asks for nodes to which there is a path from a in the given graph. The two answer substitutions that will be produced bind X to b and then to c.

It is an easy matter to specify evaluation for the untyped λ-calculus by using β-reduction. For example, the declarations in Figure 7.3 define the predicate cbn, for call-by-name evaluation, and the predicate cbv, for call-by-value eval-uation. Under both evaluation schemes, an abstraction evaluates to itself. When given the application represented by (app M N), both evaluators compute the value of M, expecting back an abstraction given by (abs R). That abstraction is instantiated with N in the call-by-name evaluator and by the value of N (i.e., the term U such that eval N U is provable) in the call-by-value evaluator. The resulting expression then is evaluated to compute the value of the original application term.

Notice that (the representation of) the term $(\lambda x\ (x\ x))\ (\lambda x\ (x\ x))$ will be associated with no value by either of these predicates because it will lead to an infinite search for a derivation. On the other hand, the call-by-name evaluator will terminate with a value when given (the representation of) the term $(\lambda x\ \lambda w\ w)((\lambda x\ (x\ x))\ (\lambda x\ (x\ x)))$, whereas the call-by-value evaluator will not terminate (because it will require a value to be computed for $(\lambda x\ (x\ x))\ (\lambda x\ (x\ x)))$. More specifically, given the query

```
?- cbn (app (abs x\ abs w\w) (app (abs x\ app x x) (abs x\ app x x))) V.
```

the binding (abs w\w) will be produced for V, whereas the query

```
?- cbv (app (abs x\ abs w\w) (app (abs x\ app x x) (abs x\ app x x))) V.
```

will result in an infinite search.

The various specifications in this section are succinct and declarative because all the details regarding object-level bound variables and object-level substitution has been relegated to the meta-level. Notice, however, that these specifications still are formal and precise: The details regarding object-level syntax have not gone away; they simply have become the burden of an implementation of a metalogic such as λProlog. The benefit of this approach is that a programmer using λProlog is relieved of dealing with the details behind such "concrete nonsense" as binder names, capture avoiding substitutions, etc. and can focus instead on the really meaningful aspects of computation.

7.3 Mobility of binders

A commonly accepted principle concerning equality between syntactic expressions is the following: If one decomposes two equal expressions into their subcomponents, then corresponding subparts also should be equal. For example, if we are given two nonempty lists that are equal, the heads and tails of these lists should be equal as well. If we apply this principle to λ-terms, it leads to the natural conclusion that we should not be able to decompose an abstraction into the variable that it binds and its body. For example, while the terms (all x\ some y\ p x ==> p y) and (all z\ some y\ p z ==> p y) are equal, the names x and z are not equal, and hence these by themselves should not be meaningful subparts of the given terms. Similarly, the bodies of the outermost abstractions, namely,

(some y\ p x ==> p y)   and   (some y\ p z ==> p y)

are also not equal. Such decompositions, in fact, have no logical status within the *hohh* language: Because equality includes α-conversion, the name for a bound variable is a fiction, and an implementation may not represent it at all.

The recursive manipulation of data objects with binding structure eventually requires a descent into the body of a binding. There is actually a rather elegant approach to realizing this in the higher-order logic programming context that exploits *mobility* among three different kinds of bindings. In particular, this approach uses the fact that during proof search, a *term-level* binding (i.e., a λ-abstraction) can be converted into a *formula-level* binding (i.e., a quantifier), which then can be converted into a *proof-level* binding (i.e., an eigenvariable). To illustrate such mobility, let us consider the problem of defining a predicate term of type tm -> o in λProlog such that it identifies expressions that are of type tm. Relying on the existing typing discipline, such a predicate can be defined simply by the following declarations:

```
type  term   tm -> o.
term T.
```

That is, type checking would enforce that the argument given to term is of type tm. Another, more flexible way to define this predicate is to reflect the structure of terms of type tm into program clauses. As described in Section 7.1.2, the type tm has two constructors given by the declarations

```
type   app   tm -> (tm -> tm).
type   abs   (tm -> tm) -> tm.
```

As a result, the term predicate can be defined by two clauses, one for each constructor. These clauses, written in a form that makes their logical content clear, would be

```
pi M\ term M => pi N\ term N => term (app M N).
pi R\ (pi x\ term x => term (R x)) => term (abs R).
```

We could have written these clauses equivalently as

```
term (app M N) :- term M, term N.
term (abs R)   :- pi x\ term x => term (R x).
```

To understand how the second definition gives rise to a mobility of binders, consider the attempt to derive the goal

```
?- (term (abs y\ app y y)).
```

This leads to an attempt to prove the goal

```
?- pi x\ term x => term ((y\ app y y) x).
```

which is equal (via β-conversion) to the goal

```
?- pi x\ term x => term (app x x).
```

This goal-reduction step, in effect, moves the term-level binder for y in the original query to the formula-level binder for x in the second query; the actual move takes place via the reduction of ((y\ app y y) x) to (app x x) that leads to a term-level bound variable being replaced by a formula-level bound variable. At this stage, the usual operational semantics of a universally quantified goal causes the formula-level binding to move to a proof-level binding via the introduction of an eigenvariable. In particular, to derive the new universally quantified goal, a new eigenvariable, say, c, is introduced, and an attempt is made to solve the query

```
?- term (app c c).
```

from a program that has been augmented with the atomic clause (term c). This reduction step evidently involves substituting a proof-level (implicitly) bound variable c for a formula-level bound variable x. Since this final goal clearly succeeds, the original goal has been established.

The preceding example illustrates an important programming idiom for the *hohh* language that can be summarized as follows:

> In order to continue a recursive analysis within the scope of a binder, first, apply that binder to a universal quantified goal variable, for which the metalogic will substitute an eigenvariable, and second, using an implicational goal, assume new clauses that extend the definition of various predicates so that they can deal with the presence of this new eigenvariable.

In the example considered, the first step is achieved by applying (y\ app y y) to the universally quantified variable x, which an interpreter will replace with an eigenvariable such as c, and the second step is achieved by assuming the clause (term c). It is in this way that the abstraction (y\ app y y) is decomposed into a (proof-level) binding c and the term (app c c).

7.4 Computing with untyped λ-terms

We consider a varied set of computations involving untyped λ-terms in this section and use these to show how binder mobility can be used to realize recursion over abstraction structure.

7.4.1 Computing normal forms

An untyped λ-term is in β-normal form if it does not contain any β-redexes. An equivalent, positive definition is the following: An untyped λ-term is in this form if it has the structure $\lambda x_1 \ldots \lambda x_n \, (v \, t_1 \ldots t_m)$, where n and m are nonnegative integers, v is a variable, and for each $i = 1, \ldots, m$, t_i is in β-normal form. The term of the form $v \, t_1 \ldots t_m$ in this context will be said to be *β-body-normal*.

This second definition translates easily into the following logic program:

```
type bnorm, bbnorm  tm -> o.

bnorm (abs M)      :- pi x\ bbnorm x => bnorm (M x).
bnorm H            :- bbnorm H.
bbnorm (app M N) :- bbnorm M, bnorm N.
```

Here, bnorm recognizes β-normal terms, and bbnorm recognizes β-body-normal terms.

If we accept this specification of β-normal forms, then the correspondence between goal-directed search and intuitionistic provability gives us a substitution lemma "for free." Assume that from this specification and a collection of assumptions Γ of the form

$$\{\text{bbnorm } c_1, \ldots, \text{bbnorm } c_n\}, \qquad (n \geq 0)$$

we can derive the goals (bnorm (abs R)) and (bbnorm S). Since derivability is based on intuitionistic logic, it must be the case that (pi x\ bbnorm x => bnorm (R x)) is provable and, by instantiating the quantifier in this formula with S and using modus ponens, (bnorm (R S)) must be provable. Thus, if an abstraction $\lambda x\, t$ is β-normal and s is β-body-normal, then the substitution $t[s/x]$ must be β-normal.

The specification in Figure 7.4 can be used to compute β-normal forms. The predicate redex relates β-redexes to their one-step reduction. The predicate red1 relates two terms if the second is the result of replacing exactly one redex somewhere in the first term. The predicate reduce relates two terms if the second is the β-normal form of the first. This predicate uses the bnorm predicate to decide whether or not to carry out an additional reduction. A second implementation of this predicate, called reduce', is also defined in Figure 7.4. Viewed procedurally, reduce' computes the reduction by using a looping computation realized through the higher-order predicate repeat that results in the predicate red1 being called repeatedly until it no longer succeeds. Notice that the definition of repeat' uses the predicate ! to prune away alternative solutions to the parent goal.

There is a natural relationship between our encoding of the untyped λ-calculus and a common approach to describing models for this calculus. This approach to semantics is based on providing a suitable domain D, an associated notion of the function space $[D \to D]$, and two mappings $f : D \to [D \to D]$ and $g : [D \to D] \to D$. The correspondence to our encoding of the untyped λ-calculus is the following: The domain D corresponds to the type tm, and the constructors app and abs correspond to f and g, respectively. The analogy can be extended a bit further. The semantic equality captured by the redex rule

```
type redex, red1, reduce  tm -> tm -> o.

redex (app (abs R) N) (R N).
red1 M N :- redex M N.
red1 (app M N) (app P N) & red1 (app N M) (app N P) :- red1 M P.
red1 (abs M) (abs N) :- pi x\ red1 (M x) (N x).

reduce M M :- bnorm M.
reduce M N :- red1 M P, reduce P N.

type repeat   (A -> A -> o) -> A -> A -> o.
type reduce'  tm -> tm -> o.

repeat Pred M N :- Pred M P, !, repeat Pred P N.
repeat Pred M M.

reduce' M N :- repeat red1 M N.
```

Figure 7.4. Specifying reduction to β-normal form.

for β-reduction (Figure 7.4) can be understood as stating that for all values $R \in [D \to D]$ and $N \in D$, $(f\ (g\ R)\ N) = (R\ N)$ or $((f \circ g)\ R)\ N = R\ N$ or, in other words, $(f \circ g)\ R = R$. Similarly, the semantic equality captured by the `redex` rule

```
redex (abs x\ app M x) M.
```

for η-reduction can be interpreted as saying that for all values $M \in D$, $(g\ (\lambda x\ (f\ M\ x))) = M$ or, in other words, $(g \circ f)\ M = M$. Thus these two redexes essentially state that $f \circ g$ is the identity mapping on $[D \to D]$ and $g \circ f$ is the identity mapping on D. These are the familiar properties stating that f and g are, in fact, retracts. Since there are strong parallels between the syntax used to encode the untyped λ-calculus and their semantical models, one should expect that formal properties of *hohh* programs that manipulate the untyped λ-calculus often would be easy to state and prove.

7.4.2 Reduction based on paths through terms

In this section we present a different way of computing β-normal forms that is based on the idea of a path through an untyped λ-term. Intuitively, a path is obtained by moving from the top of the term to a variable occurrence in it as follows: When we encounter an abstraction, we simply pass through it, whereas when we encounter an application, we choose to move either through its left argument or through its right argument. The following code introduces a type for paths, three constants for constructing them, and the predicate `path` that relates a term to each one of its paths:

```
kind path type.
type bnd            (path -> path) -> path.
type left, right    path -> path.
type path           tm -> path -> o.
```

```
path (app M _) (left P) &
path (app _ M) (right P) :- path M P.
path (abs R) (bnd S) :- pi x\ pi p\ path x p => path (R x) (S p).
```

From these definitions, it should be easy to see that the following three paths are associated with the term (abs x\ app x (abs y\ app y x)):

```
bnd u\ left u
bnd u\ right (bnd v\ left v)
bnd u\ right (bnd v\ right u)
```

It is also possible to think of this relationship in the converse direction: Given a list of paths, one can identify a λ-term that has these paths. We can, in fact, use the foreach predicate defined in Section 5.3 to pose a query that exhibits this behavior:

```
?- foreach (path N)
            ((bnd u\ left u) ::
             (bnd u\ right (bnd v\ left v))::
             (bnd u\ right (bnd v\ right u))::nil).
N = abs W1\ app W1 (abs W2\ app W2 W1);
no
```

```
?-
```

A more interesting notion of a path through a term is one that does something different when encountering a β-redex (app (abs R) N): In particular, a path through this term proceeds through the body of the abstraction R, and if the bound variable of that abstraction is encountered in this process, then the path gets redirected to N. This changed idea of a path allows for an exploration of the effect of reducing the β-redexes in a term a little bit at a time.

Suppose now that we do not explore all β-redexes in this way but only specially marked ones. Let us represent the marked redexes by representing them as (beta N R) rather than as (app (abs R) N), where beta is a new constructor for type tm. Figure 7.5 contains a generalization of the path predicate, called bpath, that explores these specially marked β-redexes in the manner just described. If we wish to explore *all* β-redexes in a given term in this way, we can use the predicate addbeta to mark them all in this way at the outset.

```
type beta              tm -> (tm -> tm) -> tm.
type addbeta           tm -> tm -> o.
type bpath             tm -> path -> o.

bpath (app M _) (left P)  &
bpath (app _ M) (right P) :- bpath M P.
bpath (abs R)   (bnd S)   :- pi x\ pi p\ bpath x p =>
                                         bpath (R x) (S p).
bpath (beta N R) P :-
  pi x\ (pi Q\ bpath x Q :- bpath N Q) => bpath (R x) P.

addbeta (app (abs R) N) (beta M S) :- addbeta (abs R) (abs S),
                                       addbeta N M.
addbeta (app (app M N) P) (app O Q) :- addbeta (app M N) O,
                                        addbeta P Q.
addbeta (abs R) (abs S) :-
  pi x\ (pi M\ pi N\ addbeta (app x M) (app x N) :- addbeta M N) =>
        (addbeta x x) => addbeta (R x) (S x).
```

Figure 7.5. Realizing β-reductions using paths.

Suppose now that we want to contract all the marked β-redexes in a given term. We can do this by first producing a list of paths (in the extended sense) in that term by using the bpath predicate and then synthesizing a new term with those paths using the path predicate. An interaction illustrating this possibility is the following:

```
?- sigma B\ addbeta (app (abs x\x) (abs x\x)) B, bpath B Path.
Path = bnd W1\ W1;
no

?- foreach (P\ path T P) (bnd (W1\ W1) :: nil).
T = abs W1\ W1;
no

?-
```

Here, the synthesis of a term was particularly simple. The next example is slightly more complicated and involves the untyped λ-term $(K(SK))$, for the usual combinators K (i.e., $\lambda x \, \lambda y \, x$) and S (i.e., $\lambda x \, \lambda y \, \lambda z \, (xz)(yz)$). The query

```
?- sigma K\ sigma S\ sigma B\  K = (abs x\ abs y\ x),
   S = (abs x\ abs y\ abs z\ app (app x z) (app y z)),
   addbeta (app K (app S K)) B, bpath B Path.
```

first marks all β-redexes in this term, after which bpath computes four paths through it. Collecting these four paths into a list allows us to partially normalize this term.

```
?- foreach (path T)
    ((bnd W1\ bnd W2\ bnd W3\ left (left (bnd W4\ bnd W5\ W4)))::
     (bnd W1\ bnd W2\ bnd W3\ left (right W3))::
     (bnd W1\ bnd W2\ bnd W3\ right (left W2))::
     (bnd W1\ bnd W2\ bnd W3\ right (right W3))::nil).
T = abs W1\ abs W2\ abs W3\
        app (app (abs W4\ abs W5\ W4) W3) (app W2 W3);
no

?-
```

The resulting term, namely, $\lambda w_1\, \lambda w_2\, \lambda w_3\, (((\lambda w_4\, \lambda w_5\, w_4)\, w_3)\, (w_2\, w_3))$, is not in β-normal form. However, we can iterate this process, marking more β-redexes in this term, generating all the bpaths in the resulting term, collecting these paths into a list, and synthesizing a term containing those paths. Since we are dealing with the untyped λ-calculus, this iterative process may not terminate, but if it does, it will yield a β-normal form.

In the description of the β-normalization procedure using paths, there is one step that is difficult to formalize using the logic programming paradigm described here, namely, the step that collects all paths into a list so that the foreach predicate can be applied to them. Turning a series of answers into a single list is not formally possible in the simple proof-theoretic framework that we have described here. Some versions of Prolog come equipped with a bagof operator that does exactly this. If a logic programming implementation comes with a persistent memory, such as a database of facts or a file system, then it is possible to realize a form of the bagof operator.

7.4.3 Type inference

Consider the following declaration of a datatype for object-level simple types and the specification of a predicate that relates an (object-level) term with an (object-level) simple type.

```
kind ty type.
type arr      ty -> ty -> ty.
type typeof   tm -> ty -> o.

typeof (app M N) A :- typeof M (arr B A), typeof N B.
typeof (abs M) (arr A B) :- pi x\ typeof x A => typeof (M x) B.
```

Based on this specification, we can have the following interaction:

```
?- typeof (abs x\ abs y\ abs z\ app (app x z) (app y z)) Ty.
Ty = arr (arr T1 (arr T2 T3)) (arr (arr T1 T2) (arr T1 T3))

?- typeof (abs x\x) Ty.
Ty = arr T1 T1

?- typeof (abs x\ app x x) Ty.
no

?-
```

Interpreting this interaction, the λ-term $\lambda x\, \lambda y\, \lambda z\,((x\ z)\ (y\ z))$ is given the (polymorphic) type $(\alpha \rightarrow \beta \rightarrow \gamma) \rightarrow (\alpha \rightarrow \beta) \rightarrow (\alpha \rightarrow \gamma)$, the term $\lambda x\, x$ is given the type $\alpha \rightarrow \alpha$, and the term $\lambda x\,(x\ x)$ cannot be assigned a type. Since the only constructor here for type ty is arr (for the functional arrow type constructor), there are no closed terms of type ty: Thus, only open expressions can be reported by λProlog for inferred types. Of course, if we add more constructors to the datatype ty, we can work with closed expressions for object-level types. For example, if i is declared to be a constant of type ty, then the following queries are derivable:

```
?- typeof (abs x\x) (arr i i).
yes

?- typeof (abs x\x) (arr i Ty).
Ty = i

?-
```

Now that we have a specification of evaluation and of typing for untyped λ-terms, it is natural to consider the *subject-reduction theorem* (also called the *type-preservation theorem*), which states that if a program P has a given type T and this program evaluates to V, then V also has type T. Given the high-level nature of our specifications and their connection to intuitionistic logic, this kind of metatheorem can be proved easily. We show below how this might be done for the call-by-name evaluation scheme formalized in Figure 7.3. The result also holds for the call-by-value evaluation scheme, but we leave the detailed proof of this to the reader.

We prove by induction on the derivation of the goal (cbn P V) that if (typeof P A) is derivable, then (typeof V A) is derivable. The base case corresponds to (cbn P V) being derived by using the first clause for cbn. In this case, P and V are equal, and the result is immediate. If, on the other hand, the second clause for cbn is used to construct this derivation, then P has the form (app M N), and we have shorter derivations of (cbn M (abs R)) and (cbn (R N) V). Since the goal (typeof (app M N) A) is derivable, it must be the case that there is a type B such that (typeof M (arr B A)) and (typeof N B) are derivable. Using the induction hypothesis, we conclude that (typeof (abs R) (arr B A)) is derivable, and hence it must be the case that the formula (pi x\ typeof x B => typeof (R x) A) is derivable. Invoking the correspondence to intuitionistic provability now to instantiate the universal quantifier in this last formula with N and then using modus ponens, we have that (typeof (R N) A) is derivable. Finally, using the induction hypothesis again, we can conclude that (typeof V A) is provable.

The proof just provided involved a straightforward induction. The hard technical part in such a proof is establishing a *substitution lemma*: In this case, given that an abstraction $\lambda x.R$ has type $\beta \to \alpha$ and that N has type β, one must show that the result of the substitution $R[N/x]$ has type α. Often establishing such a substitution lemma requires a challenging additional proof. Here, that substitution lemma is obtained essentially for free by referring to well-known properties of intuitionistic logic.

7.4.4 Translating to and from de Bruijn syntax

A popular representation of binding in implementations of the λ-calculus uses *de Bruijn numerals* or *nameless dummies*. In this representation, variables are encoded not by names but by positive integers. A variable represented by the number n is bound by the nth abstraction above it. A few examples of untyped λ-terms and their corresponding representation in de Bruijn style are given below:

$\lambda x\, x$	$\lambda 1$
$\lambda x\, (x\, x)$	$\lambda(1\ 1)$
$\lambda x\, \lambda y\, x$	$\lambda\lambda 2$
$\lambda x\, \lambda y\, y$	$\lambda\lambda 1$
$\lambda x\, \lambda y\, (y\, x)$	$\lambda\lambda(1\ 2)$
$\lambda x\, \lambda y\, \lambda z\, ((x\, z)\, (y\, z))$	$\lambda\lambda\lambda((3\ 1)(2\ 1))$
$\lambda x\, (x\, (\lambda y\, x))$	$\lambda(1\ \lambda 2)$
$\lambda x\, (x\, (\lambda y\, (x\, (\lambda w\, (w\, x)))))$	$\lambda(1\ (\lambda(2\ (\lambda(1\ 3)))))$

Notice that in the last two examples, the variable x has more than one occurrence, and because each of these occurrences is in the scope of a different number of abstractions, it is translated to a different number.

To encode this style of syntax for λ-terms, we introduce a new type (for the new syntactic category of "de Bruijn" terms) and introduce three constructors for it: one for abstraction, one for application, and one for embedding integers into the syntax.

```
kind deb      type.
type ab       deb -> deb.
type ap       deb -> deb -> deb.
type deb      int -> deb.
```

A predicate `trans` that translates between terms of type `tm` and `deb` is given by the following declarations:

```
type trans    int -> tm -> deb -> o.
type depth    int -> tm -> o.

trans D (abs M)   (ab P)   :- pi c\ depth D c =>
                                     (E is D + 1, trans E (M c) P).
trans D (app M N) (ap P Q) :- trans D M P, trans D N Q.
trans D X         (deb E)  :- depth N X, E is (D - N).
```

This example makes use of the special "built-in" predicate `is`, which, as explained previously, forces an (arithmetic) evaluation of its right argument and unifies the resulting value with its left argument. Now, the given specification supports the following interaction:

```
?- trans 1 (abs x\ app x (abs y\ app x (abs w\ app w x))) D.
D = ab (ap (deb 1) (ab (ap (deb 2) (ab (ap (deb 1) (deb 3))))))

?- trans 1 P
   (ab (ap (deb 1) (ab (ap (deb 2) (ab (ap (deb 1) (deb 3))))))).
P = abs W1\ app W1 (abs W2\ app W1 (abs W3\ app W3 W1))

?-
```

To see how this predicate computes in detail, consider attempting to solve the query

```
?- trans 1 (abs x\ abs y\ abs z\ y) P.
```

This leads to the substitution of (ab P1) for P and to the addition of depth c 1 (for some eigenvariable c) to the program before attempting the next subgoal:

```
?- trans 2 (abs y\ abs z\ y) P1.
```

In a similar fashion, this query will lead to the substitution of (ab P2) for P1 and to the additional assumption depth d 2 (for some eigenvariable d) before attempting the next (internal) query:

```
?- trans 3 (abs z\ d) P2.
```

Finally, this query will lead to the substitution of (ab P3) for P2 and to the additional assumption depth e 3 (for some eigenvariable e) before attempting the next (internal) query:

```
?- trans 4 d P3.
```

At this point, only the third clause for trans can be applied, yielding the substitution of (deb E) for P3 and the next query

```
?- depth N d, E is (4 - N).
```

Using the second assumption that was added to the program, N gets bound to 2 and E gets bound to the result of evaluating $4 - 2$, i.e., to 2. Thus the final answer substitution for the entire computation is the instantiation of P with (ab (ab (ab (deb 2)))).

It is possible to organize this same computation differently by dropping the additional auxiliary predicate depth and adding extensions to the main translation predicate directly. In particular, consider the following clauses:

```
trans D (app M N) (ap P Q) :- trans D M P, trans D N Q.
trans D (abs M)    (ab P)   :-  pi u\
   (pi N\ pi H\ trans N u (deb H) :- H is (N - D))
                          => (D' is D + 1, trans D' (M u) P).
```

This program starts out with just two clauses for trans: No clause is present for the general "variable" case. As the computation proceeds, additional clauses are added for trans in order to treat particular eigenvariables as they are generated. Attempting to solve the query

```
?- trans 1 (abs x\ abs y\ abs z\ y) P.
```

with this new specification leads to the assumption of the following three clauses for trans:

```
pi N\ pi H\ trans N c (deb H) :- H is (N - 1).
pi N\ pi H\ trans N d (deb H) :- H is (N - 2).
pi N\ pi H\ trans N e (deb H) :- H is (N - 3).
```

When the query

```
?- trans 4 d P3.
```

is called eventually, the second of these three assumed clauses will be used to finish the proof.

7.5 Computations over first-order formulas

We now illustrate the virtues of the λ-term based representation of first-order formulas by considering several different computations that one may want to perform over these formulas. The predicate vacuous, defined in Figure 7.6, can be used to recognize and drop vacuous quantifiers in such formulas. This predicate succeeds exactly when the top-level abstracted variable *does not* appear in the body of the formula and, in this case, binds the second argument to the body. The same figure shows the definition of the predicate quantfree, which succeeds on an object-level formula just in the case that that formula does not contain quantifiers. This definition uses the predicate atom, whose definition is constructed from the predicates of the object logic: See the discussion in Section 7.2 and an example definition in Figure 7.2.

To consider a more complicated example, suppose that we are interested in transforming formulas into normal forms that are useful in the implementation of theorem provers for classical logic. One such normal form is the *negation normal form*: Such a formula contains no occurrences of implications, and all occurrences of negation have only atomic scope. Another normal form is the *prenex normal form*. A formula has this form if no quantifier occurrence in it is in the scope of a logical connective; i.e., all the quantifiers occur at the outermost level. It is a theorem of first-order classical logic that every formula is equivalent to one in negation normal form and also to one in prenex normal form and hence to one that is in both negation normal and prenex normal form.

The following classical logic equivalences are useful in transforming any given formula into a negation normal form:

$$
\begin{array}{rclrcl}
\neg\neg B & \equiv & B & B_1 \supset B_2 & \equiv & \neg B_1 \vee B_2 \\
\neg\forall x\, B\, x & \equiv & \exists x\, \neg B\, x & \neg(B_1 \wedge B_2) & \equiv & \neg B_1 \vee \neg B_2 \\
\neg\exists x\, B\, x & \equiv & \forall x\, \neg B\, x & \neg(B_1 \vee B_2) & \equiv & \neg B_1 \wedge \neg B_2
\end{array}
$$

These equivalences can be oriented from left to right and used as rewrite rules. The specification of the predicate nnf in Figure 7.7 uses this idea. Since no

```
type vacuous      form -> form -> o.
type quantfree    form -> o.

vacuous (all  x\ P) P.
vacuous (some x\ P) P.

quantfree tt & quantfree ff.
quantfree F :- atom F.
quantfree (neg F) :- quantfree F.
quantfree (F && G) & quantfree (F !! G) & quantfree (F ==> G) :-
  quantfree F, quantfree G.
```

Figure 7.6. Two predicates concerning object-level formulas.

```
type nnf    form -> form -> o.

nnf A A & nnf (neg A) (neg A)  :- atom A.
nnf (neg (neg B)) D            :- nnf B D.
nnf (neg (B && C)) (D !! E)    &
nnf (neg (B !! C)) (D && E)    :- nnf (neg B) D, nnf (neg C) E.
nnf (B ==> C) (D !! E)         :- nnf (neg B) D, nnf C E.
nnf (B !! C) (D !! E)          &
nnf (B && C) (D && E)          :- nnf B D, nnf C E.


nnf (neg (all B)) (some D) &
nnf (neg (some B)) (all D)  :- pi x\ nnf (neg (B x)) (D x).
nnf (all B) (all D)         &
nnf (some B) (some D)       :- pi x\ nnf (B x) (D x).
```

Figure 7.7. Relating a formula to an equivalent formula in negation normal form.

two heads of the clauses for nnf overlap, it is easy to see that the relation nnf
specifies a partial function. A simple argument by induction shows also that the
function represented is total.

Next, consider computing prenex normal forms of formulas that are in negation normal form (this restriction to negation normal forms is not necessary
and is used only to shorten the specification of this relation). The following
equivalences of classical logic provide the basis for the transformation process:

$$(\forall x\, B_1\, x) \wedge (\forall x\, B_2\, x) \equiv \forall x\, (B_1\, x \wedge B_2\, x) \qquad (\exists x\, B_1\, x) \vee (\exists x\, B_2\, x) \equiv \exists x\, (B_1\, x \vee B_2\, x)$$

$$B_1 \wedge (\forall x\, B_2\, x) \quad \equiv \quad \forall x\, (B_1 \wedge B_2\, x) \qquad (\forall x\, B_2\, x) \wedge B_1 \quad \equiv \quad \forall x\, (B_2\, x \wedge B_1)$$

$$B_1 \wedge (\exists x\, B_2\, x) \quad \equiv \quad \exists x\, (B_1 \wedge B_2\, x) \qquad (\exists x\, B_2\, x) \wedge B_1 \quad \equiv \quad \exists x\, (B_2\, x \wedge B_1)$$

$$B_1 \vee (\forall x\, B_2\, x) \quad \equiv \quad \forall x\, (B_1 \vee B_2\, x) \qquad (\forall x\, B_2\, x) \vee B_1 \quad \equiv \quad \forall x\, (B_2\, x \vee B_1)$$

$$B_1 \vee (\exists x\, B_2\, x) \quad \equiv \quad \exists x\, (B_1 \vee B_2\, x) \qquad (\exists x\, B_2\, x) \vee B_1 \quad \equiv \quad \exists x\, (B_2\, x \vee B_1)$$

Figure 7.8 contains the specification of a binary predicate prenex that relates
a negation normal formula to an equivalent formula in prenex normal form.
An auxiliary predicate is used in this definition to merge two formulas that are
already in prenex normal form. Given this specification of prenex, the unique
prenex normal form of the formula

```
(all x\ (p x) && (all y\ q x y) && (p (f x))) !! (p a).
```

is the formula

```
all x\ all y\ ((p x) && (q x y) && (p (f x))) !! (p a).
```

In general, the predicate prenex is not functional: That is, a single formula can
have multiple prenex normal forms to which it is equivalent using the shown
equivalences. For example, the query

```
?- prenex ((all x\ q x x) && (all z\ all y\ q z y)) P.
```

```
type  prenex, merge        form -> form -> o.

prenex A A & prenex (neg A) (neg A)   :- atom A.
prenex (B && C) D   :- prenex B U, prenex C V,
                       merge (U && V) D.
prenex (B !! C) D   :- prenex B U, prenex C V,
                       merge (U !! V) D.
prenex (all B)  (all D)   &
prenex (some B) (some D) :- pi x\ prenex (B x) (D x).

merge ((all  B) && (all C)) (all D) :-
  pi x\ merge ((B x) && (C x)) (D x).
merge ((all  B) && C) (all D) &
merge ((some B) && C) (some D) :-
  pi x\ merge ((B x) && C) (D x).
merge (B && (all  C)) (all D) &
merge (B && (some C)) (some D) :-
  pi x\ merge (B && (C x)) (D x).
merge ((some B) !! (some C)) (some D) :-
  pi x\ merge ((B x) !! (C x)) (D x).
merge ((some B) !! C) (some D) &
merge ((all B) !! C)  (all D) :-
  pi x\ merge ((B x) !! C) (D x).
merge (B !! (some C)) (some D) &
merge (B !! (all C))  (all D) :-
  pi x\ merge (B !! (C x)) (D x).

merge B B :- quantfree B.
```

Figure 7.8. Computing the prenex normal form of formulas in negation normal form.

will generate the following five answer substitutions for P:

```
all z\ all y\ (q z z) && (q z y)
all x\ all z\ all y\ (q x x) && (q z y)
all z\ all x\ (q x x) && (q z x)
all z\ all x\ all y\ (q x x) && (q z y)
all z\ all y\ all x\ (q x x) && (q z y)
```

As another example of a computation over first-order formulas, consider the problem of identifying which object-level formulas are goals or definition clauses for first-order Horn clauses and for first-order hereditary Harrop formulas. The clauses in Figure 7.9 specify four (meta-level) predicates that can make these determinations: fohcG and fohcD recognize goals and clauses within the first-order Horn clause setting, and fohhG and fohhD recognize goals and clauses within the first-order hereditary Harrop formula setting. These definitions need

```
type fohcG, fohcD, fohhG, fohhD   form -> o.

fohcG tt.
fohcG A              :- atom A.
fohcG (some B)       :- pi x\ fohcG (B x).
fohcG (B && C) & fohcG (B !! C) :- fohcG B, fohcG C.

fohcD A              :- atom A.
fohcD (G ==> D)      :- fohcG G, fohcD D.
fohcD (D1 && D2)     :- fohcD D1, fohcD D2.
fohcD (all D)        :- pi x\ fohcD (D x).

fohhG tt.
fohhG A              :- atom A.
fohhG (D ==> G) :- fohhD D, fohhG G.
fohhG (B && C) & fohhG (B !! C) :- fohhG B, fohhG C.
fohhG (some B) & fohhG (all B)   :- pi x\ fohhG (B x).

fohhD A              :- atom A.
fohhD (D1 && D2)  :- fohhD D1, fohhD D2.
fohhD (G ==> D)   :- fohhG G, fohhD D.
fohhD (all D)     :- pi x\ fohhD (D x).
```

Figure 7.9. Specifying various syntactic classes of object-level formulas.

a specification of the predicate `atom` that we have already discussed in earlier
examples. The code that appears in these definitions deviates a little from the
idiom discussed at the end of Section 7.3 in that the universally quantified goals
that they contain do not have implications immediately within their scope: Such
implications are not needed because the eigenvariables introduced by those universal quantifiers correspond to terms, and the `atom` predicate does not examine
the structure of terms.

Based on the specifications provided in Figure 7.9, we get substitution theorems of the following kind for free: If $\forall x\ D$ is a first-order Horn clause and t
is a term, then $D[t/x]$ is a first-order Horn clause.

Figure 7.1 presented an interpreter for first-order Horn clauses. It is easy
to extend that interpreter to all of first-order hereditary Harrop formulas: We
simply add the two clauses

```
interp D (D1 ==> G) :- interp (D1 && D) G.
interp D (all G) :- pi x\ interp D (G x).
```

Thus, just as object-level conjunction, disjunction, and existential quantification
in goals in the *fohc* language are handled by the corresponding meta-level logical primitives, universal quantifiers in goals of the *fohh* language are handled
by meta-level universal quantifiers.

7.6 Specifying object-level substitution

We have seen that object-level substitution can be specified using meta-level
β-reduction. Thus the predicate defined by

```
type   subst (tm -> tm) -> tm -> tm -> o.
subst R N (R N).
```

can be used to substitute into the body of an abstraction over untyped λ-terms.
As we have seen in Section 4.6, full β-conversion is a complex operation on
terms. We now consider a specification of object-level substitution that does
not use general β-reduction.

Figure 7.10 provides such a specification of the subst predicate based on
an auxiliary predicate copy. This copy predicate specifies equality between two
untyped λ-terms; that is, copy is a relation between two closed terms that is
derivable if and only if those terms are equal. To illustrate in detail how copy
works, consider finding a solution to the goal

```
?- copy (abs x\ abs y\ app y x) M.
```

Backchaining using the second clause for copy reduces this query to

```
?- copy (abs y\ app y c) (M1 c).
```

where c is a new eigenvariable, after M has been unified with (abs M1), and the
clause (copy c c) has been added to the current program. Backchaining again
on the same clause yields the subgoal

```
?- copy (app d c) (M2 d).
```

where d is another new eigenvariable, after (M1 c) has been unified with
(abs M2), and the clause (copy d d) has been added to the current program.
This last goal leads to three more backchainings, one each using the copy clauses
for app, c, and d. At the end of this sequence, (M2 d) must be unified with
(app d c). Solving for all the variables yields the unique answer substitution

```
M2 = u\app u c    M1 = v\abs u\app u v    M = abs v\abs u\app u v.
```

Thus the result of "copying" (abs x\ abs y\ app y x) is (abs v\ abs
u\ app u v); these two terms are obviously equal modulo α-conversion. Viewing the clauses for copy operationally, we can say that these clauses copy the
top-level constructor from, say, the first argument to the second argument and
use recursion for copying the subterms. Of course, if the immediate subformula
is of type tm -> tm instead of tm, then we need to use the principle of binder
mobility to deal with the subexpression that is of higher type.

```
type copy  tm -> tm -> o.
type subst (tm -> tm) -> tm -> tm -> o.

copy (app M N) (app P Q) :- copy M P, copy N Q.
copy (abs M)   (abs N)   :- pi x\ copy x x => copy (M x) (N x).

subst M T S :- pi x\ copy x T => copy (M x) S.
```

Figure 7.10. Specification of substitution into untyped λ-terms.

The substitution of a term T for the bound variable in the body of an abstraction M to produce S can be realized operationally by copying the structure of the body of M into S with the exception that the outermost abstracted variable is copied to T. The specification of subst follows this prescription: First, it converts the outermost abstracted variable of M into the variable x that is universally bound at the formula level; second, it assumes that that variable copies to T by augmenting the current program with the clause (copy x T); and finally, it calls the copy goal in the context of the augmented program to compute the result of "copying" (M x).

The structure of the definitions of the subst and copy predicates in Figure 7.10 gives us an easy way to argue that if (subst M T S) is derivable, then S is equal to the term (M T). If (subst M T S) is derivable, it must be the case that

```
pi x\ copy x T => copy (M x) S
```

is derivable. As observed earlier, copy relates two equal terms in the context of the *unaugmented* definition of copy. Thus it must be the case that (copy T T) is derivable. Instantiating the preceding universally quantified goal with T and using modus ponens implies that (copy (M T) S) is derivable from the unaugmented set of clauses for copy, which implies that (M T) is equal to S.

The substitution of terms for abstracted variables in first-order formulas can be specified in a similar fashion. Suppose, for example, that our first order logic has a set of nonlogical constants given by the following declarations:

```
type  a  term.
type  f  term -> term.
type  g  term -> term -> term.
type  p  term -> form.
type  q  term -> term -> form.
```

The specification of the subst and copy predicates in this case is given by the declarations in Figure 7.11. There are actually two versions of the copy predicate now, one for terms and another for formulas. It is interesting to observe that the clauses for these predicates can be derived from the identity relation

```
kind  term, form  type.

type  copyterm    term -> term -> o.
type  copyform    form -> form -> o.
type  subst       (term -> form) -> term -> form -> o.

copyterm a        a.
copyterm (f X)    (f U)        :- copyterm X U.
copyterm (g X Y)  (g U V)      :- copyterm X U, copyterm Y V.

copyform tt tt.
copyform ff ff.
copyform (neg B)   (neg D)     :- copyform B D.
copyform (B && C)  (D && E)    &
copyform (B !! C)  (D !! E)    &
copyform (B ==> C) (D ==> E)   :- copyform B D, copyform C E.
copyform (all B)   (all D)     &
copyform (some B)  (some D) :- pi y\ copyterm y y =>
                                    copyform (B y) (D y).

copyform (p X)    (p U)        :- copyterm X U.
copyform (q X Y)  (q U V)      :- copyterm X U, copyterm Y V.

subst M T N :- pi x\ copyterm x T => copyform (M x) N.
```

Figure 7.11. Specifying substitution for first-order formulas.

on constants essentially by a process of "lowering" the type on this relation. To describe this more precisely, let $[\![t, s : \tau]\!]^+$ and $[\![t, s : \tau]\!]^-$ represent formulas defined by recursion on the structure of the type τ (which, in the present context, is assumed to be built only from the base types term and form) in the following way:

$$[\![t, s : \texttt{term}]\!]^+ = [\![t, s : \texttt{term}]\!]^- = \qquad \texttt{copyterm } t\ s$$

$$[\![t, s : \texttt{form}]\!]^+ = [\![t, s : \texttt{form}]\!]^- = \qquad \texttt{copyform } t\ s$$

$$[\![t, s : \tau \ \rightarrow \ \sigma]\!]^+ = \ \forall x\, ([\![x, x : \tau]\!]^- \supset [\![t\ x, s\ x : \sigma]\!]^+)$$

$$[\![t, s : \tau \ \rightarrow \ \sigma]\!]^- = \forall x\, \forall y\, ([\![x, y : \tau]\!]^+ \supset [\![t\ x, s\ y : \sigma]\!]^-)$$

Using this definition, we see, for example, that $[\![\texttt{all}, \texttt{all} : (\texttt{term -> form}) \to \texttt{form}]\!]^-$ is equal to

$$\forall x\, \forall y\, ([\![x, y : \texttt{term -> form}]\!]^+ \supset [\![(\texttt{all } x), (\texttt{all } y) : \texttt{form}]\!]^-)$$

Expanding this further, we get the expression

$$\forall x\, \forall y\, ((\forall z\, [\![z, z : \texttt{term}]\!]^- \supset [\![(x\ z), (y\ z) : \texttt{form}]\!]^+)$$
$$\supset [\![(\texttt{all } x), (\texttt{all } y) : \texttt{form}]\!]^-)$$

Using the equality predicate at the atomic types, we finally get

$$\forall x \, \forall y \, (\forall z \, (\texttt{copyterm} \, z \, z \supset \texttt{copyform} \, (x \, z) \, (y \, z))$$

$$\supset \texttt{copyform} \, (\texttt{all} \, x) \, (\texttt{all} \, y))$$

This clause corresponds to the one shown for the constant `all` in Figure 7.11. In fact, the clauses in that figure are exactly the formulas $[\![c, c : \tau]\!]^-$ for each of the constants $c : \tau$ of the object logic.

As we have seen with the encoding of untyped λ-terms, it is a simple matter to show that (`copyterm T S`) is derivable from the specification in Figure 7.11 if and only if T and S are equal terms and that (`copyform B C`) is derivable if and only if B and C are equal formulas. Using these facts, we can see once again that if (`subst M T S`) is provable, then S is equal to (M T).

The specifications of the `copy` predicates we have just seen are examples of *signature-dependent* logic programs in the sense that the object-level signature is used explicitly in defining the `copy` and `subst` predicates. By contrast, the earlier one-line specification of `subst` that used β-reduction does not refer to the object-level signature.

The development of the definition of a relation or predicate by the device of lowering the relation to be defined at a higher type to a version at a lower type that is already defined is, in fact, quite general. We can imagine doing this for other types: In that case, each primitive type will need to map to a distinct predicate. Notice that the relation we are defining by this process is also not restricted to being one of arity two. To take a concrete example, the definition of `term` presented in Section 7.3 can be seen as the result of applying this technique to a predicate of arity one in a context where the signature contains just `abs` and `app`.

It is possible to specify object-level substitution by a direct recursion on the structure of expressions without using a `copy` predicate. The (signature dependent) clauses in Figure 7.12 provide such a specification.

The `subst` predicate, whether given by the code in Figure 7.10, Figure 7.11, or Figure 7.12, is relational and not functional. Thus, given a term T and a formula S, it is possible to compute an abstraction M such that (`subst M T S`) is derivable. For example, the query

```
?- subst M (f a) ((p (f a)) && (q a (f a))).
```

yields the following four answer substitutions:

```
M = x\ (p x) && (q a x)
M = x\ (p x) && (q a (f a))
M = x\ (p (f a)) && (q a x)
M = x\ (p (f a)) && (q a (f a))
```

```
type subst       (term -> form) -> term -> form -> o.
type substterm   (term -> term) -> term -> term -> o.


subst (x\ tt) T tt.
subst (x\ ff) T ff.
subst (x\ neg (B x))        T (neg D)    :- subst B T D.
subst (x\ (B x) && (C x))   T (D && E)   &
subst (x\ (B x) !!  (C x))  T (D !! E)   &
subst (x\ (B x) ==> (C x))  T (D ==> E)  :- subst B T D,
                                           subst C T E.
subst (x\ all  (B x))       T (all  D)   &
subst (x\ some (B x))       T (some D)   :-
   pi y\ substterm (x\y) T y => subst (x\ B x y) T (D y).


subst (x\ p (X x))          T (p U)      :- substterm X T U.
subst (x\ q (X x) (Y x)) T (q U V)  :- substterm X T U,
                                        substterm Y T V.


substterm (x\ x) T T.
substterm (x\ a) T a.
substterm (x\ f (F x)) T (f S) :- substterm F T S.
substterm (x\ g (F x) (G x)) T (g S R) :-  substterm F T S,
                                           substterm G T R.
```

Figure 7.12. Specification of substitution without using the auxiliary copy clauses.

Notice that such a nondeterministic computation is implied by the usual statement of the rule of *existential generalization*: If a formula $M(t)$ holds for some t, then $\exists x \, M(x)$ holds. As this example illustrates, if the expression $M(t)$ denotes the formula $p(f(a)) \wedge q(a, f(a))$, then there are four possible existential generalizations of this based on the term $f(a)$, namely, $\exists x \, p(x) \wedge q(a, x)$, $\exists x \, p(x) \wedge q(a, f(a))$, $\exists x \, p(f(a)) \wedge q(a, x)$, and $\exists x \, p(f(a)) \wedge q(a, f(a))$.

7.7 The λ-tree approach to abstract syntax

The term *concrete syntax* generally refers to the syntactic representation of expressions using text or strings. Concrete syntax is intended for interactions with humans, and as a result, it contains devices that help reading, such as white space (e.g., carriage returns and indentation), parentheses, infix operators, comments, multiple typefaces, etc. While all these devices can aid in human consumption, they generally obstruct the formal manipulation based on the meanings of expressions. In order to treat syntax in a way that corresponds more closely to its intended semantics, one generally parses concrete syntax into some form of *abstract syntax*. In particular, parsing returns a representation of syntax where infix and prefix distinctions of operators are removed, where white space and comments are discarded, and where the information provided by parentheses is reflected in a treelike representation within abstract syntax.

There are many alternatives for structuring abstract syntax. One possibility involves explicitly treating the names of bound variables present in concrete syntax. If the metalanguage supports abstraction directly, then one also might map binding in the concrete syntax into the corresponding device in the metalanguage. The syntactic representation that results from doing this is often called *higher-order abstract syntax* because abstraction mechanisms in metalanguages typically arise from explicit treatments of higher-orderness. The exact meaning of this term, however, depends on the specific computational context in which it is embedded: As a result, the term *higher-order abstract syntax* denotes a range of encoding techniques. To take a specific example, as was discussed in Section 5.10, there is a significant difference between the interpretation of λ-terms and abstraction in functional programming and in logic programming. In the former setting, as also in constructive type theories that use function evaluation to determine values of expressions, meta-level abstraction is used to build rich function spaces. Because of the richness of these spaces, it is not possible to compare function-valued expressions for equality in any simple way. If such expressions are used in the representation, for example, of first-order logic formulas with quantifiers, it follows that we cannot also compare or structurally analyze formulas under such an encoding. Most logic programming languages do not, in fact, have meta-level binders that can be used within expressions, so a higher-order approach to abstract syntax is not available within them. However, abstraction is available within the λ-terms of the logic we have considered here, and these can be used to encode binding in syntactic structures. This treatment of binding uses a λ-calculus with a weak notion of functionality that makes it possible to analyze the structures of objects under the encoding.

Clearly, the two extremes in the treatment of binding—one using functions that are best thought of extensionally and the other using λ-expressions that are easily treated intensionally—can differ significantly. We shall use the term *λ-tree syntax* to denote the approach to higher-order abstract syntax that uses typed λ-terms modulo equality based on α-conversion, some sufficiently weak form of β-conversion, and possibly η-conversion. Our treatment in this chapter of the abstract syntax of object-level logics and languages is an example of this approach; β-conversion is weakened in this context by the use of simple types. In the next section we identify a subset of *hohh* in which a much weaker version of β-conversion is needed for proof search.

7.8 The L_λ subset of λProlog

Now that we have identified λ-tree syntax as an approach to syntactic representation and manipulation that is supported by the *hohh* language and its implementation in λProlog, it is natural to ask if the full power of this language is needed to support this approach to syntax. This seems not to be the case. For example, while the predicate quantification of λProlog is probably useful for manipulating λ-tree syntax, it is certainly not central to it. Can anything else be removed? As we now will illustrate, it is possible to further weaken the role of β-reduction in computations on λ-tree syntax.

This chapter has discussed two important principles for carrying out computations over syntactic structures involving binding. First, such structures can be treated more abstractly by equating two terms if they are identical up to α-conversion: As a result, the names of bound variables become a fiction. Second, binders are permitted some mobility in the sense that during a computation, they can move from term level to formula level to proof level. The movement of formula-level binding (represented specifically by universally quantified variables in goals) to a proof-level binding (corresponding to eigenvariables) was discussed in Section 7.3. We discuss next a restricted form of the *hohh* language that still caters to the mobility of term-level binders to formula-level bindings.

Let G be a goal formula. We say that a bound variable occurrence in G is *essentially universal* if it is bound by a positive occurrence of a universal quantifier, by an negative occurrence of an existential quantifier, or by a (term-level) λ-abstraction. A bound variable occurrence is *essentially existential* if it is not essentially universal. To express this positively, an essentially existential bound variable occurrence in a goal formula is one that is bound by either a negative universal quantifier or a positive existential quantifier. Occurrences of bound variables in program clauses are classified by dualizing this definition. In particular, a bound variable occurrence in such a clause is *essentially universal* if it is bound by a negative occurrence of a universal quantifier, by a positive occurrence of an existential quantifier, or by a (term-level) λ-abstraction, and it is *essentially existential* if it is bound by either a positive universal quantifier or a negative existential quantifier. Within the context of proof search, it is essentially existential bound variables that can be instantiated with general terms (via logic variables and unification), whereas essentially universal bound variables can be instantiated only with eigenvariables. It is the essentially universal bound variable occurrences that provide mobility during proof search.

The logic programming language L_λ is the result of restricting *hohh* by requiring all quantification to be over nonpredicate types and by limiting essentially existential bound variable occurrences as follows: Each such occurrence may appear applied to at most distinct essentially universal variables, all whose binding scope is contained within the scope of the quantifier binding the essentially existential variable occurrence that is in question. Expressed in another way, a program clause or goal formula B is in the L_λ class if

Every subterm in B with an essentially existential variable occurrence as its head, that is, a subterm of the form $(x\ t_1 \ldots t_n)$ $(n \geq 0)$, where x is essentially existentially quantified in B, must be such that $t_1, \ldots, t_n$ are distinct essentially universal variable occurrences bound in the scope of x.

This restriction ensures that if x is ever instantiated by some term, say, t, then the only β-redexes that follow that substitution are of the form $(t\ y_1 \ldots y_n)$, where the variables $y_1, \ldots, y_n$ are not free in t. Using α- and η-conversions, we can assume that t is of the form $\lambda y_1 \ldots \lambda y_n\ t'$. Thus β-reduction simply transforms $(\lambda y_1 \ldots \lambda y_n\ t')\ y_1 \ldots y_n$ to t'.

Let β_0-conversion be that subcase of β-conversion that is expressed as the equation

$$(\lambda x\ s)\ x = s \quad (\beta_0)$$

In the presence of α-conversion, this is equivalent to the conditional equation

$$(\lambda y\ s)\ x = s[x/y], \qquad \text{provided } x \text{ is not free in } \lambda y\ s \quad (\beta_0)$$

Almost all hohh programs presented in this chapter have been examples of L_λ programs as well. In particular, all the program clauses in Figures 7.7 through 7.12 belong to L_λ. Further, there is exactly one clause in Figure 7.4 that does not belong to L_λ, and this is the redex clause: The subterm (R N) is an example of an essentially existential variable occurrence applied to a second essentially existential variable occurrence. Of course, not all hohh program clauses and goals are L_λ program clauses and goals, respectively. For example, if the constant p has type $i \to o$ and f has type $i \to i$, then the formula

$$\forall_{i \to i} x\ \forall_i y\ (p\ (x\ y) \supset p\ (f\ y))$$

is an example of a goal in L_λ but not a program clause. As a program clause, this formula has a subterm occurrence $(x\ y)$ where both x and y are essentially existential and thus does not satisfy the L_λ restriction on such variable occurrences.

An hohh program that is not an L_λ program often can be rewritten into an L_λ program. To illustrate this, let us consider the clause

```
redex (app (abs R) N) (R N).
```

from Figure 7.4, which is not an L_λ clause. If this clause is used as is, proof search may lead to β-conversions that are not also β_0-conversions. However, if we have access to the clauses in Figure 7.10, then we can rewrite this clause as

```
redex (app (abs R) N) S :- subst R N S.
```

If we do this, we obtain a specification that is entirely within L_λ.

The translation of *hohh* programs to L_λ programs just described is, however, not without problems. First, the encoding using suitable subst and copy predicates requires reflecting the signature of the terms into which one is substituting into program clauses using the $[\![t, s : \gamma]\!]^\pm$ translation described in Section 7.6. Second, the operational behavior of the copy predicate can be quite different from that of the equality notion it encodes. For example, if M and N are variables, the query

```
?-  M = N.
```

can be solved immediately with an answer substitution that binds M to N. In contrast, the call

```
?-  copy M N.
```

will attempt to actually build terms *t* using the clauses for copy recursively and, if successful, will bind both M and N to the *t* that is constructed. To see this more vividly, consider the following code where a small signature is encoded using copy clauses:

```
kind i  type.
type a  i.
type f  i -> i.
type copyi  i -> i -> o.

copyi a a.
copyi (f X) (f Y) :- copyi X Y.
```

The goal

```
?-  copyi M N.
```

will succeed by binding M and N successively to a, (f a), (f (f a)), etc. If the order of the clauses for copyi were reversed, then this query would cause the depth-first λProlog interpreter to loop without providing any solution.

The complexity of the reduction rules based on

$$(\lambda x\, M)\, N = M[N/x] \quad (\beta) \qquad \text{and} \qquad (\lambda x\, M)\, x = M \quad (\beta_0)$$

are vastly different. When moving from the left-hand term to the right-hand term of the β_0-equality, one abstraction and application pair disappears, and the resulting term is strictly smaller: In particular, no new β-redexes are introduced. In contrast, with the β rule, the right-hand side might be smaller (if, for example, the variable x is not free in M), or it might be significantly larger (if x has several occurrences in M and N has a complex structure), and furthermore, it may contain new β-redexes (if x occurs with arguments within M).

The complexity of β-conversion naturally suggests that unification modulo $\beta\eta$-conversion also may be complex. The simplicity of β_0-conversion similarly suggests that unification in L_λ could be significantly simpler. We shall see that these observations are indeed true in Chapter 8, where we consider these forms of unification in detail. In particular, we shall see that while unification modulo $\beta\eta$-conversion is undecidable and may admit multiple, most general unifiers, unification in L_λ is much more like first-order unification in that both are decidable, and if unifiers exist, a single unifier that is most general also exists. Thus, working within the L_λ subset could have a significant impact on the implementation of the overall language. From a programming perspective, this restriction may be acceptable because an overwhelming majority of clauses in "typical" λProlog programs are within the L_λ fragment of the $\hbar o\hbar\hbar$ language.

It is useful to observe that while all L_λ unification problems are instances of unification modulo α, β_0, and η, the converse is not true: For example, the problem of finding an instance of F such that $\forall x\,(F\,x\,x = x)$ is provable requires only β_0-reduction to justify the fact that the substitution of either $\lambda u\,\lambda v\,u$ or $\lambda u\,\lambda v\,v$ for F represents a solution. This latter unification problem is not in L_λ because the variable occurrence F is applied to two essentially universal occurrences of the *same* variable. While unification modulo α-, β_0-, and η-conversion is not as complex as unification modulo α-, β-, and η-conversion, it is also not *unitary* in the sense that more than one incomparable, most general unifier can exist for particular problems.

It is sometimes of interest in a computational setting to simplify quantifier alternations in goal formulas. For example, we may wish to transform the goal formula $\forall y\,\exists x\,G$ into the form $\exists h\,\forall y\,G[(h\,y)/x]$. We have seen how to do this in Section 4.4.1 using the technique of *raising*. An interesting observation is that this technique, which is employed often in implementations of the logic, is one that preserves the class of L_λ formulas.

7.9 Bibliographic notes

A major focus in this chapter has been on using the abstraction operator that is available with λ-terms to encode the varied forms of binding that are present in syntactic structures. This idea is an old one and dates back at least to Church (1940) and his presentation of the Simple Theory of Types. Church's logic has several binding operators, such as the quantifiers, the choice operator, and the definite description operator, all of which were encoded using λ-abstraction and a suitably chosen constant. That treatment of quantifiers is used in the various logics we have presented, and as we have already mentioned, the names pi and sigma in the λProlog syntax for the universal and existential quantifiers derive from the ones Church used for them. The first six axioms in the logic that Church described yield a higher-order logic that is similar to the one we have used; the main difference is that Church developed a classical logic, whereas we principally consider intuitionistic logic. Using just these six axioms, the equality notion over λ-terms is quite weak and is akin to our treating these terms in a rather intensional manner. Church's full system includes several more axioms, especially ones for extensionality, choice, infinity, and descriptions. This richer logic is well suited to the task of formalizing mathematics but supports an equality notion over λ-terms that makes it difficult to see them as the basis for λ-tree syntax.

Two early papers that describe computing directly with λ-tree syntax are those by Huet and Lang (1978) and Miller and Nadathur (1987). These papers argued that matching, unification, and proof search over simply typed λ-terms modulo the equality theory of α-, β-, and η-conversion provides novel, interesting, and declarative approaches to manipulating object-level syntax. Pfenning and Elliott (1988) used the term *higher-order abstract syntax* to describe an approach to syntax representation that used typed λ-terms modulo α-, β-, and η-conversion as well as containing polymorphic types and equalities for products. Shortly afterwards, however, it appears that the term *higher-order abstract syntax* came to denote the general principle of using a meta-level abstraction to encode binding structure in object-level syntax. While this is an accurate description of the kind of logic specifications presented in this chapter, this principle also can be considered in the functional programming setting, where the main abstraction mechanism is that of functions. In fact, higher-order abstract syntax frequently deals with identifying term-level abstractions with such functions (Despeyroux et al., 1995; Hofmann, 1999; Honsell et al., 2001; Röckl et al., 2001). As discussed in Section 7.7, the use of a rich notion of function to encode term-level λ-bindings can be problematic. In order to differentiate the approach to encoding syntax that is described here from the other "function-based" approach, the term *λ-tree syntax* was introduced (Miller and Palamidessi 1999; Miller 2000) for the brand of higher-order abstract syntax used here.

Several of the examples in this chapter have concerned the untyped λ-calculus. A good reference for various aspects of this well-studied calculus is the book by Barendregt (1984). The approach to λ-term syntax that avoids names and uses numerical indices for bound variable occurrences was developed by de Bruijn (1972). This kind of representation of λ-terms plays a significant role in recent work that allows substitutions over such terms to be represented directly in syntax; exemplars of such work are the calculus of *explicit substitutions* (Abadi et al., 1991) and the *suspension calculus* (Nadathur and Wilson 1990, 1998).

There are a number of alternatives to using λ-tree syntax to representing and manipulating bindings in syntax. For example, Pitts (2003, 2006) and Gabbay and Pitts (2001) have developed *nominal logic* as a first-order logic containing primitives for renaming via name swapping and for the freshness of names: The notion of binding can be derived from these primitives.

The idea of copy clauses to specify object-level substitution was first used at the second-order level by Miller (1991a). Felty (1991, 1992) extended that definition to arbitrary orders and also showed how to encode a dependently typed λ-calculus (Harper et al. 1993) into hereditary Harrop formulas. The recursive definition of subst that does not use copy-clauses (Figure 7.12) is loosely based on an equational presentation of λ-conversion (Andrews 1971, 1986).

An implementation of the hohh language eventually must treat unification of simply typed λ-terms (also known as *higher-order unification*). A study of the kinds of unification problems that arise typically in this setting led Miller (1989a, 1991b) to identify the L_λ subset of hohh. The restricted form of unification that is needed for proof search in L_λ is called L_λ-*unification* or, more commonly, *higher-order pattern unification* Nipkow (1993). Unification is discussed in greater detail in Chapter 8.

8

Unification of λ-Terms

The computations that arise in the course of proof search with higher-order logic programs often require finding substitutions for essentially existentially quantified variables that make two different terms λ-convertible. In Chapter 4 we characterized such higher-order unification problems using a mixed quantifier prefix over a "matrix" involving a conjunction of equations. Specifically, unification problems are formulas of the form

$$Q_1 x_1 \ \ldots \ Q_n x_n \ [t_1 = s_1 \wedge \ldots \wedge t_m = s_m]$$

where $n, m \geq 0$, Q_i is either $\forall$ or $\exists$ for $1 \leq i \leq n$ and $t_1, s_1, \ldots, t_m, s_m$ are λ-terms such that, for $1 \leq j \leq m$, t_j and s_j are of the same type. In Chapter 4 we made a distinction between the notion of a unifier and a solution to a unification problem in this general form: Only the latter checks for the existence of closed terms and therefore embodies an actual proof of the quantified formula. Following common practice, we will limit ourselves in this chapter to the simpler task of finding unifiers.

As we discuss in the first section of this chapter, the unification of λ-terms is algorithmically complex. This complexity is to be expected because finding unifiers requires inverting β-reduction, an operation that has considerable computational power, as we observed in Section 4.3. Nevertheless, as we show in Section 8.2, a systematic way to structure the search for unifiers can be described. When applied to arbitrary unification problems, this procedure is nondeterministic and may not terminate. However, this procedure becomes both deterministic and terminating when we restrict our attention to the unification problems that arise in the setting of the L_λ subset of ℎℴℎℎ described in Chapter 7. In Section 8.3 we present a unification algorithm for proof search in L_λ. The final section of this chapter discusses pragmatic issues involving this form of unification in the context of λProlog programs.

8.1 Properties of the higher-order unification problem

The general form that we have described for unification problems allows for arbitrary alternations between universal and existential quantifiers in the prefix. In the first three sections of this chapter, we shall restrict prefixes to be of the form ∀∃∀: That is, a sequence of universal quantifiers in the prefix can be followed by a sequence of existential quantifiers that can be followed again by a sequence of universal quantifiers. As we have seen in Section 4.4, existential quantifiers in a prefix can be moved outside universal quantifiers using raising. Thus any unification problem can be transformed into an equivalent one in the ∀∃∀ form. While the outermost sequence of universal quantifiers is not strictly needed, these quantifiers provide a convenient way to represent the symbols in the ambient signature comprising the declared constants in an λProlog program, and we will interpret them as such.

Let t be a term, and let $\theta = \{\langle x_1, t_1 \rangle, \ldots, \langle x_n, t_n \rangle\}$ be a substitution. The application of the substitution θ to t, denoted by $\theta(t)$, can be given formally by the expression

$$((\lambda x_1 \ldots \lambda x_n \, t) \, t_1 \, \ldots \, t_n)$$

Given the λ-conversion rules, this term is equal to the result of replacing the free occurrences of $x_1, \ldots, x_n$ in t by the terms $t_1, \ldots, t_n$, making sure to rename bound variables within t to avoid capture of free variables in $t_1, \ldots, t_n$. Defining substitution in this way ensures that $\theta(t)$ is equal to $\theta(t')$, where t' is any term that results through λ-conversion from t. Thus, in considering questions of unification, without loss of generality, we can replace terms by their β-normal forms. Using the η-conversion rule, we can further ensure that the binders of the terms t and s in an equation $t = s$ that appears in the matrix of a unification problem are of identical length. Finally, using the equivalence between the formulas $\lambda x \, t = \lambda x \, s$ and $\forall x \, (t = s)$, the formulas $(\forall x \, (t = s)) \wedge F)$ and $\forall x \, ((t = s) \wedge F)$, and the formulas $(F \wedge (\forall x \, (t = s)))$ and $\forall x \, (F \wedge (t = s))$, we can transform the abstractions appearing at the heads of the equations in the matrix of a unification problem in a ∀∃∀ form into quantifiers that extend the inner sequence of universal ones. Using these transformations, we can convert any unification problem into a form where not only the quantifier prefix is of the form ∀∃∀, but also the equations in the matrix are between terms that have empty binders. We shall assume that all unification problems are of this kind.

We presented the notion of a most general unifier for first-order unification problems in Section 1.5. Such a unifier is one from which all other unifiers can be obtained by making further substitutions. Most general unifiers are useful in a computational setting because they satisfy all the constraints expressed in the unification problem while also allowing other possible ways of satisfying them to be easily generated at later stages. However, most general unifiers may not exist for higher-order unification problems. For example, consider the unification problem

$$\forall a \, \forall g \, \exists F \, [(F \ a) = (g \ a \ a)]$$

where the types of the variables a, g, and F are i, $i \rightarrow i \rightarrow i$, and $i \rightarrow i$, respectively, for some primitive type i. It is easy to see that this problem has four different unifiers given by the substitutions $\{\langle F, \lambda x \, (g \ x \ x)\rangle\}$, $\{\langle F, \lambda x \, (g \ a \ x)\rangle\}$, $\{\langle F, \lambda x \, (g \ x \ a)\rangle\}$, and $\{\langle F, \lambda x \, (g \ a \ a)\rangle\}$. Moreover, no other substitution can be made for F that makes the two terms in the equation identical. Finally, each of the substitutions shown replaces F with a closed term. Thus none of these unifiers can be obtained by applying a substitution to any of the others. It follows, therefore, that there cannot be a most general unifier for this unification problem.

Given that we cannot guarantee the existence of a single most general unifier, we may think of generalizing this notion to that of a covering set of unifiers. Such a set, called a *complete set of unifiers*, should satisfy two requirements: First, every substitution in the set should be a unifier for the given unification problem, and second, every other unifier should be obtainable from one in the set by applying a further substitution. A desirable property for such a set in computational settings is that it be finite. Unfortunately, this is another property that does not generally hold in the higher-order context. For example, consider the unification problem

$$\forall u \, \exists F \, \forall w \, [(u \ (F \ w)) = (F \ (u \ w))]$$

assuming that the variable w has type i, and F and u both have type $i \rightarrow i$, for some primitive type i. There is an infinite number of solutions to this problem, given by the substitution of the terms

$$\lambda y \, y, \quad \lambda y \, (u \ y), \quad \lambda y \, (u \ (u \ y)), \quad \ldots$$

for F. Since these are each closed substitutions, any complete set of unifiers for the given problem must include all of them.

We might think of weakening the desire of finiteness for complete sets of unifiers to the requirement that these sets cover all the unifiers in a nonredundant way; in particular, we might want it to be the case that no two substitutions in the set should have the same unifier as a substitution instance. It is more difficult to demonstrate this fact explicitly but once again, a general guarantee of this kind of nonredundancy cannot be given in the higher-order setting.

In a computational context, we are also often interested in just the question of unifiability, i.e., in simply determining whether or not a given unification problem has any unifiers. Considering this issue shows, yet again, the complexity of the higher-order unification problem: There is no general way to guarantee a definite response to such questions. In Section 4.6 we showed how to transform any instance of the Post correspondence problem into the task of finding a unifier for a unification problem. Since Post correspondence problems are, in general, undecidable, higher-order unification also must be undecidable.

The observation of undecidability notwithstanding, it is still possible to describe a systematic procedure for exploring the existence of unifiers for any given problem. In the next section we outline the structure of such a procedure. The properties of higher-order unification that we have described still appear quite daunting and also seem to contrast sharply with the practical usefulness of this operation that seems to be implied by the many examples we have considered in earlier chapters. In Section 8.3 we resolve this dichotomy by showing that unification problems in the L_λ subset of $\hbar o\hbar\hbar$ are much better behaved.

8.2 A procedure for checking for unifiability

In Section 4.5 we noted that a term in β-normal form can be either rigid or flexible. Applying that terminology to unification problems, a term that appears on the left or right of an equation is rigid if its head is bound by a universal quantifier in the quantifier prefix and is flexible if its head is bound by an existential quantifier.

8.2.1 Simplification of rigid-rigid equations

An important observation about a rigid term is that its head is unaffected by any substitutions that might be made for existentially quantified variables. Thus a rigid-rigid equation in a unification problem can be simplified as follows. If the heads of the terms in the equation are distinct, the entire unification problem can be marked as unprovable. If, on the other hand, the heads of the terms are identical, then the equation is logically equivalent to the conjunction of equations between the arguments of the two terms and can be replaced by this conjunction; as a special case, if the terms do not have any arguments, we can replace the equation by $\top$. In other words, an equation of the form $(c\ s_1 \ldots s_n) = (c\ t_1 \ldots t_n)$, where c is a variable that is bound by a universal quantifier in the quantifier prefix, can be replaced by $s_1 = t_1 \wedge \cdots \wedge s_n = t_n$ or by $\top$ if $n = 0$. Carrying out such a transformation also simplifies the problem in a quantifiable sense: There are two fewer symbols in the overall conjunction of equations. The process of repeatedly treating all rigid-rigid pairs in this fashion will be called *simplification*.

8.2.2 Substitutions for equations between flexible and rigid terms

The property that the head of a rigid term cannot be changed through substitution also underlies the treatment of equations in which one term is flexible and the other is rigid. Let

$$(F \ t_1 \ \ldots \ t_n) = (c \ s_1 \ \ldots \ s_m)$$

be such an equation, where F and c are variables bound by an existential and a universal quantifier, respectively. This equation can be proved only by making the head of the left term identical to c. Moreover, there are only two broad categories of substitutions for F that can result in such a transformation of the left term: that in which the head of the term substituted for F is itself c and that where this term uses one of the arguments of F to make the head of the left term identical to c.

Imitation substitutions The first kind of substitution for F, called *imitation*, is logically correct only when the quantification over F occurs within the scope of the quantifier that binds c. If this is the case, and if F and c have the types $\tau_1 \to \cdots \to \tau_n \to \beta$ and $\sigma_1 \to \cdots \to \sigma_m \to \beta$, respectively, then the *imitation substitution* for F has the form

$$\lambda x_1 \ldots \lambda x_n (c \ (H_1 \ x_1 \ \ldots \ x_n) \ (H_m \ x_1 \ \ldots \ x_n))$$

where, for $1 \le i \le m$, H_i is a new variable of type $\tau_1 \to \cdots \to \tau_n \to \sigma_i$. Moreover, we replace the quantification over F in the prefix by a sequence of existential quantifiers over the H_j variables to reflect a transformation of the obligation to find a substitution for F into ones for finding substitutions for the H_j variables under the same constraints. Notice that the proposed imitation substitution term has as its arguments flexible terms whose arguments include all the variables bound by abstractions at its head. Replacing F by this term and contracting the resulting β-redexes therefore will produce a term that has c as its head and has as its arguments flexible terms that each have as their arguments the original arguments of F. Thus this substitution has the effect of fixing only the head of the substitution term, leaving all choices of what the arguments should be to the determination of substitutions for the H_j variables in subsequent steps in the transformation process.

Projection substitutions The second kind of substitution for F, called *projection*, is used to get one of the arguments of F to become the new head of the flexible term. Assume, again, that F has the type $\tau_1 \to \cdots \to \tau_n \to \beta$. The type of the ith argument of F then is τ_i. A term that is to be substituted for F can have a head of this type only if the target type of τ_i is identical to β. Suppose that this is the case and that τ_i is, in fact, the type $\varphi_1 \to \cdots \to \varphi_k \to \beta$. Then there is an ith *projection substitution* for F that is given by the term

$$\lambda x_1 \ldots \lambda x_n (x_i \ (H_1 \ x_1 \ \ldots \ x_n) \ (H_k \ x_1 \ \ldots \ x_n))$$

where, for $1 \le j \le k$, H_j is a new variable of type $\tau_1 \to \cdots \to \tau_n \to \varphi_j$. Further, as in the case of imitation, we replace the quantification over F in the prefix with a sequence of existential quantifiers over the H_j variables. Notice that the arguments of the substitution term have been chosen so as to commit F at this stage only to projecting onto its ith argument; how the rest of the eventual substitution for F is to be structured is left entirely open, to be determined by later computations that yield substitutions for the H_j variables.

Suppose that the head of the flexible term in a flexible-rigid equation has type $\tau_1 \to \cdots \to \tau_n \to \beta$, where β is a primitive type. Then there may or may not be an imitation substitution corresponding to this equation, and there can be between 0 and n valid projection substitutions. Thus up to $n + 1$ substitutions may have to be considered for such an equation in the course of determining unifiability.

8.2.3 The iterative transformation of unification problems

We can try to check for unifiability by iterating the use of the steps described for removing rigid-rigid, flexible-rigid, and rigid-flexible equations from a given unification problem. To illustrate this process, consider the unification problem

$$\forall a \, \forall g \, \exists F \, [(F \; a) = (g \; a \; a)]$$

where the types of the variables a, g, and F are i, $i \to i \to i$, and $i \to i$, respectively, for some primitive type i. The imitation and project substitutions for this flexible-rigid equation yield the substitution terms

$$\lambda x \, (g \; (H_1 \; x) \; (H_2 \; x)) \qquad \text{and} \qquad \lambda x \, x$$

for F, where H_1 and H_2 are new variables, each of type $i \to i$. These substitutions are, respectively, the imitation and the one projection substitution. The application of the second substitution to the original unification problem transforms it (after β-normalizing) into

$$\forall a \, \forall g \, [a = (g \; a \; a)]$$

The sole equation in this case has an unprovable rigid-rigid form: Thus this choice of substitution leads to a dead end. Using the first substitution, on the other hand, leads to the problem

$$\forall a \, \forall g \, \exists H_1 \, \exists H_2 \, [(g \; (H_1 \; a) \; (H_2 \; a)) = (g \; a \; a)]$$

Simplification now can be applied, and doing so results in the problem

$$\forall a \, \forall g \, \exists H_1 \, \exists H_2 \, [((H_1 \; a) = a) \wedge ((H_2 \; a) = a)]$$

The left conjunct here leads us to consider the substitutions

$$\lambda x \, a \qquad \text{and} \qquad \lambda x \, x$$

for H_1. Using either of these reduces the problem to

$$\forall a \, \forall g \, \exists H_2 \, [\top \wedge ((H_2 \, a) = a)]$$

The only remaining equation yields $\lambda x \, a$ and $\lambda x \, x$ as the imitation and projection substitutions for H_2. Both substitutions transform the unification problem into a form where the matrix is equivalent to $\top$; i.e., they result in a formula that is obviously provable. Composing the different steps together yields four different substitutions for F—the terms $\lambda x \, (g \, a \, a), \lambda x \, (g \, a \, x), \lambda x \, (g \, x \, a)$, and $\lambda x \, (g \, x \, x)$—any one of which is a unifier for the original problem.

8.2.4 Unification problems with only flexible-flexible equations

In the problem considered in the preceding subsection, each of the possible sequences of applications of the simplification and substitution steps terminates, and each succeeds in eliminating all the equations from the matrix. However, we cannot be assured that this will happen for every unification problem. One reason why this might fail to happen is that the process might terminate, yielding a matrix that contains a nonempty conjunction of flexible-flexible equations. For example, consider the unification problem

$$\forall a \, \forall g \, \exists X \, \exists Y \, [(X \, a) = (g \, (Y \, a))]$$

where the variable a has type i and the variables X, Y and g have type $i \rightarrow i$. Using the imitation substitution $\lambda x \, (g \, (H \, x))$ for X and then simplifying yields the unification problem

$$\forall a \, \forall g \, \exists H \, \exists Y \, [(H \, a) = (Y \, a)]$$

While this problem cannot be reduced further, it has at least one unifier: Substituting the term $\lambda x \, a$ for both H and Y (thereby also refining the substitution for X to $\lambda x \, (g \, a)$) makes the two terms in the equation identical. More generally, a unifier always can be generated for a problem whose matrix is a conjunction of equations that are all of flexible-flexible form by using the following recipe: First, associate with each primitive type τ a fixed new variable H^τ of existential strength. Then, for every type $\tau_1 \rightarrow \ldots \rightarrow \tau_n \rightarrow \sigma$, where σ is a primitive type, let $\lambda x_1 \ldots \lambda x_n \, H^\sigma$ be the *canonical constant term* of that type; notice that n may be 0, in which case the proposed term has no abstractions at its head. Finally, let the *canonical substitution* relative to a unification problem be the substitution that maps each existentially quantified variable appearing in the quantifier prefix to the canonical constant term corresponding to its type. As a specific example, letting W be the selected variable for type i, this recipe yields $\{\langle H, \lambda x \, W \rangle, \langle Y, \lambda x \, W \rangle\}$ as the canonical substitution for the final unification problem shown earlier. It is easy to see that the canonical substitution for a unification problem containing only flexible-flexible equations is actually a unifier for that problem.

The reduction of a unification problem to a flexible-flexible form thus constitutes success from the perspective of determining unifiability. The process of carrying out such a reduction is known as *pre-unification*, and the substitution that leads to the corresponding success is called a *pre-unifier*. Full unification requires also finding a unifier for the remaining flexible-flexible equations. As we have just seen, it is easy to provide a unifier for a problem in this form. However, the attempt to characterize *all* its unifiers is often not a fruitful exercise. Consider, for instance, the final flexible-flexible unification problem in the example discussed earlier. Any substitution for H and Y that is obtained by picking a term t constructed using a, g, and existential variables other than H, Y, and X and abstracting over some of the occurrences of a in t would yield a unifier for this problem. This is clearly too large and uncontrolled a set to try to generate explicitly.

8.2.5 Nontermination of reductions

The iterated use of simplification and imitation or projection substitutions may not succeed in eliminating all the equations from the matrix of a unification problem for another reason: The process may be nonterminating. To illustrate this possibility, let us consider the problem

$$\forall g \, \exists F \, \forall x \, [(F \; (g \; x)) = (g \; (F \; x))]$$

where the variable x has type i and the variables g and F have types $i \rightarrow i$. This unification problem has only one flexible-rigid equation. There is exactly one projection substitution for F in this case, and this is given by the term $\lambda x \, x$. Applying this substitution yields an obviously solved unification problem. However, we also might consider using the imitation substitution $\lambda x \, (g \; (H \; x))$ for F. Applying this substitution and then simplifying results in the unification problem

$$\forall g \, \exists H \, \forall x \, [(H \; (g \; x)) = (g \; (H \; x))]$$

This problem is identical to the original problem except for the fact that the variable F has been replaced by H. It is easy to see from this that we can generate an infinite sequence of transformations by repeatedly using the imitation substitution followed by a simplification. Notice also that tracing the different paths to completion leads to the substitutions

$$\lambda x \, x, \quad \lambda x \, (g \; x), \quad \lambda x \, (g \; (g \; x)), \quad \ldots$$

for F that constitute an infinite set of unifiers for the original problem.

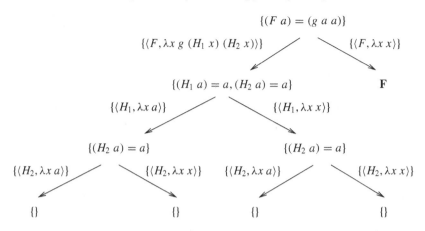

Figure 8.1. A matching tree for $\forall a \, \forall g \, \exists F \, ((F \, a) = (g \, a \, a))$.

8.2.6 Matching trees

The procedure that we have outlined for checking unifiability is nondeterministic in that it may need to make choices between substitutions generated through imitation and projection. The search space for the procedure can be depicted by a structure referred to as a *matching tree*. The nodes in this tree are the simplified equations in the matrix of the unification problem represented as multisets; the quantifier prefix is left implicit. The arcs correspond to the different possibilities in the imitation and projection substitutions. The matching tree for the unification problem $\forall a \, \forall g \, \exists F \, ((F \, a) = (g \, a \, a))$ considered earlier is shown in Figure 8.1; we have used **F** to represent failure nodes in this tree, i.e., nodes corresponding to unification problems for which it is immediately apparent that there are no solutions. The leaves in such a tree are either failure nodes or unification problems with matrices of at most flexible-flexible equations. We refer to the latter kind of leaf as a *success node*. The reduction of the original unification problem to a success node represents a pre-unification; the corresponding pre-unifier is obtained by composing the substitutions labeling the arcs leading to the success node.

An important property of a matching tree is that if the problem at its root has a unifier, then it must have a success node at a finite depth. Moreover, the unifier for the problem at the root can be obtained by composing the corresponding pre-unifier with a unifier for the problem at the success node. In creating a matching tree, we may have choices in the equation to use for generating the imitation and projection substitutions and hence the next nodes in the tree. Thus, in the matching tree in Figure 8.1, we may have selected the equation $(H_2 \, a) = a$ instead of $(H_1 \, a) = a$ at the left child of the root. The completeness property for matching trees that we have just described holds independently of how this choice is made. Matching trees may have some paths in them that go on forever. For example, from the discussion in the preceding subsection, it follows that there would be one such path in any matching tree for the problem $\forall g\,\exists F\,\forall x\,((F\,(g\,x)) = (g\,(F\,x)))$. As we have observed previously, the question of unifiability is an undecidable one in general. This implies that there are unification problems with matching trees that have at least one infinite path and no finite paths ending in success nodes. As a concrete illustration, consider the unification problem

$$\forall g\,\exists F\,\forall x\,[((F\,(g\,x)) = (g\,(F\,x))) \wedge (F\,a) = (F\,b)]$$

where a and b are constants of type i. The second equation in the matrix here causes each of the unifiers that we have seen for the first equation to be rejected. Thus the matching tree for the overall problem will have no success nodes but will have an infinite path arising from repeated attempts to unify the first equation.

8.3 Higher-order pattern unification

In Section 7.8 we introduced the L_λ subset of λProlog and discussed its utility from a programming perspective. To recall the defining characteristic of this subset, a program clause or goal formula B is in L_λ if all quantification in B is over nonpredicate types and every subterm of B of the form $(x\,t_1\,\ldots\,t_n)$ in which x is an essentially existentially quantified variable is such that $t_1,\ldots,t_n$ are distinct variables that are universally quantified within the scope of the quantifier binding x. We shall refer to this property as the L_λ *condition*. The β-reduction operation that results from substituting for an essentially existentially quantified variable in this situation corresponds to simply replacing the bound variables within the body of an abstraction with a new set of names. This operation, called β_0-*reduction*, is a particularly simple one: Transforming $((\lambda y\,s)\,x)$ into $s[x/y]$ decreases the size of the term. Consequently, we might expect its inversion, i.e., unification in the setting of L_λ, to be a better behaved operation than general higher-order unification. We will see this to be the case in this section.

L_λ unification, also known as *higher-order pattern unification*, can be realized by the procedure we have described in the preceding section refined to take into account the restriction on terms in the L_λ setting. It is easy to see that computations in L_λ (as also in $\hbar o\hbar\hbar$) yield unification problems in which essential existential quantifiers in goals and program clauses become existential quantifiers in the prefix, and essential universal quantifiers translate similarly into universal quantifiers. At the outset, the ordering of such quantifiers in the prefix can be arbitrary. However, raising substitutions can be used once again, and such substitutions obviously preserve the L_λ condition. Thus we may continue to limit our attention to problems in which the quantifier prefix has a $\forall \exists \forall$ form while simultaneously assuming that the L_λ condition is satisfied. The simplification process for rigid-rigid equations applies unchanged in the new situation. When considering a flexible-rigid equation, the special properties of the L_λ class ensure that all the projection and imitation substitutions with at most one exception will result in failure in the immediately following simplification phase. To see this, suppose that the equation being considered is

$$(F\ c_1\ \ldots c_n) = (c\ t_1\ \ldots\ t_m)$$

where F is an existentially quantified variable, and $c, c_1, \ldots, c_n$ are universally quantified variables. If F is bound within the scope of the quantifier binding c, then c must be distinct from $c_1, \ldots, c_n$. In this case, every one of the possible projection substitutions for F will lead immediately to a nonunifiable equation. On the other hand, if c is bound within the scope of the quantifier binding F, then the imitation substitution is not a possibility. Moreover, unless it is the case that c_i is identical to c, applying the ith projection substitution to the flexible term will leave it with a head that does not match that of the rigid term. Since the variables in the sequence $c_1, \ldots, c_n$ are all distinct, there can be at most one useful projection to consider.

The preceding observations can be built into the substitution selection process so as to make it entirely deterministic. Another important property to note about the class of L_λ unification problems is that the application of an imitation or projection substitution preserves this class. For example, consider the equation shown earlier. The substitutions that have to be considered for F in this situation are of the form

$$\lambda x_1 \ldots \lambda x_n\ (@\ (H_1\ x_1\ \ldots\ x_n)\ \ldots\ (H_k\ x_1\ \ldots\ x_n))$$

where $@$ is c or x_i for some i such that $1 \leq i \leq n$. Since the new variables $H_1, \ldots, H_k$ will be quantified at the same location as F, replacing F with the indicated substitution term in a context where it is applied to distinct constants and then effecting a β-reduction clearly will yield a new term that also satisfies the L_λ condition.

By using imitation or projection substitutions repeatedly, we may succeed in transforming the equations in the matrix of the unification problem into flexible-flexible ones. While it is not profitable to solve such equations in the general case, the special properties of the L_λ subset change this situation. In this setting, these equations have the form

$$(F\ c_1\ \ldots\ c_n) = (G\ d_1\ \ldots\ d_m)$$

where $c_1, \ldots, c_n$ and $d_1, \ldots, d_m$ are variables that are universally quantified within the scope of the existential quantifiers binding F and G; note that since the prefix is assumed to have a $\forall\exists\forall$ form, F and G are effectively bound "at the same place." Let us suppose first that F and G are distinct variables. Any unifier for the equation must transform both sides of it to a common term t. Such a term obviously cannot contain any of the variables $c_1, \ldots, c_n$ in it unless that variable also appears in the sequence $d_1 \ldots, d_m$. A converse property applies to the variables $d_1, \ldots, d_m$. Let $e_1, \ldots, e_\ell$ be some listing of the variables common to both $c_1, \ldots, c_n$ and $d_1, \ldots, d_m$, let H be a new variable for which an existential quantifier will be introduced in the prefix at the same place as the one for F, and consider the substitution $\lambda c_1 \ldots \lambda c_n \, (H \ e_1 \ \ldots \ e_\ell)$ for F. It is easy to see that any term of the form of t can be generated by first applying this substitution to $(F \ c_1 \ \ldots \ c_n)$ and then using a substitution for H. A similar observation applies to the term $(G \ d_1 \ \ldots \ d_m)$ with the substitution $\lambda d_1 \ldots \lambda d_m \, (H \ e_1 \ \ldots \ e_\ell)$ for G. Finally, we note that the posited substitutions for F and G make the two sides of the flexible-flexible equation equal. Thus these substitutions for F and G constitute a most general unifier for the problem posed by the equation.

Let us now consider the case where F and G are identical; notice that n then must be equal to m. The main difference in this situation from the earlier case is that the *same* substitution will be applied to the heads of the terms on *both* sides of the equation. It follows from this that a variable c_i or d_i from the sequences $c_1, \ldots, c_n$ and $d_1, \ldots, d_n$ can appear in a common instance of the terms on the two sides of the equation only if $c_i = d_i$. Let $e_1, \ldots, e_\ell$ be a listing of the variables satisfying this property. The observations that we have made then imply that the substitution of $\lambda c_1 \ldots \lambda c_n \, (H \ e_1 \ \ldots \ e_\ell)$ for F is a most general unifier for the flexible-flexible unification problem in this case.

By combining the completeness property of matching trees with the observations that there is at most one productive path in the tree and that most general unifiers can be provided for flexible-flexible pairs in the L_λ setting, it follows that the higher-order pattern unification problem possesses the property of having most general unifiers. Another property that we may desire of unification is decidability. Unfortunately, the procedure that we have sketched up to this point is not guaranteed to terminate. In fact, it may not terminate even when applied to first-order unification problems. To see this, let us consider the problem $\forall f \ \exists X \ [X = (f \ X)]$. The only potentially useful substitution for the flexible-rigid equation here is imitation, i.e., substituting the term $(f \ H)$ for X. Transforming the unification problem based on this substitution yields $\forall f \ \exists H \ [H = (f \ H)]$. This problem is identical to the one with which we started. It is clear, then, that the process we have described will go on endlessly in this case.

Nonterminating behavior of the kind just illustrated obviously is restricted in the L_λ setting to the situation where the unification problem does not have a solution. This observation can be further refined: Such behavior occurs only when the variable that is the head of the flexible term also occurs in the rigid term in a flexible-rigid equation. We therefore can ensure termination for the unification procedure by adding an "occurs-check" to the substitution-generation step that treats such equations: We examine the rigid term and reduce the problem to a nonunifiable one if the flexible head appears in it and produce the relevant imitation or projection substitution only otherwise.

The imitation and projection substitutions that are used when a flexible-rigid equation is treated realize a traversal over term structure that is also repeated many times in the course of conducting an occurs-check. It is possible to combine these different computations into a larger, more efficient substitution generation operation. We will call this operation *variable elimination* because of its similarity to an operation of the same name discussed for first-order unification in Section 1.5. Specifically, let the flexible-rigid equation under consideration be $(F \ c_1 \ \ldots \ c_n) = t$. There may be, in general, occurrences of existentially quantified variables in t. Suppose that such an occurrence is as the head of a term of the form $(G \ d_1 \ \ldots \ d_m)$. If not all the variables in $d_1, \ldots, d_m$ are contained in $c_1, \ldots, c_n$, then one part of variable elimination involves generating a substitution for G that prunes such variables. This pruning substitution replaces G with the term $\lambda d_1 \ \ldots, \lambda d_m \ (G' \ e_1 \ \ldots \ e_\ell)$, where G' is a new existentially quantified variable, and $e_1, \ldots, e_\ell$ is some listing of the variables that are common to $c_1, \ldots, c_n$ and $d_1, \ldots, d_m$. Now let the result of applying these auxiliary substitutions to the term t be t'. Then the main part of variable elimination checks whether there are occurrences in t' either of F or of variables different from the ones in $c_1, \ldots, c_n$ that are quantified universally within the scope of the quantifier binding F. If there are such occurrences, then it marks the problem as one for which no unifiers exist. Otherwise, it generates the substitution $\lambda c_1 \ \ldots \lambda c_n \ t'$ for F and replaces the equation under consideration by $\top$.

To illustrate the higher-order pattern unification algorithm in its final evolved form, let us consider the unification problem

$$\forall f \ \forall g \ \exists U \ \exists V \ \forall w \ \forall x \ \forall y \ [(f \ (U \ x \ y)) = (f \ (g \ (V \ y \ w)))]$$

assuming that x, y, and w are of type i, f and g are of type $i \to i$, and U and V are of type $i \to i \to i$. Using the simplification transformation for rigid-rigid equations, this problem reduces to

$$\forall f \ \forall g \ \exists U \ \exists V \ \forall w \ \forall x \ \forall y \ [(U \ x \ y) = (g \ (V \ y \ w))]$$

At this stage, variable elimination becomes applicable. Using it first generates the pruning substitution $\lambda y \, \lambda w \, (V' \; y)$ for V and subsequently the substitution $\lambda x \, \lambda y \, (g \; (V' \; y))$ for U. These substitutions together constitute a most general unifier for the original problem. If the unification problem had been

$$\forall f \, \forall g \, \exists U \, \exists V \, \forall w \, \forall x \, \forall y \, [(U \; x \; y) = (g \; (U \; y \; w))]$$

instead, then variable elimination would determine nonunifiability because of the occurrence of U, the head of the flexible term, in the rigid term. Similarly, the problem

$$\forall f \, \forall g \, \exists U \, \exists V \, \forall w \, \forall x \, \forall y \, [(U \; x \; y) = (g \; w)]$$

has no unifiers because the universally quantified variable w, which is not one of the arguments in $(U \; x \; y)$, appears on the right-hand side of the equation and in a position that is not the argument of a flexible term.

It is evident at this stage that higher-order pattern unification is a simpler kind of problem than general higher-order unification. It is, in fact, an operation that is computationally similar to first-order unification: In both cases, term simplification and variable elimination constitute the critical parts of the computation, although variable elimination has a more involved structure in the higher-order pattern unification case. Another interesting observation concerns the role of types. In the L_λ setting, types are needed to constrain terms and thereby to guarantee the correctness of the unification computation. However, the algorithm that we have described for higher-order pattern unification makes no use at all of type information in determining unifying substitutions. In particular, types have no bearing on the shapes of unifiers.

8.4 Pragmatic aspects of higher-order unification

Our discussion of higher-order unification has assumed that these problems are presented in a form where the quantifier prefix has a $\forall \exists \forall$ structure. The computations that result from λProlog programs often yield a prefix that does not adhere to this structure. While raising can be used to transform arbitrary prefixes into the more restricted form, such a transformation can be costly. To begin with, such raising has to be performed dynamically. Moreover, existential quantifiers may have to be raised over long lists of universally quantified variables; this is especially true of the computational paradigm discussed in Chapter 7, in which recursion over binding structures in λ-tree syntax is realized by using universal goals. A further observation is that such raising often can be redundant and may have to be undone by a pruning substitution at a later point. To illustrate this, let us consider the higher-order pattern unification problem $\forall f \, \exists U \, \forall x \, \forall y \, \forall z \, \exists V \, [(U \; x) = (f \; V)]$. The quantifier prefix for this problem can be transformed into a $\forall\exists\forall$ form by raising the existential quantifier over V to obtain the problem $\forall f\ \exists U\ \exists V'\ \forall x\ \forall y\ \forall z\ [(U\ x) = (f\ (V'\ x\ y\ z))]$. A unifier for this problem now will be computed using variable elimination that, as a first step, would apply a pruning substitution of the form $\lambda x\ \lambda y\ \lambda z\ (W\ x)$ to V'.

An alternative approach that might be better in practice is to note the possibility of raising but to delay its application up to a point where it is clear how this needs to be done. To realize this approach, it is necessary to maintain with each existentially quantified variable a list of universally quantified variables over which it can be raised. For example, consider the problem

$$\forall f\ \exists U\ \forall x\ \forall y\ \forall z\ \exists V\ [(U\ x) = (f\ V)]$$

We would record here the information that U can be raised over f and that V can be raised over x, y, z, and f. In solving this problem using higher-order pattern unification, this information would be used in variable elimination. In particular, we can immediately proceed to computing a binding for U, but noting the presence of x as an argument of the flexible term and the possibility of raising V over x, we would replace V with the term $(V'\ x)$, where V' is a new variable quantified at the same place in the prefix as U and would produce the unifying substitution $\lambda x\ (f\ (V'\ x))$ for U. This approach also seems to be costly initially because it requires us to maintain different lists of universal variables with existentially quantified ones. However, these lists are all initial segments of the sequence of variables that are universally quantified in the prefix, and thus an efficient representation based on sharing is possible. Moreover, it is mainly the alternations between universal and existential quantification that are relevant to unification, and this information can be maintained and used efficiently by attaching numerical indices to the quantified variables.

We have motivated higher order pattern unification by assuming a static adherence to the L_λ subset of the *hohh* language. While the spirit of this class underlies many practical examples, a strict imposition of the restriction can rule out some useful programming idioms. For example, consider the use of (meta-level) β-reduction to realize substitution. This idiom is epitomized by the following definition of the subst predicate that we discussed in Chapter 7:

```
type  subst (tm -> tm) -> tm -> tm -> o.
subst R N (R N).
```

Observe that R and N represent essentially existentially quantified variables in the program clause shown. The term (R N) therefore does not satisfy the L_λ condition.

A common practical resolution to this dilemma is to not impose the L_λ restriction on program clauses statically but rather to expect the condition to be satisfied by the unification problems that are encountered *dynamically*. The rationale is that while we sometimes might want to generate computations by using predicate definitions that lie outside the L_λ class, we never intend these to be used to produce general higher-order unification problems. For example, consider the clause defining subst. When we use this clause, we expect the variables R and N to be fully instantiated. Thus the term (R N) is meant only to compute the effect of substitution through reduction and is not intended to yield a unification problem. A further generalization to this "dynamic L_λ programming" idea is also possible: We can think of approaching arbitrary higher-order unification through the higher-order pattern class. In this view, we would treat any unification problem as if it is a higher-order pattern-unification one. In the course of such a treatment, we might discover that a particular equation does not respect the L_λ condition. In this case, we might defer further consideration of this equation until such time that substitutions resulting from solving other parts of the problem have altered its status.

Our desire to allow for programs outside the L_λ class is motivated by examples such as the definition of the subst predicate. Going in the other direction, we have seen in Section 7.6 that if we can make explicit the signature of object language expressions, then this predicate also can be defined within the L_λ subset of *hohh*. By an extension of this argument, it also may be possible to describe general higher-order unification as a logic program in the L_λ language. If completely developed, such an approach can yield an alternative declarative way to realize the general unification computation that could be useful in practical settings.

8.5 Bibliographic notes

Interest in higher-order unification first arose from a desire to mechanize theorem proving in higher-order logics. Early investigations of this problem are due to Guard (1964) and Gould (1966), who showed that in certain instances it was necessary to consider infinite sets of unifiers. Darlington (1971) described an incomplete algorithm called *f-matching* for the second-order case. Pietrzykowski (1973) provided a complete enumeration algorithm for this case and extended it together with Jensen (1972) to the full higher-order setting. Huet (1976) undertook a comprehensive study of higher-order unification in his doctoral dissertation. Among various results, he showed that the problem was undecidable in the third-order case (Huet 1973a) [a result that also was established independently by Lucchesi (1972)], he defined the notion of complete sets of unifiers (Huet 1975), and he showed that the search for such a set of unifiers has to be redundant (Huet 1976). Goldfarb (1981) later established undecidability of unification even for the second-order language.

A problem related to unification is that of matching, where only one of the two terms in an equation contains existentially quantified variables. Decidability for this problem was shown early for the second-order (Huet and Lang 1978) and third-order (Dowek 1992) cases, but the question remained open for a while for the general case until Stirling (2009) finally answered it in the affirmative.

The procedure for general higher-order pre-unification described in this chapter is due to Huet (1975). Snyder and Gallier (1989) provided an alternative presentation of Huet's procedure in the form of transformations of sets of equations. Huet (1973b) developed a notion of constrained resolution that uses his procedure to yield a mechanization of higher-order logic by building on the idea of resolution in type theory due to Andrews (1971). Huet's pre-unification procedure has been adapted by Dowek et al. (2000) so as to draw benefit from the idea of explicit substitutions in the λ-calculus. Dougherty (1993) developed an alternative to Huet's procedure based on translating λ-terms to combinatory logic. This procedure has the advantage that it does not use types, but it also has the drawback that it conducts a redundant search; by contrast, Huet's procedure, which is limited to determining unifiability, is nonredundant.

Unlike unification in Prolog systems, unification in *hohh* requires dealing with explicit quantifiers and their alternations. Miller (1992a) developed the notion of unification under a mixed quantifier prefix and described raising as a means for simplifying quantifier alternations in the prefix. The notion of ∀-lifting used in Isabelle (Paulson 1989) is essentially a combination of raising with a backchaining step. The effect of quantifier alternations also can be understood via hierarchies of term universes and captured directly in unification by associating universe level tags with variables and constants; see Nadathur (1993) and Nadathur and Linnell (2005) for specific uses of this idea.

The higher-order pattern unification problem was defined and first studied by Miller (1991b), who proved that such unification is decidable and possesses the property of having most general unifiers. Miller (1991a) also discussed the encoding of general higher-order unification via a logic program in the L_λ language. Qian (1996) showed that the complexity of higher-order pattern unification is linear. Nipkow (1993) provided an implementation of higher-order pattern unification in a functional programming language. Dowek et al. (1996) described an algorithm for the problem that uses a presentation of λ-terms based on explicit substitutions in an intrinsic way. All these developments treat quantifier alternations essentially through raising: The algorithm used by Nipkow assumes that the quantifier prefix has been simplified through raising in a preprocessing phase, whereas the behavior of the algorithm of Dowek et al. is more subtle but still may manifest the effect of raising in a nondiscriminating way. Avoiding such raising can be important in a situation where quantifier prefixes are created dynamically through computations. Nadathur and Linnell (2005) have developed an alternative algorithm that obviates explicit raising by encoding quantifier dependencies through universe-level tags. This algorithm has been used in several practical systems such as Bedwyr (Baelde et al. 2007), Abella (Gacek 2008), and the Teyjus implementation of λProlog (Qi 2009).

While systems that incorporate unification modulo α-, β-, and η-conversion, such as λProlog and Isabelle (Paulson 1990), contain implementations of L_λ unification, there are other systems that have focused on implementing only L_λ unification even when the term language does not satisfy the L_λ restriction on essentially existential variable occurrences. Two systems that do this are Twelf (Pfenning and Schürmann 1999) and Minlog (Schwichtenberg 2006). While the first version of the Teyjus implementation (Nadathur and Mitchell 1999) of λProlog provided for (pre-)unification in the setting of unrestricted higher-order terms, the second version (Qi 2009) only implements L_λ unification. Using L_λ unification has auxiliary practical effects such as obviating type information during execution; some of these consequences are explored by Nadathur and Qi (2005).

9

Implementing Proof Systems

We showed in Chapter 7 that λ-terms provide a natural means for representing logical formulas and, in particular, for capturing the binding aspects of quantification. We illustrated the benefits of such representations by considering structural manipulations on formulas, such as the implementation of substitution and conversion to normal forms. A common computation concerning logical formulas is that of attempting to show that they are theorems in a given proof system. In this chapter we show how a higher-order logic programming language can be used to specify and implement proof systems. In the first two sections we consider proof systems for intuitionistic logic, and in the third section we discuss a proof system for classical logic. Our main goal here is to illustrate how natural deduction and sequent calculus proof systems can be *specified* in λProlog. Occasionally, such specifications can be converted into simple theorem provers using a λProlog implementation. However, rich forms of theorem proving require more careful control over search in deduction. In the last section of this chapter we discuss an approach to encoding such control within the λProlog setting.

9.1 Deduction in propositional intuitionistic logic

In Section 1.4.2 and again in Section 7.1.1 we described a representation for propositional formulas that uses the types and constants identified by the following declarations:

```
kind   term, form  type.        % types for terms and formulas

type   ff,                      % encoding the false proposition
       tt    form.              % encoding the true proposition
type   &&,                      % encoding conjunction
       !!,                      % encoding disjunction
       ==>   form -> form -> form.  % encoding implication
```

229

$$\frac{}{\Gamma, A \longrightarrow A} \text{ initial, } A \text{ atomic} \qquad \frac{}{\Gamma, \bot \longrightarrow G} \bot L \qquad \frac{}{\Gamma \longrightarrow \top} \bot L$$

$$\frac{\Gamma, A, B \longrightarrow G}{\Gamma, A \wedge B \longrightarrow G} \wedge L \qquad \frac{\Gamma \longrightarrow A \quad \Gamma \longrightarrow B}{\Gamma \longrightarrow A \wedge B} \wedge R$$

$$\frac{\Gamma, A \longrightarrow G \quad \Gamma, B \longrightarrow G}{\Gamma, A \vee B \longrightarrow G} \vee L \qquad \frac{\Gamma \longrightarrow A}{\Gamma \longrightarrow A \vee B} \vee R \qquad \frac{\Gamma \longrightarrow B}{\Gamma \longrightarrow A \vee B} \vee R$$

$$\frac{\Gamma, A \supset B \longrightarrow A \quad \Gamma, B \longrightarrow G}{\Gamma, A \supset B \longrightarrow G} \supset L \qquad \frac{\Gamma, A \longrightarrow B}{\Gamma \longrightarrow A \supset B} \supset R$$

Figure 9.1. Inference rules for a fragment of propositional intuitionistic logic.

```
infixl   &&   5.
infixl   !!   4.
infixr   ==>  3.
```

We also will use this representation for propositional formulas in this chapter.

In Section 2.4.5 we described how a sequent calculus proof system can be turned into a λProlog specification of provability. The λProlog specification in Figure 6.8 provides another such illustration, this time including a treatment of quantifier rules; while not explicitly presented, the sequent calculus in that case can be extracted transparently from the specification. The soundness of such direct translations of a sequent proof system into a λProlog specification is often easy to verify. On the other hand, such λProlog specifications are far from being complete: Depth-first search usually steers the interpreter into endless loops when trying to work backwards from a given sequent. Consider, for example, the sequent calculus proof system in Figure 9.1 for propositional intuitionistic logic. Here, the left-hand side of the sequents are multisets. As one moves from conclusion to the premises in these rules, the number of occurrences of logical connectives in a sequent diminishes in all cases except that of the $\supset L$ rule. In the $\supset L$ rule, the formula that is the focus of the rule, $A \supset B$, appears in the conclusion as well as in the left premise. A particular instance of this rule is

$$\frac{p \supset q \longrightarrow q \quad q \longrightarrow q}{p \supset q \longrightarrow q}$$

While the right premise is proved using the initial rule, the left premise is identical to the conclusion. The straightforward translation of this rule into a λProlog clause therefore will lead to a program that loops.

Sequent calculi have been proposed for intuitionistic propositional logic that ensure that the premises of a rule are always simpler than the conclusion in some well-defined sense. For example, one can replace the $\supset L$ rule in Figure 9.1 with the four rules displayed in Figure 9.2 to produce an alternative proof system that is complete while also guaranteeing that any sequence of sequents produced

$$\frac{\Gamma, A, B \longrightarrow G}{\Gamma, A, A \supset B \longrightarrow G} \supset L_1, \; A \text{ atomic} \qquad \frac{\Gamma, C \supset D \supset B \longrightarrow G}{\Gamma, (C \wedge D) \supset B \longrightarrow G} \supset L_2$$

$$\frac{\Gamma, C \supset B, D \supset B \longrightarrow G}{\Gamma, (C \vee D) \supset B \longrightarrow G} \supset L_3 \qquad \frac{\Gamma, D \supset B \longrightarrow C \supset D \qquad \Gamma, B \longrightarrow G}{\Gamma, (C \supset D) \supset B \longrightarrow G} \supset L_4$$

$$\frac{\Gamma \longrightarrow G}{\Gamma, \bot \supset B \longrightarrow G} \supset L_5 \qquad \frac{\Gamma, B \longrightarrow G}{\Gamma, \top \supset B \longrightarrow G} \supset L_6$$

Figure 9.2. Replacements for the $\supset L$ rule.

during proof search is terminating. In particular, it is possible to attribute a weight to logical connectives and to sequents in a way that ensures that the weight assigned to the conclusion of a rule is always greater than the weight assigned to any of its premises. As a consequence, the direct translation of this proof system into the λProlog specification that is presented Figure 9.3 actually constitutes a decision procedure for proposition intuitionistic logic.

The specification in Figure 9.3 makes use of the predicate `memb_and_rest` that is defined in Section 2.4.5: The goal `memb_and_rest A Gamma Gamma'` is solvable exactly when `Gamma` is a list containing an occurrence of `A` and `Gamma'` is obtained from `Gamma` by removing that occurrence of `A`. The specification also does not include a definition of the `atom` predicate that is meant to identify all the propositional symbols. This predicate can be defined simply by adding clauses to the program that enumerate all the propositional letters that appear in a formula. For example, if we wish to prove the formula

```
(a ==> (a ==> b) ==> (a ==> b ==> c) ==> c
```

we might add to Figure 9.3 the following declaration and formula

```
type a, b, c    form.
atom a & atom b & atom c.
```

The query

```
?- pi a\ pi b\ pi c\ atom a => atom b => atom c =>
           seq nil (a ==> (a ==> b) ==> (a ==> b ==> c) ==> c).
```

achieves the same effect by introducing three new constants and assuming that each of them satisfies the `atom` predicate.

9.2 Encoding natural deduction for intuitionistic logic

We now consider the encoding of a natural deduction proof system for first-order intuitionistic logic. Formulas for this logic are encoded using the constants

```
type atom      form -> o.
type seq       list form -> form -> o.

seq Gamma A :- atom A, memb_and_rest A Gamma _.
seq Gamma tt.
seq Gamma (A && B)  :- seq Gamma A, seq Gamma B.
seq Gamma (A !! B)  &
seq Gamma (B !! A)  :- seq Gamma A.
seq Gamma (A ==> B) :- seq (A::Gamma) B.
seq Gamma _ :- memb_and_rest ff Gamma _.
seq Gamma G :- memb_and_rest (A && B) Gamma Gamma',
               seq (A::B::Gamma') G.
seq Gamma G :- memb_and_rest (A !! B) Gamma Gamma',
               (seq (A::Gamma') G; seq (B::Gamma') G).
seq Gamma G :- memb_and_rest (A ==> B) Gamma Gamma',
  ( atom A, memb_and_rest A Gamma' _, seq (B::Gamma') G;
    A = (C && D),  seq ((C ==> D ==> B)::Gamma') G;
    A = (C !! D),  seq ((C ==> B)::(D ==> B)::Gamma') G;
    A = (C ==> D), seq ((D ==> B)::Gamma') A,
                   seq (B::Gamma') G;
    A = ff,        seq Gamma' G;
    A = tt,        seq (B::Gamma') G  ).
```

Figure 9.3. An encoding of a decision procedure for propositional intuitionistic
logic.

declared in the preceding section for propositional logic along with the two
constants in the declaration

```
type  all, some      (term -> form) -> form.
```

that were introduced in Section 7.1.1 for encoding first-order existential and
universal quantifiers.

Natural deduction proof systems are usually described through rules for
introducing and eliminating logical connectives in formulas. A proof system in
this style for intuitionistic first-order logic is shown in Figure 9.4. Notice that
three rules in this collection—the $\supset I$, $\vee E$, and $\exists E$ rules—use hypothetical
judgments as premises; in particular, paths in the derivation of the premises of
these rules are allowed to start with the formula shown enclosed in parentheses.
There is also a restriction on the variable y that appears in the $\forall I$ and $\exists E$ rules:
This variable must not be free in the conclusion of the rule or in any assumption
that remains undischarged after the rule application. The hypothetical and universal goals of λProlog provide a convenient means for specifying such aspects
of a natural deduction proof system, as will become apparent presently.

Our specification of the intuitionistic natural deduction system will take the
additional step of encoding proofs together with the first-order formulas they
prove. Figure 9.5 contains λProlog declarations for building representations of

$$\frac{A \wedge B}{A} \wedge E_1 \qquad \frac{A \wedge B}{B} \wedge E_2 \qquad \frac{A \quad B}{A \wedge B} \wedge I \qquad \frac{\perp}{A} \perp E \qquad \frac{}{\top} \top I$$

$$\begin{array}{cc} (A) \\ \vdots \end{array} \qquad \begin{array}{cc} (A) \ (B) \\ \vdots \ \ \vdots \end{array}$$

$$\frac{A \quad A \supset B}{B} \supset E \qquad \frac{B}{A \supset B} \supset I \qquad \frac{A \vee B \quad C \quad C}{C} \vee E \qquad \frac{A}{A \vee B} \vee I_1 \qquad \frac{B}{A \vee B} \vee I_2$$

$$\begin{array}{c} (A[y/x]) \\ \vdots \end{array}$$

$$\frac{\forall x\, A}{A[t/x]} \forall E \qquad \frac{A[y/x]}{\forall x\, A} \forall I \qquad \frac{\exists x\, A \quad C}{C} \exists E \qquad \frac{A[t/x]}{\exists x\, A} \exists I$$

Figure 9.4. Natural deduction rules for first-order intuitionistic logic.

```
kind  proof           type.

type true_i           proof.
type false_e          form  -> proof -> proof.
type and_i            proof -> proof -> proof.
type and_e1, and_e2   form  -> proof -> proof.
type imp_i            (proof -> proof) -> proof.
type imp_e            form -> proof -> proof -> proof.
type or_i1, or_i2     proof -> proof.
type or_e             form  -> form -> proof ->
                      (proof -> proof) -> (proof -> proof) -> proof.
type all_e            term  -> (term -> form) -> proof -> proof.
type all_i            (term -> proof) -> proof.
type some_e           (term -> form) -> proof ->
                      (term -> proof -> proof) -> proof.
type some_i           term  -> proof -> proof.
```

Figure 9.5. Constructors for natural deduction proof objects.

proof objects. In addition to defining the type proof corresponding to terms that represent proofs, this set of declarations identifies one (term) constructor for each of the inference rules in Figure 9.4. These constructors take arguments whose meanings should be easy to interpret from looking at the relevant components of the inference rule in Figure 9.5 that each constructor is intended to represent.

Figure 9.6 provides a specification of the inference rules in λProlog. The infix symbol # is used here to encode the binary relation between proofs and formulas: The intention is that a goal of the form Pf # F should be derivable from the specification just in the case that Pf represents a natural deduction proof of the formula represented by F. Notice that implicational goals are used to capture

```
type #                  proof -> form -> o.
infix # 2.


true_i # tt.
(and_i P1 P2) # (A && B)   :- (P1 # A), (P2 # B).
(or_i1 P) # (A !! B)       :- P # A.
(or_i2 P) # (A !! B)       :- P # B.
(imp_i Q) # (A ==> B)      :- pi p\ (p # A) => ((Q p) # B).
(some_i T P) # (some A)    :- P # (A T).
(all_i Q) # (all A)        :- pi y\ (Q y) # (A y).
(false_e A P) # A          :- P # ff.
(and_e1 B P) # A           :- P # (A && B).
(and_e2 A P) # B           :- P # (A && B).
(or_e A B P Q1 Q2) # C     :- (P # (A !! B)),
                              (pi p1\ (p1 # A) => ((Q1 p1) # C)),
                              (pi p2\ (p2 # B) => ((Q2 p2) # C)).
(imp_e A P1 P2) # B        :- (P1 # A), (P2 # (A ==> B)).
(some_e A P1 Q) # B        :- (P1 # (some A)),
                              pi y\ pi p\ (p # (A y)) => ((Q y p) # B).
(all_e T A P) # (A T)      :- (P # (all A)).
```

Figure 9.6. Encoding of the natural deduction inference rules.

the hypothetical judgments in the $\supset I$, $\vee E$, and $\exists E$ rules, and universal goals are used to introduce and subsequently abstract over the proofs of the assumed formulas. Note also the use of universal goals to enforce the newness constraint for the variable y in the $\forall I$ and $\exists E$ rules.

To illustrate the specification in Figure 9.6, let us assume that we also have the following declarations that identify the nonlogical part of the vocabulary:

```
type a, b    form.         % propositional constants
type q       term -> form. % a predicate of one argument
type c       term.         % a first-order constant
type f       term -> term. % a term constructor
```

Then the λProlog specification can be used to carry out simple *proof checking*: That is, the predicate # can be used to see if a given term of type proof is, in fact, a natural deduction proof of a particular formula. For example, the following queries are solvable:

```
?- (imp_i w\w) # (a ==> a).

?- (imp_i x\ imp_i y\ imp_e a x y) # (a ==> ((a ==> b) ==> b)).

?- (imp_i P\ all_i y\ imp_i Q\
     (imp_e (q (f y))
         (imp_e (q y) Q (all_e y (x\ (q x) ==> (q (f x)))) P))
```

```
         (all_e (f y) (x\ (q x) ==> (q (f x))) P)))
   # ((all x\ (q x) ==> (q (f x))) ==>
     (all x\ (q x) ==> (q (f (f x)))))).
```

As the following interaction illustrates, it is possible to use the specification of natural deduction to compute formulas for which a proof object is, in fact, a proof.

```
?- (imp_i w\ (and_i (and_e2 a w) (and_e1 b w))) # R.
R = a && b ==> b && a.
```

Sometimes proofs can be incompletely described by including free variables in them: The execution of the specification or logic program can compute bindings for these variables that complete the description of the proof. As an example, consider the following interaction.

```
?- (imp_i P\ all_i y\ imp_i Q\
     (imp_e (q (f y)) (imp_e (q y) Q (all_e y A P))
            (all_e (f y) A' P))) # B.
A = w\ p w ==> p (f w)
A' = w\ p w ==> p (f w)
B = all (w\ p w ==> p (f w)) ==> all (w\ p w ==> p (f (f w)))

?-
```

One might wonder if the specification can be employed as a theorem prover simply by using a logic variable for the proof term, as in the following query:

```
?- P # (a ==> ((a ==> b) ==> b)).
```

Unfortunately, this idea will not work satisfactorily in all but the simplest of cases. For example, while there is a simple proof for the formula in the query just presented, one that is, in fact, included explicitly in an earlier query, the depth-first search strategy of λProlog paired with the specification in Figure 9.5 will lead to a looping computation for the query shown.

9.3 A theorem prover for classical logic

We now consider specifying and implementing a specialized sequent-style proof system for classical logic. This sequent calculus, which we call CL, is based on formulas in negation normal form, a form that was identified previously in Section 7.5. Formulas in this normal form are constructed from literals (i.e., atoms or negated atoms), the logical constants $\top, \bot, \wedge,$ and $\vee,$ and the existential

$$\frac{\Sigma : A, \mathcal{L};\ \Gamma;\ \Phi}{\Sigma : \mathcal{L};\ A, \Gamma;\ \Phi}\ \text{literal} \qquad \frac{\Sigma : \neg A, \mathcal{L};\ \Gamma;\ \Phi}{\Sigma : \mathcal{L};\ \neg A, \Gamma;\ \Phi}\ \text{literal} \qquad \frac{\Sigma : \mathcal{L};\ \Gamma;\ \Phi, \exists_\tau x.B}{\Sigma : \mathcal{L};\ \exists_\tau x.B, \Gamma;\ \Phi}\ \exists$$

Rules that classify formulas into separate zones in a sequent.

$$\frac{}{\Sigma : \mathcal{L};\ \top, \Gamma;\ \Phi}\ \top R \qquad \frac{\Sigma : \mathcal{L};\ B, \Gamma;\ \Phi \quad \Sigma : \mathcal{L};\ C, \Gamma;\ \Phi}{\Sigma : \mathcal{L};\ B \wedge C, \Gamma;\ \Phi}\ \wedge R$$

$$\frac{\Sigma : \mathcal{L};\ B, C, \Gamma;\ \Phi}{\Sigma : \mathcal{L};\ B \vee C, \Gamma;\ \Phi}\ \vee R \qquad \frac{\Sigma \cup \{y : \tau\} : \mathcal{L};\ B[y/x], \Gamma;\ \Phi}{\Sigma : \mathcal{L};\ \forall_\tau x\, B, \Gamma;\ \Phi}\ \forall R$$

$$\frac{}{\Sigma : A, \neg A, \mathcal{L};\ \cdot;\ \Phi}\ \text{initial} \qquad \frac{\Sigma : \mathcal{L};\ B[t/x];\ \Phi, \exists_\tau x\, B}{\Sigma : \mathcal{L};\ \cdot;\ \exists_\tau x\, B, \Phi}\ \exists R$$

The introduction and initial rules. Here, A is atomic, t is a Σ-term, and y is not in Σ.

Figure 9.7. The sequent calculus proof system CL for classical logic.

and universal quantifiers. Sequents in CL, written as $\Sigma : \mathcal{L};\ \Gamma;\ \Phi$, consist of four *zones*, described as follows:

1. The *eigenvariable signature zone*, given by Σ, that identifies the set of eigenvariables that can be used in the formulas in the sequent
2. The *literal zone*, given by $\mathcal{L}$, that consists of a *set* of literals
3. The *introduction zone*, given by Γ, that consists of a *list* of formulas in negation normal form
4. The *existential zone*, given by Φ, that consists of a *list* of existentially quantified formulas

The rules that define CL are presented in Figure 9.7. In the initial and $\exists$R rules in this collection, $\cdot$ represents an empty list. The following observations can be made about the collection of rules: (1) The introduction zone of the sequent in the conclusion is empty for both the initial and the $\exists$R rules. (2) The introduction rules act only on the first formula in the introduction zone: In particular, if the first formula in the introduction zone is $\perp$ (false), then that sequent is not provable because there is no introduction rule for $\perp$. (3) In a bottom-up reading of the $\exists$R rule, an existentially quantified formula $\exists_\tau x\, B$ is removed from the existential zone, and an instance of it, $B[t/x]$, is placed into the introduction zone of the premise. At the same time, the formula $\exists_\tau x\, B$ is reinserted into the existential zone at the end.

The CL proof system is designed to give some structure to the search for classical proofs. In particular, we can view the bottom-up construction of proofs in this proof system as being governed by the contents of the introduction zone. If that list is nonempty, then the first element in that zone completely determines which inference rule must be applied. If that zone is empty, then either the initial rule or the $\exists$R rule may be tried. If the process is started with a propositional formula, say, B, then the proof for the sequent $\cdot : \cdot$; B; $\cdot$ results in a tree whose leaves (which must be proved by the initial rule) have literal zones corresponding to the disjuncts in the conjunctive normal form of B.

The high-level description of how to conduct proof search using CL that we have just provided can lead to a never-ending computation in some cases. For example, for any one-argument predicate q, the sequent $\cdot : \cdot$; $\exists_\tau x.q(x)$; $\cdot$ is not provable. When used with this sequent, proof search as described earlier leads to the attempt to prove sequents of the form $\cdot : q(t_1), \ldots, q(t_n)$; $\cdot$; $\exists_\tau x.q(x)$, for increasingly larger sets of terms $\{t_1, \ldots, t_n\}$. Hence proof search in this case does not terminate. Nonetheless, the CL proof system can be used to provide a complete proof procedure for first-order logic by taking two steps. First, we impose a limit on the number of times any given existentially quantified expression can be instantiated by the $\exists$R inference rule. Second, if no proof is found for a given bound, we increment that bound and search again.

Our first step in specifying the proof system CL in λProlog involves specializing the representation of formulas to those in negation normal form. First, we exclude ==> from our earlier collection of declared constants because implications are not permitted in negation normal forms. Second, we shall view literals as either *positive atoms* or *negative atoms*. Formally, we introduce a new type atm that will encode atoms, and we view predicate symbols as constructors of this type. Thus, if q is a one place predicate symbol, it will have the type term -> atm. The constants p and n then are used to inject terms of type atm positively or negatively into the type of formulas. These new type and constant declarations are give by the following signature:

```
kind   atm        type.
type   p, n        atm -> form.
```

As examples of our representation, if c is a constant of type term and r is a constant of type term -> atm (denoting a predicate of one argument), then (p (r c)) and (n (r c)) correspond to a pair of complementary literals, and the term ((p (r c)) !! (n (r c))) of type form encodes an instance of the principle of the excluded middle.

The λProlog program in Figure 9.8 provides an implementation of a queue, i.e., a linear structure in which items are taken out from one end and inserted at the other. Moreover, an item that enters such a queue gets to be reused a fixed number of times that is determined by the predicate bound. However, after an item has been used by being "popped off" the front, its reuse is delayed until all other items currently in the queue have been used; this effect is realized by pushing the item back at the end of the queue. In this code, we make use of functional difference lists, discussed in Section 5.8.2, to realize a list-based data

```
kind pair    type -> type -> type.
type pr      A -> B -> pair A B.

kind que     type -> type.
type que     (list (pair A int) -> list (pair A int)) -> que A.
type qpush   A -> que A -> que A -> o.
type qpop    A -> que A -> que A -> o.
type bound   int -> o.

qpush X (que k\ Phi k) (que k\ Phi ((pr X N)::k)) :- bound N.
qpop  X (que k\ ((pr X 1)::(Phi k)))
        (que k\ Phi k).
qpop  X (que k\ ((pr X N)::(Phi k)))
        (que k\ Phi ((pr X M)::k)) :- N > 1, M is N - 1.
```

Figure 9.8. A queue that allows reinserting an item a bounded number of times.

structure with the twist that we access items from the front and add back items at the end. The empty queue in this representation is given by the term (que x\x). The code uses the constructor pr to associate the items in the queue with an integer indicating the number of (re)uses left to reach the (preset) usage bound. When an item is freshly put into the queue, something that is realized through the qpush predicate, the number to be associated with it is acquired by using the bound predicate. The predicate qpop provides the means for extracting and thereby using items in the queue; this predicate ensures that the item is put back at the end of the list if the bound to its reuse has not been reached. Of course, it also must update the number of reuses left to reach the limit. To carry out the arithmetic needed in this process, the clauses specifying the qpop predicate use the previously discussed built-in λProlog evaluation predicate is.

Our encoding of a sequent of the form $\Sigma : \mathcal{L}$; Γ; Ψ does not maintain the eigenvariable zone explicitly. Rather, it uses λProlog-level universal quantifiers and the generic constants they introduce during computation to implicitly realize the eigenvariables together with their logical properties. Similarly, the set of literals $\mathcal{L}$ is encoded implicitly by using implications in λProlog goals: Specifically, the addition of a literal A to this zone is realized by adding the predicate lit A to the collection of assumed formulas. Using these devices, the proposition "the sequent $\Sigma : \mathcal{L}$; Γ; Φ has a proof in the CL proof system" is reduced to a relation between only two explicit arguments: the introduction zone and the existential zone. We use the predicate prv that takes a list and a queue of formulas to represent this relation. Figure 9.9 presents the declarations identifying the constants lit and prv. The figure also contains clauses for prv that encode the rules for CL that were presented in Figure 9.7.

```
type lit          form -> o.
type prv          list form -> que form -> o.

prv (tt        :: Gamma) Phi.
prv ((B && C) :: Gamma) Phi :- prv (B::Gamma) Phi,
                                prv (C::Gamma) Phi.
prv ((B !! C) :: Gamma) Phi :- prv (B::C::Gamma) Phi.
prv ((all B)  :: Gamma) Phi :- pi x\ prv ((B x)::Gamma) Phi.
prv ((some B) :: Gamma) Phi :- qpush (some B) Phi Q,
                                prv Gamma Q.
prv (p A      :: Gamma) Phi :- lit (p A) => prv Gamma Phi.
prv (n A      :: Gamma) Phi :- lit (n A) => prv Gamma Phi.
prv nil Phi :- lit (n A), lit (p A).
prv nil Phi :- qpop (some B) Phi Q, prv ((B T)::nil) Q.
```

Figure 9.9. A theorem prover for classical first-order logic.

A complete theorem prover that is based on the CL proof system is now realized through the following additional clauses.

```
posints 1.
posints N :- posints M, N is M + 1.

thm B :- posints N, bound N => prv (B::nil) (que x\x).
```

More precisely, B represents a formula in negation normal form that has a CL proof if and only if the goal (thm B) is provable.

Now that we have a specification of a prover, it is possible to consider improvements. For example, when moving a literal from the introduction zone to the literal zone, one could check whether the literal zone contains a complementary literal: That is, this check does not need to be delayed until the introduction zone is empty. One could code that modification naturally by deleting the three clauses in Figure 9.9 that mention the lit predicate and replacing them with the following:

```
prv (p A :: Gamma) Phi :- lit (n A) ; lit (p A) => prv Gamma Phi.
prv (n A :: Gamma) Phi :- lit (p A) ; lit (n A) => prv Gamma Phi.
```

One also might want to insist that if the literal zone of a sequent already contains complementary literals then no additional proof search should be conducted. One thus is tempted to replace the two clauses above with the following two clauses:

```
prv (p A :: Gamma) Phi :- lit (n A), ! ; lit (p A) => prv Gamma Phi.
prv (n A :: Gamma) Phi :- lit (p A), ! ; lit (n A) => prv Gamma Phi.
```

This modification is acceptable when there are no existential quantifiers in the formula that we are trying to prove. However, when existential quantifiers are

present, their processing introduces (free) logic variables in the interpreter for
λProlog, and the interaction between such logic variables and the Prolog-cut
(!) can lead to incompleteness in the theorem prover. As a specific example,
the formula

```
((p (r c)) !! (p (r t)) !! (p (g c)) !! (some x\ (n (r x)) && (n (g x)))).
```

is a theorem of classical logic, but it is not provable by the version of this prover
that makes use of cut (!). This fails because the logic variable that instantiates
x gets bound to t first and the cut then eliminates the path in which it would
get bound to c: Unfortunately, only this second path and binding will lead to a
proof.

9.4 A general architecture for theorem provers

We have relied up to this point on a reflection of provability relations directly
into predicates in a logic programming language. This approach has the benefit
of yielding a transparently correct specification. However, it also means that we
must use the control regimen of the interpreter for the underlying language when
searching for proofs based on the deductive calculus. This actually can be quite
a severe limitation: For example, proof search within λProlog is designed to
be predictable, whereas we may want to vary the application of inference rules
depending on the formula to be proved in the setting of more general reasoning.
We can obtain such flexibility even when using λProlog if we encode inference
rules not directly as clauses but rather, for example, as atomic formulas that
describe how the goal of trying to prove the conclusion of the rule is related to
that of trying to prove its premises. Given such declarations, we can use clauses
to build flexible search engines that can put together the effects of inference
rules in any desired way. We elaborate on this approach in the rest of this
section.

9.4.1 Goals and tactics

The first step, then, is to abstract away from the particular structure of the objects
that are to be proved and to focus instead on the abstract task of proving such
objects. We shall refer to objects such as a formula, a sequent, or a typing judgment of the form (P # A) as *primitive goals*. Methods for proving primitive
goals are specific to the particular contexts to which this abstraction is applied.
In addition to the primitive goals, there are three *compound*, or *nonprimitive*,
goals: the vacuously true goal, the conjunctive goal, and the universally quantified goal. Goals of these kinds arise in the course of trying to solve primitive
goals; for example, the task of trying to prove a conjunctive formula yields the
conjoined goals of trying to prove each of the component formulas separately.

```
kind  goal    type.
type  trueg   goal.                    % vacuously true goal
type  cc      goal -> goal -> goal.    % conjunctive goal
type  allg    (A -> goal) -> goal.     % universally quantified goal
infixl cc     3.

type  goalreduce, redex, red1      goal -> goal -> o.
type  primgoal                     goal -> o.

redex (trueg cc G) G & redex (G cc trueg) G.
redex (allg x\trueg) trueg.

red1 G H :- redex G H, !.
red1 (G cc H) (Gx cc H) &
red1 (H cc G) (H cc Gx) :- red1 G Gx.
red1 (allg G) (allg Gx) :- pi x\ red1 (G x) (Gx x).

goalreduce G H :- red1 G Gx, !, goalreduce Gx H.
goalreduce G G.
```

Figure 9.10. The definition of goals and some operations on them.

The declarations in Figure 9.10 identify a type for goals and constants for representing compound goals. Also defined in the figure is a binary relation on goals called goalreduce. This relation holds between two goals when the second is reached by a sequence of simple rewrites that essentially erase true goals in conjunctive goals and lift such goals out of universally quantified ones. This approach to rewriting is discussed in Section 7.4.1.

Given the notion of goal, an inference rule is captured abstractly as a relation between a conclusion that is represented by a primitive goal and a collection of premises given by a goal that might be nonprimitive. When abstracted in this way, an inference rule represents a *tactic* for transforming a given goal. Such tactics are encoded in our λProlog programs as predicates that have the type goal -> goal -> o.

As an example of the use of goals and tactics, consider the problem of determining whether or not two nodes in a graph are connected by a path. Figure 9.11 contains a declaration for a node type and identifies five constants representing nodes. It also declares the constants adj and path to represent the adjacency and the path relationship between nodes. In the present context, expressions of the form (adj X Y) and (path X Y) are to be thought of as the primitive goals for showing, respectively, that X and Y are adjacent and that X and Y have a path between them. Edges between nodes then are defined through clauses for a basic tactic called adj_tac. Finally, path_base_tac and path_rec_tac are tactics representing steps that can be taken in calculating whether a path exists between two given nodes.

```
kind node                type.
type a, b, c, d, e       node.
type adj, path           node -> node -> goal.

primgoal (adj _ _) & primgoal (path _ _).

type adj_tac, path_base_tac, path_rec_tac    goal -> goal -> o.

adj_tac (adj a b) trueg  &  adj_tac (adj a c) trueg.
adj_tac (adj b d) trueg  &  adj_tac (adj c d) trueg.
adj_tac (adj d a) trueg  &  adj_tac (adj d e) trueg.
path_base_tac  (path X Y) (adj X Y).
path_rec_tac   (path X Y) ((adj X Z) cc (path Z Y)).
```

Figure 9.11. Graph and reachability described as goals and tactics.

```
type sq                 list form -> form -> goal.
primgoal (sq _ _).

type initial, and_r, imp_r, all_r, and_l, imp_l, all_l, all_l'
                 goal -> goal -> o.

initial (sq Gamma A) trueg :- memb_and_rest A Gamma _.
and_r   (sq Gamma (A && B)) ((sq Gamma A) cc (sq Gamma B)).
imp_r   (sq Gamma (A ==> B)) (sq (A::Gamma) B).
all_r   (sq Gamma (all A)) (allg x\ sq Gamma (A x)).
and_l   (sq Gamma A) (sq (B::C::Gamma') A) :-
               memb_and_rest (B && C) Gamma Gamma'.
imp_l   (sq Gamma A) ((sq Gamma B) cc (sq (C::Gamma') A)) :-
               memb_and_rest (B ==> C) Gamma Gamma'.
all_l   (sq Gamma A) (sq ((B T)::Gamma) A) :-
               memb_and_rest (all B) Gamma Gamma'.
all_l'  (sq Gamma A) (sq ((B T)::Gamma') A) :-
               memb_and_rest (all B) Gamma Gamma'.
```

Figure 9.12. Intuitionistic sequent calculus provability described via goals and tactics.

Another illustration of the use of goals and tactics appears in Figure 9.12. In this case, primitive goals encode the intention to prove intuitionistic sequents containing first-order formulas, and tactics represent the rules that can be applied toward carrying out this intention. Thus there are tactics corresponding to the initial rule and the left and right introduction rules for conjunction, implication, and universal quantifiers that appear in Figure 9.1. We observe that we have included two left-introduction rules for the universal quantifier. One of these rules, represented by the all_l tactic, instantiates the quantifier but also preserves the quantified formula in the sequent. The other, reflected in the all_l' tactic, instantiates the quantifier and drops the quantified formula. In each of the cases, the tactic encodes the corresponding inference rule as a binary relation that relates the conclusion to the premise.

9.4.2 Combining tactics into proof strategies

Tactics, starting with inference rules, can be combined to yield larger sequences of rule applications. It is also possible to abstract out of particular combinations and to think of strategies for realizing such combinations. Such strategies can be embedded in higher-order predicates that take tactics as arguments. We shall refer to predicates of this kind as *tacticals*. Figure 9.13 presents a few useful tacticals. As an example, the `orelse` tactical that appears here describes a method for forming the union of two tactics. Similarly, the `then` tactical describes the composition of two tactics. Notice that the `then` tactic cannot be equally described using the following simpler clause:

```
then Tac1 Tac2 In Out :- Tac1 In Mid, Tac2 Mid Out.
```

The way we use tactics here requires that their first argument be a primitive goal, whereas their second argument can be a compound goal. Thus the `Mid` goal that is obtained from the application of `Tac1` in the body of the clause just shown cannot be given directly to `Tac2` as its first argument. Rather, the application of `Tac2` must be "mapped" over all the primitive goals that appear in the instantiation of `Mid`. The predicate `maptac` in Figure 9.13 is defined to represent this kind of mapping action. The composition of tactics `Tac1` and `Tac2` then can be realized as the relational composition of the binary relations `Tac1` and (`maptac Tac2`).

Consider again the tactics in Figure 9.12 that encode the inference rules for a subset of intuitionistic first-order logic. A natural way to orchestrate their use in trying to prove a sequent is to begin by repeatedly applying the `and_r`, `and_l`, `imp_r`, and `all_r` tactics. These tactics correspond to inference rules whose premises are true if and only if their conclusions are true; such rules are said to be *invertible*, and they can be forced to appear at the end of a proof without any loss of completeness. The repeated use of these tactics can be captured in the `invertible` tactic that is defined below with the aid of some of the tactics from Figure 9.13.

```
invertible In Out :-
    repeat (orelse and_r (orelse and_l (orelse imp_r all_r))) In Out.
```

The following interaction shows applications of the `invertible` tactic.

```
?- invertible (sq [] ((a && (a ==> b)) ==> (a && b))) Out.
Out = ((sq (a :: (a ==> b) :: nil) a) cc (sq (a :: (a ==> b) :: nil) b))

?- invertible (sq [] ((all x\ (p x) ==> (p (f x)))) ==>
```

```
type maptac          (goal -> goal -> o) -> goal -> goal -> o.

maptac Tac trueg trueg.
maptac Tac (I1 cc I2) (O1 cc O2) :- maptac Tac I1 O1,
                                    maptac Tac I2 O2.
maptac Tac (allg In) (allg Out) :- pi t\ maptac Tac (In t) (Out t).
maptac Tac In Out :- primgoal In, Tac In Out.


type idtac           goal -> goal -> o.
type repeat, try     (goal -> goal -> o) -> goal -> goal -> o.
type then,
     orelse, orelse! (goal -> goal -> o) ->
                     (goal -> goal -> o) -> goal -> goal -> o.


idtac          In In.
then      Tac1 Tac2 In Out :- Tac1 In Mid, maptac Tac2 Mid Out.
orelse    Tac1 Tac2 In Out :- Tac1 In Out  ; Tac2 In Out.
orelse!   Tac1 Tac2 In Out :- Tac1 In Out, ! ; Tac2 In Out.
repeat    Tac      In Out :- orelse (then Tac (repeat Tac))
                             idtac In Out.
try       Tac      In Out :- orelse Tac idtac In Out.
```

Figure 9.13. The definition of some useful tacticals.

```
                    (all x\ (p x) ==> (p (f (f x)))))
          Out.
Out = (allg (w\ sq (p w :: (all w\ p w ==> p (f w)) :: nil)
            (p (f (f w)))))

?-
```

The goal that is produced by the second invocation of `invertible` above can be simplified by instantiating `(all w\ p w ==> p (f w))` twice. What remains at this point is a theorem of propositional intuitionistic logic that can be proved by using the theorem prover described in Section 9.1. To link with that theorem prover, we can define the following tactic:

```
ip_decide (sq Gamma A) trueg :- seq Gamma A.
```

Combining all these tactic applications, we can reduce our original goal of proving the formula

$$(\forall x. p\, x \supset p\, (f\, x)) \supset (\forall x. p\, x \supset p\, (f\, (f\, x)))$$

to wanting to establish a trivially true goal. The following interaction makes this process explicit.

```
?- then invertible (then all_l (then all_l' ip_decide))
     (sq [] ((all x\ (p x) ==> (p (f x))) ==>
             (all x\ (p x) ==> (p (f (f x))))))
```

```
    Out.
Out = allg W1\ trueg

?-
```

Thus the compound tactic

```
then invertible (then all_l (then all_l' ip_decide))
```

constitutes a script that organizes the basic tactics into a tactic that proves our original theorem.

9.5 Bibliographic notes

The specification and implementation of theorem provers described in this chapter use natural deduction and sequent calculus based presentations of intuitionistic and classical logic. Such calculi were first described by Gentzen (1969). Gentzen's sequent calculus for propositional intuitionistic logic includes a rule called *contraction* that allows formulas on the left of the sequent arrow to be duplicated in the premise. This rule does not blend well with automated theorem proving: Working backwards from the sequent to be proved, it breaks the requirement that the sequents left to be established are simpler. Kleene showed that for propositional intuitionistic logic, the contraction rule can be dispensed with in all cases except that of an implicational formula (Kleene 1952). The sequent calculus that is presented in Figure 9.1 is based on this observation. A naive implementation of this calculus can lead to a nonterminating proof search in some cases, as we have discussed. However, simple checks for loops can be built into the process, thereby yielding a decision procedure for intuitionistic propositional logic (Kleene 1952). Refinements to the inference rules that obviate such loop checks were investigated by several people, including Hudelmaier (1992) and Dyckhoff (1992), whose rules are the ones contained in Figure 9.2. The complexity of decision procedures for this logic has been studied by Statman (1979a), who has shown that the task of determining whether or not a propositional intuitionistic logic formula is provable is PSPACE complete.

The encoding of natural deduction and sequent calculus based inference systems in a higher-order logic programming language is a topic that has been studied extensively by Felty, starting with her doctoral dissertation (Felty 1989). The representation of proof objects and the specification of natural deduction rules in terms of the relation # that is discussed in Section 9.2 is modeled closely on a presentation by her (Felty 1993a). The relation P # A can be viewed as a typing judgment that is valid exactly when the object given by P is a proof *for* the formula corresponding to A. However, this kind of typing judgment is external to λProlog: At the outset, an expression of the form P # A can be a well formed even when P does not represent a proof of A. There are languages such as LF (Harper et al. 1993) that are based on the dependently typed λ-calculus in which relationships between proofs and formulas can be encoded so as to be validated directly in the type checking phase. In our case, such type checking is embodied in a logic program. Felty and Miller have elaborated on this idea more generally by showing how LF typing judgments can be translated automatically into equivalent λProlog programs (Felty 1989; Felty and Miller 1990). However, LF expressions can have highly redundant type information, and consequently, this translation turns out not to be a practical way to implement LF-style type checking. Snow, Baelde, and Nadathur have analyzed some of the type redundancy in this translation and have used their analysis to describe a more compact and more efficient translation of LF type judgments into λProlog (Snow 2010; Snow et al. 2010). Snow has developed the Parinati system based on these ideas as a practical means for realizing logic programming search within the LF framework.

The contraction rule discussed in conjunction with provability in propositional intuitionistic logic rears its head again in the quantificational setting. This time the rule cannot be eliminated while preserving completeness. Rather, its use must be controlled so as to still be able to describe complete proof procedures. The proof system for classical logic presented in Section 9.3 is based on the "systematic tableaux" used by Smullyan (1968) to prove the completeness of first-order classical logic.

The tactics and tacticals based approach to organizing proof search was developed by Gordon, Milner, and Wadsworth (1979). Their initial presentation of these ideas used the (higher-order) functional programming language ML as the vehicle for implementation. Many modern automatic and interactive theorem provers have adopted this framework; a striking example of its use appears in the system Isabelle (Paulson 1987). The implementation of tactics and tacticals in higher-order logic programming that is sketched in Section 9.4.2 is taken from Felty and Miller (1988) and Felty (1993a).

10

Computations over Functional Programs

The treatment of programs as objects is a theme common to systems such as interpreters, compilers, and program transformers. These systems typically use an abstract representation of programs that they then manipulate in accordance with the syntax-directed operational semantics of the underlying programming language. The λProlog language can capture such representation and manipulation of programs in a succinct and declarative manner. We illustrate this strength of λProlog by considering various computations over programs in a simple but representative functional language. In the first section we describe this language through its λ-tree syntax; we assume that the reader is sufficiently familiar with functional programming notions to be able to visualize a corresponding concrete syntax. In Section 10.2 we present two different specifications of evaluation with respect to this language. In Section 10.3 we consider the encoding of some transformations on programs that are driven by an analysis of their syntactic structure.

10.1 The `miniFP` programming language

The functional programming language that we use in this illustration is called `miniFP`. While `miniFP` is a typed language, in its encoding we initially treat its programs as being untyped: We later introduce a language of types and consider a program to be proper only if a type can be associated with it.

The core of the language of program expressions, then, is the untyped λ-calculus. We use the type `tm` for these expressions, and we encode them in the manner described in Section 7.1.2 for this calculus, with the difference that we use the symbol @ instead of `app` to represent the application of two expressions, and we write @ as an infix operator. The core is enhanced with two special forms corresponding to the conditional and recursion. These special forms are encoded using the constants `cond` of type `tm -> tm -> tm -> tm` and `fixpt`

```
kind tm        type.

% Lambda calculus with special forms
type abs       (tm -> tm) -> tm.        % function abstraction
type @         tm -> tm -> tm.          % application
infixl         @ 4.                     % application is infix
type cond      tm -> tm -> tm -> tm.    % conditional
type fixpt     (tm -> tm) -> tm.        % recursive functions
type cns       tm -> tm -> tm.          % list constructor

% Builtin datatypes and builtin functions over them
type i                           int -> tm. % integers coercion
type and, or, ff, tt                   tm. % for booleans
type cons, car, cdr, nullp, consp, null tm. % for lists
type greater, zerop, minus, sum, times  tm. % for integers
type equal                             tm. % general equality
```

Figure 10.1. The signature for miniFP.

of type (tm -> tm) -> tm, respectively. The first part of Figure 10.1 contains
λProlog declarations identifying these various types and constants.

Three built-in datatypes corresponding to booleans, integers, and lists are
included in miniFP. The constructors of the boolean type in miniFP are denoted
by the λProlog constants tt and ff. The integers of miniFP are represented
by an injection of the integers of λProlog using the constant i. Finally, the
λProlog constants cns and null are used to represent lists. As an illustration,
the expression

(cns (cns (i 4) null) (cns (i 5) null))

denotes a two element list in which each element is a singleton list of integers.

The miniFP language includes several built-in functions over its datatypes.
These functions are represented by constants of type tm in our encoding. Thus
we use car and cdr to denote the functions that return, respectively, the head
and tail of a list and cons to denote the function that adds an element to a list.
Similarly, there are functions over integers and booleans in our small language
that must be encoded. The declarations in Figure 10.1 identify the complete list
of constants introduced for this purpose.

Figure 10.2 uses the prog predicate to list and name four miniFP programs.
These examples denote recursive programs for computing Fibonacci numbers,
determining membership in lists, appending two lists, and mapping a function
over a list. The recursive aspect of these functions arises from the use of the
fixpt constructor, whose exact operational semantics will be given soon.

As mentioned previously, our encoding allows us to construct many λProlog
terms of type tm that do not correspond to valid miniFP expressions; thus
(cons @ (i 4) @ (i 5)) is a well-formed λProlog term of type tm, although

```
type prog        string -> tm -> o.
prog "fib" (fixpt fib\ abs n\
  cond (zerop @ n) (i 0)
       (cond (equal @ n @ (i 1)) (i 1)
             (sum @ (fib @ (minus @ n @ (i 1))) @
                    (fib @ (minus @ n @ (i 2)))))))).

prog "mem" (fixpt mem\ abs x\ abs l\
  cond (nullp @ l) ff
       (cond (and @ (consp @ l) @ (equal @ (car @ l) @ x)) tt
             (mem @ x @ (cdr @ l))))).

prog "appnd" (fixpt appnd\ abs l\ abs k\
  cond (nullp @ l) k (cons @ (car @ l) @ (appnd @ (cdr @ l) @ k))).

prog "map" (fixpt map\ abs f\ abs l\
  cond (nullp @ l) null (cons @ (f @ (car @ l)) @
                               (map @ f @ (cdr @ l))))).
```

Figure 10.2. Some named `miniFP` expressions.

it is not a valid object in `miniFP` because the second argument of `cons` does not represent a list. To identify the valid `miniFP` objects, we introduce a language of types and use this to formalize a typing judgment over terms of type `tm`. The typing discipline for `miniFP` is specified by the clauses in Figure 10.3. In particular, λProlog terms of type `ty` will denote types for `miniFP` programs. The predicate `typeof` is a binary relation that captures the relationship between a `miniFP` expression and a type.

Notice that expressions in `miniFP` may have more than one type. For example, each of the following queries is provable

```
typeof (abs w\ w) (arr int int).
typeof (abs w\ w) (arr bool bool).
pi t\ typeof (abs w\ w) (arr t t).
```

More generally, the `miniFP` expression for the identity function has type (`arr t t`) for every term `t` of type `ty`. As further examples, the query

```
?- sigma Exp\ prog Name Exp, typeof Exp Ty.
```

computes the following bindings for `Ty` for the named expressions `"fib"`, `"mem"`, `"appnd"`, and `"map"`, respectively.

```
Ty = arr int int.
Ty = arr A (arr (lst A) bool).
Ty = arr (lst A) (arr (lst A) (lst A)).
Ty = arr (arr A B) (arr (lst A) (lst B)).
```

```
kind ty                   type.
type int, bool            ty.
type lst                  ty -> ty.
type arr                  ty -> ty -> ty.
type typeof               tm -> ty -> o.


typeof (M @ N) A          :- typeof M (arr B A), typeof N B.
typeof (cond P Q R) A     :- typeof P bool, typeof Q A, typeof R A.
typeof (abs M) (arr A B)  :- pi x\ typeof x A => typeof (M x) B.
typeof (fixpt M) A        :- pi x\ typeof x A => typeof (M x) A.


typeof tt bool & typeof and (arr bool (arr bool bool)).
typeof ff bool & typeof or  (arr bool (arr bool bool)).
typeof equal (arr A (arr A bool)).


typeof null  (lst A).
typeof cons  (arr A (arr (lst A) (lst A))).
typeof car   (arr (lst A) A).
typeof cdr   (arr (lst A) (lst A)).
typeof consp (arr (lst A) bool).
typeof nullp (arr (lst A) bool).


typeof (i I) int.
typeof zerop   (arr int bool).
typeof greater (arr int (arr int bool)).
typeof minus   (arr int (arr int int)).
typeof sum     (arr int (arr int int)).
typeof times   (arr int (arr int int)).
```

Figure 10.3. Simple typing for miniFP.

Here, A and B are variables that range over type ty. Thus the last three of these expressions have *polymorphic* types.

10.2 Specifying evaluation for miniFP programs

Several different approaches have been developed for specifying evaluation in a functional programming setting. We show here how such approaches can be formalized in our logic programming language. In particular, we present logic programs for two different styles of evaluators for miniFP: *Big-step oper-ational semantics* is used in Section 10.2.1, and *evaluation contexts* are used in Section 10.2.2.

10.2.1 A big-step-style specification

We are interested here in defining a binary predicate called eval that is such that the atomic formula (eval M V) succeeds if and only if the call-by-value evalu-ation of the miniFP program M results in the value V. This kind of specification is called a *big-step specification* because the predicate eval relates a miniFP expression to its *final* value, a computation that may take several atomic steps. A contrasting style of specification, called a *small-step specification*, is one in which a term is related only to terms from which it results by applying a small number, typically just one, of atomic computation steps. The specification of the π-calculus that we provide in Section 11.2 will illustrate the small-step style of specification.

Figure 10.4 provides clauses that define the eval predicate. Some miniFP expressions are recognized as values, and they therefore evaluate to themselves. These expressions consist of the constructors for each of the built-in datatypes and the one representing abstraction. To evaluate an application, we proceed by evaluating the function and the argument and then applying the function to the argument; in the case where the function part is an abstraction, this application corresponds to a substitution that is realized elegantly through β-conversion in the specification language. Evaluation of the special forms also follows the familiar rules. For example, evaluation of a recursive definition is given by unfolding: The value of (fixpt R) is obtained by evaluating instead (R (fixpt R)). The treatment of the conditional makes use of the predicate if defined in Section 5.7. This is done only for convenience of presentation and is not essential. For example, the goal (if (U = tt) G H) can be rewritten as (U = tt, G ; U = ff, H) under the assumption that U must be bound to a term that corresponds to a miniFP boolean value. Similarly, the goal (if (M > N) G H) can be rewritten as (M > N, G ; M =< N, H) under the assumption that M and N range over integer values.

The specification of evaluation is dominated by the treatment of the built-in functions associated with the miniFP datatypes. The predicate special is introduced to identify these functions together with their arities. Moreover, the constant spec is added to the syntax of miniFP to encode the partial application of such functions to (evaluated) arguments. For example, the expression (spec 2 minus nil) denotes the functional object that is waiting for two arguments before it can apply the "subtraction" operation to those arguments. The specification of the apply predicate treats these special forms by first accumulating the necessary arguments into the spec-term and then performing the operation corresponding to the built-in function using the eval_spec predicate.

Given the specification of evaluation in Figure 10.4, the query

```
?- prog "fib" F, eval (F @ (i 12)) V.
```

computes the twelfth Fibonacci number (which is denoted by (i 144)) and binds the variable V to it. The query

```
?- prog "fib" Fib, prog "map" Map,
```

```
type eval          tm -> tm -> o.
type val           tm -> o.
type apply         tm -> tm -> tm -> o.
type eval_spec     tm -> list tm -> tm -> o.
type special       int -> tm -> o.

type spec          int -> tm -> list tm -> tm. % for specials


% Description of which expressions denote values
val (abs _) & val (i _)  & val tt   & val ff  & val null.
val (cns _ _) & val (spec _ _ _).


% eval and apply are the heart of evaluation
eval V V              :- val V.
eval (M @ N) V        :- eval M F, eval N U, apply F U V.
eval (fixpt R)   V    :- eval (R (fixpt R)) V.
eval (cond C L R) V   :- eval C B, if (B = tt) (eval L V)
                                             (eval R V).

eval F (spec I F nil) :- special I F.

apply (abs R) U V :- eval (R U) V.
apply (spec 1 F Args) U V :- eval_spec F (U::Args) V.
apply (spec C F Args) U (spec D F (U::Args)) :- C > 1, D is C - 1.


% Declaration of the arity of the built-in functions
special 2 or    & special 2 and    & special 2 equal &
special 1 car   & special 1 cdr    & special 2 cons  &
special 1 nullp & special 1 consp  & special 1 zerop &
special 2 minus & special 2 sum    & special 2 times &
special 2 greater.


% Description of how to compute the built-in functions
eval_spec car    ((cns V U)::nil) V.
eval_spec cdr    ((cns V U)::nil) U.
eval_spec cons   (U::V::nil) (cns V U).
eval_spec nullp (U::nil) V :- if (U = null) (V = tt) (V = ff).
eval_spec consp (U::nil) V :- if (U = null) (V = ff) (V = tt).
eval_spec and (C::B::nil) V :- if (B = ff) (V = ff)
                                  (if (C = ff) (V = ff) (V = tt)).
eval_spec or  (C::B::nil) V :- if (B = tt) (V = tt)
                                  (if (C = tt) (V = tt) (V = ff)).
eval_spec minus ((i N)::(i M)::nil) (i V) :- V is M - N.
eval_spec sum   ((i N)::(i M)::nil) (i V) :- V is M + N.
eval_spec times ((i N)::(i M)::nil) (i V) :- V is M * N.
eval_spec zerop ((i N)::nil) V   :- if (N = 0) (V = tt) (V = ff).
eval_spec equal (C::B::nil) V    :- if (B = C) (V = tt) (V = ff).
eval_spec greater ((i N)::(i M)::nil) V :-
                        if (M > N) (V = tt) (V = ff).
```

Figure 10.4. Evaluation for miniFP specified by using a big-step specification.

```
eval (Map @ Fib @ (cons @ (i 9) @ (cons @ (i 4) @ null))) V.
```

maps the Fibonacci function over a list of two integers and binds V to the expression

```
(cns (i 34) (cns (i 3) null)).
```

Our specification of equality for miniFP values makes use of equality as it is defined on λProlog terms. This leads to a notion of equality that is stronger that the one usually present in functional programming languages. The difference arises from the fact that equality in λProlog applies also to terms containing abstraction. Thus the goal

```
?- eval (equal @ (abs x\x) @ (abs y\y)) V.
```

in λProlog will return the value tt for V. This goal is asking if two terms that represent the identity function in the functional programming language are equal. Most realizations of functional programming do not permit this kind of comparison of functions. One way to more accurately reflect what is actually permitted is to replace the formula B = C in the clause for eval_spec for the built-in function equal with (eq B C), where eq is defined explicitly through the clauses

```
type eq     tm -> tm -> o.
eq (i N) (i N)  &  eq tt tt  &  eq ff ff.
eq null null.
eq (cns X Y) (cns U V) :- eq X U, eq Y V.
```

If we follow this approach only structures built from integers, booleans, and lists will be checked for equality.

10.2.2 A specification using evaluation contexts

Another way to describe evaluation is as the process of repeatedly replacing redexes in a term until such time that the term represents a value. In particular, let R be a closed term of type tm representing a miniFP program. Then we can specify the evaluation of R as follows. If R is a value, it evaluates to itself. Otherwise, we scan R looking for a subexpression to rewrite. Once we find such a subexpression, we replace it with what it rewrites to and then try to evaluate the overall expression again. A particular evaluation strategy such as call-by-value evaluation is determined by *how* we identify the next redex to rewrite. The location of such a redex in a given term can be characterized through the definition of an *evaluation context*.

```
type non_val, redex   tm -> o.
type reduce, evalc    tm -> tm -> o.
type context          tm -> (tm -> tm) -> tm -> o.

% Declare which expressions are not values
non_val (_ @ _) & non_val (fixpt _) & non_val (cond _ _ _).
non_val M :- special _ M.

% Declare which expressions are top-level reducible expressions
redex F          :- special _ F.
redex (U @ V) :- val U, val V.
redex (cond tt _ _) & redex (cond ff _ _) & redex (fixpt _).

% Describe how to reduce a redex
reduce ((abs R) @ N) (R N).
reduce (fixpt R) (R (fixpt R)).
reduce (cond tt L R) L.
reduce (cond ff L R) R.
reduce F (spec C F nil) :- special C F.
reduce ((spec 1 F Args) @ N) V :- eval_spec F (N::Args) V.
reduce ((spec C F Args) @ N) (spec D F (N::Args)) :-
  C > 1, D is C - 1.

% Separate an expression into an evaluation context and a redex
context R (x\ x) R :- redex R.
context (cond M N P) (x\ cond (E x) N P) R :-
  non_val M, context M E R.
context (M @ N) (x\ (E x) @ N) R :-
  non_val M, context M E R.
context (V @ M) (x\ V @ (E x)) R :-
  val V, non_val M, context M E R.

% Evaluation repeatedly uses evaluation contexts and redexes
evalc V V :- val V.
evalc M V :- context M E R, reduce R N, evalc (E N) V.
```

Figure 10.5. Evaluation for miniFP via rewriting redexes.

The declarations in Figure 10.5 show how call-by-value evaluation for miniFP can be specified in λProlog using evaluation contexts. The predicate non_val that is defined here identifies miniFP expressions that do not represent values; such expressions should contain redexes that can be rewritten. The predicate redex succeeds if its argument is a redex, and the binary predicate reduce describes how such a redex is rewritten. The most interesting relation defined here is context, which describes how to separate a nonvalue term into an evaluation context and a redex. In particular, if the goal (context M E R) succeeds, then R is the redex that must be rewritten next in a call-by-value evaluation of M, and E is a term of type tm -> tm that is obtained from M by abstracting out the occurrence of R; thus E characterizes the *context* in which R occurs. As an example, the query

```
?- context (cond ((abs x\ ff) @ tt) (i 2) (i 3)) E R.
```

succeeds exactly once, yielding the binding (abs (x\ ff) @ tt) for R and the binding (W\ cond W (i 2) (i 3)) for E. Similarly, the query

```
?- context (cond ff ((abs x\ i 2) @ (i 3)) (i 4)) E R.
```

succeeds exactly once, binding R to the redex (cond ff (abs (x\ i 2) @ i 3) (i 4)) and E to the term (w\ w); the binding for E indicates that the next redex to be rewritten is, in fact, the entire term being considered. Given the definitions of context and reduce, the evalc predicate, which is intended to specify call-by-value evaluation in this style, is defined as one that repeatedly looks for the next redex to rewrite using the context predicate and replaces this with its reduced form until such time that a value has been found.

10.3 Manipulating functional programs

It is a simple conceptual step from writing evaluators for functional programs to specifying transformations on the source code of such programs that preserve their semantics while changing, for example, their efficiency or execution behavior. We consider a few simple examples of such transformations here and show how they can be encoded transparently in λProlog programs.

10.3.1 *Partial evaluation of* miniFP *programs*

Our specifications of the evaluation of a recursive function definition made natural use of the meaning of fixed points. In particular, both styles of evaluators for miniFP reduce the fixed point expression (fixpt R) to (the semantically equivalent) expression (R (fixpt R)). From the operational point of view, reducing a fixed point expression in this way (along with β-reduction at the logic level) amounts to unfolding a recursive definition. For example,

```
?- prog "map" (fixpt Body), Unfold = (Body (fixpt Body)).
```

will bind the variable Unfold to the expression

```
abs f\ abs l\
  cond (nullp @ l) null
       (cons @ (f @ (car @ l)) @
                (fixpt map\ abs f1\ abs l1\
                       cond (nullp @ l1) null
                         (cons @ (f1 @ (car @ l1)) @
                           (map @ f1 @ (cdr @ l1))) @ f @ (cdr @ l)))
```

This expression also carries out the computation expected of the `map` function. From a pragmatic perspective, it may be useful to transform a recursive definition this way: Doing so may, for example, enable further simplifications statically in situations where the arguments to which `map` is to be applied are known.

As another example of this kind of "static" or "partial" evaluation of programs, it might be useful to simplify parts of a function body. Our earlier specifications of evaluation do not permit such simplification because they do not allow for evaluation inside abstractions: The value of the term (`abs R`) is always (`abs R`) even if there are redexes inside `R` that can be rewritten. However, it is easy to extend these evaluators to allow for evaluation within abstraction contexts. For example, consider the following simple specification of "mixed evaluation" (i.e., mixing regular evaluation with a kind of "symbolic" evaluation):

```
type mixeval    tm -> tm -> o.
mixeval (abs R) (abs S) :- pi k\ val k => eval (R k) (S k).
```

The predicate `mixeval` attempts to evaluate under a top-level binder by introducing a "new value" (denoted by the bound variable) and attempting to evaluate the resulting expression with this new assumption. As an example, the query

```
?- prog "appnd" App,
   eval (App @ (cons @ (i 1) @ (cons @ (i 5) @ null))) R,
   mixeval R S.
```

yields the single answer substitution, binding the variable `S` to

```
abs w\ cons @ (i 1) @ (cons @ (i 5) @ w).
```

Using this mixed-evaluation predicate, we have transformed the `miniFP` program that uses the `append` program to place two elements at the front of any given list into a program that does the same without using the `append` program. Notice also that there is a theorem that can be proved about this (simple) implementation of mixed evaluation: If `mixeval` relates the two `miniFP` abstractions (`abs R`) and (`abs S`), and if `T` is a value (i.e., the atomic formula (`val T`) is provable), then the evaluation of (`R T`) yields the value (`S T`). Thus a certain kind of "soundness" for `mixeval` is easy to guarantee.

10.3.2 Transformation to continuation passing style

A well-studied and useful transformation on functional programs is the *continuation passing style* (CPS) transformation. To keep our illustration of how such a transformation may be specified simple, we limit our language to the

```
type ftrans, phi    tm -> tm -> o.

ftrans (abs V) (abs k\ k @ U) :- phi (abs V) U.
ftrans (M @ N) (abs k\ P @ (abs m\ Q @ (abs n\ m @ k @ n))) :-
    ftrans M P, ftrans N Q.

phi (abs M) (abs k\ abs x\ (P x) @ k) :-
    pi x\ pi y\ ftrans x (abs k\ k @ y) => ftrans (M x) (P y).
```

Figure 10.6. The Fischer CPS transformation for the call-by-value λ-calculus.

(untyped) λ-calculus fragment of `miniFP`; in other words, the only constructors we permit are `abs` and `@`.

The *Fischer CPS transformation* for call-by-value evaluation is given by two functions $\mathcal{F}[\cdot]$ and $\Psi[\cdot]$, which are defined as follows:

$$\mathcal{F}[V] = \bar{\lambda}k\,(k\;\Psi[V])$$
$$\mathcal{F}[M\;N] = \bar{\lambda}k\,(\mathcal{F}[M]\,(\bar{\lambda}m\,(\mathcal{F}[N]\,\bar{\lambda}n\,(m\;k\;n))))$$
$$\Psi[x] = x$$
$$\Psi[\lambda x\,M] = \lambda k\,\lambda x\,(\mathcal{F}[M]\;k)$$

Here, V ranges over values that correspond to λ-abstractions and variables. The function $\mathcal{F}[\cdot]$ is defined for all untyped λ-terms, and $\Psi[\cdot]$ is defined for all values. Some of the λ-abstractions in the results of the transformations have been marked as $\bar{\lambda}$: We ignore these markings initially, treating them as the usual abstractions.

Figure 10.6 shows a straightforward encoding of these functions in a relational specification. Using this definition, the following query computes the CPS transformation of the λ-term $((\lambda u\,u)\,(\lambda u\,u))$:

```
?- ftrans ((abs u\u) @ (abs u\u)) F.

F = (abs W1\ (abs (W2\ W2 @ abs W3\ abs W4\ abs (W5\ W5 @ W4) @ W3)) @
     (abs W2\ (abs (W3\ W3 @ abs W4\ abs W5\ abs (W6\ W6 @ W5) @ W4)) @
     (abs W3\ W2 @ W1 @ W3))).
```

The result of this transformation is rather complicated because it contains many more β-redexes than there were in the original, untransformed term. Some of these redexes are introduced solely for the purpose of providing a compositional account of the transformation and therefore are often called *administrative redexes*. These redexes are marked using the $\bar{\lambda}$ symbol. It is possible to remove such redexes from the transformed expression by rewriting them away. To that end, we introduce the new constructor `adm` of type `(tm -> tm) -> tm` to denote the marked abstractions, and we add clauses to those shown in Figure 10.6 to

```
type adm                           (tm -> tm) -> tm.
type phi, ftrans, admred, red1, red  tm -> tm -> o.

ftrans (abs V) (adm k\ k @ U) :- phi (abs V) U.
ftrans (M @ N) (adm k\ P @ (adm m\ Q @ (adm n\ m @ k @ n))) :-
    ftrans M P, ftrans N Q.

phi (abs M) (abs k\ abs x\ (P x) @ k) :-
    pi x\ pi y\ ftrans x (adm k\ k @ y) => ftrans (M x) (P y).

admred ((adm R) @ N) (R N).

red1 M N :- admred M N.
red1 (M @ N) (M' @ N) & red1 (N @ M) (N @ M') :- red1 M M'.
red1 (adm R) (abs S) & red1 (abs R) (abs S)  :-
    pi x\ red1 (R x) (S x).

red M N :- red1 M P, !, red P N.
red M M.
```

Figure 10.7. Two-phase CPS transformation for the call-by-value λ-calculus.

realize the reduction of administrative redexes. The new specification of `ftrans` is given in Figure 10.7. Notice that in this transformation we eventually change all marked abstractions back to an unmarked form. Using this two-pass design, it is possible to compute more compact Fischer-style CPS transformations. Revisiting the preceding example, the query

```
?- ftrans ((abs x\x) @ (abs x\x)) T, red T S.
```

will bind S to the smaller term

```
(abs W1\ (abs W2\ abs W3\ W2 @ W3) @ W1 @ (abs W2\ abs W3\ W2 @ W3)).
```

10.4 Bibliographic notes

Denotational semantics have long been used to provide programming languages with compositional semantic specifications (Stoy 1977). Higher-order functional programming languages, such as Scheme and ML, often have been used to provide natural and immediate implementations of denotational semantics–based specifications. In recent years, operational semantics specifications of programming languages have become increasingly popular. Operational semantics specifications typically are given via inference rules based on the syntactic structure of expressions. As a result, logic programming languages are well suited for providing immediate and natural implementations of such specifications. Since the syntax of programs usually includes binding constructs, λProlog, which integrates λ-tree syntax with logic programming, is a natural setting for specifying and executing operational semantics specifications of programming languages.

Plotkin (2004) presented operational semantics via syntax-directed inference rules in a form that is often called *small-step operational semantics* or *structural operational semantics*. Big-step style specifications, used in the example in Section 10.2.1, were proposed by Kahn (1987) under the name *natural semantics*. Evaluation by evaluation contexts was first proposed by Felleisen and Hieb (1992).

The evaluators for functional programs presented in this chapter used β-reduction to implicitly realize substitution of an actual argument for a formal parameter in the body of a function. It is possible also to model substitution explicitly by using the common practice of implementing function calls via the creation of function closures. Hannan and Miller (1992) showed how to systematically transform specifications that use β-reduction to realize substitutions into specifications that use function closures instead. By doing this, they showed that it is possible to systematically translate big-step specifications of evaluation into lower-level abstract machine specifications.

The mixed-evaluation example in Section 10.3 was presented by Hannan and Miller (1989). There are many varieties of continuation passing style transformations: The example in Section 10.3 is an implementation of the transformation given by Sabry and Felleisen (1993) that is itself modeled on the transformation given by Fischer (1972). The first examples of manipulating programs based on a λ-tree syntax representation perhaps can be traced to Huet and Lang (1978), who showed that simple structural analysis of recursive programs can be realized through second-order matching. Miller and Nadathur describe an extension to such analyses by using program clauses that mix inference rules with unification (Miller and Nadathur 1987; Nadathur and Miller 1998); using this approach, they presented, for example, a λProlog program for recognizing functional programs that are tail-recursive. The master's thesis of Mottl (2000) contains several more examples of program analyses and transformations implemented using λProlog.

The functional programming language represented by miniFP does not allow for let expressions. It is easy to add such expressions by modeling a concrete syntax expression of the form let x = t in b by the λProlog term (let t (x\b)), where let is a new constructor given by the declaration

```
type    let    tm -> (tm -> tm) -> tm.
```

Evaluation can be extended to include such expressions by adding a clause such as

```
eval (let T R) V :- eval T U, eval (R U) V.
```

The typing rules typically associated with the new construct allow for a form of polymorphism called *let-polymorphism*. The usual algorithm for inferring types in this context, which is called *algorithm W* (Damas and Milner 1982), is rather difficult to specify in our logic programming setting. In particular, no simple extension to the program provided in Figure 10.3 can realize this algorithm. The doctoral thesis of Liang (1996) describes some approaches to the specification and implementation of polymorphic typing in this extended setting.

Given the logical nature of the specifications of evaluation, typing, and even program manipulations for miniFP, it is natural to consider proving formal properties about them. For example, one might think of proving that evaluation of a given miniFP program can yield at most one value, that the type of a program is preserved under evaluation, and that replacing a term by one related to it through mixed evaluation preserves the value of the embedding term. The Abella interactive theorem prover (Gacek 2008; Gacek et al. 2008) can be used to prove such theorems about (restricted) hohh specifications.

11

Encoding a Process Calculus Language

This chapter considers the encoding of a process calculus within a higher-order logic programming language. Process calculi have been proposed in the literature as a means for modeling concurrent systems. The π-calculus in particular makes use of a sophisticated binding mechanism to encode communication between processes. Our goal here is to show that such binding mechanisms can be treated naturally using λ-tree syntax in λProlog. Since we do not discuss the π-calculus itself in any detail, a reader probably would need a prior exposure to this calculus to best appreciate the nuances of our encodings. However, our primary focus is on showing how a presentation of a formal system can be transformed into a complete and logically precise description in λProlog and how such a description can be used computationally. Thus a reader who has understood the earlier chapters also should be able to follow our development and perhaps will learn something about the π-calculus from it.

The first two sections of this chapter describe an abstract syntax representation for processes in the π-calculus and the specification of the standard transition relation over such processes. A highlight of this specification is that the transition rules are encoded in a completely logical fashion through the use of λ-tree syntax: The usual side conditions involving names are captured completely using binders and their mobility. Sections 11.3 and 11.4 discuss how our encoding can be used in analyzing computational behavior. This discussion also illuminates shortcomings of the logic programming setting in specifying what is known as the *must* behavior of processes. The last section further illustrates our approach to abstract syntax by showing the translation of a mapping of the λ-calculus under a call-by-name evaluation semantics into the π-calculus.

11.1 Representing the expressions of the π-calculus

The π-calculus is a language for modeling processes that interact using names. In particular, this calculus permits communication via named channels, and the names of channels are communicated through these means. Thus there are two syntactic categories that are important to process expressions: *names* and *processes*.

Process expressions are defined by the following syntax rule.

$$P := 0 \mid P \mid P \mid P + P \mid x(y).P \mid \bar{x}y.P \mid [x = y].P \mid \tau.P \mid (y)P \mid \, ! \, P$$

In these expressions, x and y represent names. The first expression, 0, corresponds to a process that cannot perform any actions. The expressions $P \mid P$ and $P + P$ correspond, respectively, to the parallel composition and the combination via a choice of two processes. The following four expressions constitute processes with *prefixes* that support interaction: $x(y).P$ represents a process that can accept a name on the channel x and then will transform into P with y bound to the input name; $\bar{x}y.P$ is a process that can evolve by outputting the name y on the channel x; $[x = y].P$ is a process that can become P provided that the names x and y are equal; and $\tau.P$ is a process that can evolve through a silent action. The expression $(y)P$ represents the restriction of the name y to P: Interactions can take place internal to P through this name, but the process cannot communicate externally along channel $\bar{y}$ or channel y. Finally, $! \, P$ denotes the parallel composition of any number of copies of P.

To represent expressions of the π-calculus in λProlog, we shall make use of the types `name` and `proc` for names and processes. We then introduce constructors with appropriate argument types for each category of processes. The declarations for these types and constructors are shown in Figure 11.1: The order of declaration of the process constructors follows the order in which the process expression of each kind is shown in the syntax rule. Notice that the two process expressions $x(y).P$ and $(y)P$ embody a binding notion. The λ-tree syntax for these expressions accordingly will include a λ-term with an explicit abstraction. This fact is reflected in the types of the constructors for such processes: `in` and `nu` each have an argument of type `name -> proc`.

Figure 11.1 also contains illustrations of the chosen λ-tree syntax. In particular, the clauses for the `example` predicate pair representations of the following process expressions (read row-by-row) with the numbers 1 through 8:

$$(b(y).0) \mid (\bar{b}a.0) \qquad\qquad (b(y).\bar{x}a.0) + (\bar{b}a.b(y).0)$$
$$(x)((x(y).0) \mid (\bar{x}a.0)) \qquad\qquad (x)(\bar{a}x.0)$$
$$a(y).((y(w).0) \mid (\bar{b}b.0)) \qquad\qquad a(y).((y(w).\bar{b}b.0) + (\bar{b}b.y(w).0))$$
$$(y)\bar{a}y.((y(w).0) \mid (\bar{b}b.0)) \qquad\qquad (y)\bar{a}y.((y(w).\bar{b}b.0) + (\bar{b}b.y(w).0))$$

The occurrences of a and b are free in all these expressions, whereas all the occurrences of x, y, and w are bound. Free names are denoted in the abstract syntax representation by constants of type `name`.

```
kind name          type.

kind proc          type.
type null          proc.
type plus, par     proc -> proc -> proc.
type in            name -> (name -> proc) -> proc.
type out, match    name -> name -> proc -> proc.
type taup          proc -> proc.
type nu            (name -> proc) -> proc.
type bang          proc -> proc.

type a, b, c       name.
type example       int -> proc -> o.
example 1 (par (in b y\ null) (out b a null)).
example 2 (plus (in b y\ out b a null) (out b a (in b y\ null))).
example 3 (nu x\ par (in x y\ null) (out x a null)).
example 4 (nu x\ out a x null).
example 5 (in a y\ par  (in y w\ null) (out b b null)).
example 6 (in a y\ plus (in y w\ out b b null)
                        (out b b (in y w\ null))).
example 7 (nu y\ out a y (par  (in y w\ null) (out b b null))).
example 8 (nu y\ out a y (plus (in y w\ out b b null)
                        (out b b (in y w\ null)))).
```

Figure 11.1. Representing π-calculus expressions.

In all but the last section of this chapter we will restrict our attention to processes that do not include the ! operator. Processes that belong to this variant of the π-calculus are said to be *finite*.

11.2 Specifying one-step transitions

The operational semantics of the π-calculus usually is given by a small-step semantics that is presented by inference rules defining *one-step labeled transitions*. These transitions are denoted by expressions of the form $P \xrightarrow{A} Q$, where P and Q are processes, and A is an action. The intuitive meaning of such an expression is that the process P interacts with the environment via the action A and then continues as Q. The π-calculus has three kinds of actions, one each for inputting and outputting a name on a channel and a "silent" action that occurs without involving the environment. The three lines in Figure 11.2 are the λProlog declarations for expressions representing actions: action is the type for such expressions, tau denotes the silent action, (dn x y) denotes the inputting of y on channel x, and (up x y) denotes the outputting of y on channel x.

Our specification of the transition rules for the π-calculus uses two relations. One of these will describe *free* actions that transform processes; this relation will

```
kind action       type.
type tau          action.
type up, dn       name -> name -> action.

type one    proc ->            action ->              proc  -> o.
type onep   proc -> (name -> action) -> (name -> proc) -> o.

one  (taup P)       tau     P.
one  (out X Y P)    (up X Y) P.
onep (in X M)       (dn X)   M.
one  (match X X P) A P' :- one  P A P'.
onep (match X X P) A P' :- onep P A P'.
one  (plus P Q) A P'      :- one  P A P'; one  Q A P'.
onep (plus P Q) A P'      :- onep P A P'; onep Q A P'.
one  (par  P Q) A (par P' Q) &
one  (par  Q P) A (par Q P') :- one P A P'.
onep (par  P Q) A (y\ par (P' y) Q) &
onep (par  Q P) A (y\ par Q (P' y)) :- onep P A P'.
one  (nu P) A (nu P')                :- pi y\ one  (P y) A (P' y).
onep (nu P) A (x\ nu y\ P' y x)      :- pi y\ onep (P y) A (P' y).
onep (nu P) (up X) P'                :-
                  pi y\ one  (P y) (up X y) (P' y).
one  (par P Q) tau (nu y\ par (P' y) (Q' y)) &
one  (par Q P) tau (nu y\ par (Q' y) (P' y)) :-
                  onep P (up X) P', onep Q (dn X) Q'.
one  (par P Q) tau (par S (T Y)) :- one  P (up X Y) S,
                                    onep Q (dn X)   T.
one  (par P Q) tau (par (S Y) T) :- onep P (dn X) S,
                                    one  Q (up X Y) T.
```

Figure 11.2. The operational semantics of the finite π-calculus.

be given by the predicate one of type proc -> action -> proc -> o. The other relation will characterize *bound* actions that yield abstracted processes. The predicate onep of type proc -> (name -> action) -> (name -> proc) -> o will encode this relation.

The clauses that we use to specify the predicates one and onep are based directly on the one-step transition rules of the π-calculus. Consider, for example, the following rules that do not explicitly reference name bindings:

$$\text{MATCH}: \frac{P \xrightarrow{\alpha} P'}{[x = x]P \xrightarrow{\alpha} P'} \qquad \text{SUM}: \frac{P \xrightarrow{\alpha} P'}{P + Q \xrightarrow{\alpha} P'} \qquad \frac{P \xrightarrow{\alpha} P'}{Q + P \xrightarrow{\alpha} P'}$$

These two rules have the following immediate rendition as program clauses:

```
one  (match X X P) A P' :- one  P A P'.
onep (match X X P) A P' :- onep P A P'.
```

```
one   (plus P Q)    A P' :- one  P A P'; one  Q A P'.
onep  (plus P Q)    A P' :- onep P A P'; onep Q A P'.
```

In our setting, we must consider the use of the inference rules in the context of both free and bound actions. For this reason, there is a clause for each for the predicates one and onep corresponding to each rule. Notice that the type of A in these clauses is either `action` or `name -> action` and that the type of P' is, correspondingly, either `proc` or `name -> proc`.

The main difference between the usual specification of the π-calculus and the specification here is in the treatment of bindings. Consider, for example, the following inference rule.

$$\text{RES} : \frac{P \xrightarrow{\alpha} P'}{(y)P \xrightarrow{\alpha} (y)P'}$$

There is a side condition associated with this rule: y must not be a name appearing in the action α. This rule can be specified by the clauses

```
one   (nu P) A (nu P')           :- pi y\ one  (P y) A (P' y).
onep  (nu P) A (x\ nu y\ P' y x) :- pi y\ onep (P y) A (P' y).
```

In both these clauses, the variable A is implicitly universally quantified over the entire clause, and the quantifier for y appears within the scope of the quantifier for A. As a result, all legal substitution instances of these clauses will be such that y will not occur in the second argument of the atomic formula in the body of the clauses: As discussed in Section 3.3.1, logically correct substitution into quantified formulas must not permit variable capture. Thus the side condition associated with the RES rule is realized declaratively through a proper nesting of quantification in the clauses specifying it.

A more interesting situation involving binding is presented by the following rules that are part of the usual presentation of the π-calculus:

$$\text{INPUT-ACT} : \frac{}{x(z).P \xrightarrow{x(w)} P\{w/z\}} \qquad \text{OPEN} : \frac{P \xrightarrow{\bar{x}y} P'}{(y)P \xrightarrow{\bar{x}(w)} P'\{w/y\}}$$

$$\text{CLOSE} : \frac{P \xrightarrow{\bar{x}(w)} P' \quad Q \xrightarrow{x(w)} Q'}{P \mid Q \xrightarrow{\tau} (w)(P' \mid Q')} \qquad \frac{P \xrightarrow{\bar{x}(w)} P' \quad Q \xrightarrow{x(w)} Q'}{Q \mid P \xrightarrow{\tau} (w)(Q' \mid P')}$$

The INPUT-ACT rule has the side condition that w should not be a free name of $(z)P$. The OPEN rule requires y and x to be distinct and w to not be a free name in $(y)P'$. The expression $P\{w/z\}$ denotes the result of substituting w for z in P. These two rules model bound input and output actions. The OPEN rule transforms a free output action into a bound output action and also "opens" a scope represented by a restriction operator. The CLOSE rule permits a corresponding closing of scope after a bound input action has combined with a bound output action.

The preceding transition rules can be specified by the following clauses:

```
onep (in X M) (dn X) M.
onep (nu P)   (up X) P' :- pi y\ one  (P y) (up X y) (P' y).
one  (par P Q) tau (nu y\ par (P' y) (Q' y)) &
one  (par Q P) tau (nu y\ par (Q' y) (P' y)) :-
                      onep P (up X) P', onep Q (dn X) Q'.
```

The bound input and output actions require only a clause for onep. Notice also that the names bound by these actions are represented by an explicit abstraction in the abstracted processes that result. The CLOSE rule is specified by a clause only for one because it yields a τ (free) action. The illegal name capture that is prevented in the CLOSE rule by the side condition on w in the INPUT-ACT and OPEN rules is realized in the clause for CLOSE by the nesting of scope for bound variables. In particular, since the abstraction over y, the name bound by the restriction, appears within the scope of the quantifiers for P' and Q', this name cannot appear free in the abstracted processes that instantiate P' and Q'. The OPEN rule has an additional proviso that x and y must be distinct. This requirement is realized in the corresponding clause for onep by the fact that y is bound by an explicit universal quantifier within the scope of the quantifier binding X.

The full specification of the labeled transition semantics for the π-calculus is given by the declarations in Figure 11.2. This specification includes clauses for the silent and free output actions and additional actions involving parallel combination of processes, including the communication between a free output and (bound) input action.

11.3 Animating π-calculus expressions

The specification of one-step transitions via a logic program gives us the ability to *animate* the π-calculus. For example, assuming the declarations in Figures 11.1 and 11.2, the following queries show how we can explore the one-step transitions that are possible from a given π-calculus expression:

```
?- example 1 P, one P A P'.
P = par (in b W\ null) (out b a null)
A = up b a
P' = par (in b W\ null) null;
```

```
P = par (in b W\ null) (out b a null)
A = tau
P' = par null null;
no


?- example 1 P, onep P A P'.
P = par (in b W\ null) (out b a null)
A = W\ dn b W
P' = W\ par null (out b a null);
no


?- example 3 P, one P A P'.
P = nu W\ par (in W y\ null) (out W a null)
A = tau
P' = nu W\ par null null ;
no


?-
```

The first query indicates that the π-calculus process $(b(y).0) \mid (\bar{b}a.0)$ can make transitions labeled $\bar{b}a$ and τ, yielding the continuations $(b(y).0) \mid 0$ and $0 \mid 0$, respectively. The second query reveals that this same process has a bound input action $b(w)$ with continuation $(0 \mid \bar{b}a.0)$; notice, however, that this action and continuation are shown as abstractions over type name. Finally, the last query shows that the process $(w)((w(y).0) \mid \bar{w}a.0)$ can make a silent transition to the process continuation $(w)(0 \mid 0)$.

We can extend the one-step transition relation into a relation that pairs a process with sequences of actions that it can take. Such sequences, called *traces*, provide information about the structure of possible interactions that a process can have with external observers. In defining this trace relation, we have to make a choice in the treatment of processes with input prefixes. Consider, for example, the π-calculus expression $(a(y).[y = b].\bar{y}y.0)$. A simplistic approach might treat this input action as one that receives a *generic* input. Under such an approach it is not possible to reveal any additional dynamics of this process. In this particular instance, for example, traces would not be capable of showing that if the input received on name a had been b, then the process can perform a $\bar{b}b$ action.

Figure 11.3 defines a notion of traces for π-calculus expressions that permits a more liberal treatment of bound input actions in traces. In particular, these are defined to be terms of type trace and are constructed starting from empty traces represented by the constant symbol empty. Actions in a trace can be bound or

```
kind trace  type.
type empty  trace.
type tr     action -> trace -> trace.
type trp    (name -> action) -> (name -> trace) -> trace.

type trace             proc -> trace -> o.
trace P empty.
trace P (tr Act Tr) :- one P Act Q, trace Q Tr.
trace P (trp (up X) Tr) :- onep P (up X) Q,
                     pi x\ trace (Q x) (Tr x).
trace P (tr  (dn X Y) Tr) :- onep P (dn X) Q, trace (Q Y) Tr.
```

Figure 11.3. Traces in the π-calculus.

free: `trp` or `tr` is used as the constructor for extending a trace depending on the
kind of action. This figure also contains clauses defining the `trace` predicate.
Notice that it is necessary to consider an instantiation to continue the exploration
of a process after a bound action. When this bound action is a bound output,
the binding is instantiated with a generic value by using a universal quantifier
in the body of the `trace` definition. In contrast, for an input action, we would
want to consider different possible instantiations, so a free variable is used to
instantiate the bound input action and its continuation.

As with one-step transitions, we can use the `trace` predicate to compute the
possible traces from a given process. Thus, given the declarations in Figure 11.3,
the query

```
?- example 1 P, trace P Tr.
```

will produce all the following bindings for `Tr`:

```
empty
tr (up b a) empty
tr (up b a) (tr (dn b T) empty)
tr tau empty
trp (dn b T) empty
trp (dn b T) (tr (up b a) empty)
```

As a final example, the query

```
?- trace (in a Y\ plus (match Y b (out Y Y null))
                   (match Y c (out Y Y null))) Tr.
```

will enumerate the following traces (as bindings for the variable `Tr`) as the only
ones possible for the process $a(y).(([y = b].\bar{y}y.0) + [y = c].\bar{y}y.0))$:

```
empty
tr (dn a T) empty
```

```
tr (dn a b) (tr (up b b) empty)
tr (dn a c) (tr (up c c) empty)
```

From these traces, we learn that this process can do an unrestricted input and that if that input is chosen to be b or c, then further, distinct output actions can follow.

11.4 May- versus must-judgments

Up to this point, we have only considered judgments involving the possible ways in which a process can evolve. Such judgments, sometimes called *may-judgments*, correspond to identifying paths in a computation tree that a process may follow. Our logic-based encoding of the π-calculus allows the existence of a path to be closely correlated with the existence of a proof for a query from a specification of the transition relation. More generally, may-judgments usually can be given declarative logic specifications.

One often wishes also to compute *must-judgments*. These are judgments that involve meta-level universal quantification. For example, one might want to know that even though a given π-calculus process can evolve in many different ways, it can never evolve in a way that allows it to take a certain specific action. Another example of a must-judgment is that of determining whether or not all traces associated with one process can be matched by traces associated with another process. Determining whether or not a process P can make any transitions at all is another example of a must-judgment because it is a special case of judgments concerning traces: The process P cannot make a transition if and only if it has the same traces as the process 0.

The style of logic specifications that we have described in this book does not, in general, provide declarative treatments of must-judgments. Negation-as-failure can be used, however, to capture or approximate some of these judgments. We illustrate this possibility in the rest of this section.

Our first example is that of specifying a *complete trace* for a process. Such traces are ones that cannot be extended. Figure 11.4 contains clauses defining the predicate comptrace that associates with processes their complete traces represented in the manner discussed in the preceding section. Notice that the specification of comptrace is similar to that of trace in Figure 11.3 except that a trace is allowed to be empty only if no transitions are possible from the process. Negation-as-failure is used to identify processes that have this characteristic: The predicate possible is defined to succeed if its argument is a π-calculus process that can make some (free or bound) labeled transition, and a process is terminal only if possible fails on it. The following interaction shows the use of comptrace to find complete traces:

```
type possible, terminal  proc -> o.
type comptrace           proc -> trace -> o.
type separating_trace    proc -> proc -> trace -> o.
type trace_equiv         proc -> proc -> o.

possible P :- one P _ _ ; onep P _ _.
terminal P :- not (possible P).

comptrace P empty :- terminal P.
comptrace P (tr Act     Tr) :- one  P Act Q, comptrace Q Tr.
comptrace P (tr (dn X Y) Tr) :- onep P (dn X) P',
                                      comptrace (P' Y) Tr.
comptrace P (trp (up X)  Tr) :- onep P (up X) P',
                                      pi x\ comptrace (P' x) (Tr x).

separating_trace P Q T :- trace P T,  not (trace Q T).

trace_equiv P Q :- not (separating_trace P Q _),
                   not (separating_trace Q P _).
```

Figure 11.4. Some trace-based predicates on π-calculus expressions.


```
?- example 1 P, comptrace P Tr.
Tr = tr (up b a) (tr (dn b T) empty)
P = par (in b (W1\ null)) (out b a null);

Tr = tr tau empty
P = par (in b (W1\ null)) (out b a null);

Tr = tr (dn b T1) (tr (up b a) empty)
P = par (in b (W1\ null)) (out b a null);
no

?-
```

Also defined in Figure 11.4 is the predicate separating_trace, which is intended to find a trace for a given process that is not a trace for another given process (the predicate comptrace could have been used here instead of trace). Notice again the use of negation-as-failure in the body of the clause for this predicate to check if a trace found for the first process is not a trace for the second. The following interaction shows the use of this predicate.

```
?- example 5 P, example 6 Q, separating_trace P Q T.
T = tr (dn a b) (tr tau empty)
P = in a (W1\ par (in W1 (W2\ null)) (out b b null))
Q = in a (W1\ plus (in W1 (W2\ out b b null)) (out b b (in W1 (W2\ null))));
no
```

```
?- example 5 P, example 6 Q, separating_trace Q P T.
no

?-
```

The answer to the first query shows that the process given by the π-calculus expression $a(y).((y(w).0) \mid (\bar{b}b.0))$ can do an input, after which it can do an internal communication (symbolized by the `tau` action), but the process given by $a(y).((y(w).\bar{b}b.0) + (\bar{b}b.y(w).0))$ cannot do these actions in sequence. This interaction also shows that this is the only trace that separates these two processes. Moreover, if we change the initial input prefix to a (bound) output prefix in the first process—i.e., if we consider the two processes $(y)\bar{a}y.((y(w).0) \mid (\bar{b}b.0))$ and $(y)\bar{a}y.((y(w).\bar{b}b.0) + (\bar{b}b.y(w).0))$ that are encoded by examples 7 and 8 in Figure 11.1—then there are no separating traces.

```
?- example 7 P, example 8 Q, separating_trace P Q T.
no

?- example 7 P, example 8 Q, separating_trace Q P T.
no

?-
```

Finally, Figure 11.4 contains a clause defining the predicate `trace_equiv` that specifies a notion of equivalence between processes based on the commonality of their traces. This definition makes use, once again, of negation-as-failure via the `not` predicate.

For many applications, equivalence based on traces does not make enough distinctions between processes. In particular, it does not capture branch points that are internal to processes. For example, the processes $\bar{x}a.(\bar{y}b.0 + \bar{y}c.0)$ and $(\bar{x}a.\bar{y}b.0 + \bar{x}a.\bar{y}c.0)$ are trace-equivalent, but they have an important difference: After doing an $\bar{x}a$ action, the first of these processes has the potential to do two different output actions, whereas the second process can do only one output action. A more fine-grained equivalence is based on the notions of *simulation* and *bisimulation*. Roughly speaking, process P is *simulated* by process Q if whenever P can perform an action and evolve into a process P', Q can perform an identical action that transforms it into a process Q' that simulates P'. Notice that a process that makes no actions is simulated by any process. To make this description into a formal definition, the simulation relation is usually defined coinductively.

Figure 11.5 shows a collection of declarations that attempt to encode the simulation relation. The predicate `foreach2` is defined here to hold between

```
type  foreach2   (A -> B -> o) -> (A -> B -> o) -> o.
type  sim        proc -> proc -> o.

foreach2 P Q :- not (sigma X\ sigma Y\ P X Y, not (Q X Y)).

sim P Q :- foreach2 (A\P'\ one P A P')
                    (A\P'\ sigma Q'\ one Q A Q', sim P' Q'),
           foreach2 (A\P'\ onep P A P')
                    (A\P'\ sigma Q'\ onep Q A Q',
                           pi x\ sim (P' x) (Q' x)).
```

Figure 11.5. An incorrect specification of the simulation relation.

two binary relations R and S just in the case that S holds for any pair of objects
for which R holds; this definition employs the not predicate. The sim predicate,
which is defined using foreach2, is intended to hold of two processes P and Q
just in the case that any one-step transition from P can be simulated on Q. A
key part of this definition is the treatment of bound actions. The intuition that
we desire to capture here is that any bound action on P also can be performed
on Q, and the abstracted processes P' and Q' that result from these respective
actions are such that any instance of P' is simulated by the corresponding
instance of Q'. Unfortunately, this intuition is not encoded adequately in the
definition. The problem arises from the fact that the universal quantifier in goals,
the only device available for realizing quantification over all instances in the
λProlog setting, has an intensional character: The generic goal must be derived
by showing that an *identical* derivation exists for any of its instances. However,
π-calculus processes may have different evolutions for different instantiations
of an input action. As a particular example, consider the following query:

```
?- sim (in a x\ par (in x y\ null) (out c b null))
       (in a x\ plus (in x y\ out c b null) (out c b (in x y\ null))).
solved

?-
```

The answer in this case indicates that the simulation relation holds between the
processes that are given by the following π-calculus expressions:

$$a(x).(x(y).0 \mid \bar{c}b.0) \quad \text{and} \quad a(x).((x(y).\bar{c}b.0) + (\bar{c}b.x(y).0)).$$

This simulation relationship should not hold, however, because the first expression can input the name c on channel a and then do a τ action, whereas the
second process cannot do this sequence of actions. Clearly, using the universal
quantifier in the part of the definition of simulation that deals with bounded
inputs is incorrect.

The preceding discussion makes it clear that to treat the simulation relation
properly, we need a universal quantifier that has an extensional interpretation.

There is a similar uncomfortable situation in the use of negation-as-failure: This is at best an ad hoc device in the λProlog setting, and there are well-known problems with using it with goals that have uninstantiated variables in them. Extensions can be made to the underlying logic to provide a principled treatment of both these aspects, thereby leading to a theoretically sound framework for capturing must behavior. A further discussion of these issues is beyond the scope of this book.

11.5 Mapping the λ-calculus into the π-calculus

One demonstration of the expressiveness of the π-calculus as a computational paradigm is based on showing that it can naturally encode evaluation in the untyped λ-calculus. In the common approach to doing this, abstracted variables in λ-terms are treated as names of channels along which the process representing the body of the term is told where to receive its arguments. Since bound variables can have multiple occurrences in a λ-term, we shall need to use π-calculus expressions that include the replication operator ! in the translation. We add the clauses in Figure 11.6 to those in Figure 11.2 to extend the one-step transition relation to such expressions (the ! operator is written as bang).

We consider here a translation of λ-terms that is capable of capturing lazy, call-by-name evaluation over these terms. This translation is given by the following rules:

$$[\![x]\!](u) = \bar{x}u.0$$

$$[\![\lambda x\, M]\!](u) = u(x).u(v).[\![M]\!](v)$$

$$[\![(M\, N)]\!](u) = (v).([\![M]\!](v) \mid (x).(\bar{v}x.\bar{v}u.!x(w).[\![N]\!](w)))$$

This translation will produce from the λ-term M a π-calculus expression given by $[\![M]\!](u)$ that represents a process that will receive its arguments from the environment via the channel u. In the first rule, x is expected to be a variable. Further, the names v and w that appear bound in the translated forms shown are also required to be new.

We end our discussion about the π-calculus by showing that the translation function just presented has a simple and transparent specification as a logic

```
one  (bang P) A (par P1 (bang P)) :- one P A P1.
onep (bang P) X (y\ par (M y) (bang P)) :- onep P X M.
one (bang P) tau (par (par R (M Y)) (bang P)) :-
   onep P (dn X) M, one P (up X Y) R.
one (bang P) tau (par (nu y\ par (M y) (N y)) (bang P)) :-
   onep P (up X) M, onep P (dn X) N.
```

Figure 11.6. Add these clauses to account for bang.

```
type trans  tm -> (name -> proc) -> o.

trans (abs M) (u\ in u x\ in u v\ P x v) :-
   pi x\ pi y\ trans x (u\ out y u null) => trans (M x) (P y).

trans (app M N)
      (u\ nu v\ par (P v)
                    (nu x\ out v x (out v u (bang (in x Q))))) :-
      trans M P, trans N Q.
```

Figure 11.7. Translating the lazy λ-calculus into the π-calculus.

program. In fact, consider the two clauses for the trans predicate in Figure 11.7. This predicate relates the untyped λ-term M with abstraction $\lambda u.P$ if and only if it is the case that $[\![M]\!](u) = P$. Notice how the use of λ-tree syntax results in a different treatment of the base case of the translation in the encoding shown in Figure 11.7. In the conventional presentation, free variables are considered to be part of the syntax and, as such, must have a case that describes their translation. In contrast, the logic specification, with its reliance on λ-tree syntactic representation, does not formally allow free variables in syntax. Instead, the base case is embedded into the abstraction case: When recursion moves into the abstraction context, the trans predicate is given an additional clause that describes how to treat occurrences of the variable bound by the abstraction. In effect, one base case is assumed for every bound variable encountered.

To illustrate how this translation works, consider using it to transform the λ-terms $\lambda x\, x$ and $(\lambda x\, x)(\lambda x\, x)$ into process calculus expressions; note here that the latter term evaluates to the former. To observe the behavior of the resulting process expressions, we also apply them to a particular name b and then examine the list of complete traces that are possible.

```
?- trans (abs w\ w) P, comptrace (P b) T.
P = u\ in u x\ in u y\ out x y null
T = tr (dn b T1) (tr (dn b T2) (tr (up T1 T2) empty));
no

?- trans (app (abs w\ w) (abs w\ w)) P, comptrace (P b) T.
P = u\ nu u\ par
              (nu y\ out u y (out u u
                   (bang (in y w\ in w r\ in w s\ out r s null))))
              (in u z\ in u v\ out z v null)
T = tr tau (tr tau (tr tau
       (tr (dn b T1) (tr (dn b T2) (tr (up T1 T2) empty)))));
no

?-
```

Notice that the second process has three silent (tau) transitions corresponding to reduction of the term $(\lambda x\, x)(\lambda x\, x)$ to $\lambda x\, x$. After this point, the trace for the second process becomes identical to that for the first.

11.6 Bibliographic notes

The π-calculus was proposed originally by Milner, Parrow, and Walker (1992a 1992b). Two monographs by Milner (1989, 1999) provide an introduction to the structure and philosophy underlying this and some closely related specification languages for concurrent systems. The book by Sangiorgi and Walker (2001) is an encyclopedic presentation of the π-calculus and its theory.

The logic specification of the one-step transition relation for the π-calculus that is presented here has been taken from Miller and Palamidessi (1999) and from Miller and Tiu (2003, 2005).

Almost all the one-step transition rules for the π-calculus given in Figures 11.2 and 11.6 are in the L_λ fragment of *hohh*. In particular, only the last two rules of Figure 11.2 and the third rule of Figure 11.6 are not in L_λ. If one deletes these non-L_λ clauses, then one gets exactly the subset of the π-calculus that Sangiorgi (1996) called π_I (π-calculus with *internal* mobility). In this calculus, only new names are bound to inputs: As a result, the metalogic only needs to implement β_0-conversion instead of full β-conversion.

The translation of the call-by-name semantics of the λ-calculus into the π-calculus is due to Milner (1989, 1990).

There has been a body of work aimed at extending the logic associated with logic programming in order to allow for direct and declarative specifications of must-judgments. One such development views logic specifications not as theories (which, in principle, always can be extended) but as *definitions* or *fixed points* (which are not extendable). McDowell and Miller (2000) and McDowell et al. (2003) provided a proof theoretic status to negation-as-finite-failure that extended earlier work by Hallnäs and Schroeder-Heister (1991). In this setting, the usual universal quantifier can be given a natural extensional interpretation. On the other hand, the treatment of bindings in abstract syntax still requires a quantifier with an intensional or generic interpretation. Miller and Tiu (2005) introduced a new quantifier called ∇ (read as "nabla") for this purpose and showed how to include it in a logic with fixed points. In such an enriched logic, it is possible to give completely declarative descriptions of a number of may- and of must-judgments involving the π-calculus (Miller and Tiu 2005; Tiu and Miller 2004; Tiu 2005).

Appendix
The Teyjus System

We have presented sample λProlog programs to illustrate various computations throughout this book. Being able to execute and experiment with those programs should help the reader understand the λProlog programming language and the logic underlying it. To that end, this appendix presents a short introduction to the Teyjus implementation of λProlog. This system can be freely downloaded over the web. The various programs presented in the earlier chapters are also available in electronic form from the website associated with this book.

A.1 An overview of the Teyjus system

The Teyjus implementation of λProlog is based on two components. One component is the emulator of an abstract or virtual machine that has an instruction set and runtime system that realizes all the high-level computations implicit in a λProlog program. The second component is a compiler that translates λProlog programs into the instructions of the abstract machine.

Another important aspect of the Teyjus system is that it uses the modules language discussed in Chapter 6. A programmer therefore, must, organize the kind and type declarations and the clauses into modules and then attach signatures to such modules in order to mediate their external view. The compiler is responsible for taking a given module of λProlog code, certifying its internal consistency, ensuring that it satisfies its associated signature, and finally, translating it into a byte-code form. This byte-code form consists of a "header" part containing constant and type names and other related data structures as well as a sequence of instructions that can be run on the virtual machine once it has understood the header information. A critical part of the emulator is a loader that can read in such byte-code files and put the emulator in a state where it is ready to respond to user queries. The other part of the emulator is, of course, a byte-code interpreter that steps through instructions in the manner called for by the user input.

The module directives that we have described allow large systems to be constructed by composing smaller modules. The Teyjus system supports separate
compilation, meaning that the compiler processes each module separately from
any other and generates code in such a way that it later can be combined with
the compiled forms of other relevant modules to build the image that is eventually executed. This extra "composition" information that is generated by the
compiler is actually another part of the header information in byte-code files.
The task of composing these files is taken up by a third component of the Teyjus
system, the linker.

There are two other utilities that complete the suite of executables available
with the Teyjus system. One of these is a disassembler that can be used to display
byte-code files—whether linked or unlinked—in a readable form. Of course,
knowledge of the instruction set is needed to make sense of what is obtained
from disassembling. The second utility is a dependency analyzer that can look
at a module and calculate all the signatures that are needed to understand its
code and all the other modules that are needed to produce a completely linked,
executable image of the given module. This dependency analyzer is useful in
constructing a make file that exploits the separate compilation feature of Teyjus.

Once the Teyjus system has been downloaded and built, the following different executables are produced: tjcc (the compiler), tjsim (the emulator),
tjlink (the linker), tjdis (the disassembler), and tjdepend (the dependency
analyzer).

A.2 Interacting with the Teyjus system

The read-prove-print loop provides the basic mode of interaction in the logic
programming setting. As explained in Section 2.4, such an interaction occurs in
the context of a program and a signature. In the simplest case, the program and
signature may be the ambient one determined by the set of built-ins provided
by the Teyjus system. Interactions of this form are initiated by invoking tjsim
with no qualifications, as shown below:

```
% tjsim
Welcome to Teyjus
Copyright (C) 2008 A. Gacek, S. Holte, G. Nadathur, X. Qi, Z. Snow
Teyjus comes with ABSOLUTELY NO WARRANTY
This is free software, and you are welcome to redistribute it
under certain conditions. Please view the accompanying file
COPYING for more information
[toplevel] ?-
```

The name `toplevel` that appears in the prompt is used to signify that querying is taking place relative to the basic environment determined by only the built-in types and definitions.

The user can enter queries when presented with the prompt. A simple example of a query, which uses the built-in equality predicate = and the built-in types and value constructors for integers and lists, is the following:

```
[toplevel] ?- pi x:int \ (F x) = (x :: 1 :: x :: nil).

The answer substitution:
F = W1\ W1 :: 1 :: W1 :: nil

More solutions (y/n)? y
no (more) solutions

[toplevel] ?-
```

In this case, Teyjus is able to make sense of the query and hence goes about trying to solve it. If the query succeeds, the system prints out the answer substitution it has found for the implicitly existentially quantified variables. The user may, as usual, ask for more solutions at this stage.

Queries, of course, may not be well formed. In this case, Teyjus will print an error message. For example, a query may not be syntactically correct, as illustrated by the following interaction:

```
[toplevel] ?- pi x:int \ (F x) = (x :: 1 :: x :: nil.
(1,19) : Error : Unmatched parenthesis starting here
[toplevel] ?-
```

Another kind of error that is possible is that the expression does not respect the typing rules, as shown in the following query:

```
[toplevel] ?- pi x:int \ (F x) = (x x).
(1,20) : Error : operator is not a function
        operator type: int
        in expression: x x.
[toplevel] ?-
```

Teyjus also can do a certain amount of *type inference*: That is, missing types can be inferred and inserted in order to make a query or program well formed. Type inference was involved, for example, in determining that the variable F must have type `int -> list int` for the query `pi x:int \ (F x) = (x :: 1 :: x :: nil)` to be is well formed. Types for bound variables also can be omitted, as seen in the following query:

```
[toplevel] ?- pi x \ (F x) = (x :: x :: nil).
The answer substitution:
F = W1\ W1 :: W1 :: nil
More solutions (y/n)? n
yes
[toplevel] ?-
```

Teyjus uses a polymorphic type system, and therefore, the types it fills in for the abstracted variable x and the (implicitly) existentially quantified variable F are A and A -> list A, respectively, where A denotes a type variable. The type inference process assumes, as usual, that every occurrence of a bound variable must have exactly the same type at all its occurrences in the expression.

Type inference in Teyjus is limited to filling missing types for only the variables that are bound over queries or individual clauses. More specifically, constants that are used in queries must be either pervasive (i.e., built-in) or declared in the modules and signatures associated with a query or program clause. Thus, while the expression

```
pi x \ (F x) = (x :: 1 :: x :: nil)
```

which uses the predefined constants 1 and ::, is acceptable to Teyjus, the following query contains an undeclared constant and is not acceptable.

```
[toplevel] ?- pi x \ (F x) = (g x x).
(1,16) : Error : undeclared constant 'g'
[toplevel] ?-
```

Generally, we need to pose queries in contexts that contain user declared types, constants, and program clauses. The modules and signatures of Chapter 6 are used to add such declarations and clauses. Teyjus takes a file-oriented view of these notions. For example, suppose that we want to be able to use the declarations in the module shown in Figure A.1, and suppose also that we want the external view of these definitions to be given by the signature in Figure A.2. We would then have to place these definitions in files named lists.mod and lists.sig, respectively. This file-oriented view also allows for a slight simplification of syntax: The keyword end can be omitted, letting the end of file signify the end of the declarations.

Before we can use these definitions in parsing and interpreting queries, Teyjus requires us to compile them. A module is compiled using the tjcc executable with the desired module, as in the command

```
% tjcc lists
```

```
module lists.

type   append     list A -> list A -> list A -> o.
append nil L L.
append (X::L) K (X::M) :- append L K M.

type rev_aux      list A -> list A -> list A -> o.
rev_aux nil L L.
rev_aux (X::L1) L2 L3 :- rev_aux L1 (X::L2) L3.

type reverse      list A -> list A -> o.
reverse L1 L2 :- rev_aux L1 nil L2.

type member       A -> list A -> o.
member X (X::L).
member X (Y::L) :- member X L.

end
```

Figure A.1 The lists.mod file.

```
sig lists.

type append       list A -> list A -> list A -> o.
type reverse      list A -> list A -> o.
type member       A -> list A -> o.

end
```

Figure A.2 The lists.sig file.

Compilation involves checking that a module is well formed and that it matches its explicit signature. Teyjus does this by following the process described in Section 6.3 with one exception: It adds the explicit signature of the module to the type and kind declarations collected from the module and the signatures of those which it accumulates in generating the implicit signature against which the type declarations and the clauses defining predicates are checked. Concretely, this means that type and kind declarations in the explicit signature do not have to be replicated in the module. Thus, in the case of the lists module, the type declarations for append and reverse can be omitted because these appear in the signature qualifying the module. However, the type declaration for rev_aux is essential; not providing it will result in an undefined constant error.

If the declarations in a module are deemed to be well formed, and if the module matches the associated signature, then tjcc produces a compiled version of the module in a file with the extension lpo; thus the compiled form of the module lists will be left in the file lists.lpo. This code now needs to be linked using tjlink, a process that yields a file with the extension lp. The linked version then can be provided to tjsim to produce a context in which queries can be posed against the relevant module. The following interaction illustrates these steps.

```
% tjlink lists
% tjsim lists
Welcome to Teyjus
Copyright (C) 2008 A. Gacek, S. Holte, G. Nadathur, X. Qi, Z. Snow
Teyjus comes with ABSOLUTELY NO WARRANTY
This is free software, and you are welcome to redistribute it
under certain conditions. Please view the accompanying file
COPYING for more information
[lists] ?- append (1::2::nil) (3::4::nil) L.

The answer substitution:
L = 1 :: 2 :: 3 :: 4 :: nil
More solutions (y/n)? y

no (more) solutions

[lists] ?-
```

In addition to supplying clauses defining predicates, the module also provides a set of constants and types that can be used in constructing queries. Notice, however, that the available such symbols are limited to those identified by the explicit signature. Thus, while the preceding query, which uses the symbol append, is well formed, a query using the symbol rev_aux is not well formed.

```
[lists] ?- rev_aux (1::2::nil) nil L.
(1,0) : Error : undeclared constant 'rev_aux'

[lists] ?-
```

The queries posed at the prompt in the examples in this section have all taken the form of atomic goals. More complex goals also can be presented. The only limitation in Teyjus with respect to the logical structure discussed in this book is that these goals cannot contain embedded implications; i.e., they cannot have the symbols :- or => in them. This is a restriction that applies only to top-level goals: Implications *can be* embedded in the bodies of clauses that appear within modules.

The user eventually would want to quit an interactive session. Teyjus provides the special predicate halt for this purpose. Invoking it as a goal terminates execution of the simulator and returns control to the command level.

A.3 Using modules within the Teyjus system

The module lists that we considered in the last section has a rather simple structure. This might lead us to wonder whether it is really necessary to produce the file lists.lpo that needs to be linked before it can be used by the simulator; perhaps the compiler can produce the file lists.lp directly. The reason for this intermediate step is that Teyjus allows modules to be composed to produce larger collections of definitions. The two step process is needed in this context to support separate compilation.

The composition of code is realized through the accumulation of signatures and modules discussed in Chapter 6. An example illustrating module accumulation is provided by the code in Figure A.3, which implements a simple form of association lists. One part of the compilation of the associst module involves checking that it is well formed. To do this, it is necessary to know the declarations that are available from the lists module. This information is obtained by consulting the lists signature. The other effect of compilation is to produce byte code for the clauses in the module. To exhibit the intended execution profile, the byte code for the clauses that appear in the associst module also must have access to the byte code for the clauses in the lists module. One way to realize this effect is to combine the declarations in the two modules explicitly into one large unit and to compile that unit. Teyjus does not do this, choosing instead to produce separate compiled forms for the associst and lists modules that can be combined later to yield a version ready for execution. Notice that for such a scheme to work, the result of compiling even a

```
sig associst.

kind pair      type -> type -> type.
type pr        A -> B -> pair A B.
type assoc     A -> B > list (pair A B) -> o.
type addassoc  A -> B -> list (pair A B) -> list (pair A B) -> o.
end

module associst.

accumulate lists.

kind pair      type -> type -> type.
type pr        A -> B -> pair A B.

type assoc     A -> B -> list (pair A B) -> o.
assoc X Y L :- member (pr X Y) L.

type addassoc  A -> B -> list (pair A B) -> list (pair A B) -> o.
addassoc X Y L ((pr X Y)::L).

end
```

Figure A.3 A simple example of module composition.

seemingly stand-alone module such as lists must include additional "header" information that allows its code to be incorporated into a larger context. The linker (tjlink) later uses this auxiliary information in producing the desired executable in the file accumlist.lp.

Module interactions can take two broad forms, as discussed in Section 6.5. In one form, a large program may be constructed by incrementally extending a collection of predicate definitions to cover more and more cases. The example of the theorem prover discussed in Section 6.5.2 has this structure. In this case, one module typically will need to accumulate a few other modules, add to the definitions provided by them, and then pass a view of the result on outward, possibly filtered by a specialized signature. The other kind of interaction is one where different modules implement disjoint functionalities but may need to share some of those functionalities. The assoclist example illustrates this kind of interaction at a conceptual level: The clauses in assoclist need some of the definitions available from the lists module, but these are only to be used, not modified. While accumulating lists directly into assoclist as done in Figure A.3 can achieve this effect, there is a better way to do this, as discussed in Section 6.5.3. In this approach, we indicate the dependency by including declarations for the parts to be "imported" in the signature of the module concerned but delaying the actual module accumulation. Here, we would drop the accumulation of the lists module from the assoclist module, adding the declaration

```
type   member   A -> list A -> o.
```

to the assoclist signature instead. The module that needs to use the functionality of assoclist eventually must provide a definition of the member predicate, which it can do by accumulating the "library" module lists. For example, a testing harness for the assoclist module might have the structure

```
module testassoc.
accumulate  lists,assoclist.
end
```

The kind of interaction just described involves one module making available predicate definitions that it expects to be used unchanged and another module using those definitions without modifying them. It can be beneficial to make such expectations explicit: This provides for better documentation, and a compiler also can check adherence to such expectations. Toward this end, Teyjus includes two variants to type declarations for predicate constants in signature files. One of these variants uses the keyword exportdef in place of type, signifying thereby that the associated module expects the relevant predicate constants to be used but without adding clauses to their definitions in any context into which the module is accumulated. The converse form, needed for checking conformity with such restrictions in a separate compilation model, uses the keyword useonly in place of type to indicate that the module in which the declaration appears will use the concerned predicate constants without modifying their definitions. Using these variants, the lists signature might be changed to

```
sig lists.

exportdef append      list A -> list A -> list A -> o.
exportdef reverse     list A -> list A -> o.
exportdef member      A -> list A -> o.

end
```

Correspondingly, the type declaration for member in the assoclist signature would be replaced by

```
useonly  member   A -> list A -> o.
```

Sometimes it is more convenient to accumulate entire signatures rather than to include individual type (or kind) declarations. To this end, Teyjus allows the keyword use_sig to be used as a variant of accum_sig. When this variant is used, declarations that have the exportdef form are changed to the useonly form before the signature is accumulated.

A large Teyjus project may involve interactions between many modules and signatures. Building the executable for such a project may require keeping track of many module dependencies. Moreover, to obtain the benefit of separate compilation, it also would be necessary to record whether or not a module has changed since it was last compiled. Many of these aspects can be automated in an environment that supports the make facility. The Teyjus web page provides the skeleton of a make file that can be used in such a setting. In order to use this capability, it is necessary to calculate module and signature dependencies manifest through accumulation declarations. The Teyjus program tjdepend realizes this functionality: Given a module name, it produces all the signatures and modules that are needed for building an executable version of that module.

A.4 Special features of the Teyjus system

We discuss in this section some of the basic programming capabilities that the Teyjus system provides through its pervasive types and predicates. The language that is implemented also differs in a few respects from the one assumed in the examples earlier in this book, and we discuss these differences as well.

A.4.1 Built-in types and predicates

In addition to the type o for propositions, the Teyjus system provides built-in support for the type int representing integers, the type real representing reals, and the type string representing strings. Constants of the first two types are denoted in the usual way, and string constants are given syntactically by sequences of characters enclosed between double quotes. Several function constants over these types are also supported: Examples include the usual infix arithmetic operators such as +, -, and * that are overloaded between the types of integers and reals; div that corresponds to division over integers; / that represents division over reals; and ^ that represents (infix) concatenation between strings and coercion operators such as int_to_string. These symbols are treated *intensionally*, as is typical in the logic programming setting (see Section 2.7.1). Evaluation can be forced by using the is predicate familiar from Prolog; this predicate is also overloaded among integers, reals, and strings. The following interaction indicates the distinction:

```
[toplevel] ?- X = "every" ^ "thing".

The answer substitution:
X = "every" ^ "thing"

More solutions (y/n)? y
no (more) solutions

[toplevel] ?- X is "every" ^ "thing".

The answer substitution:
X = "everything"

More solutions (y/n)? y
no (more) solutions

[toplevel] ?-
```

Finally, at the predicate level, Teyjus includes the comparison operators <, =<, >, and >=; these are, once again, overloaded among the int, real, and string types.

Beyond the basic types, Teyjus supports lists and streams. The lists that are permitted are polymorphic in the parametric sense and are realized through the unary type constructor list and the constants nil and :: that we have seen numerous times already. Streams can be of two kinds: in_stream for input and `out_stream` for output. The constant `std_in` denotes the predefined standard input stream, `std_out` denotes the predefined standard output stream, and `std_err` denotes the standard error (output) stream. It is often useful to open new streams that are bound to files so as to read or write from them. Teyjus provides the built-in predicate `open_in` for binding an `in_stream` variable to a file and `open_out` for binding an `out_stream` variable to a file. Streams opened in this way can be closed using the predicates `close_in` and `close_out`, respectively. The predicate `input` and `output` can be used, respectively, for reading from and writing to streams that are open. The full details of these and other predicates can be found in the documentation provided with the Teyjus system.

Teyjus also includes some logical and metalogical predicates. The former category includes the equality predicate = that we have already encountered: This predicate attempts to unify the two terms that appear to its left and right. At the metalogical level, Teyjus supports the *cut* predicate ! familiar from Prolog, the `fail` predicate that always fails, and the `halt` predicate that terminates execution of the simulator. Teyjus also provides the `not` predicate, although this should be used with more care than in Prolog: Negation-by-failure has a problematic semantics in a situation where implicational goals are used in an essential way.

Teyjus does not support predicates such as `assert` and `retract` that are used in Prolog for realizing a notion of state. The scoping capability obtained by using these predicates in tandem can be partially realized by using implicational goals. Some effects of state can be simulated, albeit in a roundabout way, by writing data to a file and later reading from the file.

A.4.2 Deviations from the language assumed in this book

The reader wanting to experiment with examples in this book should be aware of two important differences between the language discussed here and the one implemented in Teyjus. One difference was mentioned earlier: Teyjus does not permit implications to be used in top-level goals. This is a characteristic that may change in the future when the compilation model is also extended to these goals, but for now it means that some of the examples presented, e.g., in Section 3.2, cannot be run directly using this system. Notice that implications are disallowed only in top-level goals: They can be used freely in goals that appear in the body of program clauses. Thus this limitation can be overcome by first building a suitable program clause and then using it to pose the desired query. For example, instead of posing the query

```
?- p a => p b => p X.
```

one can create the clause

```
test X :- p a => p b => p X.
```

and then use the query

```
?- test X.
```

The second difference is that Teyjus does not implement higher-order unification completely, taking the approach to realizing it partially through higher-order pattern unification, as discussed in Section 8.4. As a result, examples such as those in Section 5.9 that rely on the extended form of higher-order unification will not display the kind of behavior presented there if they are run using the Teyjus system.

Bibliography

Martín Abadi, Luca Cardelli, Pierre-Louis Curien, and Jean-Jacques Lévy. Explicit substitutions. *Journal of Functional Programming* 1(4):375–416, October 1991.

Hassan Aït-Kaci. *Warren's Abstract Machine: A Tutorial Reconstruction.* Logic Programming Research Reports and Notes. MIT Press, Cambridge, MA, 1991.

Jean-Marc Andreoli. Logic programming with focusing proofs in linear logic. *Journal of Logic and Computation* 2(3):297–347, 1992.

Peter B. Andrews. Resolution in type theory. *Journal of Symbolic Logic* 36:414–432, 1971.

Peter B. Andrews. General models, descriptions, and choice in type theory. *Journal of Symbolic Logic* 37:385–394, 1972.

Peter B. Andrews. *An Introduction to Mathematical Logic and Type Theory.* Academic Press, New York, 1986.

K. R. Apt and M. H. van Emden. Contributions to the theory of logic programming. *Journal of the ACM* 29(3):841–862, 1982.

L. Bachmair and H. Ganzinger. Resolution theorem proving. In A. Robinson and A. Voronkov, editors, *Handbook of Automated Reasoning*, vol. I, chap. 2, pp. 19–99. Elsevier Science, New York, 2001.

David Baelde, Andrew Gacek, Dale Miller, Gopalan Nadathur, and Alwen Tiu. The Bedwyr system for model checking over syntactic expressions. In F. Pfenning, editor, *21th Conference on Automated Deduction (CADE)*, number 4603 in LNAI, pp. 391–397. Springer, New York, 2007.

Henk Barendregt. *The Lambda Calculus: Its Syntax and Semantics*, volume 103 of *Studies in Logic and the Foundations of Mathematics*, revised edition. Elsevier, New York, 1984.

Henk Barendregt. Lambda calculus with types. In S. Abramsky, Dov M. Gabbay, and T. S. E. Maibaum, editors, *Handbook of Logic in Computer Science*, vol. 2, pp. 117–309. Oxford University Press, Oxford, England, 1992.

Kenneth A. Bowen and Robert A. Kowalski. Amalgamating language and metalanguage in logic programming. In K. L. Clark and S.-A. Tarnlund, editors, *Logic Programming*, vol. 16 of *APIC Studies in Data Processing*, pp. 153–172. Academic Press, New York, 1982.

Pascal Brisset and Olivier Ridoux. Naïve reverse can be linear. In *Eighth International Logic Programming Conference*, Paris, France, June 1991. MIT Press, Cambridge, MA, 1992.

Pascal Brisset and Olivier Ridoux. The architecture of an implementation of λProlog: Prolog/Mali. In Dale Miller, editor, *Proceedings of the 1992 λProlog Workshop*, 1992.

M. Bugliesi, E. Lamma, and P. Mello. Modularity in logic programming. *Journal of Logic Programming* 19–20:443–502, 1994.

Daniel Cabeza and Manuel V. Hermenegildo. A new module system for Prolog. In John Lloyd et al., editors, *Computational Logic, CL 2000*, vol. 1861 of *LNCS*, pp. 131–148. Springer, New York, 2000.

Luís Caires and Luis Monteiro. Higher-order polymorphic unification for logic programming. In P. Van Hentenryck, editor, *Logic Programming, 11th International Conference, S. Margherita Ligure, Italy*, pp. 419–433. MIT Press, Cambridge, MA, 1994.

Weidong Chen, Michael Kifer, and David S. Warren. HILOG: A foundation for higher-order logic programming. *Journal of Logic Programming* 15(3):187–230, 1993.

Alonzo Church. An unsolvable problem of elementary number theory. *American Journal of Mathematics* 58:354–363, 1936.

Alonzo Church. A formulation of the simple theory of types. *Journal of Symbolic Logic* 5:56–68, 1940.

Alonzo Church. *The Calculi of Lambda-Conversion*. Princeton University Press, Princeton, NJ, 1941.

W. F. Clocksin and C. S. Mellish. *Programming in Prolog*. Springer-Verlag, New York, 1984.

Alain Colmerauer. Prolog and infinite trees. In Keith Clark and Sten-Åke Tärnlund, editors, *Logic Programming*, pp. 231–251. Academic Press, New York, 1982.

Thierry Coquand and Gérard Huet. The calculus of constructions. *Information and Computation* 76(2–3):95–120, February–March 1988.

Michael A. Covington. *Natural Language Processing for Prolog Programmers*. Prentice-Hall, Englewood Cliffs, NJ, 1994.

Luis Damas and Robin Milner. Principal type schemes for functional programs. In *Proceedings of the ACM Conference on Principles of Programming Languages*, pp. 207–212, 1982.

J. L. Darlington. A partial mechanization of second-order logic. In *Machine Intelligence* 6, pp. 91–100. American Elsevier, New York, 1971.

N. G. de Bruijn. Lambda calculus notation with nameless dummies, a tool for automatic formula manipulation, with application to the Church-Rosser Theorem. *Indagationes Mathematicae*, 34(5):381–392, 1972.

Joëlle Despeyroux, Amy Felty, and Andre Hirschowitz. Higher-order abstract syntax in Coq. In *Second International Conference on Typed Lambda Calculi and Applications*, pp. 124–138, April 1995.

Kees Doets. *Basic Model Theory*. CSLI Publications, Stanford, CA, 1996.

D. J. Dougherty. Higher-order unification via combinators. *Theoretical Computer Science* 114(2):273–298, 1993.

G. Dowek, Th. Hardin, C. Kirchner, and F. Pfenning. Higher-order unification via explicit substitutions: the case of higher-order patterns. In M. Maher, editor, *Joint International Conference and Symposium on Logic Programming*, pp. 259–273, 1996.

G. Dowek, T. Hardin, and C. Kirchner. Higher order unification via explicit substitutions. *Information and Computation* 157(1–2):183–235, 2000.

Gilles Dowek. Third order matching is decidable. In *7th Symposium on Logic in Computer Science*, pp. 2–10, Santa Cruz, CA, June 1992. IEEE Computer Society Press, New York.

Roy Dyckhoff. Contraction-free sequent calculi for intuitionistic logic. *Journal of Symbolic Logic* 57(3):795–807, September 1992.

Matthias Felleisen and Robert Hieb. The revised report on the syntactic theories of sequential control and state. *Theoretical Computer Science* 103:235–271, 1992.

Amy Felty. *Specifying and Implementing Theorem Provers in a Higher-Order Logic Programming Language.* Ph.D. thesis, University of Pennsylvania, August 1989.

Amy Felty. Transforming specifications in a dependent-type lambda calculus to specifications in an intuitionistic logic. In Gérard Huet and Gordon D. Plotkin, editors, *Logical Frameworks.* Cambridge University Press, Cambridge, England, 1991.

Amy Felty. Higher-order conditional rewriting in the L_λ logic programming language. Preprint of talks given at the Third International Workshop on Extensions to Logic Programming, February 1992.

Amy Felty. Implementing tactics and tacticals in a higher-order logic programming language. *Journal of Automated Reasoning* 11(1):43–81, August 1993a.

Amy Felty. Encoding the calculus of constructions in a higher-order logic. In M. Vardi, editor, *8th Symposium on Logic in Computer Science*, pp. 233–244. IEEE, New York, June 1993b.

Amy Felty and Dale Miller. Specifying theorem provers in a higher-order logic programming language. In *Ninth International Conference on Automated Deduction*, number 310 in *LNCS*, pp. 61–80. Springer-Verlag, New York, May 1988.

Amy Felty and Dale Miller. Encoding a dependent-type λ-calculus in a logic programming language. In Mark Stickel, editor, *Proceedings of the 1990 Conference on Automated Deduction*, vol. 449 of *LNAI*, pp. 221–235. Springer, New York, 1990.

Michael J. Fischer. Lambda calculus schemata. *ACM SIGPLAN Notices* 7(1):104–109, January 1972.

Melvin Fitting. Resolution for intuitionistic logic. In *Proceedings of the International Symposium of Methodologies for Intelligent Systems ISMIS'87*, pp. 400–407, 1987.

Melvin C. Fitting. *Intuitionistic Logic Model Theory and Forcing.* North-Holland, Amsterdam, 1969.

D. M. Gabbay and U. Reyle. N-Prolog: An extension of Prolog with hypothetical implications. I. *Journal of Logic Programming* 1:319–355, 1984.

M. J. Gabbay and A. M. Pitts. A new approach to abstract syntax with variable binding. *Formal Aspects of Computing* 13:341–363, 2001.

Andrew Gacek. The Abella interactive theorem prover (system description). In A. Armando, P. Baumgartner, and G. Dowek, editors, *Fourth International Joint Conference on Automated Reasoning*, vol. 5195 of *LNCS*, pp. 154–161. Springer, New York, 2008.

Andrew Gacek, Dale Miller, and Gopalan Nadathur. Reasoning in Abella about structural operational semantics specifications. In A. Abel and C. Urban, editors, *International Workshop on Logical Frameworks and Meta-Languages: Theory and Practice (LFMTP 2008)*, number 228 in *ENTCS*, pp. 85–100, 2008.

Jean H. Gallier. *Logic for Computer Science: Foundations of Automatic Theorem Proving.* Harper & Row, New York, 1986.

Gerhard Gentzen. Investigations into logical deductions. In M. E. Szabo, editor, *The Collected Papers of Gerhard Gentzen*, pp. 68–131. North-Holland, Amsterdam, 1969. Translation of articles that appeared in 1934–35.

L. Giordano and A. Martelli. A modal reconstruction of blocks and modules in logic programming. In *Proceedings of the International Logic Programming Symposium*, pp. 239–253, San Diego, 1991.

Jean-Yves Girard. The system F of variable types: Fifteen years later. *Theoretical Computer Science* 45:159–192, 1986.

Jean-Yves Girard. Linear logic. *Theoretical Computer Science* 50:1–102, 1987.

Jean-Yves Girard, Paul Taylor, and Yves Lafont. *Proofs and Types*. Cambridge University Press, Cambridge, England, 1989.

Kurt Gödel. On formally undecidable propositions of the principia mathematica and related systems, part I. In Martin Davis, editor, *The Undecidable*. Raven Press, New York, 1965.

Warren Goldfarb. The undecidability of the second-order unification problem. *Theoretical Computer Science* 13:225–230, 1981.

Michael J. Gordon, Arthur J. Milner, and Christopher P. Wadsworth. *Edinburgh LCF: A Mechanised Logic of Computation*, vol. 78 of *LNCS*. Springer-Verlag, New York, 1979.

W. E. Gould. A matching procedure for ω-order logic. Technical Report Scientific Report No. 4, AFCRL, 1966.

J. R. Guard. Automated logic for semi-automated mathematics. In *Scientific Report No 1*, pp. 64–411. AFCRL, 1964.

Rémy Haemmerlé and François Fages. Modules for Prolog revisited. In S. Etalle and M. Truszczynski, editors, *ICLP: Logic Programming, 22nd International Conference*, vol. 4079 of *LNCS*, pp. 41–55. Springer, New York, August 2006.

Lars Hallnäs and Peter Schroeder-Heister. A proof-theoretic approach to logic programming. I. Clauses as rules. *Journal of Logic and Computation* 1(2):261–283, December 1990.

Lars Hallnäs and Peter Schroeder-Heister. A proof-theoretic approach to logic programming. II. Programs as definitions. *Journal of Logic and Computation* 1(5):635–660, October 1991.

John Hannan and Dale Miller. Deriving mixed evaluation from standard evaluation for a simple functional programming language. In Jan L. A. van de Snepscheut, editor, *1989 International Conference on Mathematics of Program Construction*, vol. 375 of *LNCS*, pp. 239–255. Springer-Verlag, New York, 1989.

John Hannan and Dale Miller. From operational semantics to abstract machines. *Mathematical Structures in Computer Science* 2(4):415–459, 1992.

Michael Hanus. The integration of functions into logic programming: From theory to practice. *Journal of Logic Programming* 19–20:583–628, 1994.

Robert Harper and Frank Pfenning. A module system for a programming language based on the LF logical framework. *Journal of Logic and Computation* 8(1):5–31, February 1998.

Robert Harper, Furio Honsell, and Gordon Plotkin. A framework for defining logics. In *2nd Symposium on Logic in Computer Science*, pp. 194–204, Ithaca, NY, June 1987.

Robert Harper, Furio Honsell, and Gordon Plotkin. A framework for defining logics. *Journal of the ACM* 40(1):143–184, 1993.

R. Harrop. Concerning formulas of the types $A \rightarrow B \vee C$, $A \rightarrow (Ex)B(x)$ in intuitionistic formal systems. *Journal of Symbolic Logic* 25:27–32, 1960.

Leon Henkin. Completeness in the theory of types. *Journal of Symbolic Logic* 15:81–91, 1950.

Jacques Herbrand. *Recherches sur la Théorie de la Démonstration.* Ph.D. thesis, University of Paris, 1930.

Pat Hill and John Lloyd. *The Gödel Programming Language.* MIT Press, Cambridge, MA, 1994.

J. Roger Hindley and Jonathan P. Seldin. *Introduction to Combinatory Logic and Lambda Calculus.* Cambridge University Press, Cambridge, England, 1986.

Joshua Hodas and Dale Miller. Logic programming in a fragment of intuitionistic linear logic. *Information and Computation* 110(2):327–365, 1994.

W. Hodges. *A Shorter Model Theory.* Cambridge University Press, Cambridge, England, 1997.

M. Hofmann. Semantical analysis of higher-order abstract syntax. In *14th Symposium on Logic in Computer Science*, pp. 204–213. IEEE Computer Society Press, New York, 1999.

Steven Holte and Gopalan Nadathur. Modularity and separate compilation in logic programming. Technical Report DTC Research Report 2006/19, University of Minnesota, November 2006.

Furio Honsell, Marino Miculan, and Ivan Scagnetto. An axiomatic approach to metareasoning on systems in higher-order abstract syntax. In *Proceedings of ICALP'01*, number 2076 in *LNCS*, pp. 963–978. Springer-Verlag, New York, 2001.

Jörg Hudelmaier. Bounds on cut-elimination in intuitionistic propositional logic. *Archive for Mathematical Logic* 31:331–353, 1992.

Gérard Huet. The undecidability of unification in third order logic. *Information and Control* 22:257–267, 1973a.

Gérard Huet. A mechanization of type theory. In *Proceedings of the Third International Joint Conference on Articifical Intelligence*, pp. 139–146, 1973b.

Gérard Huet. A unification algorithm for typed λ-calculus. *Theoretical Computer Science* 1:27–57, 1975.

Gérard Huet. *Résolution d'équations dans les langages d'ordre* $1, 2, \ldots, \omega$. Thèse de doctorat d'état, Université Paris 7, 1976.

Gérard Huet and Bernard Lang. Proving and applying program transformations expressed with second-order patterns. *Acta Informatica* 11:31–55, 1978.

ISO/IEC. Prolog. 13211. Part 2: Modules, 2000.

Gilles Kahn. Natural semantics. In *Proceedings of the Symposium on Theoretical Aspects of Computer Science*, vol. 247 of *LNCS*, pp. 22–39. Springer, New York, March 1987.

Stephen Cole Kleene. *Introduction to Metamathematics.* North-Holland, Amsterdam, 1952.

Keehang Kwon, Gopalan Nadathur, and Debra Sue Wilson. Implementing polymorphic typing in a logic programming language. *Computer Languages* 20(1):25–42, 1994.

T. L. Lakshman and Uday S. Reddy. Typed Prolog: A semantic reconstruction of the mycroft-O'keefe type system. In Vijay A. Saraswat and Kazunori Ueda, editors, *Logic Programming, Proceedings of the 1991 International Symposium*, pp. 202–217, San Diego, CA, 1991. MIT Press, Cambridge, MA, 1992.

Daniel Leivant. Higher-order logics. In Dov M. Gabbay, C. J. Hogger, and J. A. Robinson, editors, *Handbook of Logic in Artificial Intelligence and Logic Programming*, vol. 2, pp. 229–321. Oxford University Press, Oxford, England, 1994.

Chuck Liang. *Object-Level Substitution, Unification and Generalization in Meta-Logic*. Ph.D. thesis, University of Pennsylvania, Philadelphia, PA, 1996.

Chuck Liang and Dale Miller. Focusing and polarization in linear, intuitionistic, and classical logics. *Theoretical Computer Science* 410(46):4747–4768, 2009.

C. L. Lucchesi. The undecidability of unification for third order languages. Technical Report Report CSRR 2059, Department of Applied Analysis and Computer Science, University of Waterloo, Ontario, Canada, 1972.

David Maier and David S. Warren. *Computing with Logic: Logic Programming with Prolog*. Addison-Wesley, Reading, MA, 1988.

Alberto Martelli and Ugo Montanari. An efficient unification algorithm. *ACM Transactions on Programming Lanuages and Systems* 4(2):258–282, April 1982.

L. T. McCarty. Clausal intuitionistic logic: I. Fixed point semantics. *Journal of Logic Programming* 5:1–31, 1988a.

L. T. McCarty. Clausal intuitionistic logic: II. Tableau proof procedure. *Journal of Logic Programming* 5:93–132, 1988b.

Raymond McDowell and Dale Miller. Cut-elimination for a logic with definitions and induction. *Theoretical Computer Science* 232:91–119, 2000.

Raymond McDowell, Dale Miller, and Catuscia Palamidessi. Encoding transition systems in sequent calculus. *Theoretical Computer Science* 294(3):411–437, 2003.

Dale Miller. A theory of modules for logic programming. In Robert M. Keller, editor, *Third Annual IEEE Symposium on Logic Programming*, pp. 106–114, Salt Lake City, Utah, September 1986.

Dale Miller. Hereditary Harrop formulas and logic programming. In *Proceedings of the VIII International Congress of Logic, Methodology, and Philosophy of Science*, pp. 153–156, Moscow, August 1987a.

Dale Miller. A compact representation of proofs. *Studia Logica* 46(4):347–370, 1987b.

Dale Miller. A logic programming language with lambda-abstraction, function variables, and simple unification: Extended abstract. In Graham M. Birtwistle, editor, *Proceedings of the 1989 Banff Meeting on "Higher-Orders,"* Banff, Canada, September 1989a.

Dale Miller. Lexical scoping as universal quantification. In *Sixth International Logic Programming Conference*, pp. 268–283, Lisbon, Portugal, June 1989b. MIT Press, Cambridge, MA, 1990.

Dale Miller. A logical analysis of modules in logic programming. *Journal of Logic Programming* 6(1-2):79–108, January 1989c.

Dale Miller. Abstractions in logic programming. In Piergiorgio Odifreddi, editor, *Logic and Computer Science*, pp. 329–359. Academic Press, New York, 1990.

Dale Miller. Unification of simply typed lambda-terms as logic programming. In *Eighth International Logic Programming Conference*, pp. 255–269, Paris, France, June 1991a. MIT Press, Cambridge, MA, 1992.

Dale Miller. A logic programming language with lambda-abstraction, function variables, and simple unification. *Journal of Logic and Computation* 1(4):497–536, 1991b.

Dale Miller. Unification under a mixed prefix. *Journal of Symbolic Computation* 14 (4):321–358, 1992a.

Dale Miller. Abstract syntax and logic programming. In *Logic Programming: Proceedings of the First and Second Russian Conferences on Logic Programming*, number 592 in *LNAI*, pp. 322–337. Springer-Verlag, New York, 1992b.

Dale Miller. A proposal for modules in λProlog. In R. Dyckhoff, editor, *4th Workshop on Extensions to Logic Programming*, number 798 in *LNCS*, pp. 206–221. Springer-Verlag, New York, 1994.

Dale Miller. Forum: A multiple-conclusion specification logic. *Theoretical Computer Science* 165(1):201–232, September 1996.

Dale Miller. Abstract syntax for variable binders: An overview. In John Lloyd et al., editors, *CL 2000: Computational Logic*, number 1861 in *LNAI*, pp. 239–253. Springer, New York, 2000.

Dale Miller. Higher-order quantification and proof search. In Hélène Kirchner and Christophe Ringeissen, editors, *Proceedings of AMAST 2002*, number 2422 in *LNCS*, pp. 60–74, 2002.

Dale Miller. Collection analysis for Horn clause programs. In *Proceedings of PPDP 2006: 8th International ACM SIGPLAN Conference on Principles and Practice of Declarative Programming*, pp. 179–188, July 2006.

Dale Miller. A proof-theoretic approach to the static analysis of logic programs. In *Reasoning in Simple Type Theory: Festschrift in Honor of Peter B. Andrews on His 70th Birthday*, number 17 in *Studies in Logic*, pp. 423–442. College Publications, London, 2008.

Dale Miller and Gopalan Nadathur. Higher-order logic programming. In Ehud Shapiro, editor, *Proceedings of the Third International Logic Programming Conference*, pp. 448–462, London, June 1986.

Dale Miller and Gopalan Nadathur. A logic programming approach to manipulating formulas and programs. In Seif Haridi, editor, *IEEE Symposium on Logic Programming*, pp. 379–388, San Francisco, September 1987.

Dale Miller and Catuscia Palamidessi. Foundational aspects of syntax. *ACM Computing Surveys* 31, September 1999.

Dale Miller and Alwen Tiu. A proof theory for generic judgments: An extended abstract. In Phokion Kolaitis, editor, *18th Symposium on Logic in Computer Science*, pp. 118–127. IEEE, New York, June 2003.

Dale Miller and Alwen Tiu. A proof theory for generic judgments. *ACM Transactions on Computational Logic* 6(4):749–783, October 2005.

Dale Miller, Gopalan Nadathur, and Andre Scedrov. Hereditary Harrop formulas and uniform proof systems. In David Gries, editor, *2nd Symposium on Logic in Computer Science*, pp. 98–105, Ithaca, NY, June 1987.

Dale Miller, Gopalan Nadathur, Frank Pfenning, and Andre Scedrov. Uniform proofs as a foundation for logic programming. *Annals of Pure and Applied Logic* 51:125–157, 1991.

Robin Milner. *Communication and Concurrency*. Prentice-Hall International, England, Cliffs, NJ, 1989.

Robin Milner. Functions as processes. In *Automata, Languages and Programming 17th International Collection*, vol. 443 of *LNCS*, pp. 167–180. Springer-Verlag, New York, July 1990.

Robin Milner. *Communicating and Mobile Systems: The π-Calculus*. Cambridge University Press, New York, 1999.

Robin Milner, Mads Tofte, and Robert Harper. *The Definition of Standard ML*. MIT Press, Cambridge, MA, 1990.

Robin Milner, Joachim Parrow, and David Walker. A calculus of mobile processes, part I. *Information and Computation* 100(1):1–40, September 1992a.

Robin Milner, Joachim Parrow, and David Walker. A calculus of mobile processes, part II. *Information and Computation* 100(1):41–77, 1992b.

J. C. Mitchell and G. D. Plotkin. Abstract types have existential type. *ACM Transactions on Programming Languages and Systems*, 10(3):470–502, 1988.

L. Monteiro and A. Porto. Contextual logic programming. In *Proceedings of the 6th International Conference on Logic Programming*, Lisbon, Portugalo. MIT Press, Cambridge, MA, 1989.

Markus Mottl. Automating functional program transformation. Master's thesis, University of Edinburgh, September 2000.

A. Mycroft and R. A. O'Keefe. A polymorphic type system for Prolog. *Artificial Intelligence* 23:295–307, 1984.

G. Nadathur and G. Tong. Realizing modularity in λProlog. *Journal of Functional and Logic Programming* 1999(9), April 1999.

Gopalan Nadathur. *A Higher-Order Logic as the Basis for Logic Programming*. Ph.D. thesis, University of Pennsylvania, May 1987.

Gopalan Nadathur. A proof procedure for the logic of hereditary Harrop formulas. *Journal of Automated Reasoning* 11(1):115–145, August 1993.

Gopalan Nadathur and Natalie Linnell. Practical higher-order pattern unification with on-the-fly raising. In *ICLP 2005: 21st International Logic Programming Conference*, vol. 3668 of *LNCS*, pp. 371–386, Sitges, Spain, October 2005. Springer, New York, 2006.

Gopalan Nadathur and Dale Miller. An Overview of λProlog. In *Fifth International Logic Programming Conference*, pp. 810–827, Seattle, August 1988. MIT Press, Cambridge, MA, 1989.

Gopalan Nadathur and Dale Miller. Higher-order Horn clauses. *Journal of the ACM* 37 (4):777–814, October 1990.

Gopalan Nadathur and Dale Miller. Higher-order logic programming. In Dov M. Gabbay, C. J. Hogger, and J. A. Robinson, editors, *Handbook of Logic in Artificial Intelligence and Logic Programming*, vol. 5, pp. 499–590. Clarendon Press, Oxford, England, 1998.

Gopalan Nadathur and Dustin J. Mitchell. System description: Teyjus — A compiler and abstract machine based implementation of λProlog. In H. Ganzinger, editor, *16th Conference on Automated Deduction (CADE)*, number 1632 in *LNAI*, pp. 287–291, Trento, 1999. Springer, New York, 2000.

Gopalan Nadathur and Frank Pfenning. The type system of a higher-order logic programming language. In Frank Pfenning, editor, *Types in Logic Programming*, pp. 245–283. MIT Press, Cambridge, MA, 1992.

Gopalan Nadathur and Xiaochu Qi. Optimizing the runtime processing of types in polymorphic logic programming languages. In G. Sutcliffe and A. Voronkov, editors, *LPAR: Logic Programming and Automated Reasoning, International Conference*, vol. 3835 of *LNCS*, pp. 110–124. Springer, New York, December 2005.

Gopalan Nadathur and Debra Sue Wilson. A representation of lambda terms suitable for operations on their intensions. In M. Wand, editor, *Proceedings of the 1990*

ACM Conference on Lisp and Functional Programming, pp. 341–348. ACM Press, New York, 1990.

Gopalan Nadathur and Debra Sue Wilson. A notation for lambda terms: A generalization of environments. *Theoretical Computer Science* 198(1–2):49–98, 1998.

Tobias Nipkow. Functional unification of higher-order patterns. In M. Vardi, editor, *8th Symposium on Logic in Computer Science*, pp. 64–74. IEEE, New York, June 1993.

Richard A. O'Keefe. Towards an algebra for constructing logic programs. In J. Cohen and J. Connery, editors, *Proceedings of the IEEE Symposium on Logic Programming*, pp. 152–160. IEEE Computer Society Press, New York, 1985.

Richard A. O'Keefe. *The Craft of Prolog*. MIT Press, Cambridge, MA, 1990.

M. S. Paterson and M. N. Wegman. Linear unification. *Journal of Computer and System Sciences* 16:158–167, 1978.

Lawrence C. Paulson. *Logic and Computation: Interactive Proof with Cambridge LCF*. Cambridge University Press, Cambridge, England, 1987.

Lawrence C. Paulson. The foundation of a generic theorem prover. *Journal of Automated Reasoning* 5:363–397, September 1989.

Lawrence C. Paulson. Isabelle: The next 700 theorem provers. In Piergiorgio Odifreddi, editor, *Logic and Computer Science*, pp. 361–386. Academic Press, New York, 1990.

Fernando C. N. Pereira and Stuart M. Shieber. *Prolog and Natural-Language Analysis*, vol. 10. CLSI, Stanford, CA, 1987.

Frank Pfenning. Elf: A language for logic definition and verified metaprogramming. In *4th Symposium on Logic in Computer Science*, pp. 313–321, Monterey, CA, June 1989.

Frank Pfenning, editor. *Types in Logic Programming*. MIT Press, Cambridge, MA, 1992.

Frank Pfenning and Conal Elliott. Higher-order abstract syntax. In *Proceedings of the ACM-SIGPLAN Conference on Programming Language Design and Implementation*, pp. 199–208. ACM Press, New York, June 1988.

Frank Pfenning and Carsten Schürmann. System description: Twelf—A meta-logical framework for deductive systems. In H. Ganzinger, editor, *16th Conference on Automated Deduction (CADE)*, number 1632 in *LNAI*, pp. 202–206, Trento, 1999. Springer, New York, 2000.

T. Pietrzykowski. A complete mechanization of second-order type theory. *Journal of the Association for Computing Machinery* 20:333–364, 1973.

T. Pietrzykowski and D. C. Jensen. A complete mechanization of ω-order type theory. In *ACM '72: Proceedings of the ACM annual conference*, pp. 82–92. ACM, New York, 1972.

Andrew M. Pitts. Nominal logic, A first order theory of names and binding. *Information and Computation* 186(2):165–193, 2003.

Andrew M. Pitts. Alpha-structural recursion and induction. *Journal of the ACM*, 53(3): 459–506, 2006.

Gordon D. Plotkin. A structural approach to operational semantics. *Journal of Logic and Algebraic Programming*, 60-61:17–139, 2004.

E. L. Post. A variant of a recursively unsolvable problem. *Bulletin of the American Mathematical Society* 52:264–268, 1946.

X. Qi. *An Implementation of the Language λProlog Organized around Higher-Order Pattern Unification*. Ph.D. thesis, University of Minnesota, 2009.

Zhenyu Qian. Unification of higher-order patterns in linear time and space. *Journal of Logic and Computation* 6(3):315–341, 1996.

Uday S. Reddy. Higher-order aspects of logic programming. In P. Van Hentenryck, editor, *Logic Programming, 11th International Conference, S. Margherita Ligure, Italy*, pp. 402–418. MIT Press, Cambridge, MA, 1994.

J. A. Robinson. A machine-oriented logic based on the resolution principle. *Journal of the ACM* 12:23–41, January 1965.

C. Röckl, D. Hirschkoff, and S. Berghofer. Higher-order abstract syntax with induction in Isabelle/HOL: Formalizing the pi-calculus and mechanizing the theory of contexts. In F. Honsell and M. Miculan, editors, *Proceedings FOSSACS'01*, vol. 2030 of *LNCS*, pp. 364–378. Springer, New York, 2001.

Amr Sabry and Matthias Felleisen. Reasoning about programs in continuation-passing style. *Lisp and Symbolic Computation* 6(3-4):289–360, 1993.

Davide Sangiorgi. π-Calculus, internal mobility and agent-passing calculi. *Theoretical Computer Science* 167(2):235–274, 1996.

Davide Sangiorgi and David Walker. π-*Calculus: A Theory of Mobile Processes*. Cambridge University Press, Cambridge, England, 2001.

D. T. Sannella and L. A. Wallen. A calculus for the construction of modular Prolog programs. *Journal of Logic Programming* 12(1–2):147–178, January 1992.

Helmut Schwichtenberg. Minlog. In Freek Wiedijk, editor, *The Seventeen Provers of the World*, vol. 3600 of *LNCS*, pp. 151–157. Springer, New York, 2006.

Ehud Y. Shapiro. *Algorithmic Program Debugging*. MIT Press, Cambridge, MA, 1983.

Steward Shapiro. Second-order languages and mathematical practice. *Journal of Symbolic Logic* 50(3):714–742, September 1985.

Raymond M. Smullyan. *First-Order Logic*. Springer-Verlag, New York, 1968.

Zachary Snow. Realizing the dependently typed lambda calculus. Master's thesis, University of Minnesota, 2010.

Zachary Snow, David Baelde, and Gopalan Nadathur. A meta-programming approach to realizing dependently typed logic programming. In *ACM SIGPLAN Conference on Principles and Practice of Declarative Programming (PPDP)*, pp. 187–198, 2010.

Wayne Snyder and Jean H. Gallier. Higher order unification revisited: Complete sets of transformations. *Journal of Symbolic Computation* 8(1-2):101–140, 1989.

Richard Statman. Intuitionistic propositional logic is polynomial-space complete. *Theoretical Computer Science* 9:67–72, 1979a.

Richard Statman. The typed λ-calculus is not elementary recursive. *Theoretical Computer Science* 9:73–81, 1979b.

Leon Sterling and Ehud Shapiro. *The Art of Prolog: Advanced Programming Techniques*. MIT Press, Cambridge MA, 1986.

Colin Stirling. Decidability of higher-order matching. *Logical Methods in Computer Science* 5(3):1–52, 2009.

Joseph E. Stoy. *Denotational Semantics: The Scott-Strachey Approach to Programming Language Theory*. MIT Press, Cambridge, MA, 1977.

M. Takahashi. A proof of cut-elimination theorem in simple type-theory. *Journal of the Mathematical Society of Japan* 19:399–410, 1967.

Paul Tarau. Program transformations and WAM-support for the compilation of definite metaprograms. In *Proceedings of the First and Second Russian Conference on Logic Programming*, number 592 in *LNAI*, pp. 462–473. Springer-Verlag, New York, 1992.

Alwen Tiu. Model checking for π-calculus using proof search. In Martín Abadi and Luca de Alfaro, editors, *Proceedings of CONCUR'05*, vol. 3653 of *LNCS*, pp. 36–50. Springer, New York, 2005.

Alwen Tiu and Dale Miller. A proof search specification of the π-calculus. In *3rd Workshop on the Foundations of Global Ubiquitous Computing*, vol. 138 of *ENTCS*, pp. 79–101, September 2004.

Anne S. Troelstra and Helmut Schwichtenberg. *Basic Proof Theory*. Cambridge University Press, Cambrdige, England, 1996.

Maarten H. van Emden and Robert A. Kowalski. The semantics of predicate logic as a programming language. *Journal of the ACM* 23(4):733–742, 1976.

William W. Wadge. Higher-order Horn logic programming. In *Proceedings of the 1991 International Symposium on Logic Programming*, pp. 289–303, October 1991.

D. H. D. Warren. An abstract Prolog instruction set. Technical Report 309, SRI International, October 1983.

D. S. Warren. Database updates in Prolog. In *Proceedings of the International Conference on Fifth Generation Computer Systems*, pp. 244–253, 1984.

David H. D. Warren. Higher-order extensions to Prolog: Are they needed? In *Machine Intelligence 10*, pp. 441–454. Halsted Press, Chichester, England, 1982.

Index

Abella, 228
abstract datatypes, 165
abstract logic programming language, 73
abstraction
  body of, 97
  bound variable of, 97
`accum_sig` keyword, 156, 285
`accumulate` keyword, 154
∀∃ unification problems, 32
∀∃∀ unification problems, 106, 212
algorithm W, 260
α-conversion, 37, 100
α-rewriting, 100
anonymous variable, 47, 51
answer substitution, 43, 52
`append` predicate, 50
application of a term, 17
argument type, 13
`assert`, Prolog predicate, 287
atomic formula, first-order, 34

backchaining, 3, 44
backslash \
  as λ-binder, 97
  as quantifier binder, 36
`bagof`, 190
Bedwyr, 228
β-conversion, 6, 7, 100
β-expansion, 100
β-normal form, 101, 185
  arguments of, 111
  binder of, 111
  flexible, 111
  head of, 111
  rigid, 111
β-redex, 101
β-reduction, 2, 100

β_0-conversion, 206, 220
$\beta\eta$-long normal form, 111
$\beta\eta$-normal form, 102
big-step specification, 250
binary clauses, 130, 148
binder mobility, *see* mobility of binders
bisimulation, 271
`bnorm`, β-normal form, 186
bound variable, 36
bound variable renaming, 37

Calculus of Constructions, 148
call-by-name evaluation, 182, 273
call-by-value evaluation, 182
candidats de réductibilité, 5
capture avoiding substitution, 86, 183
Church numerals, 102, 115
Church, Alonzo, 6, 74, 116, 147, 208
classical logic, 4, 41, 235
classical logic theorem prover, 239
classical vs intuitionistic logic, 89
clausal order, 76
`close_in`, built-in predicate, 287
`close_out`, built-in predicate, 287
closed formula, 38
closed term, 98
closed-world assumption, 94
comparisons `<`, `>`, `=<`, `>=`, 49
complete set of unifiers, 213
complete trace, 269
`compose`, 130
comprehension, 5
computation via proof normalization, 2
computation via proof search, 2
computation-as-deduction, 2
computation-as-model, 2
concrete nonsense, 183